Second Edition

Writing That Works

How to Write Effectively on the Job

Second Edition

Writing That Works

How to Write Effectively on the Job

Walter E. Oliu
U.S. Nuclear Regulatory Commission

Charles T. Brusaw
NCR Corporation

Gerald J. Alred
University of Wisconsin—Milwaukee

St. Martin's Press
New York

For information, write St. Martin's Press, Inc.
175 Fifth Avenue, New York, NY 10010

cover design: Tom McKeveney

ISBN: 0–312–89506–2

Acknowledgments

BIOSPHERICS, INC., for business letters on pp. 224–227.

POPULAR SCIENCE for the passage on windmills, p. 57. Reprinted from
Popular Science with permission © 1979 Times Mirror Magazines, Inc.

RANDOM HOUSE, INC., for the sample dictionary entry, p. 442. Reproduced
by permission from *The Random House College Dictionary,* Revised Edition.
Copyright © 1975, 1979 by Random House, Inc.

Preface

Writing That Works, Second Edition, is designed for students of varied academic backgrounds and occupational interests whose jobs will, or already do, require writing skills. Each chapter provides abundant and realistic examples drawn from a wide range of occupations, as well as carefully structured exercises and writing assignments. The text is unusually comprehensive, and probably few instructors will wish to assign every chapter. We have, therefore, built into the book sufficient flexibility to enable instructors to choose the sections they consider most important for any particular class. (In addition, our Instructor's Manual contains a suggested syllabus for a 16-week course.) At the same time, we feel that a text such as this should be made inclusive enough to serve as a reference tool for the student long after the course is over, since no course can possibly cover all the writing concerns students will encounter once they are actually on the job.

For the Second Edition we have organized the text in three parts— a new organization designed to facilitate both the teaching and learning of various types of writing. Part One is an introduction to the writing process. The five chapters in this part guide the student through all the steps of the process—planning, organizing, writing (including a separate chapter on achieving the proper emphasis), and revising—with special emphasis on the questions a writer must ask when approaching any writing task: What is my purpose in writing? For whom is the writing intended? How much information must I include? By page 36 the student is familiar with the most common organizational patterns; by page 54 he or she has been introduced to the principles of effective paragraph writing, including transition between sentences and paragraphs and successful openings and closings. And by page 72 the student has studied the ways of achieving emphasis in writing—with the active and passive voices, subordination, word order, and introductory words and phrases.

Part Two—chapters 6 through 15—looks at the writing process at work, considering in particular the various kinds of on-the-job writing and the strategies appropriate to each one. We have expanded the original chapter on business correspondence to two full chapters, allowing for more thorough treatment of memorandums and of types of business letters. Chapter 6 discusses the principles of business correspondence, focusing on the importance of goodwill and on the "you" viewpoint and includes typical letter and memo formats. Chapter 7 then goes on to describe the various types of business correspondence, including order letters, inquiry letters, transmittal letters, acknowledgment letters, complaint letters, adjustment letters, collection letters, and sales letters. Chapter 8 presents the range of rhetorical strategies that should be a part of every writer's basic equipment: instructions, process explanation, description, comparison, definition, division and classification, cause and effect, and persuasion. Each rhetorical method is illustrated by one or more job-related examples.

Chapters 9 through 11 discuss reports, with separate chapters on the informal report, the formal report, and research techniques (not only library research but interviews and questionnaires). For the Second Edition, we have expanded the formal report chapter to include the executive summary and the abstract, as well as excerpts from an actual formal report, and we have added to the research chapter a new section on computerized information retrieval. Chapter 12 looks at proposal writing, with coverage of both internal proposals (including those for capital expenditures) and external, or sales, proposals (both solicited and unsolicited). Comprehensive examples of both internal and external proposals are provided.

Chapter 13 takes up the preparation of tables, charts, and other visual aides. Chapter 14 discusses not only the preparation and delivery of oral presentations but also a vitally important skill that is too often ignored: effective listening. The last text chapter is a practical, step-by-step guide to finding a job, with special emphasis on the preparation of effective résumés and of application and follow-up letters. Sample résumés are provided both for students with little or no job experience and for those with a great deal of experience.

Finally, Part Three of *Writing That Works* is a highly accessible Writer's Guide, with instructional material on spelling and vocabulary building, as well as a handbook of grammar, punctuation, and mechanics. The handbook is based on materials drawn from our *Handbook of Technical Writing* and *The Business Writer's Handbook* (both published by St. Martin's Press). In an effort to make the handbook section as useful and accessible as possible, we have cross-referenced it with the chapter on revising. Last, at the very end of the book is a correction chart, with page references to appropriate passages in the text discussion and the handbook.

For valuable assistance in preparation of the Second Edition of *Writing That Works,* we wish to thank Donna Gorrell, Francis Hubbard, and William Van Pelt, all of the University of Wisconsin-Milwaukee. In addition, we would like to express our appreciation to the following instructors for their helpful comments and recommendations: Kevin Harty, La Salle College; Mark Johnston, Quinnipiac College; Judith Kaufman, Eastern Washington University; Richard Profozich, Prince George's Community College; Mary Scotto, Kean College of New Jersey; Phyllis Sheldon, Virginia Polytechnic Institute and State University; Douglas Taylor, California State College at Stanislaus; and Jackie Zrubek, Texas State Technical Institute of Waco. Finally, we want to thank Nancy Perry, Marilyn Moller, and Charles Thurlow, of St. Martin's Press, for their editorial guidance.

Walter E. Oliu
Charles T. Brusaw
Gerald J. Alred

Contents

Part One   THE WRITING PROCESS   1

1 **Getting Started**   3
Determining Your Purpose 5
Determining Your Reader's Needs 5
Generating Ideas and Recording Facts 8
Establishing Your Scope 11
Organizing Your Ideas 12
Successful Writing 13
Chapter Summary 16
Exercises 16

2 **Organizing Your Information**   19
Outlining 19
Methods of Organization 23
Chapter Summary 36
Exercises 36

3 **Writing the Draft**   41
Paragraph Unity 42
Coherence 44
Paragraph Length 48
Writing an Opening 48
Writing a Closing 51
Chapter Summary 54
Exercises 54

4 **Achieving Emphasis**   58
Active and Passive Voice 58
Subordination 61
Unusual Word Order 66
Introductory Words and Phrases 66
Parallel Structure 67
Lists 69
Other Ways to Achieve Emphasis 70
Chapter Summary 72
Exercises 72

5 Revising 76

Effective Revision *77*
Checking for Precision *78*
Checking for Conciseness *86*
Checking for Accuracy *93*
Checking for Completeness *93*
Checking Grammar *93*
Checking Spelling *104*
Physical Appearance *107*
Final Checklist *108*
Chapter Summary *109*
Exercises *110*

Part Two THE PROCESS AT WORK 115

6 Principles of Business Correspondence 117

Writing Letters *118*
The Memorandum *136*
Chapter Summary *142*
Exercises *143*

7 Types of Business Letters 144

The Order Letter *144*
The Inquiry Letter *145*
Response to an Inquiry Letter *148*
The Transmittal Letter *150*
The Acknowledgment Letter *155*
The Complaint Letter *155*
The Adjustment Letter *158*
The Refusal Letter *160*
The Collection Letter Series *163*
The Sales Letter *166*
Chapter Summary *171*
Exercises *172*

8 Writing Strategies 176

Instructions *176*
Explaining a Process *180*
Description *186*
Comparison *189*
Division and Classification *191*
Definition *195*
Cause and Effect *200*

Persuading Your Reader *203*
Chapter Summary *205*
Exercises *207*

9 Informal Reports **209**
Writing the Report *210*
The Parts of the Report *210*
Types of Reports *211*
Chapter Summary *227*
Exercises *228*

10 Researching Your Subject **231**
In the Library *232*
Taking Notes *244*
Plagiarism *251*
Interviewing *251*
Using a Questionnaire *254*
Other Sources of Information *260*
Documentation *261*
Chapter Summary *272*
Exercises *273*

11 Formal Reports **276**
Order of Elements in a Formal Report *276*
Front Matter *277*
Body *286*
Back Matter *307*
Graphic and Tabular Matter *308*
Chapter Summary *309*
Exercises *309*

12 Proposals and Other Kinds of On-the-Job Communication **311**
Proposals *311*
Minutes of Meetings *339*
Job Descriptions *343*
Creating Business Forms *344*
Chapter Summary *350*
Exercises *351*

13 Creating Tables and Illustrations **353**
Tables *355*
Graphs *356*

Drawings   *369*
Photographs   *371*
Flowcharts   *373*
Organizational Charts   *376*
Maps   *377*
Chapter Summary   *378*
Exercises   *379*

14   **Making an Oral Presentation**   **382**
Preparing an Oral Presentation   *383*
Delivering an Oral Presentation   *389*
Effective Listening   *393*
Chapter Summary   *395*
Exercises   *396*

15   **Finding a Job**   **397**
Locating the Job You Want   *397*
Preparing an Effective Résumé   *400*
Writing an Effective Letter of Application   *408*
Conducting Yourself During the Interview   *414*
Sending Follow-up Letters   *416*
Chapter Summary   *420*
Exercises   *421*

Part Three   **WRITER'S GUIDE**   **423**

Section A   **Spelling and Vocabulary**

1   **Spelling**   **425**
1.1   The Silent *e* Rule of Thumb   *428*
1.2   Hard and Soft Sounds   *429*
1.3   Adding to Basic Words   *430*
1.4   Doubling Final Consonants   *433*
1.5   Prefixes and Suffixes   *434*
1.6   Words with *ie* or *ei*   *435*
1.7   Contractions   *435*
1.8   Abbreviated Spellings   *436*
1.9   Word Groups of Frequently Misspelled Words   *436*

2   **Vocabulary**   **438**
Choosing the Right Word   *439*
Word-Part Approach   *442*

2.1   Roots   *443*
2.2   Prefixes   *448*
2.3   Suffixes   *457*

Section B   Handbook of Grammar, Punctuation, and Mechanics

3   Parts of Speech   **460**
3.1   Nouns   *461*
3.2   Pronouns   *464*
3.3   Adjectives   *473*
3.4   Verbs   *475*
3.5   Adverbs   *488*
3.6   Conjunctions   *492*
3.7   Prepositions   *493*
3.8   Interjections   *495*

4   Phrases, Clauses, Sentences, and Paragraphs   **495**
4.1   Phrases   *495*
4.2   Clauses   *497*
4.3   Sentences   *500*
4.4   Paragraphs   *516*

5   Punctuation   **519**
5.1   Commas   *520*
5.2   Semicolons   *527*
5.3   Colons   *528*
5.4   Periods   *530*
5.5   Question Marks   *533*
5.6   Exclamation Marks   *534*
5.7   Parentheses   *534*
5.8   Hyphens   *535*
5.9   Quotation Marks   *537*
5.10   Dashes   *539*
5.11   Apostrophes   *540*
5.12   Slashes   *542*
5.13   Brackets   *543*

6   Mechanics   **543**
6.1   Numbers   *544*
6.2   Acronyms and Initialisms   *547*
6.3   Abbreviations   *548*
6.4   Ampersands   *551*

6.5 Capital Letters *552*
6.6 Dates *557*
6.7 Italics *557*
6.8 Symbols *560*
6.9 Proofreaders' Marks *562*

Index   **565**

Second Edition

Writing That Works

How to Write Effectively on the Job

part one

THE WRITING PROCESS

1

Getting Started

Christine Thomas was aware of both an opportunity and a potential problem at HVS Data Processing Services. An administrative assistant, she knew that the computer service offered by HVS could easily attract new customers if only the president and founder of the small company, Harriet Sullivan, would expand HVS's equipment and staff. Christine had, in fact, turned customers away because HVS's computer equipment was loaded to capacity handling 49 current business customers. Even more troubling, HVS had promised to cover emergency or overload backups for its present customers. Christine knew it was only a matter of time before HVS would be forced to refuse computer time to a valued customer. Something had to be done.

Christine had for the last month kept careful records of the number of customers she turned away. She had also researched the costs of new equipment and additional staff. She was convinced that even though HVS was just over two years old, the time to expand had come.

So, with all the information at hand and confident of the value of her suggestion, Christine wrote the following memo to Harriet Sullivan, president of HVS Data Processing Services:

DATE: December 3, 19--

TO: Harriet Sullivan

FROM: Christine Thomas *CT*

SUBJECT: Expansion of HVS Capabilities

> The number of customers being turned away is steadily growing. Further, we may need to refuse computer time for emergency or overload backups for our present customers.
>
> By purchasing a VT-8000 computer and expanding our staff by two, we could triple the number of customers and ensure emergency and overload backup for new and current clients.
>
> Please consider my suggestion that we expand HVS.

Two days later, Christine Thomas's memo was returned to her with the note "Too soon to make such a move" written across the bottom.

Christine Thomas was not only disappointed but also puzzled. She knew that her suggestion was timely and reasonable because she had checked all the facts before writing the memo. Yet she had failed to convince Harriet Sullivan.

In writing her memo, Christine Thomas committed the most common of all mistakes made by people who write on their jobs: she lost sight of the purpose of her memo and overlooked the needs of her reader. Christine had been so convinced of the rightness of her suggestion that she forgot that her reader was not familiar with the information her research had produced and could not see the situation from Christine's perspective. Had she kept her purpose and her reader clearly in mind, Christine would then have been able to generate ideas, establish her scope, and organize her ideas in a way that might have achieved her objective.

The last three steps are important: even with her reader and her purpose clearly in mind, Christine would still not have been ready to write her memo to Harriet. She would simply have established a framework in which to develop her memo. Some writers, once they have identified their purposes and their readers, don't know where to go next and stare at a blank piece of paper waiting for inspiration.

A systematic approach helps writers over this hurdle. Before writing her memo, Christine should not only have identified her purpose and reader but should have thought seriously about the content of her memo and the form this information should take. This process involves first listing all the ideas and facts that you might wish to include, refining the list by examining each item in it from the perspectives of reader and purpose, and then organizing the resulting list in a way that satisfies your purpose and your reader's needs. Careful writers complete each of the following steps before they begin to compose any important document.

1. They determine their purpose.
2. They determine their reader's needs.

3. They generate ideas and record facts.
4. They establish their scope.
5. They organize their ideas.

DETERMINING YOUR PURPOSE

Everything you write is written for a purpose. You want your reader to know, to believe, or to be able to do something when he or she has finished reading what you have written. Determining your purpose is the first step in preparing to write, for unless you know what you hope to accomplish by your writing, you cannot know what information should be presented.

Purpose, then, gives direction to your writing: the more precisely you can state your purpose at the outset, the more successful your writing is likely to be. Christine Thomas, if asked, might have said that her purpose was "to expand HVS's computer facilities"—but expansion was the *result* she wanted, not the precise *purpose* of her memo. Further thought on her part would have led her to recognize the more specific goals of the memo itself.

To make sure that your purpose is precise, try to put it in writing. In most cases, you can use the following formula to guide you:

My purpose is to _____ so that my reader _____.

Using this formula, Christine Thomas might have come up with the following statement of purpose:

My purpose is *to explain the advantages of expanding our equipment and staff* so that my reader *will be persuaded to buy the VT-8000 and hire two new employees.*

With this statement of purpose, Christine would have recognized that her purpose was more complicated than it had at first appeared and that she would have to present persuasive evidence if her writing were to be effective.

DETERMINING YOUR READER'S NEEDS

Remember that your job as a writer is to express your ideas so clearly that your reader cannot misinterpret them and that an important element of the purpose formula is the phrase "so that my reader. . . ." Simply identifying the response you would like is very different from actually achieving it. Although a purpose statement addresses a problem from the writer's point of view, the reader's needs must also be taken into account. Yet all too often writers forget that they have readers and write essentially to themselves, focusing solely on their purposes.

After you have stated your purpose, ask yourself "Who is my reader?" Often you will know who your reader is. For example, if you are writing a memo to your boss attempting to convince him to fund a project you would like to do, you know who your reader is. In another situation, however, you might be writing a letter to someone you do not know in another company. In this case, you would try to imagine your reader, taking into consideration what you know about that company, your reader's position in the company or department, and your reader's responsibilities regarding the topic you are writing about. You could not know what his needs were until you knew at least this much about him.

Obviously, when you know enough about your reader that you can actually picture him or her responding to what you have written, you have an advantage. But even when you know your reader very well, a little reflection is necessary. In Christine Thomas's case, without careful thought she might have answered the question from only one point of view:

> My reader is Harriet Sullivan, and she's been my boss for two years. We've worked together since she founded the company, so she'll no doubt understand that I have her best interest in mind.

Had Christine thought more carefully about Harriet *as the reader of the memo* rather than as her friend and boss she might have answered the question differently:

> My reader is Harriet Sullivan, president of HVS Data Processing Service. Harriet founded HVS two years ago with modest savings and a substantial loan. Cautious, industrious, and a stickler for detail, Harriet has built HVS into a sound business and is now beginning to see some return on her investment. She is not an expert in the technical aspects of data processing and has had little time to keep up with innovations in the field. Instead, Harriet is an able manager, but one who is sometimes slow to recognize the value of the advice her more technically oriented subordinates can offer.

This portrait of Harriet would have enabled Christine to raise two essential questions, the answers to which would have helped her frame her memo:

1. What information does my reader need in order to understand what I'm writing about?
2. What is my reader's basic attitude likely to be toward what I'm writing about?

These questions—which might be rephrased "What does my reader probably know?" and "What does my reader probably think?"—are always worth investigating. If your purpose were to explain to an associate your plan for bypassing a malfunctioning piece of equipment that is causing a production bottleneck, these questions are easier to answer than if your purpose were to submit your plan to the president of your company, someone you know only by name and title. In the first case, your reader is a colleague who understands the equipment, the terminology you will use, and the production system. In the second case, your reader is a decision maker primarily interested in the "big picture"—the broader implications of the bottleneck and the feasibility of your plan to correct it. This reader would probably not know the technical details of the day-to-day operation of your production system and would likely have neither the time nor the inclination to learn them simply to understand your explanation. You would have to write to the company president in terms that would be comprehensible to a typical executive. The company president, having read your explanation, would want to know whether to investigate your plan further or to replace the malfunctioning equipment.

Keep in mind that your reader, whether a coworker, a customer, or a company president, is more interested in the problem you are addressing from his or her own point of view than from yours. Imagine yourself in your reader's position.

If you were working for a bicycle manufacturer and your purpose were to write a set of assembly instructions so that people who buy your new model 1050J could get from opening the carton to riding the bicycle with a minimum of frustration, you would have to break the assembly process down into a sensible series of easy-to-follow steps. You would avoid technical language and anticipate questions that your readers would be likely to have. You would make it unnecessary for them to consult other sources in order to follow your directions. You would not explain the engineering theory that is responsible for the bicycle's unique design; your reader would be more interested in riding the bicycle than in reading such details, however fascinating they might be to you. If you ventured into theory at all, it would be for a specific reason such as to explain why a particular step had to be completed before the next. You would also include assembly diagrams, a list of parts, and a list of the tools necessary for assembly.

You would approach the situation differently if you were preparing assembly instructions for a bicycle dealer. You could feel free to use standard technical terms without defining them, and you would probably reduce the number of steps necessary for assembly by combining related steps because your reader, the dealer, would be familiar with bicycle assembly and be able to follow a more sophisticated set of instructions. Your reader would not need a list of tools required for assembly; the dealer's shop would no doubt have all the necessary tools and the dealer would know which ones to use. You might well, in a separate section, include some theoretical detail, too. The dealer could possibly use this information to explain to customers the advantages of your bicycle over a competitor's.

When you write for a group of readers who are similar in background and knowledge—all operators, for example, or all programmers—picture in your mind a typical representative of that group. Then write directly to that person. Occasionally, however, you may write a document that will be used by many different types of people. For example, you might write a technical report that would be used by technicians, salespeople, and executives. In such a situation, you might deal with each audience separately in clearly identified sections of your document: you might write an executive summary for the executive, include an appendix for the technician, and address the body of the report to the salespeople. When you cannot segment your writing this way, determine who your primary reader is and then make certain that you meet all of that reader's needs. Then meet the needs of your other readers only if you can do so without placing a burden on your primary reader. For example, if your primary reader were the executive, you would not include a full page of technical detail for the technician, even though the technician is a secondary reader. But you could include a single paragraph of detailed technical information for the technician without interfering seriously with your message to the executive (who would probably skip over the technical paragraph).

GENERATING IDEAS AND RECORDING FACTS

When you have determined your purpose and analyzed your reader's needs, you must decide what information will satisfy the demands of both. A good way to start is to make a list of everything that comes to mind about the general subject of the document that you plan to write. At this stage, don't worry about writing complete sentences. Don't even hesitate to list humorous or even silly items—they might suggest other points that your document should cover. Some of the items that you put in your list will trigger other ideas. Include every-thing you can think of—you will have plenty of time to eliminate material that does not suit your purpose or your reader's needs.

One useful device for generating ideas is expressed in a short poem by Rudyard Kipling:

> I keep six honest serving-men
> (They taught me all I knew);
> Their names are What and Why and When
> And How and Where and Who.

Newspaper reporters have long used "the five W's and How" as a guide to make sure that they have answered the questions their readers are likely to have about a particular story: *What* happened? *Why* did it happen? *When* did it happen? *How* did it happen? *Where* did it happen? *Who* was involved? Rarely will you be able to apply all "five W's and How" to any single on-the-job writing situation, but the range of information that these questions cover can be useful in helping you to start getting your ideas down on paper.

This type of brainstorming may not produce all the information you need. You may need to conduct formal, systematic research into your subject in order to get enough information to meet your reader's needs adequately. In such cases, you would need some idea of the thoroughness with which you will cover your subject. In other words, you would have to know how much detail you needed in order to consult the appropriate sources. If you know what you are looking for and you know where to find it, research presents few problems. Chapter 10 contains a full range of research techniques for gathering information.

Once you have assembled a list of ideas, examine each item and decide whether it contributes to your purpose or satisfies your reader's needs. Mark the item with a "P" for purpose or an "R" for reader. Some items will be required by both your purpose and your reader; other items will appear to apply to only one, and still others will appear to have nothing to do with either your purpose or your reader's needs. Often you will mark items first with one letter and then see that the other applies as well. The order in which you write the letters down will indicate whether you consider the item to be more important for your reader or for your purpose.

Those items that relate clearly to both your purpose and your reader's needs are, of course, easiest to deal with. Trickier are items that your reader might need but that would get in the way of your purpose. Harriet Sullivan, for example, would want to know that the VT 8000 Computer's printer is noisier than the printer that VHS is presently using; Christine Thomas, on the other hand, would be reluc-tant to mention this fact, since it would appear to be counterproductive

Items for Memo to Harriet Sullivan

R,P Harriet needs to see financial benefits of expansion

P,R Our old computer showing signs of rheumatoid arthritis

P,R Employee morale down because of overwork

R,P We could triple number of customers (give estimate)

R ~~How the VT-8000 was developed~~ List costs of data entry person and operator

R,P Income would more than pay for expansion (give estimate)

~~R VT-8000 can be color coordinated~~

RP We can't attract new customers with old equipment

R,P Easy to implement VT-8000 (see brochure)

~~R,P VT-8000 service people use radio-dispatched trucks~~

R,P Peripheral VT-3033 equipment could be added later

R,P Buying an entire new system would disturb routine

~~P VT-8000 would make my job easier~~

R VT-8000 is noisy

P,R VT-8000 is compact and easy to operate

P ~~Soundproofing~~ would be inexpensive and we need it anyway

   Our office furniture will be adequate

R ~~List~~ costs of new equipment and operation

R,P (~~Give number of~~ money direct requests turned away

   We run 3 shifts on our VT-3400 but don't keep up

P,R Briefly describe VT-8000 capacity

R,P Buying now will give us a edge on our competitors

R,P We could advertise in: Computer Times for new staff

to her own purpose. To reconcile Harriet's interests and her own, Christine would have to note the noise problem but also point out that soundproofing can be installed easily and inexpensively.

Before you eliminate any item from your list, look at it from the perspectives of both your purpose and your reader's, and make certain that it fits neither. Your ideal goal is to come up with a comprehensive list of items beside which you can place both a "P" and an "R," although many items will no doubt belong more to one than the other, and some will belong exclusively to one or the other. The more common ground your purpose and your reader's needs share, the more effective your writing is likely to be.

Turning a writer's list of ideas into a reader's list of information should be neither difficult nor mysterious; thoroughness is the key. Christine Thomas, for example, might have generated the list on the previous page, using one or more of the methods described here.

ESTABLISHING YOUR SCOPE

Having refined your list of ideas and facts, you must review it once again to establish your scope. Your scope is the degree of detail in which you decide to cover each item in your list; and, as before, you must consider this aspect of preparation in terms of your purpose and your reader's needs. This step is really a refinement of the last: as you contemplate each item, ask yourself, "Am I including enough information to support my purpose? Am I including enough information to satisfy my reader's needs? Have I included unnecessary information that only gets in the way of meeting my purpose and my reader's needs?" Often you will find that you are omitting important facts or figures and will have to research your subject further in order to come up with them. At other times, you will find that your list is cluttered with unnecessary detail.

Had Christine Thomas drawn up the list on page 10 and then reviewed it to establish her scope, she would have discovered that many of the items on her list needed detailed information to satisfy her reader's concerns. Entries such as "Harriet needs to see financial benefits of expansion" would tell her that she had to provide some figures. However, other items requiring more detail might be more difficult to identify: "Income would more than pay for expansion" sounds reasonable enough, but Harriet would want to know how much more and in what period of time. On page 12 is an example of the preceding list after the scope has been established.

Be on guard, though, when establishing your scope. Writers who have much knowledge of a subject tend to "unload" information on

> *Increase in number of customers: 45 in 1st yr – 50 in 2nd yr*
> *Six customers turned away equal to our largest account*
> *21 direct requests refused*
> *VT-8000 easy to maintain and is expandable*
> *Give Harriet Sullivan copy of brochure on VT-8000*
> *Increased income: $26,000 (1st yr) – $48,000 (2nd yr)*
> *Cost of operator ($9,000/yr) and data entry person ($8,000)*
> *VT-8000 would triple our capacity*
> *Surplus income expected: $30,270 (underline)*
> *Current systems can't handle state-of-art VRX software*
> *Can't attract new customers with our VT-3400*
> *VT-8000 is fast, reasonably priced, and high capacity*
> *VT-8000 costs $16,330 (break out items)*
> *We can't offer improved service to current customers with VT-3400*
> *VT-8000 is compact and will not disturb routine.*

readers who have no time or need to wade through a boring catalog of topics or a mass of details in order to get to the point. In establishing your scope, always be guided by your reader's needs and your purpose.

ORGANIZING YOUR IDEAS

When you have established your scope, you should have a list of the ideas and facts to be included in your writing. Examine this list and look for relations among the items in it. Group the related ideas and arrange them under headings—short phrases that identify the kind of items in each group. Once you have established these groups, consider the order in which you would like to present them. In other words, determine which arrangement of groups would most effectively serve your purpose and your reader's needs. As you assemble and arrange the groups of ideas, feel free to rework the items in your groups—adding, deleting, and moving ideas around until you feel that you have the best possible organization. Following is a satisfactory organization of the preceding list.

Problems with Present System

Turning away customers (21 last month)–6 equal to our biggest accounts

Current computer can't handle state-of-the-
art VRX software
We can't offer improved services to our best
customers
We can't attract new customers with an old,
limited system

VT-8000 as a Solution

VT-8000 is a fast, reasonably priced, high-
capacity computer
VT-8000 would triple our capacity
Cost of new equipment (list) and operating
personnel (list)
Increased income produced by expansion (list
for projected two years)

Advantages of Expansion

Surplus income would be $30,270
VT-8000 requires little maintenance
VT-8000 requires less-skilled staff than VT-
3400
VT-8000 is compact and fits our space
VT-8000 can expand with peripherals
Expansion will not disturb routine (VT-8000
is compatible)
Include brochure for Harriet

To organize larger and more complex subjects a more formal outline
is often helpful. Chapter 2 discusses outlining techniques in detail.

From these groups of items, presented in the order shown, Christine could have written a rough draft and polished it into a final
memo that not only might have achieved its purpose but also would
have demonstrated Christine's skill and effectiveness to her boss.

SUCCESSFUL WRITING

Soon after she received the disappointing response to her memo,
Christine found the courage to step into Harriet's office. Christine
explained, "I've really investigated the situation, and I'm sure my
suggestion would be to our best interests. Perhaps if I gave you more
information, you'd reconsider my suggestion." Harriet thought for a
moment and then said, "All right. Give me the figures and major
benefits tomorrow. If they are convincing, I'll talk to Fred Sadowski,
our accountant, as soon as I get the chance." Christine Thomas left
Harriet Sullivan's office both relieved and determined that this time
she would convince Harriet.

After writing a statement of purpose, determining the needs of
her reader, generating ideas, recording facts, and establishing her
scope, Christine organized the items that she wanted to cover. She

then wrote the following memo. Notice that as she drafted and revised the memo, Christine found it advantageous to alter her original headings.

DATE: December 5, 19--

TO: Harriet Sullivan

FROM: Christine Thomas   CT

SUBJECT: Advantages of Expanding HVS Computing
            Facilities

As we discussed earlier, because our computing facilities currently operate at maximum capacity, we are turning new customers away in growing numbers and will soon have to deny present customers computer time for emergencies or overload backups. By purchasing a new VT-8000 minicomputer and expanding our staff, we could respond to new service requests, provide better service to valued customers, and attract new customers who would not have previously considered using our service.

Last month we turned away 21 new service requests. At least 6 of these requests were equal to the largest accounts we currently serve. Furthermore, since our aging mainframe computer cannot handle the latest software available from VRX Systems, we can neither offer improved, faster services to our most profitable accounts (such as First International Savings and Loan) nor attract the new customers who are eager to take advantage of the most recent advances in computer technology.

The VT-8000 is a very fast, reasonably priced minicomputer with massive peripheral memory capacity in the form of removable disk packs. This machine would triple our current processing capacity and enable us to use the full range of new VRX software now available. The following details show how purchasing the VT-8000 system would triple our number of customers and pay for itself within two years.

Cost of New Equipment

VT-8000 minicomputer	$12,500
Two 3033 disks and disk drives	1,800
One VT80 computer terminal	980
New VRX software	1,050
Total cost of equipment	$16,330

Increases in Annual Operating Budget

Salaries: Computer operator	$9,000
Data entry technician	8,200
Total increase in annual operating budget	$17,200

Total Costs

First year	$33,530
Second year	17,200
Two-year total cost	$50,730

Increased Income Generated by Expansion

First-year estimate (45 new customers)	$26,010
Second-Year estimate (50 new customers) plus the 45 of the first year	54,900
Total	$81,000

Since the purchase of the VT-8000 system is a one-time investment a profit of over $30,270 could be generated by the end of the second year. The estimates are based on the $578 average annual value of accounts over the past two years.

Other advantages of the VT-8000 minicomputer are as follows:
- It requires little maintenance and therefore suffers minimal downtime.
- It is easy to operate and thus requires less highly trained staff.
- It is extremely compact and will easily fit into space already available in our computer room.
- Additional peripheral equipment, such as disk drives and remote terminals, can be added at minimal cost if we decide to expand the facility again at a later date.

Because this system is reliable, easy to install, and easy to operate, we could have it running in three weeks with little disturbance of our normal office routine. More importantly, buying the VT-8000 will provide a cost-effective solution to the current problem of overburdened computing resources and will clear the way for meeting the demands of a growing base of customers. Although

> the VT-8000 printer is somewhat noisier than the
> VT-3400 printer, soundproofing the computer room
> is something that we had planned to do anyway.
>
> On the basis of these details, I recommend that we
> expand HVS services by purchasing the VT-8000
> system. An enclosed brochure describes the system
> in more detail. I will be happy to provide addi-
> tional information about the system at your re-
> quest.

Christine's story had a happy ending: Harriet was impressed with Christine's memo and within a month ordered the VT-8000. Furthermore, Christine was promoted to office manager, taking over many of Harriet's duties in the expanded organization.

CHAPTER SUMMARY

Successful writing on the job is the result of careful preparation. Successful writers prepare by precisely defining the purpose of their writing, determining the identity and needs of their reader or readers as specifically as possible, generating a list of ideas and facts, and establishing their scope. Then they organize their writing by logically grouping their facts and ideas. Once organized, the facts and ideas can be converted to a rough draft, then polished into final form. These two steps—writing and revising—are the subjects of Chapters 3 and 5.

EXERCISES

1. Using the pattern suggested in this chapter, create a statement of purpose for a memo you could write. Select a problem at your place of employment (past or present) or on your campus—for instance, inadequate parking, poor cafeteria services, or lack of tuition reimbursement for job-related courses. Aim your memo at a reader who could make a decision regarding your suggestion. Be sure to give the reader's name and position in your statement of the objective.

2. Using the method for generating ideas described in this chapter, create a list of items for the subject selected for Exercise 1. Try to list at least 15 to 20 items—don't worry if some seem inappropriate, just keep listing.

3. Eliminate the items in your list from Exercise 2 that clearly do not meet the reader's needs or contribute to your objective. Then establish your scope, and rewrite the resulting list.

4. Group the items in your revised list from Exercise 3 in three or more categories. Next arrange the items in each category in sequence.

5. Using the outline created in Exercise 4, write the memo suggesting a solution to the problem.

6. You are involved in a local charity or volunteer group (select an area with which you are familiar) and have an idea for raising funds. You find, however, that you must submit the idea to the board of directors. If they approve, you will outline the procedure for volunteers who will execute the campaign door to door. You also plan a letter that will be given to potential donors. First, identify your three groups of readers. Next, make a list of needs and attitudes that each group of these readers might have.

7. Find an article on a subject of interest to you in two different types of publications—for example, a newspaper and a newsmagazine, a magazine like *Popular Science* and a technical journal, and so on. After you have read the two articles, respond to the following:

   a. Compare the approaches taken in each article toward the intended audience. Look specifically for the presence or absence of technical terms, the kind and number of illustrations used, and the audience's apparent knowledge of the subject.
   b. Create statements of purpose for each article, as if you had been the writer.
   c. How well do you think the writers met the needs of their readers? (Respond only after you have completed *a* and *b*.)

8. Using the techniques described in this chapter, write a description of your job (or a job you've had) for an employee who may be replacing you while you are on vacation. Write two versions of this assignment:

   a. For an employee hired through a temporary job service from outside the organization.
   b. For an employee who works in your department but not in the same job.

9. Discuss similarities and differences between writing for the reader in 8*a* and writing for the reader in 8*b*.

10. Discuss the similarities and differences between writing on the job and writing for a general composition class.

2

Organizing Your Information

When a motion picture is filmed, the scenes are usually shot out of the sequence in which they will appear in the finished film. Different shooting locations, actors' schedules, weather conditions, and many other circumstances make shooting out of sequence necessary. If it were not for a skilled film editor, the completed film would be a jumble of randomly shot scenes. The film editor, following the script, carefully splices the film together so that the story moves smoothly and logically from one event to the next, as the screen writer planned. Without a plan, no such order would be possible: the film editor would have no guide for organizing the thousands of feet of film.

Organizing a film and organizing a written document are obviously different tasks, but they have one element in common—both must be planned ahead of time. For a film, planning means creating a script. For a written document, it means organizing the information into a sequence appropriate to the subject, the purpose, and the reader.

Organizing your information before you write has two important advantages. First, it forces you to reexamine the information that you plan to include in your writing to be sure that you have sufficient facts and details to satisfy your reader's needs and achieve the purpose of your writing. Second, it forces you to order the information logically, so that your reader understands it as clearly as you do.

OUTLINING

For relatively short items, like memos and letters, you may need to jot down only a few notes to make sure that you haven't left out any important information and that you have arranged the information in a logical order. Longer documents generally require more elaborate planning; when such planning is necessary, the formal outline provides the best means.

An outline consists of phrases arranged according to the logical development of your subject. To create an outline, you begin by dividing your topic into its major sections. If these sections need to be subdivided, you divide them into their major parts. Then you identify all items by a number or a letter, according to the following system.

```
I. Major section
   A. First-level subsection
      1. Second-level subsection
         a. Third-level subsection
            1) Fourth-level subsection
```

This system permits you to recognize at a glance the relative importance of divisions within your subject. Your subject will seldom require this many divisions, but the system allows for a highly detailed outline if one is necessary.

When you are ready to write, you should know your topic well enough that you can identify its major sections. Write them down. Then consider them carefully to make sure that they divide the topic logically. Assume, for example, that you are writing an article about computers for a company magazine. You might start with the following major sections.

```
  I. Development of computers
 II. Varied types of present applications
III. Future and potential benefits
 IV. Potential benefits to mankind
```

After a moment's reflection, you might decide that you can combine "present" and "future." A few more moments of thought might convince you that you can also combine "applications" and "benefits." So you might substitute the following two major sections for the original four.

```
 I. Development of computers
II. Present and future applications and benefits
```

You quickly decide, however, that you have put too much into your second major section, so you make another effort.

```
  I. Development of computers
 II. Present applications
III. Future benefits
```

Now you are satisfied that you have arrived at the appropriate major sections for your topic.

Once you have established your major sections, look for minor divisions within each section. For example, you might first arrive at the following minor divisions within your first major section.

```
  I. Development of computers
     A. Early efforts not practical
     B. New industry created
 II. Present applications
     A. Business
     B. Social
III. Future benefits
     A. Economic
     B. Social
```

This outline is a start, but it is weak. The minor divisions are too vague to be useful. As a result of considering these weaknesses, you might produce the following revision.

```
  I. Development of computers
     A. History of computing aids
     B. Development of the computer to a practical
        size
     C. New industry created around the computer
 II. Present applications
     A. Business applications of the computer
     B. Social and scientific applications of the
        computer
III. Future benefits
     A. Potential business impact of the computer
     B. Potential social impact of the computer
```

Now you are ready to insert any notes that you may have compiled under the appropriate major and minor divisions.

```
  I. Development of computers
     A. History of computing aids
        1. Abacus as man's first computing tool
        2. First electronic computer patented in
           1944
     B. Development of the computer to a practical
        size
        1. Early computers very large, impractical
           for commercial use
        2. First electronic computer weighed 30
           tons, took 1,500 square feet of floor
           space
        3. Introduction of transistor in 1958 made
           computer commercially practical
```

II. Present applications
    A. Business applications of the computer
        1. Used to navigate ships and planes
        2. Used to route long-distance telephone calls and set newspaper type
        3. Used to monitor airline reservations
    B. Social and scientific applications of the computer
        1. Prepare weather forecasts
        2. Direct city traffic
        3. Maintain data banks on crime and criminals
        4. Monitor the condition of patients in hospitals
        5. Compare chemical characteristics of drugs
III. Future benefits
    A. Potential impact of the computer on business and industry
        1. More efficient operation of business and industry
        2. More production from business and industry
        3. More leisure time for employees, enhancing the recreation industry
    B. Potential social impact of the computer
        1. Will greatly change society
        2. Can make education and government considerably more effective
        3. May one day help find cures for diseases, translate languages, land jetliner without human aid
        4. Potential limited only by man's imagination

When you have finished, you have a complete rough outline. It is only a rough outline, however, because you still must check for a number of things. For example, you will need to make sure that your major divisions are all of equal importance, and that all your minor divisions are also equal to one another.

NOT
    II. Present applications
        A. Economic applications of the computer
        B. Social and scientific applications of the computer
        C. Future benefits

BUT
    II. Present applications
        A. Economic applications of the computer
        B. Social and scientific applications of the computer
    III. Future benefits

Make sure that all division heads at any one level are in parallel form. If you begin one with a noun phrase, for example, make sure that all heads at that level begin with noun phrases.

NOT   A. Potential economic impact of the computer
PARALLEL   B. The computer's potential social impact

PARALLEL   A. Potential economic impact of the computer
             B. Potential social impact of the computer

Make sure that all topics are divided logically. A head must be divided into at least two parts if it is to be divided at all.

NOT   A. Retailer benefits
SUBDIVIDED   1. Permits direct transfer of purchase price to retail-
                   er's account

SUBDIVIDED   A. Retailer benefits
                1. Permits direct transfer of purchase price to retail-
                   er's account
                2. Provides daily printout of vital records

Scan your outline for completeness, determining whether you need additional information. If you find that your research is not really complete, now is the time to return to your sources and dig out the missing data.

Finally, the outline is only a means to an end, not an end in itself. Don't view it as being cast in concrete. If you suddenly see a better way to organize your material while you are writing the draft, depart from your outline and choose the better approach. The main purpose of the outline is to bring order and shape to your writing *before* you begin to write the draft. But don't hesitate to improve upon the outline *as* you write the draft.

METHODS OF ORGANIZATION

The method of organization comes naturally for some types of writing. Instructions for operating a piece of machinery are arranged step by step. A trip report usually follows a chronological sequence. When a subject does not lend itself to one particular sequence, you can choose the best sequence, or combination of sequences, by considering your purpose in writing and your reader's needs. Suppose, for example, that you report on a trip to several offset-printing companies to gather information on the most efficient way to arrange equipment in the printing shop where you work. You would probably organize the report of the trip chronologically, but your description of the various shop layouts, emphasizing the physical locations of the equipment, would be organized spatially. If you went on to make recommendations about the most workable arrangement for your shop, you would present the most efficient arrangement first, the second most efficient arrangement next, and so on. Thus the recommendations portion of the report would be organized according to decreasing order of importance.

The most common ways to organize, or sequence, information in on-the-job writing are the following:

- step by step, chronological, spatial, decreasing order of importance, increasing order of importance, general to specific, and specific to general.

Step by Step

In the step-by-step sequence, you divide your subject into steps and then present the steps in the order in which they occur. This arrangement is the most effective way to describe the operation of a mechanism such as an internal combustion engine, or to explain a process such as the administration of cardiopulmonary resuscitation. Step by step is also the logical method for writing instructions. For example, the instructions for using a pay telephone follow a step-by-step sequence.

For local calls:

1. Deposit coin.
2. Listen for dial tone.
3. Dial number.

The greatest advantage of presenting your information in a step-by-step sequence is that it is easy for your reader to understand and follow because the sequence of steps in your writing corresponds to the natural sequence of the process. If you were to write instructions for the proper way to process film, for example, you would present the information in a step-by-step sequence:

OUTLINE

Processing Black-and-White Film

        I. Developing
            A. In total darkness, load film in developing
               tank
            B. Do not let film touch tank or other film
            C. Add developing solution

        D. Turn lights on
        E. Start timer, set for seven minutes
        F. Agitate for five seconds; then agitate for
           five seconds every half minute
   II. Stopping
        A. Drain developer from tank
        B. Add stop bath
        C. Rinse 30 seconds in stop bath, agitating
           continually
  III. Fixing
        A. Drain stop bath from tank
        B. Add fixing solution
        C. Fix for two to four minutes
        D. Agitate for five seconds, then agitate for
           five seconds every half minute
   IV. Washing
        A. Remove tank top
        B. Wash for 30 minutes under running water
    V. Drying
        A. Hang film
        B. Sponge gently to remove excess water
        C. Allow film to dry completely

PROCESSING FILM

Developing. In total darkness, load the film on
the spindle and enclose it in the developing tank.
Be careful not to allow the film to touch the tank
walls or other film. Add the developing solution,
turn the lights on, and set the timer for seven
minutes. Agitate for five seconds initially and
then every half minute.

Stopping. When the timer sounds, drain the developing solution from the tank and add the stop
bath. Agitate continually for 30 seconds.

Fixing. Drain the stop bath and add the fixing
solution. Allow the film to remain in the fixing
solution for two to four minutes. Agitate for five
seconds initially and then every half minute.

Washing. Remove the tank top and wash the film
for at least 30 minutes under running water.

Drying. Suspend the film from a hanger to dry.
It is generally advisable to place a drip pan below the rack. Sponge the film gently to remove
excess water. Allow the film to dry completely.

**When you present your information in steps, you must carefully
consider the needs of your reader. Do not assume that your reader**

is as familiar with your subject as you are. Even for a simple process, be sure that you list *all* steps and that you explain in adequate detail how each step is performed. Sometimes you must also indicate the purpose or function of each step.

In some instructions or process descriptions, the steps can be presented in one sequence only. The steps for using a pay telephone, for example, must be carried out in the sequence in which they are listed. In other instructions or process descriptions, the steps can be presented in the sequence that the writer thinks is most effective.

Chronological

In a chronological sequence, you arrange events in the order in which they occur in time, beginning with the first event, going on to the next event, and so on until you have reached the last event. Trip reports, work schedules, minutes of meetings, and certain accident reports are among the types of writing in which information may be organized chronologically.

In the following report, a firefighter describes the events of a fire at a lumber mill. After providing important background information, the writer presents the events according to their time of occurrence.

OUTLINE

Woodworking Plant Fire

```
    I. Setting
       A. Pile of combustible by-products stored
          near two buildings
       B. Fire building used as electric shop and
          storage area for lumber
       C. Fire building contained flammable liquids
       D. Fire building contained sprinkler system
   II. Cause of fire
       A. Spontaneous ignition of combustible by-
          products, which spread to second building
       B. Fire aided by 40-mph wind
  III. Events of fire
       A. 6 A.M.: Fire first noticed
       B. 7 A.M. (approx.): Plant superintendent ar-
          rived and wet smoldering area
       C. 1:20 P.M. Fire resumed in same area
       D. 1:25 P.M. (approx.): Fire department
          called
       E. Fire spread to second building; pumping
          equipment activated 15 to 30 minutes later
```

WOODWORKING PLANT FIRE[1]

Exposed Building Destroyed
Notification Delayed

July 24, 19--
Burney, California

Wood bark, sawdust, and wood chips were stored in three piles about 100 feet south of one building at this lumber mill and 150 feet west of a second building. The second building, called the "panel plant," consisted of one story and a partial attic and was used in part as an electric shop and in part for the storage of finished lumber. About six pallet loads of Class I flammable liquids in 55-gallon drums were stored in the western section. The building contained a sprinkler system.

Fire, caused by spontaneous ignition of the piled bark, spread to sawdust and chip piles, then to the chip-loading facilities, and finally to the panel plant. A 40-mph wind was blowing in the direction of the panel plant.

A watchman first noticed the fire in the bark pile about 6:00 A.M. He notified the plant superintendent, who arrived more than an hour later, hosed down the smoldering bark pile, and set up several irrigation sprinklers to wet the area.

At about 1:20 P.M., smoke was seen at the further end of the bark pile. The hose was not long enough to reach this area and the local fire department was called, nearly eight hours after the fire was originally discovered.

The fire burned up into the hollow joisted roof of the panel plant. The sprinklers were on a dry system and, from accounts of witnesses, it is estimated that the fire pump was not started until after the fire had been burning in the panel plant for 15 to 30 minutes.

The plant was a $350,000 loss. . . .

This report follows a chronological sequence because the time in which the events occurred and the intervals between events are crucial to an understanding of how the fire developed. Consequently, the chronological sequence is the best method for organizing this report.

Spatial

In a spatial sequence, you describe an object or a process according to the physical arrangement of its features. Depending upon the subject, you may describe the features from top to bottom, from side to side, from east to west (or west to east), from inside to outside, and so on. Descriptions of this kind rely mainly on dimension (height,

[1] "Bimonthly Fire Record," *Fire Journal* 72 (March 1977), p. 24.

width, length), direction (up, down, north, south), shape (rectangular, square, semicircular), and proportion (one-half, two-thirds). Features are described in relation to one another:

One end is raised six to eight inches higher than the other end to permit the rain to run off.

Features are also described in relation to their surroundings:

The lot is located on the east bank of the Kingman River.

The spatial method of organization is commonly used in descriptions of buildings and laboratory equipment, in proposals for landscape work, in construction-site progress reports, and, in combination with a step-by-step sequence, in many types of instructions.

The following description of a small house relies on a bottom-to-top, clockwise (south to west to north to east) sequence, beginning with the front door:

OUTLINE

Interior of a Two-Story, Five-Room House

I. Ground floor
   A. Front hall and stairwell
   B. Dining room
   C. Kitchen
   D. Bathroom
   E. Living room
II. Second floor
   A. Hallway
   B. Southwest bedroom
   C. Northwest bedroom
   D. Bathroom
   E. Bathroom
   F. Master bedroom

INTERIOR OF A TWO-STORY, FIVE-ROOM HOUSE

The front door faces south and opens into a hallway seven feet deep and ten feet wide. At the end of the hallway is the stairwell, which begins on the right-hand (east) side of the hallway, rises five steps to a landing, and reverses direction at the left-hand (west) side of the hallway. To the left (west) of the hallway is the dining room, which measures 15 feet along its southern exposure and 10 feet along its western exposure. Directly to the north of the dining room

is the kitchen, which measures ten feet along its
western exposure and 15 feet along its northern
exposure. To the east of the kitchen, along the
northern side of the house, is a bathroom that
measures 10 feet (west to east) by 5 feet. Parallel to this bathroom is a passageway having the
same dimensions as the bathroom and leading from
the kitchen to the living room. The living room,
which measures 15 feet (west to east) by 20 feet
(north to south), occupies the entire eastern end
of the floor.
    On the second floor, at the top of the stairs
is an L-shaped hallway, 5 feet wide. The base of
the "L," over the front door, is 15 feet long. The
vertical arm of the "L" is 13 feet long. To the
west of the hall is the southwest bedroom, which
measures 10 feet along its southern exposure and 8
feet along its western exposure. Directly to the
north, over the kitchen, is the northwest bedroom,
which measures 12 feet along its western exposure
and 10 feet along its northern exposure. To the
east, at the end of the hall, is a bathroom, which
is 5 feet wide along the northern side of the
house and 7 feet long. To the east of this bathroom and also along the northern side of the house
is the master bathroom, which is 10 feet square
and is entered from the master bedroom, which is
directly over the living room. Like the living
room, the master bedroom measures 15 feet along
the northern and southern exposures of the house
and 20 feet along the eastern exposure.

Decreasing Order of Importance

When you organize your information in decreasing order of importance, you begin with the most important fact or point, then go on
to the next most important, and so on, ending with the least important.
Newspaper readers are familiar with this sequence of information.
The most significant information always appears first in a news story,
with related but secondary information completing the story.

Decreasing order of importance is an especially appropriate
method of organization for a report addressed to a busy decision-maker,
who may be able to reach a decision after considering only the most
important points—and who may not even have time to read the entire
report. This sequence of information is useful, too, for a report written
for a variety of readers, some of whom may be interested in only
the major points and others in all the points. The following outline
presents an example of such an approach.

OUTLINE

Candidates for Chief of Claims Processing Section

I. Most qualified candidate: Mildred Bryant,
acting chief
   A. Positive factors
      1. Twelve years' experience in claims pro-
         cessing
      2. Thoroughly familiar with section's op-
         eration
      3. Strong production record
      4. Continually ranked "outstanding" on
         job appraisals
   B. Negative factors
      1. Supervisory experience limited to pres-
         ent tenure as acting chief
      2. Lacks college degree required by job
         description
II. Second most qualified candidate: Michael Bas-
tick, claims coordinator
   A. Positive factors
      1. Able administrator
      2. Seven years' experience in section's
         operation
      3. Currently enrolled in management-train-
         ing course
   B. Negative factors
      1. Lacks supervisory experience
      2. Most recent work indirectly related to
         claims processing
III. Third most qualified candidate: Jane Fine,
administrative assistant
   A. Positive factors
      1. Skilled administrator
      2. Three years' experience in claims pro-
         cessing
   B. Negative factors
      1. Lacks broad knowledge of claims proce-
         dures
      2. Lacks supervisory experience

MEMORANDUM

To: Mary Vincenti, Chief, Personnel Department
From: Frank W. Russo, Chief, Claims Department *FWR*
Date: November 13, 19--
Subject: Selection of Chief of the Claims Pro-
          cessing Section

The most qualified candidate for Chief of the
Claims Processing Section is Mildred Bryant, who

is at present Acting Chief of the Claims Processing Section. In her twelve years in the Claims
Department, Mrs. Bryant has gained wide experience
in all facets of the department's operations. She
has maintained a consistently high production record and has demonstrated the skills and knowledge
that are required for the supervisory duties she
is now handling in an acting capacity. Another
consideration is the continual rating of "outstanding" she has received in all categories of
her job-performance appraisals. However, her supervisory experience is limited to her present
three-month tenure as acting chief of the section,
and she lacks the college degree required by the
job description.

Michael Bastik, claims coordinator, my second
choice, also has strong potential for the position. An able administrator, he has been with the
company for seven years. For the past year he has
been enrolled in several management-training
courses at the university. He is ranked second,
however, because he lacks supervisory experience
and because his most recent work has been with the
department's maintenance and supply components. He
would be the best person to take over many of
Mildred Bryant's responsibilities if she should be
made full-time chief of the Claims Processing
Section.

Jane Fine, my third-ranking candidate, has shown
herself a skilled administrator in her three years
with the Claims Consideration Section. Despite her
obvious potential, my main objection to her is
that, compared with the other top candidates, she
lacks the breadth of experience in claims processing that would be required of someone responsible for managing the Claims Processing Section.
Jane Fine also lacks on-the-job supervisory experience.

Increasing Order of Importance

When you want the most important of several ideas to be freshest
in your reader's mind at the end of your writing, organize your information by increasing order of importance. This sequence is useful
in argumentative writing when saving your strongest points until the
end suits your purpose and your perception of your audience. The
sequence begins with the least important point or fact, then moves
to the next least important, and builds finally to the most important

point at the end. You lead your reader to the conclusion you want him or her to reach by building your case inductively.

Writing organized by increasing order of importance has the disadvantage of beginning weakly, with the least important information. This can cause your reader to become impatient before reaching your main point. But for writing in which the ideas lead, point by point, to an important conclusion, increasing order of importance is an effective method of organization. Reports on production or personnel goals are often arranged by this method, as are oral presentations. Below are an outline and a memorandum in which this approach is used.

OUTLINE

Recruiting Electronics Technicians

    I. Staffing problem
        A. Too few qualified electronics technicians
        B. New recruiting program necessary
   II. Recruiting veterans
        A. Relied heavily on veterans in past
        B. Fewer veterans now available
        C. Want ads less successful than in past
  III. Apprentice program
        A. Providing insufficient numbers
        B. Fewer high school graduates entering program
   IV. Technical colleges
        A. Provide pool of trained technicians
        B. Recommend recruiting from this group

MEMORANDUM

To: William D. Vane, Vice President, Operations
From: Harry Matthews, Personnel Department *HM*
Date: December 3, 19--
Subject: Recruiting Qualified Electronics Technicians

To keep our company staffed with qualified electronics technicians, we will have to redirect our recruiting program.

In the past dozen years, we have relied heavily on the recruitment of skilled veterans. An end to the military draft, as well as attractive reenlistment bonuses for skilled technicians now in uniform, have all but eliminated veterans as a source of trained employees. Our attempts to reach this group through ads in service and daily newspapers have not been successful recently. I think that the

want ads should continue, although each passing
month brings fewer and fewer veterans as job applicants.

Our in-house apprentice program has not provided
the needed personnel either. High school enrollments in the area are continually dropping. Each
year, fewer high school graduates, our one source
of trainees for the apprentice program, enter the
shop. Even vigorous Career Day recruiting has
yielded disappointing results. The number of students interested in the apprentice program has
declined proportionately as school enrollment has
dropped.

The local and regional technical schools produce
the greatest number of qualified electronics
technicians. These graduates tend to be highly
motivated, in part because many have obtained
their education at their own expense. The training
and experience they have received in the technical
programs, moreover, are first-rate. Competition
for these graduates is keen, but I recommend that
we increase our recruiting efforts and hire a
larger share of this group than we have been doing.

I would like to meet with you soon to discuss the
details of a more dynamic recruiting program in
the technical schools. I am certain that with the
right recruitment campaign we can find the skilled
personnel essential to our expanding role in
electronics products and services.

General to Specific

In a general-to-specific sequence, you begin your writing with a
general statement and then provide facts or examples to develop and
support that statement. For example, if you begin a report with the
general statement "Companies that diversify are more successful than
those that do not," the remainder of the report would offer examples
and statistics that prove to your reader that companies that diversify
are, in fact, more successful than companies that do not.

A memorandum or report organized in a general-to-specific sequence discusses only one point—the point made in the opening general statement. All other information in the memo or report supports
the general statement, as in the following example.

OUTLINE

Locating Additional Circuit Suppliers

The company needs to locate additional suppliers of circuits because of several related events.

    I. The current supplier is reducing output.
   II. Domestic demand for our calculators continues to increase.
 III. We are expanding into the foreign market.

LOCATING ADDITIONAL CIRCUIT SUPPLIERS

General statement

On the basis of information presented at the Supply Committee meeting on April 14, we recommend that the company locate additional suppliers of integrated circuits. Several related events make such an action necessary.

Our current supplier, ABC Electronics, is reducing its output. Specifically, we can expect a reduction of between 800 and 1,000 units per month for the remainder of this fiscal year. The number of units should stabilize at 15,000 units per month thereafter.

Supporting information

Domestic demand for our calculators continues to grow. Demand during the current fiscal year is up 25,000 units over the last fiscal year. Sales Department projections for the next five years show that demand should peak next year at 50,000 units and then remain at that figure for at least the following four years.

Finally, our overseas expansion into England and West Germany will require additional shipments of 5,000 units per quarter to each country for the remainder of this fiscal year. Sales Department projections put calculator sales for each country at double this rate, or 20,000 units in a fiscal year, for the next five years.

Examples and data that support the general statements are frequently accompanied by charts and graphs. Guidelines for creating and presenting illustrations are given in Chapter 13.

Specific to General

When you organize information in a specific-to-general sequence, you begin with a specific statement and build to a general conclusion. The examples, facts, and statistics that you present in your writing support the general conclusion that comes at the end. For example, if your subject were highway safety, you might begin with details of a specific highway accident, go on to generalize about how that accident was similar to many others, and then present recommendations for reducing the probability of such accidents. For example, if your subject were highway safety, you might begin with details of a specific highway accident, go on to generalize about how that accident was similar to many others, and then present recommendations for reducing the probability of such accidents. If your purpose is to persuade a skeptical reader by providing specific details, this method is useful because it suspends the general point until your case has been made. This method of organization is somewhat like increasing order of importance in that you carefully build your case and do not actually make your point until the end. Here is an example:

OUTLINE

The Facts About Seat Belts

    I. Study of 4,500 accidents involving nearly 13,000 people showed only 20 percent of those involved wore seat belts
  II. Shoulder belts worn by only 4 percent
 III. Studies show passengers without belts are 4 times as likely to be killed as passengers wearing belts
  IV. Estimated 40 percent of front-seat passenger car deaths could be prevented if seat belts were worn
   V. Survival chances in an accident are greater with seat belts

THE FACTS ABOUT SEAT BELTS[2]

Statistic   Recently the Highway Safety Foundation studied the use of seat belts in 4,500 accidents involving nearly 13,000 people. Nearly all these accidents occurred on routes which had a speed limit of at least 40 mph. Only 20 percent of all the vehicle occupants were wearing any kind of seat belt.

Statistic   The shoulder-type belts were even more unpopular than the lap belts, and only 4 percent of the occupants who had shoulder belts were wearing them.

[2] *The Safe Driving Handbook* (New York: Grosset & Dunlap, 1970), pp. 84–85.

Statistic In this study, as in other studies, it was found that vehicle passengers not using seat belts were more than 4 times as likely to be killed as those using them. The driver in some cases escaped a more serious injury by being thrown against the steering wheel.

General conclusion A conservative estimate is that 40 percent of the front-seat passenger car deaths could be prevented if everyone used the seat belts, which the law requires the manufacturer to put into each automobile. If you are in an accident, your chances of survival are far greater if you are using your seat belt.

CHAPTER SUMMARY

This chapter has presented the most commonly used methods of organizing information in job-related writing: step by step, chronological, spatial, decreasing order of importance, increasing order of importance, general to specific, and specific to general. Some subjects lend themselves naturally to a particular method. Other subjects can be organized in more than one way; you must choose the best method on the basis of your reader's needs and the purpose of your writing.

A simple outline will help you to organize the information into a logical sequence before you begin to write. Preparing an outline gives you a chance to reexamine your information and order it in such a way that your reader will understand it as clearly as you do.

EXERCISES

1. Below is a sample of a poorly developed outline. Prepare a new outline in which the weaknesses are corrected.

COMPANY SPORTS

I. Intercompany sports
   A. Advantages to the company
      1. Publicity
      2. Intercompany relations
   B. Disadvantages
      1. Misplaced emphasis
      2. Athletic participation restricted
II. Intracompany sports
   A. Wide participation
   B. Physical fitness

   C. Detracts from work
   D. Risk of injuries

2. The following list contains both major and minor topic heads for a report entitled "Plan to Remodel a 50-Year-Old House to Make It Energy Efficient." Select the heads that you think should be major heads and arrange them in the appropriate sequence. Then select the heads that should go under each major head and arrange them too in the appropriate sequence. Assign Roman numerals to the major heads and capital letters to the minor heads, creating an outline.

   - Insulation
   - Introduction
   - Heat loss through conduction
   - Scope of the report
   - Storm doors and windows
   - The proposed solutions
   - Procedure used to prepare the report
   - Heat loss through air infiltration
   - The problems
   - Weatherstripping
   - Purpose of the report
   - Caulking

3. Insert the following notes into the appropriate places in the outline you created for Exercise 2.

   - Specific costs are not discussed.
   - Caulking is a flexible adhesive.
   - Fiberglass (six inches thick) should be installed between the unfinished basement and the floor.
   - To recommend a remodeling plan to make the house more energy-efficient.
   - Window sashes and casings are loose.
   - The best weatherstripping is the spring-bronze or felt-hair type.
   - The cost of insulating is recovered in fuel savings in five years.
   - The proposed plan does not specify methods or materials.
   - Doors do not close tightly.
   - Such openings allow cold air to enter and heated air to escape.
   - Insulation provides comfort and a sense of well-being.
   - Storm windows and doors should be installed to help reduce air infiltration.
   - Conduction through doors and windows is even worse.
   - The structure of the building and its foundation were studied.

- The house was built at a time when little insulation was used.
- A storm window or door is an extra window or door in an outside wall to help insulate against air infiltration.
- Insulation is material that resists the conduction of heat and cold; it is installed in attics and walls of homes.
- Lack of insulation means that much of the heat passes through the walls and ceilings by conduction.
- Caulking should be done after weatherstripping.
- The history of the house was studied.
- The windows and doors were checked for air leaks.
- Storm windows and doors also reduce conduction through the glass by half.
- Weatherstripping is material that is installed around windows and doors in an outside wall to help insulate against air infiltration.
- Each cavity between the studs in the walls should be filled with foam.
- To recommend improvements that should lower the fuel bills and increase the comfort of residents.
- Doors and windows that are made of thin materials waste vast amounts of heat.
- Eight inches of insulation should be installed in the attic.
- To ensure watertight weatherstripping, windows should be sealed and new window latches should be installed.
- Caulking provides an airtight seal between the doors and windows and the building materials.
- The report deals with the causes of heat loss and the solutions being recommended to solve the problem.

4. Create an outline for one of the following topics, organizing it in a *step-by-step* sequence. Using the outline, write a paper of assigned length on the topic.

   a. Changing a washer in a wash basin faucet
   b. Starting and banking a fire in a wood-burning stove
   c. Tuning a six-string acoustic guitar
   d. Opening a checking account
   e. Sharpening a chain-saw blade
   f. Splicing together two pieces of movie film
   g. Bathing a bedridden adult
   h. Repairing a broken window
   i. Borrowing money on a life insurance policy
   j. How a monarch butterfly egg becomes an adult

5. Create an outline for one of the following topics, organizing it by a *chronological* sequence. Using the outline, write a paper of assigned length on the topic.

   a. A report on an accident
   b. Instructions for breeding, raising, and selling puppies or other pets
   c. A description of the life cycle of a typical fruit, from blossom to ripe fruit, in one growing season

6. Create an outline for one of the following topics, organizing it in a *spatial* sequence. Using the outline, write a paper of assigned length on the topic. Without relying on illustrations, describe the topic clearly enough so that a classmate, if asked, could create an accurate drawing or diagram based on your description.

   a. The layout of your apartment or of a floor in your home
   b. The layout of the reference room or other area of the school library
   c. The dimensions and pertinent features of the grounds of a public building
   d. The layout of a vegetable or flower garden
   e. The layout of the shop, office, or laboratory where you work
   f. Instructions for disinfecting a hospital room, exterminating insects in a kitchen or other area, or painting or wallpapering a room

7. Create an outline for one of the following topics, organizing it by a *decreasing-order-of-importance* sequence. Using the outline, write a paper of assigned length on the topic.

   a. Your job qualifications
   b. The advantages to you of living in a particular city or area of the country
   c. The importance of preventive maintenance of a machine or piece of equipment with which you are familiar
   d. The importance of preventive care in one health-related area (diet, exercise, dental care, and so on)

8. Create an outline for one of the following topics, organizing it by an *increasing-order-of-importance* sequence. Using the outline, write a paper of assigned length on the topic.

   a. The college courses that you believe will be most important to your career (discuss no more than five)

   b. Why smoking should or should not be permitted in the classroom or on the job

   c. The advantages of learning to pilot a small airplane

   d. The reasons why you need a pay raise

   e. The advantages of a home solar-heating system

   f. A proposal to change a procedure where you work

9. For this exercise, use a *general-to-specific* sequence. Choose one
of the following statements, then support it with pertinent facts,
examples, anecdotes, and so on. Outline the information and write
a paper of assigned length based on the outline.

   a. Volunteer jobs provide valuable experience in the working
world

   b. For families on limited means, budgeting is essential

   c. The mark of a capable administrator is willingness to delegate
authority

10. For this exercise, use a *specific-to-general* sequence. For one of
the following sets of data, study the trends or patterns that are
presented, draw your own conclusions, and state the conclusions
in a plausible general statement. Outline the information that
supports your main point, and write a paper of assigned length
based on your outline. Alternatively, as a basis for this exercise
you may select other information from lists and tables in current
yearbooks, almanacs, or newspapers.

   a. Deaths from Motor Vehicle Accidents in the United States

1978	51,500
1977	48,849
1976	44,520
1975	45,853
1974	46,402
1973	55,511
1972	56,278

   b. Vocational Training in the United States, 1979

Type of Training	*Men (18–24)*	*Women (18–24)*
Office	300,000	1,100,000
Nursing, health	63,000	432,000
Trades	1,100,000	384,000
Engineering	277,000	19,000
Agriculture and home economics	83,000	46,000
Other	153,000	93,000

3

Writing the Draft

As illustrated in Chapter 1, grouping the facts and details that you wish to include in your writing is essential to effective organization. But this grouping process also serves a further function. Once you have determined which facts and details illustrate and support which main ideas of your writing, you are ready to construct your paragraphs—the major building blocks of any piece of writing. At this stage, clear groupings of the pertinent points can be extremely helpful.

Suppose you were responsible for writing the report of a committee examining possible locations for a new distribution center. One group of details might concern the way in which the committee narrowed thirty possible locations to three.

- Committee considered 30 locations
- Twenty locations eliminated because of labor supply, tax structure, and so forth
- Committee selected three cities to visit
- Committee visited Chicago, Minneapolis, and Philadelphia
- Committee's observations follow in the report

From this group of items, you could write the following paragraph:

The committee narrowed 30 possible locations for the new distribution center to three. Twenty possibilities were eliminated almost immediately for reasons ranging from unfavorable tax structures to inadequate labor supplies. Of the remaining ten locations, the committee selected for intensive study the three cities that seemed to offer the best transportation and support facilities: Chicago, Minneapolis, and Philadelphia. The committee then visited these three cities, and its observations on each follow in this report.

Because the sentences in the paragraph evolved from the items listed in the group, every sentence is directly related to one central idea—narrowing the selection of possible locations for the distribution center to three cities. Notice that the paragraph does not contain the committee's final recommendation or the specific advantages of each of the three cities. Those details will follow later in the report. To include such details in this paragraph would make the paragraph stray from its one central idea. In fact, the function of any paragraph is to develop a single thought or idea within a larger piece of writing.

PARAGRAPH UNITY

When every sentence in a paragraph contributes to developing one central idea, the paragraph has *unity*. If a paragraph contains sentences that do not develop the central idea, it lacks unity. The following is a later paragraph from the report in which possible locations for the new distribution center are evaluated. Does this paragraph have unity?

Probably the greatest advantage of Chicago as the location for our new distribution center is its excellent transportation facilities. The city is served by three major railroads. In fact, Chicago was at one time the hub of cross-country rail transportation. Chicago is also a major center of the trucking industry, and most of the nation's large freight carriers have terminals there. We are concerned, however, about the delivery problems that we've had with several truck carriers. We've had far fewer problems with air freight. Both domestic and international air cargo services are available at O'Hare International Airport. Finally, except in the winter months when the Great Lakes are frozen, Chicago is a seaport, accessible through the St. Lawrence Seaway.

Every sentence in this paragraph should have been about *the advantages of Chicago's transportation facilities*. Three sentences, however, do not develop that central idea: the sentence about Chicago as the former hub of rail transportation, and the two sentences about delivery problems. These sentences are italicized below:

Probably the greatest advantage of Chicago as the location for our new distribution center is its excellent transportation facilities.

The city is served by three major railroads. *In fact, Chicago was at one time the hub of cross-country rail transportation.* Chicago is also a major center of the trucking industry, and most of the nation's large freight carriers have terminals there. *We are concerned, however, about the delivery problems that we've had with several truck carriers. We've had far fewer problems with air freight.* Both domestic and international air cargo services are available at O'Hare International Airport. Finally, except in the winter months when the Great Lakes are frozen, Chicago is a seaport, accessible through the St. Lawrence Seaway.

Now read the paragraph without the italicized sentences. Each of the remaining sentences is directly related to the central idea, and the paragraph has unity.

Probably the greatest advantage of Chicago as the location for our new distribution center is its excellent transportation facilities. The city is served by three major railroads. Chicago is also a major center of the trucking industry, and most of the nation's large freight carriers have terminals there. Both domestic and international air cargo services are available at O'Hare International Airport. Finally, except in the winter months when the Great Lakes are frozen, Chicago is a seaport, accessible through the St. Lawrence Seaway.

One way to make sure that your paragraph has unity is to provide a *topic sentence,* which is a sentence within a paragraph that clearly states the central idea of that paragraph. If every sentence in the paragraph directly relates to the topic sentence, the paragraph will have unity.

Notice that all the sentences in the following paragraph directly relate to the topic sentence:

Probably the greatest advantage of Chicago as the location for our new distribution center is its excellent transportation facilities. The city is served by three major railroads. Chicago is also a major center of the trucking industry, and most of the nation's large freight carriers have terminals there. Both domestic and international air cargo service is available at O'Hare International Airport. Finally, except in the winter months when the Great Lakes are frozen, Chicago is a seaport, accessible through the St. Lawrence Seaway.

Beginning a paragraph with the topic sentence helps both the writer and the reader. The writer has no difficulty constructing a unified paragraph because every sentence can be measured against the topic sentence and the central idea it expresses. And the reader knows immediately what the paragraph is about because the opening sentence states the central idea. Busy readers, especially, appreciate being told at once what a paragraph will deal with. For this reason, topic sentences are usually the first sentences of paragraphs in on-the-job writing.

Occasionally, however, a topic sentence may be placed somewhere other than at the beginning of a paragraph. A topic sentence may be the last sentence of a paragraph, for example. Placing the topic sentence at the end of a paragraph emphasizes the central idea because all the sentences build up to that idea. Notice how the sentences in the following paragraph lead up to the topic sentence:

> A study by the Department of Agriculture revealed that insect damage in our region increased from 15% to 23% between 1975 and 1977. During this past year, many farmers reported a 30% increase in insect damage over damage that had occurred the previous year. Furthermore, another recent study found that certain destructive insects are migrating north into our area. *Clearly, we should prepare for increased insect damage in the coming year.*

Although a topic sentence placed at the end of a paragraph provides a forceful conclusion, it also makes reading the paragraph more difficult. Especially in on-the-job situations, where time is at a premium, the reader may become irritated at having to plow through details to reach the main point of a paragraph. Therefore, it is best to place topic sentences at the ends of paragraphs only occasionally.

COHERENCE

An effective paragraph has not only unity but *coherence;* that is, it takes the reader logically and smoothly from one sentence to the next. When a paragraph is coherent, the reader clearly recognizes that one sentence or idea leads logically to the next, that that sentence or idea leads to the following one, and so on. Consider the following paragraph. Does each sentence or idea lead logically and clearly to the one that follows?

> Most adjustable office chairs have nylon hub tubes that hold metal spindle rods. To ensure trouble-free operation, lubricate these spindle rods occasionally. Loosen the set screw in the adjustable bell. Lift the chair from the base so that the entire spindle rod is accessible. Apply the lubricant to the spindle rod and the nylon washer, using the lubricant sparingly to prevent dripping. Replace the chair and tighten the set screw.

Because each sentence in the paragraph says something about how to lubricate an adjustable office chair, the paragraph has unity. Yet the paragraph does not move as smoothly from one sentence to the next as it could. Nor does the paragraph make as clear as possible how each idea relates to the others. Transitional devices, as discussed below, will achieve both these goals.

Transitions Between Sentences

Transitional devices are words and phrases that help the reader to move smoothly from one sentence to the next and to see the logical relationships between the sentences. Notice how the simple technique of putting the steps in sequence (see the italicized words and phrases) provides effective transitions between ideas in the sample paragraph:

> Most adjustable office chairs have nylon hub tubes that hold metal spindle rods. To ensure trouble-free operation, lubricate these spindle rods occasionally. *First,* loosen the set screw in the adjustable bell. *Then* lift the chair from the base so that the entire spindle rod is accessible. *Next,* apply the lubricant to the spindle rod and the nylon washer, using the lubricant sparingly to prevent dripping. *When you have finished,* replace the chair and tighten the set screw.

Now, because the transitional devices provide coherence, the reader can follow the writer's step-by-step instructions easily. The word *first* indicates that the statement following is the first step in lubricating the rods. The words *then* and *next* point out the logical, step-by-step relationship of the instructions that follow. The phrase *when you have finished* tells the reader that the lubricating process is finished and that a new instruction will follow.

The following list includes other words and phrases that commonly function as transitional devices:

- To express result: *therefore, as a result, consequently, thus, hence*
- To express example: *for example, for instance, specifically, as an illustration*
- To express comparison: *similarly, likewise*
- To express contrast: *but, yet, still, however, nevertheless, on the other hand*
- To express addition: *moreover, furthermore, also, too, besides, in addition*
- To express time: *now, later, meanwhile, since then, after that, before that time*
- To express sequence: *first, second, third, then, next, finally*

Some of the above words and phrases are nearly synonymous but imply somewhat different logical connections. Be sure that the transitional device you choose conveys the precise meaning you intend.

Another transitional device is the use of pronouns, such as *he, she, they,* and *it.* Because pronouns refer to a person or thing mentioned in a previous sentence, they bind sentences and ideas together. Notice the use of pronouns as transitional devices in the following paragraph:

It **refers to punch press**	We have recently discovered a problem with the #41 *punch press. It* consistently fails to retract fully when *it* is shut off at the end of the second shift. *First-shift employees* are concerned that this condition poses a safety hazard. *They* believe that the press could go
They **refers to first-shift employees**	through a cycle after the power has been turned on. *Bill Taylor,* a second-shift supervisor, reports that the maintenance department does not consider the problem to be a safety hazard. *He* has pointed
He **refers to Bill Taylor**	out to me, however, that when the power is turned on, the safety shield is not in place. *He* believes that this fact warrants a thorough analysis of the problem.

Although pronouns can be excellent transitional devices, they confuse the reader if the person or thing to which the pronoun refers is not perfectly clear.

CONFUSING   Midcity College is located in the central business district of the city. *It* is very large.

It is confusing because the reader must guess whether *it* refers to the college, the business district, or the city. In such a case, repeating a word is better.

BETTER   Midcity College is located in the central business district of the city. The *college* is very large.

The problem of pronoun reference is discussed in Chapter 5.

Another transitional device that links sentences and ideas is the repetition of key words and phrases. Notice how repetition of the key words and phrases in the paragraph below moves the paragraph forward:

Over the past several months, I have heard complaints about the Merit Award *Program.* Specifically, many employees feel that this *program* should be linked to annual *salary increases.* They believe that *salary increases* would provide a much better incentive than the current $150 to $300 *cash awards* for exceptional service. In addition, these *employees believe* that their supervisors consider the *cash awards* a satisfactory alternative to salary increases. Although

I don't think this practice is widespread, the fact that the *employees believe* that it is justifies a reevaluation of the Merit Award Program.

Transitions Between Paragraphs

Transitional devices used to link sentences can also be effective for transition between paragraphs. The repetition of a key phrase, for example, connects the first paragraph below with the one that follows.

Consumers spend more money for plumbing repairs than for any other home repair service. The most common repair that plumbers make is the clearing of drains. Since the kitchen *sink drain* is used more often than any other drain in the home, that is the drain that is most often clogged.

Clearing the *sink drain* yourself is easier than you might expect. You probably have all the tools you need. . . .

Another transitional device for linking paragraphs is to begin a paragraph with a sentence that summarizes the preceding paragraph. In the following excerpt from a report, notice how the first sentence in the second paragraph summarizes the ideas presented in the first paragraph:

Each year, forest fires in our region cause untold destruction. For example, wood ashes washed into streams after a fire often kill large numbers of fish. In addition, the destruction of the vegetation along stream banks causes water temperatures to rise, making the stream unfit for several varieties of cold-water fish. Forest fires, moreover, hurt the tourist and recreation business, for vacationers are not likely to visit flame-blackened areas.

The opening sentence summarizes the examples from the preceding paragraph

These losses, and many other indirect losses caused by forest fires, damage not only the quality of life but also the economy of our region. They also represent a huge drain on the resources and manpower of the Department of Natural Resources. For example, our financial investment last year in fighting forest fires. . . .

If used sparingly, another effective transitional device between paragraphs is to ask a question at the end of one paragraph and answer it at the beginning of the next. This device works well in the following example:

Transition using a question and answer

Automation has become an ugly word in the American vocabulary because it has sometimes meant the displacement of employees from their jobs. But the all-important fact that is so often overlooked is that automation invariably creates many more jobs than it eliminates. The vast number of people employed through automation in the American automobile industry, compared with the number of people who had been employed in the harness-and-carriage-making business, is a classic example. Almost always, the jobs that have been eliminated by automation have been menial, unskilled jobs, and the people who have been displaced have been forced to increase their skills. The result has been better and higher-paying jobs for many workers. *In view of these facts, is automation really bad?*

> *There is no question that automation has made our country the wealthiest and most technologically advanced nation the world has ever known. Furthermore, it has freed many people from boring and repetitive work. . . .*

When you use this transitional device, make sure that the second paragraph does, in fact, answer the question posed in the first. And, again, do not use this device too often. Your reader may find it monotonous and gimmicky.

PARAGRAPH LENGTH

Paragraph length should be tailored to the reader's convenience. Specifically, a paragraph should help the reader by providing a physical break on the page as well as by signaling a new idea. Long paragraphs can intimidate your reader by failing to provide manageable subdivisions of thought. Overly short paragraphs have a disadvantage too: they may make it difficult for the reader to see the logical relationships between ideas in your writing. A series of short paragraphs can also sacrifice unity by breaking a single idea into several pieces.

Although there are no fixed rules for the length of paragraphs, paragraphs in on-the-job writing average about one hundred words each, with two or three paragraphs to a double-spaced, typewritten page. Paragraphs in letters tend to be shorter; two- or even one-sentence paragraphs are not unusual in letters. The best advice is that a paragraph should be just long enough to deal adequately with the central idea stated in its topic sentence. A new paragraph should begin whenever the subject changes significantly.

WRITING AN OPENING

What should the opening statement of your writing do? It should (1) identify your subject and (2) catch the interest of your reader.

Most readers of on-the-job writing are preoccupied with other business when they begin to read a memo, letter, or report. Therefore, you must catch their interest and focus their attention on the subject you are writing about. Even if your readers are required to read what you've written, catching their interest at the outset will help ensure that they pay close attention to what follows. And if you are attempting to persuade your readers, you *must* catch their interest if your writing is to succeed.

To catch your reader's interest, you first must know your reader's needs (as discussed in Chapter 1). An awareness of those needs will help you to determine which details your reader will find important and thus interesting. Consider the following opening from a memo written by a personnel manager to her supervisor. This opening not only states the subject of the report but also promises that the writer will offer solutions to a specific problem. And solutions to problems are always of interest to a reader.

MEMORANDUM

```
To:    Paul Route, Corporate Relations Director
From:    Sondra L. Rivera, Personnel Manager SLR
Date:    November 1, 19--
Subject:    Decreasing Applications from Local Col-
            lege Graduates

This year only 12 local college graduates have
applied for jobs at Benson Tubular Steel. Last
year over 30 graduates applied, and the year be-
fore 50 applied. After talking with several col-
lege counselors, I am confident that we can solve
the problem of decreasing applications from local
colleges.

First, we could resume our advertisements in local
student newspapers . . .
```

For most types of writing done in offices, shops, and laboratories, openings that simply get to the point are more effective than those that provide detailed background information. Furthermore, the subject of a memo or report is often, by itself, enough to catch the reader's interest. The following openings are typical; however, do not feel that you must slavishly follow these patterns. Rather, always first consider the purpose of your writing and the needs of your reader and then tailor your opening accordingly.

Correspondence

Mr. George T. Whittier
1720 Old Line Road
Thomasbury, WV 26401

Dear Mr. Whittier:

You will be happy to know that we have corrected
the error in your bank balance. The new balance
shows . . .

Progress Report Letter

William Chang, M.D.
Phelps Building
9003 Shaw Avenue
Parksville, MD 29099

Dear Dr. Chang:

To date, 18 of the 26 specimens you submitted for
analysis have been examined. Our preliminary
analysis indicates . . .

Longer Progress Report

PROGRESS REPORT ON REWIRING THE SPORTS ARENA

The rewiring program at the Sports Arena is
continuing ahead of schedule. Although the cost of
certain equipment is higher than our original bid
had indicated, we expect to complete the project
without exceeding our budget, because the speed
with which the project is being completed will
save labor costs.

Work Completed

As of August 15th, we have . . .

Memorandum

MEMORANDUM

To: Jane T. Meyers, Chief Budget Manager
From: Charles Benson, Assistant to the Personnel *CB*
        Director
Date: June 12, 19--
Subject: Budget Estimates for Fiscal Year 19--

```
The personnel budget estimates for fiscal year
19-- are as follows: . . .
```

Notice that all these openings get directly to the point; they do not introduce irrelevant subjects or include unnecessary details. They give the readers exactly what they need to focus their attention on what is to follow. (For examples of openings for special types of writing, such as application letters, complaint letters, and formal reports, refer to specific entries in the index.)

WRITING A CLOSING

A closing not only ties your writing together and ends it emphatically but also may make a significant point. A closing may recommend a course of action, offer a value judgment, speculate on the implications of your ideas, make a prediction, or summarize your main points. Even if your closing only states, "If I can be of further help, please call me" or "I would appreciate your comments," you are showing consideration for your reader and thereby gaining your reader's goodwill.

The way you close depends on the purpose of your writing and the needs of your reader. For example, the committee report on possible locations for a new distribution center could end with a recommendation. A report studying a company's annual sales could end with a judgment about why sales are up or down. A report for a retail department store about consumer buying trends could end by speculating on the implications of these trends, perhaps even suggesting new product lines that the store might carry in the future. A lengthy report could end with a summary of the main points covered to pull the ideas together for the reader.

The following closings, shown paired with the openings previously illustrated to provide a context, are typical.

Correspondence

```
Mr. George T. Whittier
1720 Old Line Road
Thomasbury, WV 26401

Dear Mr. Whittier:

You will be happy to know that we have corrected
the error in your bank balance. The new balance
shows . . .
```

Polite, helpful **closing**	Please accept our thanks for your continued business, and let us know if we can be of further help.

Sincerely,

Michael Fosse

Michael Fosse
Branch Manager

Progress Report Letter

William Chang, M.D.
Phelps Building
9003 Shaw Avenue
Parksville, MD 29099

Dear Dr. Chang:

To date, 18 of the 26 specimens you submitted for analysis have been examined. Our preliminary analysis indicates . . .

Closing that **recommends a** **response**	These results indicate that you may need to alter your testing procedure to eliminate the impurities we found in specimens A-G and K.

Sincerely,

Marion Lamb

Marion Lamb
Research Assistant

Longer Progress Report

PROGRESS REPORT ON REWIRING THE SPORTS ARENA

The rewiring program at the Sports Arena is continuing ahead of schedule. Although the cost of certain equipment is higher than our original bid had indicated, we expect to complete the project without exceeding our budget, because the speed with which the project is being completed will save labor costs.

Work Completed

As of August 15th, we have . . .

Closing that makes a prediction

Although my original estimate on equipment ($20,000) has been exceeded by $2,300, my original labor estimate ($60,000) has been reduced by $3,500; therefore, I will easily stay within the limits of my original bid. In addition, I see no difficulty in having the arena finished in time for the December 23 Christmas program.

Memorandum

MEMORANDUM

To: Jane T. Meyers, Chief Budget Manager
From: Charles Benson, Assistant to the Personnel _CB_
         Director
Date: June 12, 19--
Subject: Budget Estimates for Fiscal Year 19--

The personnel budget estimates for fiscal year 19-- are as follows: . . .

Closing that offers a judgment

Although our estimate calls for a substantially higher budget than in the three previous years, we believe that it is justified by our planned expansion.

MEMORANDUM

To: Paul Route, Corporate Relations Director
From: Sondra L. Rivera, Personnel Manager _SLR_
Date: November 1, 19--
Subject: Decreasing Applications from Local College Graduates

This year only 12 local college graduates have applied for jobs at Benson Tubular Steel. Last year over 30 graduates applied, and the year before 50 applied. After talking with several college counselors, I am confident that we can solve the problem of decreasing applications from local colleges.

First, we could resume our advertisements in local student newspapers . . .

Closing that summarizes main points

As this report has indicated, we could attract more recent graduates by (1) increasing our advertising in local student newspapers, (2) re-

suming our co-op program, (3) sending a representative to career day programs at local
colleges and high schools, (4) inviting local
college instructors to teach in-house courses
here in the plant, and (5) encouraging our employees to attend evening classes at various
colleges.

As these examples show, a good closing is concise and ends your
writing emphatically, making it sound finished. Any of the methods
for closing can be effective, depending on the purpose of your writing
and the needs of your reader. Be careful, however, not to close with
a cliché or a platitude, such as "While profits have increased with
the introduction of this new product, *the proof is in the pudding."*
Also be careful not to introduce a new topic in your closing. A closing
should always relate to and reinforce the ideas presented in the opening and body of your writing.

CHAPTER SUMMARY

Grouping the facts and details you wish to include in your writing
(discussed in Chapter 1) leads naturally to the construction of paragraphs. To be effective, paragraphs must have unity and coherence.
Unity is achieved when every sentence in a paragraph relates to the
single central idea stated in the topic sentence. *Coherence* is achieved
when the ideas are arranged in a logical order and transitional devices
link sentences and paragraphs, enabling the reader to move smoothly
from sentence to sentence and from paragraph to paragraph.

Good openings identify the subject of the writing and catch the
reader's interest. Good closings not only show consideration for the
reader but may recommend a course of action, make a prediction,
offer a judgment, speculate on the implications of the ideas presented
in the writing, or summarize the main points.

EXERCISES

1. Underline the topic sentences in the following paragraphs.

a.   Whether you use a hand mower, a power reel mower, or a
rotary power mower to cut your lawn, the blades should be sharp
enough to trim the grass cleanly without bruising or tearing the
leaves. Both the cutting edge of the bedknife or reel-type mower
and the reel blades should be sharp, and the reel should be set
firmly against the bedknife. Make any necessary adjustments of
the bedknife or of the roller (which determines the height of cut)

on a flat surface, such as a concrete walk or floor. Rotary mower blades in particular require frequent sharpening. On most rotary mowers, height of cut is fixed by adjusting the wheels in holes or slots on the mower frame.

b.   One property of material considered for manufacturing processes is hardness. Hardness is the internal resistance of the material to the forcing apart or closing together of its molecules. Another property is ductility, the characteristic of material that permits it to be drawn into a wire. The smaller the diameter of the wire into which the material can be drawn, the greater the ductility. Material may also possess malleability, the property that makes it capable of being rolled or hammered into thin sheets of various shapes. Engineers, in selecting materials to employ in manufacturing, must consider the materials' properties before deciding which ones are most desirable for use in production.

c.   People who raise houseplants must periodically replace the soil that serves as the growing medium for most indoor plants. When the soil of plants housed in small pots needs to be replaced, the plant is usually "potted up"—that is, transplanted to a pot of the next largest size. The plant, with its root ball intact, is removed from the small pot, and fresh dirt is piled into the larger container, with space allowed for the root ball. The plant is then carefully inserted into the new soil. For plants already in the largest-sized pots, the indoor gardener may take the plant, along with its root ball, out of the pot, discard the remaining earth, put in a similar amount of fresh dirt, and then return the plant to its original container.

2. Read the following paragraph and then complete the exercises pertaining to it.

Frequently, department managers and supervisors recruit applicants without working through the corporate personnel office. Personnel departments around the country have experienced this problem. Recently, the manager of our tool design department met with a graduate of MTI to discuss an opening for a tool designer. The graduate was sent to the personnel department, where she was told that no such position existed. When the tool design manager asked the personnel director about the matter, the manager learned that the company president had ordered a hiring freeze for two months. I'm sure that our general employment situation will get better. As a result of the manager's failure to work through proper channels, the applicant was not only disappointed but bitter.

a. Underline the topic sentence of the paragraph.
b. Cross out any sentences that do not contribute to paragraph unity.

3. Underline the transitional words and phrases in the following paragraphs.

a.   Homeowners should know where the gutters on their houses are located and should be sure to keep them in good repair, because gutters are vulnerable to various weather conditions. On many houses, gutters are tucked up under or into the eaves, so that they appear as little more than another line or two of trim. As a result, many homeowners are not even aware that their houses have gutters. Unless the gutters are well maintained, however, the thousands of gallons of water that may fall onto the roof of the average house each year can easily damage or weaken the gutters. During the winter months, the weight of snow and ice may pull gutters away from the house or loosen the down-spout straps. Clogged and frozen down spouts may also develop seam cracks. When spring comes, these seam cracks sometimes create leaks that may allow heavy rains to flood the yard or the house instead of draining properly into the sewer system. In addition, melting snow that flows freely off the roof may go down the house wall, wetting it sufficiently to cause interior wall damage.

b.   The causes of global climate change remain in dispute. Existing theories of climate, atmospheric models, and statistical data are inadequate to provide planners with information on future weather patterns. In the long run, research may lead to reliable forecasts of climate. For the present, however, planners have no choice but to heed expert judgments about the world's future climate and its effect on agriculture and other sectors of the economy.

4. Each of the following pairs of sentences lacks a transition from the first sentence to the second. From the list of transitional devices on page 45, select the most appropriate one for each sentence pair. Then rewrite the sentences as necessary.

a. Ms. Silvenski arrived at the post office just before closing time. She was not able to mail her package because it had not been wrapped according to post office specifications.

b. An improperly cut garment will not hang attractively on the wearer.
When you sew, you should be sure to lay out and cut your pattern accurately and carefully.

c. The Doctors Clinic was able to attain its fund-raising goal on time this year.
Mercer Street Hospital was forced to extend its fund-raising deadline for three months.

d. When instructing the new tellers, the branch manager explained how to deal with impatient customers.
The personal-banking assistant told the new employees that they should consult her if they had difficulty handling those customers.

e. There are several reasons why a car may skid on ice.
The driver may be going faster than road conditions warrant.

5. The sentences in the following paragraphs have been purposely placed in the wrong order. Rearrange the sentences in each paragraph so that the paragraphs move smoothly and logically from one sentence to the next. Indicate the correct order of the sentences by placing the sentence numbers in the order in which the sentences should appear.

   a.   (1) When wind speed exceeds the maximum that the mill is designed to handle, the propeller is positioned at an angle to the wind so that it no longer turns. (2) Because of their aerodynamic characteristics, vertical-axis windmills go into a stall in high winds. (3) To balance cost and performance, windmills are designed to obtain power from winds within certain speed ranges. (4) If this did not occur, the propeller would continue to speed up and the machine would eventually be destroyed.

   b.   (1) Each atrium is connected to the ventricle below by a valve that allows blood to flow in only one direction. (2) The two upper chambers are called atria, and the two lower chambers are called ventricles. (3) The ventricles are also connected by one-way valves to the main outgoing blood vessels. (4) The organ is divided into four chambers. (5) The heart is a fist-sized, heavily muscled organ located approximately in the center of the chest.

6. Write a paragraph in which you develop one of the following topic sentences. Be sure that the paragraph is unified and coherent; follow the guidelines offered in the text.

   a.   In order to keep physically fit, I regularly do a number of different exercises (or participate in a number of different sports).
   b.   Of the magazines that I read regularly, I get the most out of _____ .
   c.   Every successful industrial organization has at least one "bread and butter" product that sells well year in and year out.
   d.   A _____ technician must perform a variety of duties.

7. Write an opening paragraph for two of the following topics. The audience for each topic is specified in parentheses.

   a.   Safety on the job (your immediate supervisor)
   b.   Ways to save energy on the job (your immediate supervisor)
   c.   The advantages of budgeting (a spendthrift friend)
   d.   What to look for in a first apartment (a friend who's looking)
   e.   The advantages and disadvantages of your school's career-counseling program (the administrator in charge of the program)
   f.   Job opportunities in your locality for people in your career field (article for the student newspaper of the high school from which you graduated)

4

Achieving Emphasis

Effective writing is *emphatic* writing—it highlights the facts and ideas that the writer considers to be most important and downplays those that the writer considers less significant. By focusing the reader's attention on the key elements in a sentence, emphatic writing enables the reader to determine how one fact or idea in a sentence is related to another. Emphatic writing, then, is a technique by which writers can make their material more accessible to their readers.

Writers employ a number of methods to achieve emphasis in their sentences. This chapter discusses the use of the active voice, subordination, unusual word order, introductory words and phrases, parallel structure, lists, and a number of other devices.

ACTIVE AND PASSIVE VOICE

If you were going to relate the information contained in the following two sentences to someone in conversation, which version would you use?

EXAMPLE 1 The complicated equipment is operated skillfully by the x-ray technician.

EXAMPLE 2 The x-ray technician operates the complicated equipment skillfully.

You would probably choose Example 2 because it conveys its message more directly than Example 1. By making the x-ray technician the *actor* (or *doer*) in the sentence, Example 2 readily communicates the fact that it is the technician's initiative that turns the equipment into a working tool. Example 1, in contrast, downplays the role of the operator; the focus of the sentence is on the x-ray equipment as the *receiver* of the action. The technician, though still the performer of the action, appears in a *by* phrase at the end of the sentence, rather than as the subject of the sentence.

What accounts for the difference in "feel" between the two sentences is that Example 2 is in the active voice, while Example 1 is in the passive. A sentence is in the *active voice* if the subject of the sentence acts; it is in the *passive voice* if the subject is acted upon.

In general, the active voice is the more emphatic of the two. The reader can move quickly and easily from *actor* to *action performed* (the verb) to *receiver of the action* (direct object); in passive-voice sentences, the reader often has to reach the end of the sentence to find out who (or what) performed the action that the subject received.

ACTIVE
VOICE
  Sheila Cohen *prepared* the layout design for the new pump. (The subject, *Sheila Cohen*, acts on *the layout design*—the direct object.)

PASSIVE
VOICE
  The layout design for the new pump *was prepared* by Sheila Cohen. (The subject, *the layout design*, receives the action.)

Passive-voice sentences tend to be longer than active-voice sentences for two reasons. First, a verb in the active voice often consists of only one word (in this example, *prepared*), whereas a verb in the passive voice always consists of at least two words (*was prepared*). Second, passive-voice sentences tend to be longer because they frequently require a *by someone* or *by something* phrase to complete their meanings. The active-voice version of the Sheila Cohen sentence contains 10 words; the passive-voice version contains 12.

Note the word order and verb forms in these examples:

PASSIVE
  Up to 460 pages of text *can be stored* on a single disk.

ACTIVE
  A single disk *can store* up to 460 pages of text.

PASSIVE
  Instructions on how to use the automatic teller *are described* in the brochure.

ACTIVE
  The brochure *describes* how to use the automatic teller.

PASSIVE
  The circuit-breaker switches *are lubricated* by maintenance personnel every three months.

ACTIVE
  Maintenance personnel *lubricate* the circuit-breaker switches every three months.

The chief advantage of the active voice is that, by clearly stating who is doing what, it gives the reader information quickly and emphatically. A straightforward style is especially important in writing instructions. Compare the following two versions of a paragraph that provides nurses with directions for treating a serious burn. The first version is written entirely in the passive voice; the second uses the active.

PASSIVE VOICE
The following action must be taken when a serious burn is treated. Any loose clothing on or near the burn is removed. The injury is covered with a clean dressing, and the area around the burn is washed. Then the dressing is secured with tape. Burned fingers or toes are separated with gauze or cloth so that they are prevented from sticking together. Medication is not applied unless it is prescribed by a doctor.

ACTIVE VOICE
Take the following action when treating a serious burn. Remove any loose clothing on or near the burn. Cover the injury with a clean dressing and wash the area around the burn. Then secure the dressing with tape. Separate the person's fingers or toes with gauze or cloth to prevent them from sticking together. Do not apply medication unless a doctor prescribes it.

If you were the nurse who had to follow these instructions, which version would you find easier to read and understand?

Occasionally, of course, the passive voice can be useful. There are times, for example, when the doer of the action is less important than the receiver of the action, and the writer can emphasize the receiver of the action by making it the subject of the sentence.

EXAMPLE
The new medical secretary was recommended by several doctors.

The important person in this sentence is the medical secretary, not the doctors who made the recommendation. To give the secretary—the receiver of the action—the needed emphasis, the sentence should be written in the passive voice.

The passive voice is also useful when the performer of the action either is not known or is not important.

EXAMPLE
The valves were soaked in kerosene for twenty-four hours. (*Who* soaked them is not important.)
The wheel was invented thousands of years ago. (*Who* invented it is not known.)

The passive voice is also commonly used when the writer wants to avoid identifying the performer of an action.

EXAMPLE   The guilty employee was placed on disciplinary probation. (The writer does not want to say *who* placed the guilty employee on probation.)

As you write—and as you revise—select the voice, active or passive, that is appropriate to your purpose. In most cases you can express your ideas more simply and more emphatically in the active voice, especially if you are writing instructions or making a report in which you intend to emphasize *who did what* (for example, which employee performed which subtask of a large project). And if you are describing a complicated piece of equipment, the active voice will probably provide better clarification of how one part interacts with another part. If, on the other hand, you are explaining a process in which the *doer* is not known or is not important, the passive voice is likely to be more effective. In whatever kind of writing you do, be careful to maintain consistency of voice. Avoid making an awkward switch from active to passive (or vice versa), either within a sentence or between sentences.

REVISE   After the test for admission to the training program had been taken by ten applicants, each one wrote a brief essay on his or her career plans.

TO   After the ten applicants had taken the test for admission to the training program, each one wrote a brief essay on his or her career plans.

SUBORDINATION

Read the following passage.

The computer is a calculating device. It was once known as a mechanical brain. It has revolutionized industry.

Reading the passage—a group of three short, staccato sentences—is something like listening to a series of drum beats of identical tone. The writing, like the music, is monotonous, because every sentence has the same subject-verb structure. Further, the writing is unemphatic, because every idea is given equal weight. The passage can be revised to eliminate the monotonous sentence structure and to place stress on the most important idea, that the computer has revolutionized industry.

The computer, *a calculating device once known as a mechanical brain,* has revolutionized industry.

The key to transforming a series of repetitive, unemphatic sentences is *subordination,* a technique in which a fact or an idea is subordinated to—that is, made less important than—another fact or idea in the same sentence. You can subordinate an element in a sentence in three basic ways:

- make it a dependent clause
- make it a phrase
- make it a single modifier

With all three methods, the less-important element can be combined with the more-important element to form one unified sentence.

Ways of Subordinating

Clauses. A *subordinate clause* (also called a *dependent clause*) has a subject and a predicate, but by itself is not a sentence. Rather, it must be joined to a sentence (called an *independent clause*) by a connecting word. That is, when two sentences are joined by subordination, one sentence becomes the independent clause, and the other sentence, introduced by a connecting word, becomes the dependent clause. The words most commonly used to introduce subordinate clauses are *who, that, which, whom, whose* (relative pronouns) and *after, although, because, before, if, unless, until, when, where, while* (subordinating conjunctions). A few word groups are also used to introduce subordinate clauses—*as soon as, even though, in order that, so that.*

In the following examples, two sentences are turned into one sentence that contains a subordinate clause.

REVISE   Virginia Kelly has become a printing press operator at the Granger Printing Company. She graduated from the Midcity Graphic Arts School last month.

TO   Virginia Kelly, *who graduated from the Midcity Graphic Arts School last month,* has become a printing press operator at the Granger Printing Company.

REVISE   Their credit union has a lower interest rate on loans. Our credit union provides a fuller range of services.

TO   *Although their credit union has a lower interest rate on loans,* our credit union provides a fuller range of services.

Phrases. The second type of subordination is the phrase. A *phrase* is a group of related words that does not have either a subject or a predicate and that acts as a modifier. In the following groups of two-sentence passages, one sentence is turned into a subordinate phrase that modifies an element in the other sentence.

REVISE The Beta Corporation now employs 500 people. It was founded ten years ago.

TO The Beta Corporation, *founded ten years ago,* now employs 500 people.

REVISE Roger Smith is a forest ranger for the State of Michigan. He spoke at the local Kiwanis Club last week.

TO Roger Smith, *a forest ranger for the State of Michigan,* spoke at the local Kiwanis Club last week.

Single Modifiers. The third type of subordination is the single modifier, which may be either a one-word modifier or a compound modifier.

REVISE The file is obsolete. It is taking up valuable storage space.

TO The *obsolete* file is taking up valuable storage space.

REVISE The police radio was out of date. It was auctioned to the highest bidder.

TO The *out-of-date* police radio was auctioned to the highest bidder.

Subordination to Achieve Emphasis

Depending on the context of your writing—your subject, your purpose, and your reader—you may find that, in a sentence, one type of subordination is more effective than another. In general, a subordinate single modifier achieves some emphasis, a subordinate phrase achieves more emphasis, and a subordinate clause achieves the most emphasis of all. In the following example, one idea has been subordinated in three ways.

REVISE The display designer's report was carefully illustrated. It covered five pages.

TO The display designer's *five-page* report was carefully illustrated. (single modifier)

OR The display designer's report, *covering five pages,* was carefully illustrated. (phrase)

OR The display designer's report, *which covered five pages,* was carefully illustrated. (clause)

Just as you can determine the kind of subordinate element that you think is most appropriate in a given sentence, so you can decide, according to the context in which you are writing, which ideas you should emphasize and which ones you should subordinate. In the following sets of examples, two sentences have been combined into one, in two different ways. Notice how the emphasis varies in each set.

REVISE   Blast furnaces are used mainly in the smelting of iron. They are employed all over the world.

TO   Blast furnaces, *which are in use all over the world,* are employed mainly in the smelting of iron. (Subordinates the extent of their use and emphasizes the purpose for which they are used.)

OR   Blast furnaces, *which are used mainly in the smelting of iron,* are employed all over the world. (Subordinates the purpose and emphasizes the extent.)

REVISE   The document explains how to install the gear. It is written for the mechanic.

TO   The document, *which is written for the mechanic,* explains how to install the gear. (Subordinates the intended reader and emphasizes the purpose.)

OR   The document, *which explains how to install the gear,* is written for the mechanic. (Subordinates the purpose and emphasizes the intended reader.)

REVISE   Henry Ford was a pioneering industrialist. He understood the importance of self-esteem.

TO   Henry Ford, *who understood the importance of self-esteem,* was a pioneering industrialist. (Subordinates the subject's understanding and emphasizes his pioneering work.)

OR   Henry Ford, *who was a pioneering industrialist,* understood the importance of self-esteem. (Subordinates the subject's pioneering work and emphasizes his understanding.)

Avoiding Overloaded Sentences

Subordination is a helpful technique that can enable you to write clear, readable sentences. But, like many useful devices, it can be overdone. Be especially careful not to pile one subordinating clause on top of another. A sentence that is overloaded with subordination will force your reader to work harder than necessary to understand what you are saying. The following sentence is difficult to read because the bottleneck of subordinate clauses prevents the reader from moving easily from one idea to the next.

REVISE   When the two mechanics, who had been trained at the company's repair center in Des Moines, explained to Margarita that the new word-processing machine, which Margarita had told them was not working properly, needed a new part, Margarita decided that until the part arrived the department would have its sales letters reproduced by an independent printing supplier.

TO   Margarita told the two mechanics that the new word-processing machine was not working properly. The mechanics, who had been trained at the company's repair center in Des Moines, examined the machine and explained to Margarita that it needed a new part. Margarita decided that until the part arrived, the department would have its sales letters reproduced by an independent printing supplier.

Subordinating everything is as bad as subordinating nothing. For example, study the next three sample paragraphs of a letter from a garage owner to a parts supplier. The first paragraph has too little subordination, the second has too much subordination, and the third illustrates effective subordination.

Example 1: Too Little Subordination

I am returning the parts you sent me, and I am enclosing the invoice that came with them. You must have confused my order with someone else's. I ordered spark plugs, condensers, and points, and I received bearings, piston rings, head gaskets, and valve-grinding compound. I don't need these parts, but I need the parts I ordered. Please send them as soon as possible.

Example 2: Too Much Subordination

You must have confused my order with someone else's, because although I ordered spark plugs, condensers, and points, I received bearings, piston rings, head gaskets, and valve-grinding compound; therefore, I am returning the parts you sent me, along with the invoice that came with them, in the hope that you will send me the parts that I need as quickly as possible because this delay has already put me behind schedule.

Example 3: Effective Subordination

I am returning the parts you sent me, along with the invoice that came with them, because you must have confused my order with someone else's. Although I ordered spark plugs, condensers, and points, I received bearings, piston rings, head gaskets, and valve-grinding compound. Since I need the parts that I ordered and this mix-up is causing an unexpected delay, please send me the parts that I ordered as quickly as possible.

UNUSUAL WORD ORDER

You can sometimes call attention to an idea simply by stating it in a sentence that varies from the most common word orders in our language. Most sentences, of course, follow a subject-verb-object pattern.

EXAMPLE   I (subject) never saw (verb) a smoother-running machine (object).

Because so many sentences follow this pattern, readers learn to expect it, and their familiarity with the pattern helps them to understand what they are reading. In the sample sentence, the reader recognizes the subject and the object by their positions in relation to the verb. But a reader who comes across a sentence like this

EXAMPLE   A smoother-running machine (object) I (subject) never saw (verb).

may sit up and take notice. The rearrangement of the three sentence elements prompts the reader to pay more attention to the sentence—to think about it more carefully—than he or she ordinarily would.

In your work, you may find that an unusual word order can be an effective way of stressing an idea. Keep two cautionary notes in mind, however: (1) an unusual word order has the greatest impact in relatively short sentences, and (2) like any technique that depends upon deviation from a normal pattern, it should not be overused.

INTRODUCTORY WORDS AND PHRASES

Another way to achieve emphasis is to begin a sentence with an introductory element—a modifying word or phrase that contains the idea you wish to stress. Such a modifier would normally occur later in the sentence.

EXAMPLES   Sales have been good recently.
Recently, sales have been good.

You must work hard to advance.
To advance, you must work hard.

> She found several errors while reading the report.
> *While reading the report,* she found several errors.

When you use introductory words and phrases, though, there are two dangers to watch for. First, beginning a sentence with a modifying word or phrase may lead you to write a dangling modifier. The first sentence below, for instance, contains a dangling modifier, because the phrase *to advance* cannot logically modify *hard work.* The second sentence corrects the error by making it clear that *to advance* modifies the pronoun *you.*

REVISE   To advance, hard work is required.

TO   *To advance,* you must work hard.

A second danger is that if you begin a sentence with a modifying word or phrase, the meaning of the sentence may accidentally be changed. The first of the following sentences instructs the reader to measure the oil that drains over a time period of fifteen seconds. The second sentence instructs the reader to wait fifteen seconds before measuring the amount of oil that drains into the container—a completely different thought.

EXAMPLES   Measure the amount of oil that drains into the container in fifteen seconds.
                 In fifteen seconds, measure the amount of oil that drains into the container.

Once again, make sure that your sentences say exactly what you intend them to say.

PARALLEL STRUCTURE

Parallel structure requires that sentence elements—words, phrases, and clauses—that are alike in function be alike in structure as well. In the following example, the three locations in which a cable is laid are all expressed as prepositional phrases.

EXAMPLE   The cable was laid *behind the embankment, under the street,* and *into the building.*

Parallel structure can produce an economy of language, clarify meaning, indicate the equality of related ideas, and, frequently, achieve emphasis. Parallel structure allows your reader to anticipate a series of units within a sentence. The reader realizes, for instance, that the relationship between the second unit (*under the street,* in the *cable* sentence) and the subject (*cable*) is the same as that between the first unit (*behind the embankment*) and the subject. A reader who has sensed the pattern of a sentence can go from one idea to another more quickly and confidently.

Parallel structure can be achieved with words, with phrases, and with clauses. Whether you use words, phrases, or clauses in parallel structure depends, as it does with subordination, upon the degree of emphasis you wish to create. In general, words in parallel structure produce some emphasis, phrases produce more emphasis, and clauses produce the most emphasis of all.

EXAMPLES   If you want to earn a satisfactory grade in the training program, you must be *punctual, courteous,* and *conscientious.* (parallel words)

If you want to earn a satisfactory grade in the training program, you must recognize the importance *of punctuality, of courtesy,* and *of conscientiousness.* (parallel phrases)

If you want to earn a satisfactory grade in the training program, *you must arrive punctually, you must behave courteously,* and *you must study conscientiously.* (parallel clauses)

To make the relationship among parallel units clear, repeat the word (or words) that introduces the first unit.

REVISE   The advantage is not in the pay but the greater opportunity.

TO   The advantage is not *in* the pay but *in* the greater opportunity.

REVISE   The study of electronics is a necessity and challenge to the technician.

TO   The study of electronics is *a* necessity and *a* challenge to the technician.

Parallel structure can contribute greatly to the clarity of your writing. But it is more than just a helpful device—sentences that contain faulty parallel structure are often awkward and difficult to read.

REVISE   Adina Wilson was happy about her assignment and getting a pay raise.

TO   Adina Wilson was happy *about her assignment* and *about her pay raise.*

REVISE   Jason advises his employees to work hard and against relying on luck.

TO — Jason advises his employees *to work hard* and not *to rely* on luck.

REVISE — Check the following items: The dip stick for proper oil level, the gas tank for fuel, the spark plug wire attachment, and that no foreign objects are under or near the mower.

TO — Check the following items: The dip stick *for proper oil level,* the gas tank *for fuel,* the spark plug wire *for proper attachment,* and the lawn *for foreign objects.*

LISTS

You can also consider using lists to achieve emphasis. Lists break up complex statements and allow key ideas to stand out. Be aware, however, that lists are most effective when they are grammatically parallel in structure. When you use a list of phrases or short sentences, each should begin with the same part of speech:

REVISE — Because expenses for the past month have far exceeded budget, the business manager has recommended the following reforms:

1. Employees will not use company telephones for personal calls.
2. For any written copy that is not to go out of house, use low-grade yellow paper rather than bond.
3. Make carbon copies rather than photocopies of all correspondence.

TO — Because expenses for the past month have far exceeded budget, the business manager has recommended the following reforms:

1. Do not use company phones for personal calls.
2. Use low-grade yellow paper rather than bond for any written copy that is not to go out of house.
3. Make carbon copies rather than photocopies of all correspondence.

Notice how much more smoothly the revised version reads, with all items beginning with imperative verbs.

To ensure that the reader understands how a list fits with the surrounding sentences, always provide adequate transitions before and after any lists. If you do not wish to indicate rank or sequence, which numbered lists suggest, you can use bullets, as shown in the list of tips that follows. To type a bullet, use a small "o" and fill it with ink. Following are some tips for using lists:

- List only comparable items.
- Use parallel structure throughout.
- Use only words, phrases, or short sentences.
- Provide adequate transitions before and after lists.
- Use bullets when rank or sequence is not important.
- Do not overuse lists.

OTHER WAYS TO ACHIEVE EMPHASIS

You can create a feeling of anticipation in your reader by arranging a series of facts or ideas in *climactic order*. Begin such a series with the least important idea and end it with the most important one.

REVISE   The hurricane destroyed thousands of homes, ruined some crops, and interrupted traffic.

TO   The hurricane interrupted traffic, ruined some crops, and destroyed thousands of homes.

Emphasis is added at each step as the reader is led from the minor inconvenience of traffic tie-ups, to the more serious problem of partial crop failure, and finally to the hurricane's most devastating impact: the destruction of thousands of homes.

An abrupt change in sentence length can also achieve effective emphasis.

EXAMPLE   We have already reviewed the problems that the bookkeeping department has experienced during the past year. We could continue to examine the causes of our problems and point an accusing finger at all the culprits beyond our control, but in the end it all leads to one simple conclusion. *We must cut costs.*

Sometimes, simply labeling ideas as important creates emphasis.

EXAMPLE   We can do a number of things that will help us to achieve our goal. We can conduct sales contests in the field; in the past, such contests have been quite successful. We can increase our advertising budget and hope for a proportionate increase in sales. We can be prepared to step up production when the increase in sales makes it necessary. But *most important,* we can do everything in our power to make sure that we are producing the best dictating equipment on the market.

If you don't overuse them, direct statements like *most important* should make your reader take particular notice of what follows.

Another kind of direct statement is the warning to your reader that something dangerous is about to follow. Warnings most often appear in instructions, where they may be brought to the reader's attention by a special format—the material may be boxed off, for instance—or by attention-attracting devices like all-capital letters or a distinctive typeface. Many offices are equipped with typewriters, like the IBM Selectric, that have changeable type (usually a "golf ball" that contains the letters of the alphabet in **boldface** and *italic*) as well as standard typefaces.

WARNING

DO NOT proceed to the next instruction until you have checked to be sure that the equipment has been unplugged. The electrical power generated by this unit CAN KILL!

Other mechanical devices can achieve a certain amount of emphasis. A dash within a sentence, for example, can alert the reader to what follows it. (On the typewriter, the dash is made by striking the hyphen twice, with no space between the two.)

EXAMPLES The job will be done--after we are under contract.
The manager pointed out that our conduct could have only one result--dismissal.

Italics (indicated on the typewriter by underlining) can be used occasionally to emphasize a word or phrase.

EXAMPLE Sales have <u>not</u> improved since we started the new procedure.

The problem with devices like italics and the dash is that they are so easy to use that we tend to rely on them too readily.

EXAMPLE Sales have <u>not improved</u> since we started the new procedure and are <u>not likely</u> to improve unless we initiate a more <u>aggressive</u> advertising campaign.

Overuse of mechanical devices may cancel their effectiveness. The reader quickly learns that the writer is using the signals to point out unimportant as well as truly important material.

CHAPTER SUMMARY

Effective writing is *emphatic* writing—it places stress on those facts and ideas that the writer wishes to highlight. Writers can use a number of techniques to make their sentences emphatic.

Ordinarily, the *active voice*, in which the subject of a sentence *performs* the action, provides greater emphasis than the *passive voice*, in which the subject *receives* the action. Unless you have a particular reason for using the passive voice, use the active.

Subordination is a device in which one element in a sentence is given greater stress than another. The less-important element may be expressed as a clause (introduced by words like *who, which, that,* and *although, when,* or *where*), as a phrase, or as a single modifier. Subordination can turn a series of short, subject-verb sentences into one emphatic sentence that pinpoints the relationship of the sentence elements.

To emphasize the key ideas in a sentence, a writer may sometimes use unusual word order (as in the sentence *Never would I have expected such a result*) or introductory words and phrases (*By keeping a record of the traffic flow through the office,* staff members can better determine the department's space needs).

Another device is parallel structure, which can achieve economy of language, clarify meaning, indicate the equality of related ideas, and, often, create emphasis. Like subordination, parallel structure may be expressed in words, phrases, and clauses. Note, too, that parallel structure is not just a stylistic device; it is often a necessity in avoiding an awkward or unclear sentence.

Other devices for lending emphasis include lists (in which the items should be grammatically parallel), the use of climactic order, a change in sentence length, labeling of ideas as important, and several mechanical devices.

EXERCISES

1. Rewrite each of the following sentences so that the verb is in the *active voice*. Whenever a potential subject is not given in a sentence, supply one as you rewrite.

  a. The report should be submitted to Sid Miner on Friday.
  b. The motion was passed by the delegates unanimously.
  c. A bonus of $1,000 for every year of service was voted by the board.
  d. Relocation pay must be approved by company officials.
  e. The sink in the bathroom has just been scrubbed.
  f. The new board of directors was approved by the stockholders at the annual meeting on May 22.
  g. It is greatly feared by employees that those who lose their jobs will not receive adequate compensation.
  h. It was felt by the committee that Jim Talbott should represent the company in New York.
  i. At the end of the presentation, the speaker was greeted with a loud burst of applause.
  j. It was announced by the advertising agency that the new package is an effective sales tool.
  k. The process of oxidation is speeded up by the presence of certain metals.
  l. You have been given an additional week by the vice president to finish the interim report.
  m. After the operator inserts a check, the check-endorsement message is printed by the terminal.
  n. All current data should be analyzed before the decision is made.

2. In each of the following, combine the series of short sentences into one unified sentence. Use *subordination* (1) to indicate how the ideas expressed in the sentence relate to each other, and (2) to emphasize the most important idea or ideas.

  a. I recorded my speech on a cassette tape. The cassette tape can be recorded over. It does not need to be erased.
  b. It rained this morning. The construction crew stayed indoors. Members played a game of hearts. Valdez won.
  c. It had snowed for a week. I like to ski. I was delighted.
  d. He studied drafting at a technical school. He joined his brother's firm as a draftsman in 1969.
  e. Thomas Edison was one of America's greatest inventors. Teddy Roosevelt was the twenty-sixth president of the United States. Edison and Roosevelt were friends.
  f. Sales of sewing machines were declining. The management of Presto-Seam became worried. The management decided to initiate a TV ad campaign.
  g. The word-processing group had a backlog of work. No one could type my report. My report is due in two days.

    h. The cost of cotton has increased. All the suppliers have increased their prices. The suppliers are wholesalers.

3. Rewrite the following sentences to eliminate *excessive* subordination.

    a. It was the security guard who warned the police who arrived in time to catch the man who was robbing the safe.
    b. Never before have I known a student who was so ready to help a friend who had gotten into trouble that involved money.
    c. Will your report, in which you outline new developments in the field, be one of the papers which will be put on the agenda that is planned for the conference?

4. Rewrite the following sentences to make elements within them parallel in construction.

    a. The system is large and convenient, and it does not cost very much.
    b. The processor sends either a ready function code or standby function code.
    c. The log is a record of the problems which have occurred and of the services performed.
    d. The committee feels that the present system has three disadvantages: it causes delay in the distribution of incoming mail, duplicates work, and unnecessary delays are created in the work of several other departments.
    e. In our first list we inadvertently omitted the seven lathes in room B-101, milling machines in room B-117, and from the next room, B-118, we also forgot to include sixteen shapers.
    f. This product offers ease of operation, economy, and it is easily available.
    g. The manual gives instructions for operating the machine and to adjust it.
    h. Three of the applicants were given promotions, and transfers were arranged for the other four applicants.
    i. To analyze the data, carry out the following steps: examine all the details carefully, eliminate all the unnecessary details, and a chart showing the flow of work should then be prepared.
    j. We have found that the new system has four disadvantages: too costly to operate, it causes delays, fails to use any of the existing equipment, and it permits only one in-process examination.
    k. The design is simple, inexpensive, and can be used effectively.

l. Management was slow to recognize the problem and even slower understanding it.

5. Rewrite the following lists to make them parallel in structure.

   a. Carry this emergency equipment in your car during long winter trips:

      - Chains for tires and towing
      - Snow shovel
      - Scraper
      - Sand or salt
      - For minor repairs, a car tool kit
      - Flashlight—be sure to check for fresh batteries
      - Flares, reflectors
      - First aid kit
      - Blankets
      - Jumper cables are also a good idea

   b. Keep these safety tips in mind as you work on your car:

      - Wear safety goggles when working under the hood, especially when dealing with the battery.
      - The engine should be operated only in a well-ventilated area.
      - Fans and belts are dangerous when moving—you or your clothing could get caught in them.
      - Avoid contact with hot metal parts, such as the radiator and the exhaust manifold.

5

Revising

One of the enduring legends of American history is that Abraham Lincoln wrote the Gettysburg Address as he made the train trip from Washington, D.C., to Gettysburg. The address is a remarkable accomplishment, even for a writer as gifted as Lincoln. It is the eloquent testimony of a leader with a powerful intellect and a compassionate heart.

But the facts of how the Gettysburg Address was composed do not support the legend. Lincoln actually worked on the address for weeks and revised the draft many times.[1] What Lincoln was doing on the train to Gettysburg was nothing more than what any of us must do before our writing is finally acceptable: he was revising. What is remarkable about the address is that Lincoln made so many revisions of a speech of well under 300 words. Obviously he wanted it to fit the occasion for which it was intended, and he knew that something written "off the cuff" would not satisfy his purpose and audience.

This principle is as true for anyone who writes on the job (which, of course, is what the president was doing) as it was for Lincoln. Unlike the Gettysburg Address, however, most on-the-job writing should not strive for oratorical elegance; the more natural a piece of writing sounds to the reader, the more effort the writer has probably put into revising it.

---

[1] Tom Burnam, *The Dictionary of Misinformation* (New York: Ballantine Books, 1977), pp. 104–106.

EFFECTIVE REVISION

Have you ever written a first draft that you knew wasn't the best you could do, but that you did not know how to improve? If your answer is yes, you are not alone. All writers—even professional writers—have the same problem at some time or another.

The problem has a simple explanation. Immediately after you write a rough draft, the ideas are so fresh in your mind that you cannot read the words, sentences, and paragraphs objectively. That is, you cannot sufficiently detach yourself from the ideas to be able to look at the writing critically. And to revise effectively, you *must* be critical. You cannot allow yourself to think, "Because my ideas are good, the way I've expressed them must also be good." The first step toward effective revision, then, is to develop a critical frame of mind—to become objective.

As professional writers have learned, there are a number of ways to put distance between yourself and your writing and become objective. Here are two methods that you should always employ:

1. *Allow for a "cooling" period.* Allow a period of time to go by between writing a rough draft and revising it. The ideas will not be as fresh in your mind then, and you can look at the writing itself more objectively. A "cooling" period of a day or two is best, but if you are pressed for time, even a few hours will help.
2. *Pretend that a stranger has written your draft.* Since it is always easier to see faults in others than in yourself, pretend that you are revising someone else's draft. If you can look at your writing and ask, "How could *he* or *she* have written that?" you are in the right frame of mind to revise.

Of course, you may discover your own methods of becoming objective. One student, for example, finds that she can be more critical if she writes her first draft on yellow paper. Another student types his first draft because he cannot be critical when looking at his own handwriting. Some students like to revise with felt-tip pen; others prefer using red or green pencils. Experiment and find out what helps you. The particular methods that work for you are not important. What *is* important is that you develop some technique for becoming objective about your writing—and then use it.

Once you have put the necessary distance between yourself and your writing, you are ready to revise. Again, there is no single method that every writer uses. The following two techniques, however, invariably prove effective:

1. *Revise in passes.* Make several passes through your draft as you revise. The first time you read the draft, look at only one aspect of your writing, such as accuracy or completeness. Then make additional passes, looking at a different aspect, such as grammar or spelling, each time. Often, you can spot problems more quickly if you look for only one than if you look for several at the same time.

2. *Be alert for your most frequent errors.* Closely related to revising in passes is looking first for the errors that you typically make. One of the most important benefits of taking a writing course is that you can learn what your weak points are. Make a list of the problems that your instructor has pointed out in your writing, and use that list to guide you as you revise. Also, you might wish to use this chapter as a checklist and run through the headings as you review your draft. A more general "final checklist" appears at the end of this chapter.

CHECKING FOR PRECISION

Writing that is precise is so clear that your reader should have no difficulty understanding exactly what you want to say. In checking for precision, look for three likely trouble spots, enemies of precision that may give rise to misinterpretation on your reader's part: ambiguity, unclear pronoun reference, and imprecise word choice.

Ambiguity

The following sign once hung on the wall of a restaurant.

> *CUSTOMERS WHO THINK OUR WAITERS ARE RUDE*
> *SHOULD SEE THE MANAGER*

Several days later the sign was removed after customers continued to chuckle at the sign's unintended suggestion: that the manager was even ruder than the waiters.

In the case of the sign, of course, the customers understood the point that the restaurant owner wanted to make. But in many types of job-related communication—a report or a letter, for instance—the reader may have difficulty deciding which of several possible meanings the writer intended to convey. When a sentence (or a passage) can be interpreted in two or more ways and the writer has given the reader no clear basis for choosing from among the alternatives, the writing is *ambiguous*. Ambiguity is a common source of vagueness in on-the-job writing. Two of the most frequent causes of ambiguity in writing are faulty comparisons and misplaced modifiers.

Faulty comparisons.   When you make a comparison, be sure that your reader understands which elements are included in the comparison.

REVISE   Ms. Jones values rigid quality-control standards more than Mr. Johnson. (Does Ms. Jones value the standards more than she values Mr. Johnson, or does she value the standards more than Mr. Johnson values them?)

TO   Ms. Jones values rigid quality-control standards more than Mr. Johnson *does*.

When you compare two persons, things, or ideas, be sure that they are elements that can logically be compared with each other.

REVISE   The *accounting textbook* is more difficult to read than *office management*. (A textbook is not the same as a field of study.)

TO   The *accounting textbook* is more difficult to read than the *office management textbook*.

Misplaced modifiers.   Another source of ambiguity occurs in the placement of modifiers. Modifiers are words that describe, explain, or qualify an element in a sentence.

The simple modifiers that are most likely to create ambiguity are *only, almost, just, hardly, even,* and *barely*. When you use one of these terms in a sentence, be sure that it modifies the word or element that you intend it to. In most cases, place the modifier directly in front of the word it is supposed to qualify. (See Section 4.3.4.d of the Writer's Guide at the end of the book for a more extensive discussion of modifiers.)

EXAMPLES   Katrina was the *only* engineer at Flagstead Industries. (The sentence says that Flagstead had one engineer, and she was Katrina.)

Katrina was *only* the engineer at Flagstead Industries. (The sentence says that Katrina had a position at Flagstead no higher than that of engineer.)

Anna Jimenez *almost* wrote $1 million in insurance policies last month. (The sentence says that although Anna Jimenez came close to writing $1 million in insurance policies, she actually didn't write *any*.)

Anna Jimenez wrote *almost* $1 million in insurance policies last month. (The sentence says that Anna Jimenez wrote *nearly* $1 million in insurance policies last month—a very different matter.)

Misplaced phrases can also cause problems. As with simple modifiers, place phrases near the words they modify. Note the two meanings possible when the phrase is shifted in the following sentences:

EXAMPLES   The equipment *without the accessories* sold the best. (Different types of equipment were available, some with and some without accessories.)

The equipment sold the best *without the accessories*. (One type of equipment was available, and the accessories were optional.)

Either of these sentences could be correct, of course, depending on the meaning the writer intends.

A third type of misplaced modifier is a *misplaced clause*. To avoid confusion, clauses should also be placed as close as possible to the words they modify.

REVISE   We sent the brochure to four local firms *that had three-color illustrations.*

TO   We sent the brochure *that had three-color illustrations* to four local firms.

A different kind of ambiguous modifier is the "squinting modifier"—a modifier that could be interpreted as qualifying either the sentence element before it or the sentence element following it.

EXAMPLE   We agreed *on the next day* to make the adjustments.

The reader doesn't know which of the following possible interpretations the writer intended.

MEANING 1   *On the next day* we agreed to make the adjustments.
MEANING 2   We agreed to make the adjustments *on the next day.*

Unclear Pronoun Reference

A *pronoun* is a word that is used as a substitute for a noun. The noun for which the pronoun substitutes is called its *antecedent*. Using a pronoun to replace a noun eliminates the monotonous repetition of the noun. When you use a pronoun, though, be sure that your reader knows which noun the pronoun refers to. If you do not clearly indicate what word, or group of words, a pronoun stands for, your reader may be uncertain of your meaning. When you revise your sentences to correct unclear pronoun references, look especially for three types of errors: ambiguous reference, general (or broad) reference, and hidden reference. (For a further discussion of pronoun reference, see Section 3.2.3b of the Writer's Guide at the end of the book.)

In *ambiguous reference,* there is uncertainty as to which of two or more nouns a pronoun is referring to.

REVISE   Studs and thick treads make snow tires effective. *They* are installed with an air gun. (*What* are installed with an air gun—studs, treads, or snow tires? The reader can only guess.)

TO   Studs, which are installed with an air gun, and thick treads make snow tires effective. (Now it is clear that only studs are installed with an air gun.)

REVISE   We made the sale and delivered the product. It was a big one. (Does *It* refer to the sale or to the product?)

TO   We made the sale, which was a big one, and delivered the product. (Now it is clear that the sale, not the product, was a big one.)

REVISE   Jim worked with Tom on the report, but *he* wrote most of it. (*Who* wrote most of the report, Tom or Jim?)

TO   Jim worked with Tom on the report, but Tom wrote most of it.

In a *general* (or *broad*) *reference,* the pronoun—which is frequently a term like *this, that, which,* or *it*—does not replace an easily identifiable antecedent. Instead, it refers in a general way to the preceding sentence or clause.

REVISE   He deals with social problems in his work. *This* helps him in his personal life. (The pronoun *this* refers to the entire preceding sentence.)

TO   Dealing with social problems in his work helps him in his personal life.

REVISE   Mr. Bacon recently retired, *which* left an opening in the accounting department. (The pronoun *which* refers to the entire preceding clause.)

TO   Mr. Bacon's recent retirement left an opening in the accounting department. (Revising the sentence to eliminate the pronoun makes the meaning clear.)

The third cause of unclear pronoun reference is the *hidden reference.* In sentences that contain a hidden reference, the antecedent of the pronoun is implied but never actually stated.

REVISE	Despite the fact that our tractor division had researched the market thoroughly, we didn't sell *many*. (Many what? The pronoun *many* has no stated antecedent in the sentence. The writer assumes that the reader understands that *many* refers to tractors.)
TO	Despite the fact that we had thoroughly researched the market for tractors, we didn't sell *many*. (Now the pronoun *many* has an antecedent, *tractors*.)
OR	Despite the fact that our tractor division had researched the market thoroughly, we didn't sell many *tractors*. (Revising the sentence so that *many* becomes an adjective modifying *tractors* makes the meaning clear too.)

The Right Word

As Mark Twain once said, "The difference between the right word and almost the right word is the difference between 'lightning' and 'lightning bug.'" Precision requires that you choose the right word.

When you write, be alert to the effect that a word may have on your reader—and try to avoid words that might, by the implications they carry, confuse or distract your reader. For example, in describing a piece of machinery that your company recently bought, you might refer to the item as *cheap*—meaning inexpensive. But because *cheap* often suggests "of poor quality" or "shabbily made," your reader may picture the new piece of equipment as already needing repairs.

In selecting the appropriate word, you will want to keep in mind the context—the setting in which the word appears. Suppose you call the new machine "inexpensive" or "moderately priced." Your reader may have confidence that the equipment will work, but may ask, "What does the writer *mean* by inexpensive?" An electric typewriter at $300 might be inexpensive; a small printing press at $30,000 would also be a good buy. The exact meaning of *inexpensive* would depend on the context. For readers who are unfamiliar with the cost of heavy machinery, it might be surprising to learn that a $30,000 press was reasonably priced. It would be up to you, the writer, to provide your readers with a context—to let them know, in this case, what the relative costs of printing equipment are.

The context will also determine whether a word you choose is *specific* enough. When you use the word *machine,* for instance, you might be thinking of an automobile, a lathe, a cash register, a sewing machine—the variety of mechanical equipment we use is almost endless. *Machine,* in other words, is an imprecise term that must be qualified, or explained, unless you want to refer in a general way to every

item included in the category *machine.* If you have a particular kind
of machine in mind, then you must use more precise language.

REVISE The maintenance contract covers all the *machines* in
Building D.

TO The maintenance contract covers all the *electric typewriters* in Building D.

Depending on the context, you might need to choose a term even
more specific than *electric typewriters.* Figure 5–1 illustrates just how
specific a particular context might require you to be. The terminology
goes from most general, on the left, to most specific, on the right.
Seven levels of specificity are shown; which one would be appropriate
depends on your purpose in writing and on the context in which you
are using the word.

For example, a person writing a company's annual report might
logically use the most general term, *assets,* to refer to all the property
and goods owned by the firm: shareholders would probably not expect
a further breakdown. Interoffice memos between the company's accounting and legal departments would appropriately call the firm's
holdings *real estate* and *inventory.* To the company's inventory-control
department, however, the word *inventory* is much too broad to be
useful; a report on inventory might contain the more specific categories
equipment and *parts in stock.* But to the assistant inventory-control
manager in charge of equipment, that term is still too general; he
or she would speak of several particular kinds of equipment—*office
furniture, office machines,* and *factory equipment.* The breakdown of
the types of *office machines* for which the inventory-control assistant
is responsible might include *copiers, typewriters,* and *calculators.*

However, even this classification wouldn't be specific enough to
enable the company's purchasing department to obtain service contracts for the normal maintenance of its typewriters. Because the
department must deal with different typewriter manufacturers, *typewriters* would have to be listed by brand name: *Olivetti, IBM,* and
Smith-Corona. And the Smith-Corona technician who performs the
maintenance must go one step further and identify each Smith-Corona
typewriter by serial number. As Figure 5–1 shows, then, a term may

FIGURE 5–1.

be sufficiently specific at one of the seven levels—but at the next level it becomes too broad. Your purpose in writing and your intended reader will determine how specific you should be.

Purpose and audience may sometimes require a general rather than a specific term. To include typewriter serial numbers in a company's annual report, a detailed parts list in a sales brochure, or highly technical language in a letter to the accounting department would, of course, be inappropriate. In all the writing you do, you must decide what your purpose is and who your reader will be, and then select the term that is neither too general nor too specific for the context.

Remember that you must sometimes define terms for your reader. Say you are making a proposal to your boss, who must pass your proposal along to his or her boss for final approval. You may be using terms that your boss's superior will not recognize, because you work with details that will be unfamiliar to someone interested in only the big picture. If you want your proposal to be approved, you would be wise to do everything you can to be sure that your ideas are readily understandable. In some cases you may define specific terms; in others, you may prefer to omit them and write at a more general level.

How you go about defining the terms that need explanation depends on the context. It may often be sufficient to give a brief explanation, in everyday language, of a technical or specialized term.

EXAMPLE   The program then spools the first file (stores the file on magnetic tape until the program is ready to print it) and opens the second file.

Or you may find it easiest to provide a dictionary-type definition.

EXAMPLE   The property includes approximately 1,700 feet of waterside (land bordering any body of water).

Sometimes it may be necessary to provide a formal definition of a word. (See Chapter 8 for a complete discussion of formal definition.) To write such a definition, place the term in a category and show how the term differs from other members of that category.

EXAMPLE   A lease [*term*] is a contract [*category*] that conveys real estate for a specified period of time at a specified rent [*how* a lease *differs from other contracts*].

Technical Terminology

Technical terms are standard, universally recognized words that are used in a particular field to refer to specific principles, processes, or devices. Technical terms are useful and sometimes essential in communicating clearly and concisely. For example, the term *divestiture* has a specific, generally understood meaning among readers who have studied management strategies. Similarly, the term *logic gate* would be understood by readers who have studied computer science. If you are certain that *all* your readers (and potential readers) would understand a technical term, use it as an efficient means of communication. If you are at all uncertain, however, you should define the term in everyday language when you first use it.

If your readers are unlikely to understand the concept that a technical term represents, you should explain the concept, perhaps including easy-to-understand examples. Although digressing into an explanation is not as efficient as simply using a technical term, your goal of making your writing easily understandable should be paramount.

Jargon

Jargon is highly specialized technical slang that is unique to an occupational group. If *all* your readers are members of a particular occupational group, jargon (like technical terminology) may provide a time-saving and efficient means of communicating with them. For example, if you were writing to printers or publishers, you might use the term "repro" and be understood. (*Repro* is short for *reproduction,* which in the printing business means the camera-ready copy from which the printing plate is cut.)

Jargon enters the language for a variety of reasons, only some of which are defensible. Often, technical terms are cumbersome and abbreviation is desirable. For example, automobiles have a device called a pollution-control valve, which people who work in the automobile industry have shortened to PCV. If you doubt that your reader would understand this technical shorthand, spell the words out.

Also common are words that already have established meanings in everyday speech but have only recently been applied to new concepts and devices. For example, *access*—a noun meaning the ability to enter, approach, communicate with, or pass to or from—has always been part of our language. However, as a transitive verb meaning to get at something, such as a computer file, *access* is very new and should only be used in a specific discussion of computers. Although you can access a computer file, you cannot access a novel. Understandably, the developers of new concepts and devices, in their need to name their creations, rarely have time for elegance. Just remember that this technical shorthand is not a satisfactory substitute for everyday language outside the field in which it is standard.

Yet another type of jargon is used to define occupations euphemistically, and this jargon also must be kept in its place. Good manners dictate that if you are writing to an undertaker and must refer to him by trade, you had best use the term "mortician." Similarly, a garbage collector is a sanitation worker when politeness requires it.

A type of jargon that is indefensible is the useless elongation of standard words. Frequently one hears *analyzation, summarization,* and *notation;* the correct words are *analysis, summary,* and *note.* The additions to such words do not make them mean anything more precise; they simply make them incorrect.

When jargon becomes so specialized that it applies only to one company or subgroup of an occupation, it is referred to as "shop talk." For example, an automobile manufacturer might produce a "pollution-control valve—Model LV-20." In the department where the device is built, it may be referred to as an "LV-20." Obviously, shop talk is appropriate only for those familiar with its special vocabulary and should be reserved for speech and informal memorandums.

CHECKING FOR CONCISENESS

Vagueness and ambiguity interfere with communication by requiring the reader to decide which of two (or more) possible ideas the writer intended. Choosing the wrong word for your reader and using jargon when standard English would better serve your purpose also reduce the precision of your writing. Similar to precision is conciseness: the more concise—that is, free of unnecessary words—your writing is, the more effective it will be. Wordiness, the opposite of conciseness, can act as a barrier between reader and writer. Writing that is wordy or that employs stilted or pretentious language can slow the reader down and make relatively straightforward ideas difficult to understand. You can achieve conciseness by eliminating any words, phrases, or clauses that do not contribute to your meaning and any expressions that are excessively fancy or obscure. While a concise sentence is not guaranteed to be an effective one, a wordy sentence, because of the extra load it carries, always loses some of its readability and clarity. As you revise your work, be on the alert in particular for four types of wordiness: *redundancy,* or the use of a word or words that do no more than repeat the meaning of something already stated (*round circle* is an example of redundancy—*circle* contains the idea of roundness); *padded phrases,* which express in several words an idea that could easily be said in one (*due to the fact that* for *because* is an example of a padded phrase); *affectation,* which results in the senseless inflation of language for the sake of making a message sound more important than it really is (*pore over a tome* for *read a book* is an example of affectation); and *excessive formality* (*The writer believes* instead of *I believe*).

Redundancy

When a modifying word, phrase, or clause adds no new information to what a sentence already says, the modifier is redundant.

REVISE   To complete the circuit, join the wires *together* with solder. (The word *together* repeats the thought contained in the word *join.*)

TO   To complete the circuit, join the wires with solder.

REVISE   *Modern* students of *today* consider work experience to be as valuable as classroom attendance. (The phrase *of today* repeats the thought expressed by the word *modern.*)

TO   *Modern* students consider work experience to be as valuable as classroom attendance.

OR   Students *of today* consider work experience to be as valuable as classroom attendance.

REVISE   Our imported products, *which come from abroad,* all have limited warranties. (Since *imported products* can be assumed to be manufactured *abroad,* the clause is not needed.)

TO   Our imported products all have limited warranties.

REVISE   We moved the storage cases into the empty warehouse, *which had nothing in it.* (An *empty warehouse* is understood to have *nothing in it.*)

TO   We moved the storage cases into the empty warehouse.

When they are selected carefully, modifiers—whether adjectives, adverbs, prepositional phrases, or subordinate clauses—can make the words they describe vivid and specific. Modifiers to avoid are those that simply repeat the idea contained in the word they modify. Studying the following list of redundant expressions may sharpen your ability to spot this kind of wordiness.

blue *in color*	to resume *again*
square *in shape*	brief in *duration*
to plan *ahead*	*tall* high rise
basic essentials	small *in size*
descended *down*	to attach *together*
visible *to the eye*	to cooperate *together*

Padded Phrases

When an idea that could be stated in one word is buried in an expression that takes several words—and is no clearer than the single word—a padded phrase results.

REVISE   The committee will meet *at an early date*.

TO   The committee will meet *soon*.

REVISE   The contractor will issue regular progress reports *during the time that* the contract is in effect.

TO   The contractor will issue regular progress reports *while* the contract is in effect.

REVISE   I recently met with the city attorney *with reference to* your case.

TO   I recently met with the city attorney *about* your case.

REVISE   We missed our deadline *due to the fact that* a strike occurred.

TO   We missed our deadline *because* a strike occurred.

REVISE   We cannot accept new clients *at the present time*.

TO   We cannot accept new clients *now*.

REVISE   We have received four complaints *in connection with* the project.

TO   We have received four complaints *about* the project.

REVISE   *In order* to meet the deadline, we must work overtime.

TO   *To* meet the deadline, we must work overtime.

REVISE   She was thinking *in terms of* subcontracting much of the work.

TO   She was thinking *of* subcontracting much of the work.

There are times, however, when the longer wording is desirable.

EXAMPLES   The committee must know the estimated costs *in order to* evaluate the feasibility of the project.

In terms of gross sales, the year has been successful; *in terms of* net income, however, it has been discouraging.

Expressions like these must be evaluated individually. If the expression does not contribute to the meaning of the sentence, use its simpler substitute.

A half-dozen terms are the particular villains of wordiness. When they occur, you should examine your work critically for padded phrases. The words are *case, fact, field, factor, manner,* and *nature*.

REVISE	*In many cases,* students profit from writing a term paper.
TO	Students *often* profit from writing a term paper. (Sometimes it is necessary, when revising a sentence, to shift the location of the modifier.)
REVISE	I was not certain *of the fact that* your cousin is a steelworker.
TO	I was not certain *that* your cousin is a steelworker.
REVISE	I have been interested *in the fields of* drafting and electronics for several years.
TO	I have been interested *in* drafting and electronics for several years.
REVISE	Speed is also *an important factor.*
TO	Speed is also *important.*
REVISE	The skids were stacked *in an unsafe manner.*
TO	The skids were stacked *unsafely.*
REVISE	The committee seldom considered grievances *of a controversial nature.*
TO	The committee seldom considered *controversial* grievances.

Affectation

Affectation is the deliberate inflation of language to make it more technical or showy than is necessary to communicate information to the reader.

Affectation can be a serious problem in on-the-job writing because it creates a smokescreen that the reader must penetrate to discover the writer's meaning. The following example illustrates the problem.

REVISE	It is the policy of the company to provide the proper telephonic apparatus to enable each employee to conduct the interoffice and intra-business communication necessary to discharge his or her responsibilities; however, it is contrary to company practice to permit telephones to be utilized for personal employee communications.
TO	Your telephone is provided for company business; do not use it for personal calls.

Most people would have to read the first version of the sentence several times before deciphering its message. The meaning of the revised version, which uses direct, simple, and precise language, is evident at a glance.

In your own writing, avoid obscure and legal-sounding words ("discharge responsibilities," "aforesaid," "hereto," and so on). Avoid trendy, vogue words such as "parameters" and "up to speed." Do not use big, imprecise words as a substitute for simple, well-thought-out language. You won't fool anyone. Take a critical look at what you've written to see whether any of the wording should be deflated—replaced with clearer, shorter, down-to-earth words and phrases. Consider the following example.

REVISE   The Model 3211 is a device which provides the capability of performing the printing function to produce reports.

TO   The Model 3211 can print reports.

The first sentence reads like an important pronouncement. Stripped of its pretentious phrases, however, it is actually a simple statement.

In recent years, consumer interest groups and lawmakers have become concerned about the problem of affectation and legal-sounding language in insurance policies, contracts, and other documents. As a result, many states have created "plain English laws," which require that documents be written in clear, understandable language. The following sentences show the effect of revising "legalese" into plain language.

REVISE   I hereby authorize the above repair work to be done along with the necessary material, and hereby grant you and/or your employees permission to operate the car or truck herein described on streets, highways, or elsewhere for the purpose of testing and/or inspection.

TO   You have my permission to make repairs listed on this work order and to use the necessary materials. You or your employees may drive my car or truck to test its performance.

In the revised version, notice the absence of the "high-sounding" phrases *I hereby authorize, hereby grant, herein described, the above repair work,* and *and/or.* Notice that when it is translated into straightforward English, the statement gains in clarity what it loses in pomposity.

Excessive Formality

Some writers feel that, especially in job-related writing, it is immodest or inappropriate to use the first-person point of view—that is, to speak of themselves as *I* or *me.* They believe that their material will sound more "objective" or "businesslike" if they refer to themselves in the third person (employing such terms as *the writer, the technician,* or *the reporter*) or if they use the passive voice. Writing of this sort tends to sound stuffy and unnatural, however. In most cases your message will be clearer and easier to follow if you speak of yourself as *I.*

REVISE	*The technician* will complete the wiring and test the system at the end of June.
TO	*I will* complete the wiring and test the system at the end of June.
REVISE	The tests described in the attached report *were all performed by the writer.*
TO	*I* performed all the tests described in the attached report.

Also, in on-the-job writing, avoid the use of *one* as a pronoun, because it is inexact, is indirect, and sounds pretentious. The use of *one* does not make your writing more objective; it merely makes a statement sound impersonal, almost as if some nameless, formless being, rather than you yourself, were expressing an idea or making a suggestion.

REVISE	*One* can only conclude that the new valves are not effective on the old fire trucks.
TO	*I* can only conclude that the new valves are not effective on the old fire trucks.

The use of an impersonal *it is* expression to avoid the pronoun *I* has the same kind of stuffy effect as *the writer* and *one.*

REVISE	*It is regrettable that* the material shipped on the 12th is unacceptable.
TO	*I regret that* we cannot accept your shipment of the 12th.

The second version is more direct, and suggests that the writer is not trying to avoid taking responsibility for what he or she has stated.

Some writers, looking for ways to make their work sound more authoritative or more serious, introduce expressions like *It should be noted that* or *I am inclined to think that* in their writing. Expressions like these only add wordiness.

REVISE	*It should be noted that* the gaskets tend to turn brittle after six months in the warehouse.
TO	The gaskets tend to turn brittle after six months in the warehouse.
REVISE	*I am inclined to think that* each manager should attend the meeting to hear the committee's recommendations.

TO   I think that each manager should attend the meeting to hear the committee's recommendations.

The more natural your writing sounds, the more effectively it will communicate.

Causes of Affectation and Excessive Formality

If affectation and excessive formality are relatively easy to cure, as the previous examples suggest, why are they so difficult to eliminate from on-the-job writing? The answer is that affectation has so many causes, only some of which are addressed in the following list.

- *Impression.* As suggested earlier, one reason writers use pretentious language is that they wish to impress the reader. Creating an impression begins in school, when students try to impress their teachers with fancy words instead of evidence and logic. Later, an employee may want to impress superiors or clients with how well he or she performs on the job.
- *Insecurity.* Writers who are insecure about their facts, conclusions, or arguments may try to protect themselves with a smokescreen of pretentious words.
- *Imitation.* Perhaps unconsciously, some writers imitate poor writing they see around them. In one company, for example, everyone referred to himself or herself in memos as "the writer" instead of "I." Each new person who joined the company unthinkingly followed the style until the president of the company noticed the practice and told the employees that they could refer to themselves with the normal "I."
- *Intimidation.* A few writers, consciously or unconsciously, try to intimidate or overwhelm their reader with words—often to protect themselves from criticism. Such writers seem to feel that the best defense is a good offense.
- *Initiation.* Those who have just completed their training for an occupation often feel that one way to prove their membership is to use technical terminology and jargon as much as possible. Usually, after a few years pass and the novice feels respected by co-workers, the impulse for affectation passes. Supervisors, however, wish the process did not take so long.
- *Imprecision.* Because a writer is having trouble being precise, he or she may find that an easy solution is to use a vague but trendy, pretentious word. It is easier to say "the policy will have a positive impact upon the department" than to explain precisely how the policy will affect the department.

Knowing the causes of affectation is important. If you know the possible reasons for affectation in your writing, you will be taking the first step toward curing the problem.

CHECKING FOR ACCURACY

Above all else, your information must be accurate. Although accuracy is important in all types of writing, it takes on special significance when you write on the job. One misplaced decimal point, for example, can create a staggering budgetary error. Incorrect or imprecise instructions can cause injury to a worker. At the very least, you will quickly lose the confidence of your reader if your writing is not accurate. Your reader will be annoyed, for example, if a figure or fact in your writing differs from one in a chart or graph. These kinds of inaccuracies are easily overlooked as you write a first draft, so it is essential that you correct them during revision.

CHECKING FOR COMPLETENESS

Revision is the time to insert any missing facts or ideas. When you finish your draft, check it against your outline. If any of the main ideas or supporting details you listed are missing from your draft, rewrite your sentences and paragraphs as necessary to incorporate the information.

In revising your draft for completeness, you may also think of new information that you failed to include when you were preparing and writing your draft. Always carefully consider such new information in light of your reader and purpose. If the information will help satisfy your reader's need and accomplish the purpose of your writing, by all means add it now. But if the information—no matter how interesting—does not serve these ends, it has no place in your writing.

CHECKING GRAMMAR

Grammatical errors, like inaccurate facts or incomplete information, can confuse or irritate your reader and cause him or her to lose confidence in you. Even worse, many of the errors discussed in this chapter are so severe that they can actually alter the meaning of a sentence. Therefore, it is essential that in revising your draft, you check for grammatical correctness.

Following is a survey of common grammatical errors. Each type of error is described briefly here, and is explained in detail in the Handbook section of the Writer's Guide. If you find it helpful, use the survey below as a checklist for grammatical revisions that may be needed.

Agreement

Agreement means that the parts of a sentence, like the pieces of a jigsaw puzzle, fit together properly. The following discussion points out the types of sentences in which problems of agreement occur often.

Subject-Verb Agreement. A *verb* must agree with its *subject* in number. A singular subject requires a singular verb; a plural subject requires a plural verb. Do not let intervening phrases and clauses mislead you. (See Section 3.4.5 of the Handbook.)

REVISE   The *use* of insecticides, fertilizers, and weed killers, although they offer unquestionable benefits, often *result* in unfortunate side effects.

TO   The *use* of insecticides, fertilizers, and weed killers, although they offer unquestionable benefits, often *results* in unfortunate side effects. (The singular verb *results* must agree with the singular subject of the sentence, *use*, not with the plural subject of the preceding clause, *they*.)

Be careful not to make the verb agree with the noun immediately in front of it if that noun is not its subject. This problem is especially likely to occur when a modifying phrase containing a plural noun falls between a singular subject and its verb.

EXAMPLES   Only *one* of the emergency lights *was* functioning when the accident occurred. (The subject is *one*, not *lights*.)

The *advice* of two engineers, one lawyer, and three executives *was* obtained prior to making a commitment. (The subject is *advice*, not *engineers*, *lawyer*, and *executives*.)

Words like *type, part, series,* and *portion* take singular verbs even when such words precede a phrase containing a plural noun.

EXAMPLE   A *series* of meetings *was* held to decide the best way to market the new product.

Subjects expressing measurement, weight, mass, or total often take singular verbs even though the subject word is plural in form. Such subjects are treated as a unit.

EXAMPLE   *Four years is* the normal duration of the apprenticeship program.

However, when such subjects refer to the individuals that make up the unit, a plural verb is required.

EXAMPLE   If you're looking for oil, *three quarts are* on the shelf in the garage.

Similarly, collective subjects take singular verbs when the group is thought of as a unit and plural verbs when the individuals are thought of separately.

EXAMPLES   The *committee is* holding its meeting on Thursday. (*Committee* is thought of as a unit.)

The *majority are* opposed to delivering their reports at the meeting. (*Majority* is thought of as separate individuals.)

A relative pronoun (*who, which, that*) may take either singular or plural verbs depending on whether its antecedent (the noun to which it refers) is singular or plural.

EXAMPLES   He is an *employee* who *takes* work home at night.

He is one of those *employees* who *take* work home at night.

A *compound subject* is one that is composed of two or more elements joined by a conjunction such as *and, or, nor, either . . . or,* or *neither . . . nor.* Usually, when the elements are connected by *and,* the subject is plural and requires a plural verb.

EXAMPLE   *Chemistry and accounting are* prerequisites for this position.

There is one exception to the *and* rule. If the elements connected by *and* form a unit or refer to the same person, the subject is regarded as singular and takes a singular verb.

EXAMPLES   *Bacon and eggs is* a high-cholesterol meal.

His *secretary and biographer was* also his toughest critic. (The same person was his secretary and his biographer.)

A compound subject with two singular elements joined by *or* or *nor* requires a singular verb.

EXAMPLES   Either a *ruler* or a *tape measure is* in the drawer.

Neither the *wiring* nor the *plumbing was* completed on schedule.

A compound subject with a singular and a plural element joined by *or* or *nor* requires that the verb agree with the element nearest to it.

EXAMPLES   Neither the office manager nor the *secretaries were* there.

Neither the secretaries nor the office *manager was* there.

Either they or *I am* going to write the report.

Either I or *they are* going to write the report.

Pronoun-Antecedent Number Agreement. A *pronoun* must agree with its *antecedent,* the noun to which it refers. Like subjects and their verbs, a pronoun must agree with its antecedent in number (singular or plural). (See Section 3.2.3a of the Writer's Guide.)

REVISE   Although the typical *engine* runs well in moderate temperatures, *they* often stall in extreme cold.

TO   Although the typical *engine* runs well in moderate temperatures, *it* often stalls in extreme cold.

Use a singular pronoun when its antecedent is a word like *everybody, everyone, each,* or *anyone,* unless to do so would be illogical because the meaning is obviously plural.

EXAMPLE   *Everyone* pulled *his* share of the load.

Collective nouns may be singular or plural, depending on meaning.

EXAMPLES   The *committee* arrived at the recommended solutions only after *it* had deliberated for days.

The *committee* quit for the day and went to *their* respective homes.

A compound antecedent joined by *or* or *nor* is singular if both elements are singular and plural if both elements are plural.

EXAMPLES   Neither the *technician* nor the *draftsman* could do *his* job until *he* understood the new concept.

Neither the *supervisors* nor the *employees* were pleased at the performance of *their* division.

When one of the antecedents connected by *or* or *nor* is singular and the other is plural, the pronoun agrees with the nearer antecedent.

EXAMPLES   Either the supervisor or the *operators* will have *their* licenses suspended.

Either the operators or the *supervisor* will have *his* license suspended.

A compound antecedent with its elements joined by *and* requires a plural pronoun.

EXAMPLE   *Jim and Ed* took *their* layout drawings with *them.*

Pronoun-Antecedent Gender Agreement and Sexist Language. A pronoun must also agree with its antecedent in gender—masculine, feminine, or neuter. (See Section 3.2.2b of the Writer's Guide.)

EXAMPLE   Mr. Swivet in the accounting department acknowledges *his* responsibility for the misunderstanding, but Ms. Barkley in the research division should acknowledge *her* responsibility for *it* also.

There is a long-standing tradition of using a masculine, singular pronoun to agree with such indefinite antecedents as *each, one, anyone,* and *person.*

EXAMPLE   *Each* may stay or go as *he* chooses.

Many people are now sensitive to implied sexual bias in such usage. When graceful alternatives are available, use them. One solution is to rewrite the sentence in the plural.

REVISE   Every *employee* will have *his* supervisor sign *his* slip.
TO   All *employees* will have *their* supervisors sign *their* slips.

Be careful not to change the pronoun to the plural but leave its antecedent in the singular. The pronoun and its antecedent must always agree.

REVISE   A *technician* can expect to advance on *their* merit.
TO   *Technicians* can expect to advance on *their* merit.

Other possible solutions are to use *his or her* instead of *his* alone or to omit the pronoun completely if it isn't essential to the meaning of the sentence.

REVISE   *Everyone* must submit *his* expense report by Monday.
TO   *Everyone* must submit *his or her* expense report by Monday.
OR   Everyone must submit *an* expense report by Monday.

However, *he or she* can become monotonous when constantly repeated, and a pronoun cannot always be omitted without changing the meaning of a sentence. The best solution, then, is the first one—to use the plural whenever possible.

Consistency of Tense and Person

Much like agreement errors, illogical shifts in *person* or *tense* can confuse the reader. You would be confused, for example, if someone wrote to you: "If *you* show the guard *your* pass, *one* will be allowed to enter the gate" (shift in person) or "When the contract *was* signed, the company *submits* the drawings" (shift in tense). Your confusion would disappear, however, if the sentences were revised as follows:

EXAMPLES   If *you* show the guard your pass, *you* will be allowed to enter the gate. (consistent use of person)

WHEN the contract *was* signed, the company *submitted* the drawings. (consistent use of tense)

Tense.   *Tense* refers to the forms of a verb that indicate time distinctions. A verb may express past, present, or future time. Be consistent in your use of tense; an unnecessary and illogical change of tense within a sentence confuses the reader. (See Section 3.4.3d of the Writer's Guide).

EXAMPLE   Before he *installed* the circuit board, he *cleans* the contacts.

This sentence, for no apparent reason, changes from the past tense (*installed*) to the present tense (*cleans*). To be both correct and logical, the sentence must be written with both verbs in the same tense.

REVISE   Before he *installed* the circuit board, he *cleans* the contacts.

TO   Before he *installed* the circuit board, he *cleaned* the contacts.

OR   Before he *installs* the circuit board, he *cleans* the contacts.

The only acceptable change of tense within a sentence records a real change of time.

EXAMPLE   After you *have assembled* Part A [past tense, because the action occurred in the past], *assemble* Part B [present tense because the action occurs in the present].

Person.   *Person* refers to the forms of a personal pronoun that indicate whether the pronoun represents the speaker, the person spoken to, or the person (or thing) spoken about. If the pronoun represents the *speaker,* the pronoun is in the *first person.* (See Section 3.2.2a of the Writer's Guide.)

EXAMPLE   *I* could not find the answer in the manual.

If the pronoun represents the person or persons spoken *to,* the pronoun is in the *second person.*

EXAMPLE   *You* are going to be a good supervisor.

If the pronoun represents the person or persons spoken *about,* the pronoun is in the *third person.*

EXAMPLE   *They* received the news quietly.

Identifying pronouns by person helps you avoid illogical shifts from one person to another. A very common error is to shift from the third person to the second person.

REVISE   *People* should spend the morning hours on work requiring mental effort, for *your* mind is freshest in the morning.

TO   *People* should spend the morning hours on work requiring mental effort, for *their* minds are freshest in the morning.

OR   *You* should spend the morning hours on work requiring mental effort, for *your* mind is freshest in the morning.

Dangling Modifiers

As noted at the beginning of this chapter, modifiers are words that describe, explain, or qualify an element in a sentence. Modifiers can be adjectives, adverbs, phrases, or clauses. A dangling modifier is a phrase that does not clearly refer to another word or phrase in the sentence. You have seen that misplaced modifiers can result in ambiguity; dangling modifiers, by contrast, result in illogical sentences. (See Section 3.3.4d of the Writer's Guide.)

EXAMPLE   While eating lunch in the cafeteria, the computer malfunctioned.

Although the idea of a computer eating lunch in a cafeteria is ridiculous, that is what the sentence actually states. With the dangling modifier corrected, the sentence would read as follows:

EXAMPLE   While *I* was eating lunch in the cafeteria, the computer malfunctioned.

Dangling modifiers often can be humorous, as in the first example. But they can also cause such confusion that your reader misinterprets the meaning of your sentence completely.

One way to correct a dangling modifier is to add a noun or pronoun for the phrase to modify.

REVISE   After finishing the research, the job was easy. (The phrase *after finishing the research* has nothing to modify. Who finished?)

TO	After finishing the research, *we* found the job easy. (The pronoun *we* tells the reader who finished.)
REVISE	Having evaluated the feasibility of the project, the centralized plan was unanimously approved. (Who evaluated the feasibility of the project?)
TO	Having evaluated the feasibility of the project, the *committee* unanimously approved the centralized plan.
REVISE	Keeping busy, the afternoon passed swiftly. (Who was keeping busy?)
TO	Keeping busy, *I* felt that the afternoon passed swiftly.

A dangling modifier can also be corrected by making the phrase a clause.

REVISE	After finishing the research, the job was easy.
TO	*After we finished the research* [clause], the job was easy.
REVISE	Having evaluated the feasibility of the project, the centralized plan was unanimously approved.
TO	*Once the committee had evaluated the feasibility of the project* [clause], the centralized plan was overwhelmingly approved.
REVISE	Keeping busy, the afternoon passed swiftly.
TO	*Because I kept busy* [clause], the afternoon passed swiftly.

Sentences

A number of errors can make a sentence ungrammatical. The most common such errors are sentence fragments, run-on sentences, and sentences with comma errors.

Fragments.   A sentence that is missing an essential part (*subject* or *predicate*) is called a *sentence fragment*. (See Section 4.3.4c in the Writer's Guide.)

EXAMPLES	He quit his job. (Sentence: *He* is the subject; *quit his job* is the predicate.)
	And left for Australia. (Fragment: subject is missing.)

But having a subject and a predicate does not automatically make a group of words a sentence. The word group must also make an independent statement. "If I work" is a fragment because the subordinating conjunction *if* turns the statement into a dependent clause.

Sentence fragments are often introduced by relative pronouns (*who, whom, whose, which, that*) or subordinating conjunctions (such as *although, because, if, when,* and *while*). The presence of any one of these words should alert you to the fact that what follows is a dependent clause, not a sentence, and must be combined with a main clause.

REVISE   The new manager instituted several new procedures.
                  Many of which are impractical. (*Many of which* must
                  be linked to *procedures.*)

TO   The new manager instituted several new procedures,
                  many of which are impractical.

A sentence must contain a main, or finite, verb. *Verbals,* which are forms derived from verbs but different in function, will not do the job. The following examples are sentence fragments because they do not contain main verbs. *Providing, to work,* and *waiting* are verbals and cannot perform the function of a main verb.

REVISE   *Providing* all employees with hospitalization insurance.

TO   The company *provides* all employees with hospitalization
                  insurance.

REVISE   *To work* a 40-hour week.

TO   The new contract *requires* all employees to work a 40-
                  hour week.

REVISE   The customer *waiting* to see you.

TO   The customer waiting to see you *is* from the Labatronics
                  Corporation.

Fragments usually reflect incomplete and sometimes confused thinking. The most common type of fragment is the careless addition of an afterthought.

REVISE   These are my coworkers. A fine group of people.

TO   These are my coworkers, a fine group of people.

Run-on Sentences.   A *run-on sentence,* sometimes called a *fused sentence,* is made up of two or more independent clauses (sentence elements that contain a subject and a predicate and could stand alone as complete sentences) without punctuation to separate them. (See Section 4.3.4b in the Writer's Guide.)

INCORRECT   The new manager instituted several new procedures some
                  were impractical.

Run-on sentences can be corrected in the following ways:

1. Create two separate sentences.

CORRECT   The new manager instituted several new procedures. Some were impractical.

2. Join the two clauses with a semicolon if they are closely related.

CORRECT   The new manager instituted several new procedures; some were impractical.

3. Join the two clauses with a comma and a coordinating conjunction.

CORRECT   The new manager instituted several new procedures, but some were impractical.

4. Subordinate one clause to the other.

CORRECT   The new manager instituted several new procedures, some of which were impractical.

5. Join the two clauses with a conjunctive adverb preceded by a semicolon and followed by a comma.

CORRECT   The new manager instituted several new procedures; however, some were impractical.

Comma Errors.   The most common punctuation problem is the misuse of the comma. This is understandable because the comma has such a wide variety of uses: it links, it encloses, it separates, and it indicates omissions. (For a complete discussion of the comma, see Section 5.1 of the Writer's Guide. Other marks of punctuation are covered there as well.) The following guidelines will help you to use the comma correctly and effectively.

When two independent clauses are joined with only a comma, the error is known as a *comma splice*. Like a run-on sentence, which also contains improperly connected clauses, a comma splice can be corrected in several ways: (1) joining the two clauses with a comma and a coordinating conjunction, (2) subordinating one clause to the other, (3) joining the two clauses with a semicolon if they are closely related, (4) joining the two clauses with a conjunctive adverb preceded by a semicolon and followed by a comma, or (5) creating two separate sentences.

REVISE   It was 500 miles to the facility, we made arrangements to fly. (comma splice)

TO   It was 500 miles to the facility, so we made arrangements to fly. (comma plus coordinating conjunction)

OR   Because it was 500 miles to the facility, we made arrangements to fly. (one clause subordinated to the other)

OR   It was 500 miles to the facility; we made arrangements to fly. (semicolon)

OR   It was 500 miles to the facility; therefore, we made arrangements to fly. (semicolon, conjunctive adverb, comma)

OR   It was 500 miles to the facility. We made arrangements to fly. (two sentences)

When correcting a comma splice, be sure that the solution you choose correctly conveys the intended meaning of the original sentence.

Do not place a comma everywhere you pause. Although it is true that commas usually signal pauses, *it is not true that pauses necessarily call for commas.* A number of common errors involve placing commas where they do not belong.

Do not place a comma between a subject and its verb or between a verb and its object.

REVISE   The cold conditions, made accurate readings difficult. (The comma incorrectly separates the subject, *conditions,* from its verb, *made.*)

TO   The cold conditions made accurate readings difficult.

REVISE   He has often said, that one company's failure is another's opportunity. (The comma incorrectly separates the verb, *said,* from its object, *that one company's failure is another's opportunity.*)

TO   He has often said that one company's failure is another's opportunity.

Do not place a comma between the two parts of a compound subject or a compound predicate.

REVISE   The director of the engineering department, and the supervisor of the quality control section were both opposed to the new schedules. (The comma incorrectly separates the parts of the compound subject, *director* and *supervisor.*)

TO   The director of the engineering department and the supervisor of the quality control section were both opposed to the new schedules.

REVISE   The director of the engineering department listed five major objections, and asked that the new schedules be reconsidered. (The comma incorrectly separates the parts of the compound predicate, *listed five major objections* and *asked that the new schedules be reconsidered.*)

TO	The director of the engineering department listed five major objections and asked that the new schedules be reconsidered.

In most cases, do not place a comma after a coordinating conjunction such as *and* or *but*.

REVISE	The chairman formally adjourned the meeting, but, the members of the committee continued to argue. (The word *but* is part of the second clause and should not be separated from it by a comma.)
TO	The chairman formally adjourned the meeting, but the members of the committee continued to argue.
REVISE	I argued against the proposal. And, I gave good reasons for my position. (The word *and* is part of the sentence and should not be separated from it by a comma.)
TO	I argued against the proposal. And I gave good reasons for my position.

Do not place a comma before the first item in a series or after the last item in a series.

REVISE	We are considering a number of new products, such as, calculators, typewriters, and cameras.
TO	We are considering a number of new products, such as calculators, typewriters, and cameras.
REVISE	It was a fast, simple, inexpensive, process.
TO	It was a fast, simple, inexpensive process.

CHECKING SPELLING

Following is a list of words that are frequently misspelled in on-the-job writing. This list can serve as a handy reference if you are in doubt about a particular word. If you have trouble with spelling, study the spelling section of the Writer's Guide at the end of the book.

Commonly Misspelled Words

aberration	achieve	actual
absorption	acknowledgment	address
accelerate	acquaint	advice (*noun*)
accessible	acquire	advise (*verb*)
accommodate	across	adviser

aerate
aggravate
aisle (*of theater*)
a lot (*two words*)
alcohol
all right (*two words*)
altar (*noun*)
alter (*verb*)
altogether
amateur
ambivalent
analysis
analyze
annual
anonymous
answer
antiseptic
apparatus
appear
appetite
appreciable
appropriate
architectural
arguing
around
arouse
arrangement
ascend
assert
assistant
athlete
attach
author
auxiliary
belief (*noun*)
believe (*verb*)
benefit
benefited
breathe (*verb*)
brilliant
buried
business
cafeteria
calendar

captain
carburetor
careful
carrying
category
ceiling
cemetery
certain
changeable
characteristic
chief
choose (*present*)
chose (*past*)
climbed
clothes
column
coming
commit
committed
committee
common
comparatively
conceivable
conceive
concentration
confidant, confidante
    (*noun*)
confident (*adjective*)
conquer
conscience
conscientious
conscious
consistent
continual
continuous
controlled
convenience
copies
corroborate
course
courteous
criticism
criticize
crowd

crystal
cylinder
dealt
dependent
desirable
despair
desperate
develop
development
diesel
dietitian
difference
different
dilemma
disappear
disappoint
disapprove
disastrous
discipline
discriminate
discussed
disease
dissatisfied
dissection
distinction
dormitories
drunkenness
ecstasy
efficiency
eighth
electricity
electronics
eligible
eliminate
embarrass
embarrassment
emphasize
enemy
engines
environment
equipment
equipped
especially
essential

exaggerate
exceed
excellent
except
exercise
exhilaration
existence
expense
experience
experiment
explanation
extremely
fascinate
fascinating
February
financial
flourish
forcibly
foreign
foresee
formally (*in a formal way*)
formerly (*earlier*)
forth (*forward*)
forty
fundamental
further
gardener
gauge
government
grammar
grateful
grievous
guarantee
guard
guidance
height
identify
imitation
immediately
incidentally
increase
incredible
indelible

independence
indispensable
inevitable
influential
initiate
inoculate
insistent
intellectual
intelligence
interfere
interrupt
invitation
irrelevant
irresistible
irritable
jealous
judgment
knowledge
laboratory
led (*verb*)
leisure
length
library
license
lightning
likable
likelihood
likely
loneliness
loose (*adjective*)
lose (*verb*)
lying
maintenance
manageable
management
maneuver
mathematics
meant
miniature
mischievous
misdemeanor
misspelled
morale
mortgage

mysterious
naturally
necessarily
ninety
ninth
noticeable
obstacle
occurred
occurrence
omission
omitted
operate
opportunity
optimistic
origin
oscillate
parallel
particularly
partner
peculiar
perceive
perform
perhaps
permanent
perseverance
persistent
persuade
pertain
piece
possess
possession
potato
potatoes
practicable
precede
preceding
preference
preferred
prejudice
presence
prevalent
privilege
procedure
proceed

prominent	seize	therefore
pronunciation	separate	thorough
propeller	sergeant	thought
protein	shepherd	through
prove	shoulder	together
psychology	signal	toward
publicly	similar	transferred
pursue	site	tries
realize	sophomore	truly
really	specimen	Tuesday
receipt	speech	twelfth
receive	statement	undoubtedly
recognize	stopped	unnecessary
recommend	straight	until
referred	strategy	usually
relevant	strength	vacuum
relieve	studying	vegetable
religious	succeed	vertical
repetition	suddenness	vitamin
resemblance	superintendent	Wednesday
resistance	suppress	weird
restaurant	surprise	wholly
rhythm	syllable	woman
ridiculous	symmetrical	women
safety	technique	writing
salary	temperament	written
scene	temperature	
schedule	tendency	

Also, as you check spelling be sure that you have not substituted a homophone—a word that sounds like another word—for the word that you ought to use. In other words, be sure that you have not used "too" when you meant "two." (Section 1 of the Writer's Guide provides a list of many of these words.) The ear can play tricks on you, and these mistakes are often hard to catch, since the wrong word is perfectly legitimate when it is used correctly. Further, if you type, be aware of your most frequent typographical errors.

PHYSICAL APPEARANCE

The most thoughtfully prepared, carefully written, and conscientiously revised writing will quickly lose its effect if it has a poor physical appearance. In the classroom or on the job, a sloppy appearance will invariably lead your reader to assume that your work is also sloppy. In the classroom, that carelessness will reflect on you; on the job, it can reflect on your employer as well.

Consider Christine Thomas's memo to Harriet Sullivan in Chapter 1. Christine wanted to persuade Harriet. A memo written in sloppy or illegible handwriting on coffee-stained paper would not have helped Christine accomplish her purpose. Similarly, your writing will not accomplish its purpose if it has a poor physical appearance. Neatness counts!

Unless your instructor provides other specific instructions, use the following guidelines to give your writing a neat and pleasing appearance:

1. Use good-quality paper—ruled if you write by hand or non-erasable white bond if you type.
2. Type if at all possible. Otherwise, make sure that your handwriting is neat and readable.
3. If you type, make sure that the ribbon is fresh and the keys are clean so the letters will not fade or smudge.
4. Use at least one-inch margins on the sides of the paper and one-and-a-half-inch margins on the top and bottom.
5. Handle the paper carefully with clean hands so it does not get crumpled or marked with fingerprints.
6. Make sure that the writing is not crowded and that ample white space separates sections.

Good physical arrangement of specific types of writing, such as letters or formal reports, is discussed elsewhere in the book. Refer to the table of contents or the index for page numbers.

FINAL CHECKLIST

The following revision checklist may help you remember in the future the various aspects of revision that this chapter has covered. Refer to it both before and after you write the final draft of any document; you must fix any problems before your reader sees them.

_____Have I revised all ambiguous passages, paying particular attention to comparison and the placement of modifiers?

_____Have I made all pronoun references clear?

_____Have I used language that suits my purpose and my reader's needs throughout?

_____Have I removed all redundancies and padded phrases?

_____Have I revised all affected and excessively formal passages?

_____Is my content complete and accurate?

_____Is my grammar correct?

_____Is my spelling correct?

_____Is the physical appearance of the document satisfactory?

CHAPTER SUMMARY

Like all good writers, you must revise your writing carefully. The first step toward careful revision is to become objective about your writing—allow for a "cooling" period and then view your draft as if it were written by a stranger. Revise your draft in passes, examining one aspect of your writing at a time, and look for your worst errors first.

In revising, make sure that you have expressed the exact meaning that you intended to express and that you have trimmed your writing of unnecessary words and stilted phrases. Make sure, in other words, that your writing is *precise* and *concise.*

As you check for *precision,* eliminate the ambiguity that faulty comparisons and inaccurately placed modifiers may produce; supply an immediately recognizable antecedent for a pronoun whenever it is not clear which word or words the pronoun is referring to; and, according to the context, select words that have no inappropriate associations and are neither too general nor too specific for the context. And, if you use specialized or technical terms that your reader may be unfamiliar with, provide definitions or explanations of the terms.

As you check for *conciseness,* strike from your work any redundant modifiers (modifiers that contribute no additional meaning to the words they qualify) and any padded phrases (expressions that take several words to convey an idea that one or two words would express just as effectively). Also, do not use inappropriate jargon as a substitute for direct, well-thought-out language, and avoid excessive formality; in most cases it is better to speak of yourself as *I* than as *the writer* or *one.*

As you revise, be sure to check your writing for accuracy and completeness. In addition, you need to examine your writing for grammatical correctness. Check for agreement of subjects and verbs and of pronouns and antecedents, consistency of tense and of person, and clear pronoun reference; eliminate dangling and misplaced modifiers;

and correct sentence fragments, run-on sentences, and comma errors.

Even with the most careful revision, however, you will lose your reader's confidence unless your writing has a neat and pleasing physical appearance.

EXERCISES

1. Each of the following sentences contains a faulty comparison. Rewrite each sentence to eliminate the error.

   a. The word-processing machine in the direct mail department operates more efficiently than the customer relations department.
   b. The production manager expressed greater appreciation for the temporary help than the sales manager.
   c. Julia Valenti, the personnel manager, felt that the applicant was better qualified than Charles Crane, the director of office services.

2. Each of the following sentences contains a "squinting modifier"— that is, a modifier that may qualify either of two elements within the sentence. Locate the squinting modifier and rewrite the sentence in two ways.

   a. The transformer that was sparking violently shocked the line operator.
   b. The man who was making calculations hastily rose from the desk and left the room.
   c. After the committee decided that the work must be completed by Monday, in spite of other commitments, it adjourned immediately.
   d. He planned after the convention to take a short vacation.

3. Each of the following sentences contains an unclear pronoun reference. Rewrite the sentences as necessary to eliminate the errors.

   a. Many members complained that their representatives made decisions secretly without considering them.
   b. Technology has so simplified computer operation that it is now being used in homes.
   c. The crane operator did not file a safety grievance and does not plan it.
   d. Our company decided to relocate in Grandview Hills, after rejecting Westville and Dale City, which was a difficult decision to make.

    e. Anita has held stenographic positions in two insurance companies and in an auto-rental firm, and it should help her in finding a new job.

    f. Mrs. Jardina wanted to dictate a letter to her assistant, Mrs. Sanfredini, but she was unable to begin work until after lunch.

    g. If you feel that you would like to become a dental hygienist, by all means take a course in it.

4. Each of the following sentences contains a redundant word, phrase, or clause. Rewrite the sentences to eliminate the redundant elements.

    a. Our experienced salespeople, who have many years of work behind them, will plan an aggressive advertising campaign to sell the new product.

    b. Any two raceway assemblies can be connected together with the plate as shown.

    c. The radio announcer kept repeatedly saying, "Buy PDQ brand pretzels!"

    d. Dissatisfied employees should give their complaints to the manager who is in charge as supervisor.

    e. If you are interested in economics, do not neglect to read the above-mentioned book, which was discussed previously.

5. Each of the following sentences contains at least one padded phrase. Rewrite the sentences to eliminate such phrases.

    a. We began the project in the month of April.

    b. He opened the conversation with a reference to the subject of inflation.

    c. The field of engineering is a profession that offers great opportunities.

    d. The process was delayed because of the fact that the chemicals were impure.

    e. The personnel manager spoke to the printing-plant supervisor with regard to the scheduling of employee vacations.

    f. Due to the fact that Monday was a holiday, we will not be able to complete the job until Wednesday.

6. Each of the following passages contains unnecessary jargon, padded phrases, and excessive formality. Revise the passages.

    a. With reference to the matter that management has declared to be in the best interest of the furtherance of company–employee relations, the president has been authorized and empowered to grant each and every employee, upon the attainment of 30 years of continued and uninterrupted service to the company, an additional period of vacation that shall be of one week's duration.

b. I hereby designate Mr. Samson, who has been holding the position and serving in the capacity of assistant technical supervisor, to be named and appointed to the position and function of deputy director of customer relations. In his newly elevated position Mr. Samson will report, in the first instance, directly to the department director—that is, to me.

c. Purchasers of the enclosed substance should carefully and thoroughly follow the instructions provided herein for the use of the substance, and should in no case whatsoever consume, or otherwise partake of, said substance without proceeding in the manner set forth on the accompanying circular of instructions.

7. In each of the following sentences, select the correct word or words from the two items in parentheses. In some sentences, the choice involves the correct pronoun; in other sentences, it involves the correct verb.

a. The supervisor asked each employee to decide whether (he/they) wanted to work overtime to finish the project.

b. Her job during the negotiations (was/were) to observe and then report her observations to the manager.

c. Our line of products (is/are) sold in the West and in the Midwest.

d. Neither John nor Peter remembered to submit (his/their) work on time.

e. The Association of Corporate Employees failed because (they/it) never received full support from the member companies.

f. Any employee who has not completed (his/their) time sheet must do so now.

g. A number of beneficial products (has/have) resulted from the experiment.

h. That these figures are contradictory anyone in (their/his) right mind can see.

i. A staff member is held responsible for any errors that (he or she/they) may introduce.

8. Revise the following sentences to correct any errors in agreement. The errors may be in subject–verb agreement or in pronoun–antecedent agreement.

a. A survey of residents in the selected communities show a large potential market for our product.

  b. After each of the printed characters are translated, the report is given to the word-processing department.
  c. The committee is planning to submit their recommendations before the end of the week.
  d. The course instructs students in the basics of the subject and provides him with hands-on time.
  e. A project engineer must be able to justify the changes they make in a technician's drawing.

9. Each of the following sentences contains either a dangling modifier or a misplaced modifier. Locate the errors and correct them. Add any necessary words.

  a. An experienced technician, the company was anxious to hire her.
  b. Before taking the training course, it is recommended that the operator read the *Operator's Manual.*
  c. After evaluating the 38 answers, the test was found by the production manager to reveal a serious deficiency.
  d. Hoping to be promoted for her contribution to the project, the vice president's report represents three months of work.
  e. We purchased the store's merchandise that was going out of business.
  f. We are going to install a desk chair for our assistant with a swivel seat.

10. Correct any sentence fragments or run-on sentences in this exercise. Add words and punctuation as necessary.

  a. You cannot consider submitting the report. If you have not typed it.
  b. Hoping to hear from you soon.
  c. Supplies are needed to operate and maintain the printout device. Among them ribbon shields, forms, and print bands.
  d. I spray the trees twice a year. Once in the late spring and again in early fall.
  e. The stenographic reporter read back the transcript. Because the members of the jury wanted to hear the evidence once more.
  f. Use these accepted signs consistently the typesetter will not understand any others.
  g. You are not a physician you should not act like one.

11. Correct the comma faults in the following sentences by adding, changing, or deleting words and punctuation as needed.

a. The electric voltage in the line was too high, he dared not risk touching it.
b. An emergency occurs, another committee is born.
c. Members may pay their dues immediately, they may choose to have a statement mailed to their homes or offices.
d. The computer's printer has a red, and tan cabinet.
e. One should never be ashamed to be somewhat sentimental, for, a certain amount of sentimentality makes a person human.
f. The new law did not put all accountants behind bars, it did make some accountants fearful, though.
g. The engine overheated, the operator turned it off.

part two

THE PROCESS AT WORK

6

Principles of Business Correspondence

Business letters are an essential means of communication between organizations and their customers; memorandums (or memos) are an essential means of communication within organizations. Because of their importance, letters and memos that are poorly written may waste considerable time and money. For example, the following poorly written letter was actually sent to a law firm. The staff at the law firm could not understand it, even though a number of attorneys, paralegal assistants, and secretaries were familiar with the case.

```
Mr. Stewart R. Cassidy
Smith and Jones, Attorneys at Law
1212 Broadway
Hartford, CT 06119

Dear Mr. Cassidy:

In regard to claim on Account #5-861 see enclosed
copy of letter received and copy of delivery re-
ceipt regarding same. There had been a claim which
was disallowed and debtor withheld payment on the
bill, and the one we referred to your office for
collection, as no pro was mentioned but the one
the claim was on was referred to the bill is still
open and they still owe Universal, please review
and advise.

Sincerely,

Ralph Madison
Ralph Madison
```

Staff members wrote to Ralph Madison and others at his company without success, and finally the law firm had to send someone to the company to find out what the letter was about.

A letter like this wasted the time of a highly paid staff—and may well have caused a delay in legal services to Ralph Madison's company. Further, carelessly written letters, because they project such a poor image of the writer, can result in loss of another kind. A reader's negative reaction to an unclear or messy letter can cost a firm an important contract or an employee his or her job.

If so much hinges on the preparation of an acceptable letter, why do business people write letters at all? Why don't they rely on the telephone, usually a quicker and easier means of communication? (A letter may be even more expensive than a call: a single business letter can cost well over $5 in labor, stationery, and postage.) A good deal of the time, of course, a telephone call is more appropriate than a letter—when, for instance, an immediate response is needed, or when a person-to-person exchange might smooth over a touchy situation. But there are times when a telephone call cannot replace a letter.

1. Letters provide a permanent, written record of a business transaction.
2. Letters represent a commitment on the part of the writer, as the expression "Put it in writing" indicates. A written promise, conveyed above the signature of an employee who has the authority to act, carries weight that a recollection of a telephone call cannot.
3. Letters provide traveling salespeople, busy executives, and others with a convenient way to receive information and respond (they may be out of the office, or not at their desks, when the phone rings). They can usually set aside time to answer their mail.
4. Letters that are carefully planned can create goodwill—and sometimes stimulate business—even in a situations where customers or clients are dissatisfied with a product or service.
5. Often a message is complicated, and the writer wishes to reduce the possibility of confusion by providing clear documentation of his position. Similarly, in many cases a recipient of a message needs time to study it. A phone call cannot accommodate careful reflection: if a complicated question is raised on the phone, the answer is often "I'll get back to you on that one."

WRITING LETTERS

The process of writing letters involves basically the same steps that go into most other on-the-job writing. *First,* establish your purpose, your reader's needs, and your scope (see Chapter 1). *Second,* prepare an outline. (For a letter, an outline may involve little more than jotting down, on a note pad, the points you wish to make and the order in which you wish to make them.) *Third,* write a rough draft from the outline. *Fourth,* set the draft aside for a "cooling" period (see Chapter 5). The cooling period is especially important in the case of a letter written in response to a problem. Business letters are not the place to vent emotions. A cooling period, even if it is only a lunch hour, gives the writer a chance to remove any hasty and inappropriate statements made in the heat of the situation. One chief executive of a large company always allows the rough draft of a crucial letter to "cool" overnight before revising and mailing it— regardless of the pressure to send it out right away. This executive believes that a slightly delayed—but appropriate—response is preferable to an immediate reply that may cause misunderstanding later.

For the *fifth* step, revising the rough draft, go over your work carefully, checking for sense as well as for grammar, spelling, and punctuation. Since *format* (the arrangement of the parts of a letter on the page) is a basic element in letter writing, it's a good idea, if you can, to type out a preliminary copy of the letter on paper that is the same size as the stationery you will be using. Set the typewriter at the margins you will use and, as you type, insert the correct spacing between parts of the letter (see pages 135–136). If a secretary or an assistant does your typing, be sure to check his or her work; you will sign the letter, and therefore you are responsible for its appearance and accuracy.

Tone: Goodwill and the Reader's Point of View

A business letter differs in one important way from other kinds of job-related writing: it usually represents a direct communication between one person and another. As a letter writer addressing yourself directly to your reader, you have an opportunity that the writer of, say, a report doesn't have: you are in a very good position to take your reader's needs into account. If you ask yourself, "How might I feel if I were the recipient of such a letter?" you can gain some insight into the likely needs and feelings of your reader—and then tailor your message to fit those needs and feelings. Furthermore, you have a chance to build goodwill for your business or organization. Many companies spend millions of dollars to create a favorable public image. A letter to a customer that sounds impersonal and unfriendly can quickly tarnish that image, but a thoughtful letter that seems sincere can greatly enhance it.

Suppose, for example, you are a department-store manager who receives a request for a refund from a customer who forgot to enclose the receipt with the request. In a letter to the customer, you might write, "The sales receipt must be enclosed with the merchandise before we can process the refund." However, if you consider how you might keep the goodwill of the customer, you might word the request this way: "Please enclose the sales receipt with the merchandise, so that we can send your refund promptly." Notice that the second version uses the word *please* and the active voice ("Please enclose the sales receipt,") while the first version contains the passive voice ("The sales receipt must be enclosed"). In general, the active voice creates a friendlier, more courteous tone than the passive, which tends to sound impersonal and unfriendly. (For a discussion of the active and passive voices, see Chapter 4.) And polite wording, such as the use of *please,* also helps to create goodwill.

However, as a business-letter writer, you can go one step further. You can put the reader's needs and interests at the center by writing from the reader's point of view. Often, but not always, doing so means using the words *you* and *your* rather than the words *we, our, I,* and *mine.* That is why the technique has been referred to as the "you" attitude or "you" viewpoint. For example, consider the point of view of the original sentence in the example just given:

> The sales receipt must be enclosed with the merchandise before <u>we can process</u> the refund.

The underlined words suggest that the point of view centers on the writer's need to process the refund. Even the second version, although its tone is more polite and friendly, emphasizes the writer's need to get the receipt "so we can send your refund promptly." (The writer, of course, may want to get rid of the problem quickly.)

But what is the reader's interest? The reader is not interested in helping the business to process its paperwork. He or she simply wants the refund—and by emphasizing that need, the writer encourages the reader to act quickly. Consider the following revision, which is written from the "you" viewpoint:

> So you can receive your refund promptly, please enclose the sales receipt with the merchandise.

In this sentence, the reader's benefit is stressed as the reason he or she should act. Consider another example:

> So that we can complete our file records, please send your Form 1040-A by March 10.

Even though the recipient has little incentive to send the form, the "you" viewpoint can suggest that the recipient's interests are at stake:

> So that your file is complete, please send your Form 1040-A by March 10.

Be aware, however, that *both goodwill and the "you" viewpoint can be overdone.* Used thoughtlessly, both techniques can produce a fawning, insincere tone—what might be called "plastic goodwill." Consider the following:

> Thank you so very much for ordering the Trend-Setter Personalized Labels. Obviously, you're a person of extraordinary judgment and good taste. You are to be congratulated on your fine selection of the one- by three-inch size. You are the kind of wonderful person who makes working a joy. Please work with us again.

Obviously, the language is full of false praise and sickeningly sweet phrases. Any attempt at goodwill that is transparently insincere will be counterproductive.

Direct and Indirect Patterns

In a speech to the Japan Business English Association, Professor Francis W. Weeks identified one of the most difficult problems in business correspondence and illustrated it with an anecdote:

> The number one problem, in my opinion, will always be the manner and style of our approach to people through the medium of written communication. One aspect of this problem can be expressed this way: "How direct or indirect should our communications be?"
>
> To be completely direct and forthright, striking to the heart of the matter immediately, is also to be blunt and perhaps offensive. To be indirect is to be polite and considerate to the reader. "Oh, no" say some writers. "To be direct is to be efficient, to save time, effort, words, and money. To be indirect is to waste time and be wordy."
>
> Nearly ten years ago when I had a sabbatical leave of absence from the University of Illinois, I was at the Douglas Aircraft Company in California studying the communications of their Marketing Department. I remember one day reading a letter from Japan—two pages long—written in very good English, but I could not determine what the writer was talking about. He seemed to go round and round his subject matter without ever coming to the point. I put the letter

aside intending to go back to it later; then several hours afterwards, "the light dawned." He was saying "No." And he was saying it as politely and tactfully and indirectly as he knew how.

I know an American executive who would have handled the situation far differently. He would have written "No" in big letters across the face of the letter he was answering and sent it back to the writer.

Even direct, efficient American writers would characterize that as brutal treatment of a correspondent.[1]

Part of the problem, of course, is that notions of courtesy in Japanese business dealings are quite different from those prevailing in the United States. Yet research has shown that, even in America, it is more effective to present good news directly and bad news indirectly.

This principle is true because readers form their impressions and attitudes very early in letters. As an example, a college student who had applied for a scholarship received a letter explaining that he had not won it. The letter began: "I'm sorry, but you were not awarded the Smith Scholarship." In disappointment, the student threw the letter on his desk and left his apartment. Three days later he picked up the letter and read further. It went on to say that the committee thought his record was so strong that he should call immediately if he were interested in another, but lesser-known, scholarship. The student called but was told that the other scholarship had been awarded to someone else. Since the student had not called immediately, everyone had assumed he was not interested.

Many readers do finish a letter when bad news is presented at the outset, but they generally continue to read with a predetermined opinion concerning what follows. They may be very skeptical about an explanation, or they may reject a reasonable alternative presented by the writer. Furthermore, even when you refuse a request or say "no" one time, you may wish to work with the reader in the future. An abruptly phrased rejection early in the letter may prevent you from reestablishing an amicable relationship.

Consider the thoughtlessness of the rejection letter shown in Figure 6–1. Although the letter is direct and uses the pronouns *you* and *your,* the writer has apparently not considered how the recipient will feel as she reads the letter. There is no expression of regret that Mrs. Mauer is being rejected for the position, nor any appreciation of her efforts in applying for the job: "Sincerely" at the close almost seems hostile. The letter is, in short, rude. The pattern for this letter is

[1] Francis W. Weeks, "Current Issues in the Practice of Business Communication in the USA," *Journal of Business Communication* 13, No. 3, Spring 1976, pp. 62–63. Professor Weeks was the executive director of the American Business Communication Association at the time.

Southtown Dental Center

3221 Ryan Road   San Diego, CA 92217
(714) 321-1579

November 11, 19--

Mrs. Barbara L. Mauer
157 Beach Drive
San Diego, CA 92113

Dear Mrs. Mauer:

Your application for the position of dental receptionist at Southtown Dental Center has been rejected. We have found someone more qualified than you.

Sincerely,

Mary Hernandez

Mary Hernandez
Office Manager

MH/bt

FIGURE 6–1. A poor "bad news" letter.

Bad news/Explanation/Close. A better general pattern for "bad news" letters is as follows:

> Buffer
> Bad news
> Goodwill

The "buffer" may be either neutral information or an explanation that makes the bad news *understandable*. Bad news is never pleasant; however, information that either puts the bad news in perspective or makes the bad news seem reasonable maintains goodwill between the writer and the reader.

Consider the revision of the rejection letter shown in Figure 6–2. This letter carries the same disappointing news as the first, but the writer is careful to thank the reader for her time and effort, to explain why she was not accepted for the job, and to offer her encouragement in finding a position in another office.

Presenting good news is, of course, easier. It is important to remember that good news should be presented early—at the outset, if at all possible. The pattern for "good news" letters should be as follows:

1. Good news
2. Explanation or facts
3. Goodwill

By presenting the good news first, you increase the likelihood that the reader will pay careful attention to details, and you achieve goodwill from the start. Figure 6–3 shows an example of a "good news" letter.

The following additional tips will help you to achieve a tone that builds goodwill with the reader:

1. *Be respectful, not demanding.*

CHANGE   Submit your answer in one week.

TO   I would appreciate receiving your answer within one week.

2. *Be modest, not arrogant.*

CHANGE   My report is thorough, and I'm sure that you won't be able to continue efficiently without it.

TO   I have tried to be as thorough as possible in my report, and I hope you find it useful.

3. *Be polite, not sarcastic.*

Southtown Dental Center

3221 Ryan Road   San Diego, CA 92217
(714) 321-1579

November 11, 19--

Mrs. Barbara L. Mauer
157 Beach Drive
San Diego, CA 92113

Dear Mrs. Mauer:

Buffer   Thank you for your time and effort in applying for the position of dental receptionist at Southtown Dental Center.

Bad news   Since we needed someone who can assume the duties here with a minimum of training, we have selected an applicant with over ten years of experience.

Goodwill   I am sure that with your excellent college record you will find a position in another office.

Sincerely,

Mary Hernandez

Mary Hernandez
Office Manager

MH/bt

FIGURE 6-2. A courteous "bad news" letter.

Southtown Dental Center

3221 Ryan Road   San Diego, CA 92217
(714) 321-1579

November 11, 19--

Mrs. Barbara L. Mauer
157 Beach Drive
San Diego, CA 92113

Dear Mrs. Mauer:

Good News   Please accept our offer of the position of dental receptionist at Southtown Dental Center.

Explanation   If the terms we discussed in the interview are acceptable to you, please come in at 9:30 a.m. on November 15. At that time we will ask you to complete our personnel form, in addition to. . . .

Goodwill   I, as well as the others in the office, look forward to working with you. Everyone was very favorably impressed with you during your interviews.

Sincerely,

Mary Hernandez

Mary Hernandez
Office Manager
MH/bt

FIGURE 6–3. A "good news" letter.

CHANGE I just received the shipment we ordered *six months ago.* I'm sending it back—we can't use it now. Thanks!

TO I am returning the shipment we ordered on March 12, 1984. Unfortunately, it arrived too late for us to be able to use it.

4. *Be positive and tactful, not negative and condescending.*

CHANGE Your complaint about our prices is way off target. Our prices are definitely not any higher than those of our competitors.

TO Thank you for your suggestion concerning our prices. We believe, however, that our prices are competitive with, and in some cases below, those of our competitors.

Writing Style in Business Letters

Letter-writing style may legitimately vary from informal, in a letter to a close business associate, to formal, or restrained, in a letter to someone you do not know. (Even if you are writing a business letter to a close associate, of course, you should always follow the rules of standard grammar, spelling, and punctuation.)

INFORMAL It worked! The new process is better than we had dreamed.

RESTRAINED You will be pleased to know that the new process is more effective than we had expected.

You will probably find yourself relying on the restrained style more frequently than on the informal, since an obvious attempt to sound casual, like overdone goodwill, may strike the reader as insincere. Do not adopt such a formal style, however, that your letters read like legal contracts. Using legalistic-sounding words in an effort to impress your reader will make your writing seem stuffy and pompous—and may well irritate your reader.

Consider the letter shown in Figure 6-4. The excessively formal writing style is full of largely out-of-date business jargon; expressions like *query* (for *request* or *question*), *I wish to state, be advised that,* and *herewith* are both old-fashioned and pretentious. Good business letters today have a more personal, down-to-earth style, as the revision of the letter in Figure 6-5 illustrates.

The revised version not only is less stuffy but more concise. Being concise in writing is important, but don't be so concise that you become blunt. If you respond to a written request that you cannot understand with "Your request was unclear" or "I don't understand your ques-

---

Amex Laboratories

327 Wilson Avenue   Birmingham, AL 35211
(205) 743-6218

September 7, 19--

Mr. Roland E. Forbes
772 South Wilton Street
Birmingham, AL 35207

Dear Mr. Forbes:

In response to your query, I wish to state
that we no longer have an original copy of
the brochure requested. Be advised that a
photographic reproduction is enclosed herewith.

Address further correspondence to this office
for assistance as required.

Sincerely yours,

E. T. Hillman

E. T. Hillman

ETH:knt
Enclosure

FIGURE 6–4. Poor letter-writing style.

Amex Laboratories

327 Wilson Avenue   Birmingham, AL 35211
(205) 743-6218

September 7, 19--

Mr. Roland E. Forbes
772 South Wilton Street
Birmingham, AL 35207

Dear Mr. Forbes:

Because we are currently out of original copies of our brochure, I am sending you a photocopy of it.

If I can be of further help, please let me know.

Sincerely,

E. T. Hillman

E. T. Hillman

ETH:knt
Enclosure

FIGURE 6-5. Better letter-writing style.

tion," you will probably offend your reader. Instead of attacking the writer's ability to phrase a request, consider that what you are really doing is asking for more information. Say so. "I will need more information before I can answer your request. Specifically, can you give me the title and the date of the report you are looking for?" The second version is a little longer than the first, but it is both more polite and more helpful.

Accuracy in Business Letters

Since a letter is a written record, it must be accurate. Facts, figures, dates, and explanations that are incorrect or misleading may cost time, money, and goodwill. Remember that when you sign a letter, you are responsible for what it says. Always allow yourself time to review a letter before mailing it. Whenever possible, ask someone who is familiar with the situation to review an important letter. Listen with an open mind to any criticisms of what you have said. Make whatever changes you believe are necessary. Again—if you sign the letter, you are responsible for its contents.

A second kind of accuracy to check for is the mechanics of writing—punctuation, grammar, and spelling. In business as elsewhere, accuracy and attention to detail are equated with carefulness and reliability. The kindest conclusion a reader can come to about a letter containing mechanical errors is that the writer was careless. Do not give your reader cause to form such a conclusion.

Appearance in Business Letters

Just as the clothes you wear to job interviews play a part in the first impression potential employers have of you, so the appearance of a business letter may be crucial in influencing a recipient who has never seen you. The rules for preparing a neat, attractive letter are not difficult to master, and they are important—particularly if you type your own letters. First, be sure that the typewriter keys are clean and that the ribbon is fresh. Type as neatly as possible and handle the paper with clean hands to avoid smudges. Type on unruled, white bond paper of standard size and use envelopes of the same quality. Center the letter on the page so that the space between the top of the page and the first line of typing is about equal to the space between the last line of typing and the lower edge. When you use company letterhead, consider the bottom of the letterhead as the top edge of the paper.

A neat appearance alone will not improve a poorly written letter, but a sloppy appearance will detract from a well-written one.

Parts of the Letter

Almost all business letters have at least five major parts. According to variations in the alignment of the parts on the page, letters may be of one format or another. If your employer recommends or requires a particular format and typing style, use it. Otherwise, follow the guidelines provided here.

Heading. The *heading* is the writer's full address (street, city and state, zip code) and the date. The writer's name is not included in the heading because it appears at the end of the letter. In giving your address, do not use abbreviations for words like *Street*, *Avenue*, *First*, or *West* (as part of a street or city name). You may either spell out the name of the state in full or use the Postal Service abbreviations shown in Figure 6–6. The date usually goes directly beneath the last line of the address. Do not abbreviate the name of the month.

If you are writing on company letterhead, omit the heading. Type in only the date, placing it two double spaces above the inside address.

EXAMPLE   1638 Parkhill Drive East
Great Falls, MT 59407
April 8, 19--

Inside address. The *inside address* is the recipient's full name and address. You can begin the inside address a double space below the date if the letter is long, or on the fifth line below the date if the letter is quite short. The inside address should be flush with (or aligned with) the left margin—and the left margin should be at least one inch wide. Include the reader's full name and title (if you know them) and his or her full address, including zip code.

EXAMPLE   Ms. Gail Silver
Production Manager
Quicksilver Printing Company
14 President Street
Sarasota, FL 33546

Salutation. Place the *salutation* (or "greeting") two spaces below the inside address, also flush with the left margin. In most business letters, the salutation contains the recipient's title (*Mr.*, *Ms.*, *Dr.*, etc.) and last name, followed by a colon. If you are on a first-name basis

Alabama	AL	Montana	MT
Alaska	AK	Nebraska	NE
Arizona	AZ	Nevada	NV
Arkansas	AR	New Hampshire	NH
American Samoa	AS	New Jersey	NJ
California	CA	New Mexico	NM
Canal Zone	CZ	New York	NY
Colorado	CO	North Carolina	NC
Connecticut	CT	North Dakota	ND
Delaware	DE	Ohio	OH
District of Columbia	DC	Oklahoma	OK
Florida	FL	Oregon	OR
Georgia	GA	Pennsylvania	PA
Guam	GU	Puerto Rico	PR
Hawaii	HI	Rhode Island	RI
Idaho	ID	South Carolina	SC
Illinois	IL	South Dakota	SD
Indiana	IN	Tennessee	TN
Iowa	IA	Trust Territories	TT
Kansas	KS	Texas	TX
Kentucky	KY	Utah	UT
Louisiana	LA	Vermont	VT
Maine	ME	Virginia	VA
Maryland	MD	Virgin Islands	VI
Massachusetts	MA	Washington	WA
Michigan	MI	West Virginia	WV
Minnesota	MN	Wisconsin	WI
Mississippi	MS	Wyoming	WY
Missouri	MO		

SOURCE: U. S. Postal Service.

FIGURE 6–6. U.S. Postal Service abbreviations of state names.

with the recipient, you would include his or her title and full name in the inside address but use only the first name in the salutation.

EXAMPLES
```
Dear Ms. Silver:
Dear Mr. Smith:
Dear Dr. Smith:
Dear Captain Smith:
Dear Professor Smith:
```
(Note that titles like *Captain* and *Professor* are not abbreviated.)
```
Dear George:
```
(if you are on a first-name basis)

For women who do not have a professional title, use *Ms.* (for either a married or an unmarried woman). If the woman has expressed a preference for *Miss* or *Mrs.,* honor her preference. In cases where you do not know whether the recipient is a man or a woman, you may use a title appropriate to the context of the letter. The following are examples of the kinds of titles you may find suitable:

EXAMPLES   Dear Customer:
(letter from a department store)
Dear Homeowner:
(letter from an insurance agent soliciting business)
Dear Parts Manager:
(letter to an auto-parts dealer)

In the past, writers to large companies or organizations customarily addressed their letter to "Gentlemen." Today, however, writers who do not know the name or the title of the recipient often address the letter to an appropriate department in the attention line or identify the subject in a subject line in place of a salutation.

EXAMPLES   National Business Systems
501 West National Avenue
Minneapolis, MN 55107

Attention: Customer Relations Department

I am returning three calculators we purchased that failed to operate when . . . .

National Business Systems
501 West National Avenue
Minneapolis, MN 55107

Subject: Defective Parts for XL-100

I am returning three calculators we purchased that failed to operate when . . . .

The Body.   The *body* of the letter is, of course, what the letter is about. Begin the body two spaces below the salutation (or below the heading if no salutation appears). Single-space within paragraphs and double-space between paragraphs. If a letter is very short and you want to suggest a fuller appearance, you may double-space throughout and indicate paragraphs by indenting the first line of each paragraph five spaces from the left. The right margin should be approximately as wide as the left margin. (In very short letters you may increase both margins to about an inch and a half.)

Complimentary Close. Start the *complimentary close* (or conventional "goodbye") a double space below the body. Use a standard expression like *Yours truly, Sincerely,* or *Sincerely yours.* (If the recipient is a friend as well as a business associate, you can use a less formal close: *Best wishes, Best regards.*) Only the first word of the complimentary close is capitalized, and the expression is followed by a comma. Two double spaces below the complimentary close, and aligned at the left with the close, type your full name. On the next line you may type in your business title, if it is appropriate to do so. Then sign your name in the space between the complimentary close and your typed name. If you are writing to someone with whom you are on a first-name basis, it is acceptable to sign only your given name; otherwise, sign your full name.

EXAMPLE   Yours truly,

Gail Silver

Gail Silver
Production Manager

Second Page. If a letter requires a second page, carry at least two lines of the body over to page 2. Do not use a continuation page to type only the complimentary close of the letter. The second page should have a heading too, containing the recipient's name, the page number, and the date (never use letterhead for a second page). The heading may go in the upper-left-hand corner or across the page, as shown in the following examples.

```
Ms. M. C. Marks
Page 2
March 12, 19--
```

```
Ms. M. C. Marks              2              March 12, 19--
```

Additional Information. Business letters sometimes require additional information—the typist's initials, an enclosure notation, or a notation that a copy of the letter is being sent to one or more named people. Place any such information flush left with the margin, a double space below the last line of the complimentary close in a long letter, two double spaces below in a short letter.

Typist's initials follow two basic patterns. No matter which style you choose, however, the letter writer's initials should appear in capital letters and the typist's initials should appear in lower-case letters. (When the writer is also the typist, no initials are needed.)

EXAMPLES   JTR/pst
(Typist's initials are separated from the writer's initials by a slash.)
JTR:pst
(Typist's initials are separated from the writer's initials by a colon.)

Enclosure notations, which indicate that the letter writer is sending material along with the letter (an invoice, an article, and so on), may take several forms. Choose the form that seems most helpful to your readers. Remember, though, that no matter which form of enclosure notation you select, you should still make a reference in the body of the letter to the fact that material is enclosed.

EXAMPLES   Enclosures: Preliminary report invoice
                Draft contract
(Enclosures are described briefly if the letter is long and formal, or if the nature of the enclosed items is not obvious.)
Enclosures (2)
or
Encs. (two or more items)
or
Enc. (a single item)

(Enclosures are not described if the letter is short and the nature of the enclosures is obvious to the reader.)

A *copy notation* tells the reader that a copy (either carbon or photocopy) of the letter is being sent to one or more named individuals.

EXAMPLE
        cc: Ms. Marlene Brier
           Mr. David Williams

A business letter may, of course, contain all three items of additional information.

EXAMPLE   Sincerely yours,

Jane T. Rogers

Jane T. Rogers
JTF/pst
Enclosures: Preliminary report invoice
                    Draft contract
cc: Ms. Marlene Brier

Sample Letter Styles

An important factor in the appearance of a letter is its overall format—the arrangement on the page of the five major parts of the letter. The two most common styles of business letters are the full block and the modified block. The *full block style,* which is easier to type because every line begins at the left margin, is suitable only with letterhead stationery (see Figure 6–7). In the *modified block style* the return address, date, and complimentary close are placed just to the right of the center of the page (see Figure 6–8). The remaining elements are aligned at the left margin. All other letter styles are variations of these two basic styles. Again, if your employer recommends or requires a particular style, follow it carefully. Otherwise, choose the style you are most comfortable with and follow it consistently.

Preparing the Envelope

The most widely used form for typing envelopes is the *block* form. Figure 6–9 shows the block form used on business envelopes. When you insert the letter into an envelope, be careful not to smudge or crumple the paper. The following illustration shows the proper technique for folding 8½" × 11" stationery into a standard (#10 size) business envelope.

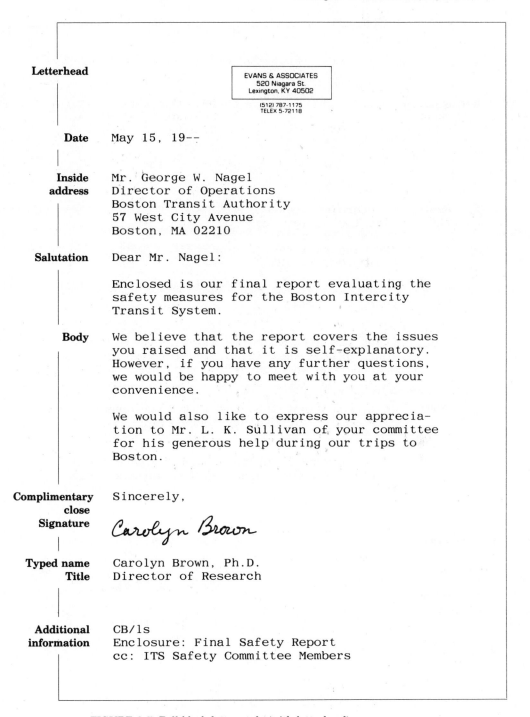

Letterhead

EVANS & ASSOCIATES
520 Niagara St.
Lexington, KY 40502

(512) 787-1175
TELEX 5-72118

Date   May 15, 19--

Inside address   Mr. George W. Nagel
Director of Operations
Boston Transit Authority
57 West City Avenue
Boston, MA 02210

Salutation   Dear Mr. Nagel:

Enclosed is our final report evaluating the safety measures for the Boston Intercity Transit System.

Body   We believe that the report covers the issues you raised and that it is self-explanatory. However, if you have any further questions, we would be happy to meet with you at your convenience.

We would also like to express our appreciation to Mr. L. K. Sullivan of your committee for his generous help during our trips to Boston.

Complimentary close   Sincerely,

Signature   *Carolyn Brown*

Typed name   Carolyn Brown, Ph.D.
Title   Director of Research

Additional information   CB/ls
Enclosure: Final Safety Report
cc: ITS Safety Committee Members

FIGURE 6–7. Full block letter style (with letterhead).

<table>
<tr><td>

**Heading just
right of
center**

</td><td>

3814 Oak Lane
Lexington, KY 40514
December 8, 19--

</td></tr>
<tr><td>

**Inside
address**

</td><td>

Dr. Carolyn Brown
Director of Research
Evans & Associates
520 Niagara Street
Lexington, KY 40502

</td></tr>
<tr><td>

Salutation

</td><td>

Dear Dr. Brown:

</td></tr>
<tr><td>

Body

</td><td>

Thank you very much for allowing me to tour your testing facilities. The information I gained from the tour will be of great help to me in preparing the report for my class at Marshall Institute. The tour has also given me some insight into the work I may eventually do as a laboratory technician.

I especially appreciated the time and effort Steven Dement spent in showing me your facilities. His comments and advice was most helpful.

Again, thank you.

</td></tr>
<tr><td>

**Complimentary
close aligned
with heading**

**Signature
Typed name**

</td><td>

Sincerely,

Leslie Warden

Leslie Warden

</td></tr>
</table>

FIGURE 6-8. Modified block letter style (without letterhead).

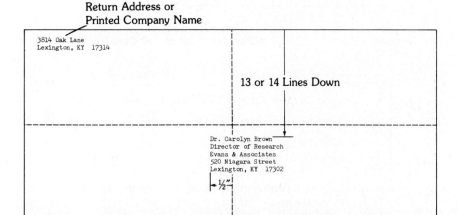

FIGURE 6–9. A #10 envelope, addressed.

THE MEMORANDUM

The most frequently written type of communication between members of the same organization is the memorandum, called the memo for short. Memos are routinely used for internal communications of all kinds—from short notes to brief reports (these memos will be discussed in the chapters dealing with reports). Memos are used to announce policies or meetings, request information, confirm conversations, transmit documents internally, and exchange information.

The format of memos varies from organization to organization, although memos normally contain lines for the sender's name, recipient's name, date, and subject. Some companies buy preprinted, standard forms; other companies have memos printed with the company name included, as in Figure 6–10.

The title of the memo in the "subject" line should be as specific as possible, and a memo should deal only with the subject specified in that line. In a long memo, you can insert headings where appropriate in order to focus the reader's attention on particular topics. Headings, such as those appearing in Figure 6–10, divide the material into manageable segments, call attention to the main topics, and signal changes of topic. They should also aid you in organizing your material. If your memo presents a series of items for consideration, you may list them in a numbered sequence. Generally, a memo is either signed at the bottom or initialed by the sender beside his or her typed name on the "From" line.

Some organizations also have memo forms on half sheets, as shown in Figure 6–11. Short forms encourage conciseness by limiting the

INTEROFFICE CORRESPONDENCE
INDUSTRIAL PUBLISHING CORPORATION

Date: April 14, 19--

To: Hazel Smith, Publications Manager

From: Herbert Kaufman, Vice President HK

Subject: Time Estimate for Acme Electronics
Brochure

Acme Electronics has asked us to prepare a
comprehensive brochure for their Milwaukee
office by August 1 of this year. We have
worked with electronic firms in the past, so
this job should be relatively easy to prepare. My guess is that the job will take
nearly two months. Ted Harris has requested
time and cost estimates for the project. Fred
Moore in accounting will prepare cost estimates, and I would like you to prepare a
schedule for the estimated time.

Schedule
In preparing the schedule, check production
schedules for all staff writers, compile a
list of available free-lance writers we can
depend on, and contact local graphic designers for art work, since our art department is
heavily scheduled through July. Also, don't
forget to take staff vacation time into account. Let me emphasize that we must finish
by our estimated date (most important), that
the overall design must have a uniform format, and that the artwork must blend properly
with the copy.

Time Estimates
Please give me time estimates by April 19. A
successful job done on time will give us a
good chance to obtain the contract to do Acme's publications for their annual stockholders' meeting this fall.

I know your staff can do the job.

Copies: Ted Harris, Senior Vice President
Fred Moore, Accounting Manager

FIGURE 6–10. A long memorandum.

```
                         MEMORANDUM


        To:    Ben Johnson, Systems Design
        From:   Linda Coleman, Sales and Service  LC
        Date:   February 12, 19--

        Subject:   Meeting with Ackley Brothers & Co.

        I thought you'd like to know that the meeting
        with Ackley went very well. In fact, I think
        they'll accept our proposal.

        Keep your fingers crossed.
```

FIGURE 6–11. A short memorandum.

amount of space the writer can use. Short memos are organized in simple paragraph form and do not require headings. The example in Figure 6–11 was written by the manager of the Sales and Service Department and is addressed to the manager of the Systems Design Department. Job titles or department names ("Systems Design" and "Sales and Service") are occasionally omitted if the sender and receiver know each other well. Since memos are often used as records of information, however, it is usually best to include the appropriate titles.

As the memos shown in Figures 6–10 and 6–11 illustrate, the tone of a memo can range from formal to informal, depending on your purpose and your reader. A memo to your general manager would be more formal than a memo to an employee of equal rank in another department who is also a friend. Often, a memo from one person to another person is much like a business letter—therefore, the strategies for writing letters apply to many memos as well. A memo written as an internal proposal to several readers, however, is more likely to use the less personal style of a report. Obviously, the level of formality and familiarity will depend entirely on the reader and the purpose.

In writing a memo, follow the processes for effective writing described in Chapters 1 and 2. An outline is essential, even though for a short memo the outline may be no more than a number of items jotted down and arranged in a logical sequence. A rough outline will help you to stick to your topic. As with other writing, if your reader is not familiar with your subject or with the background of the problem being discussed, provide a brief introductory paragraph or an introduction. In doing so, you not only are informing the reader but are supplying necessary information that will be available months (or even years) later if the memo must be reviewed and you are not there. Generally, longer memos dealing with complex subjects benefit most from such introductory information. However, even when you are writing a short memo and the recipient will be familiar with the situation, it is important to remind him or her of the context ("As we discussed at yesterday's meeting . . ."). Assume that your reader will be too busy to ponder what information might be missing from the memo.

CHAPTER SUMMARY

To write effective business letters, follow the steps of the writing process discussed in Chapters 1–3: make an outline (which may simply be a list of the points you wish to include in the letter); prepare a first draft and then set it aside for a "cooling" period; revise your work, paying attention to both content and mechanics; and type your final copy according to standard business-letter form.

To establish a tone that is effective and builds goodwill, write from the reader's point of view (the "you" viewpoint). Be careful, however, that you do not overuse these techniques and produce "plastic goodwill." For "good news" letters, be direct; for "bad news" letters, use an indirect pattern.

Writing style in business letters can be informal (in a letter to a close business associate) or formal (in a letter to someone the writer has never met). The level of formality depends on your purpose and your reader. In general, though, it is best to avoid a style that seems overly chatty.

Because a business letter is a formal written record, it must be accurate. Make sure that your facts, figures, and dates are correct. Every business letter should follow one of the standard letter formats. The two most common ones are the *full block style,* in which all parts of the letter begin at the left margin, and the *modified block style,* in which the return address, the date, and the complimentary close appear just to the right of the center of the page.

A *memorandum,* or *memo* for short, is the chief means of written communication between members of the same organization. A memo may take the form of a brief note; a longer, letter-like correspondence; or an informal report.

EXERCISES

1. Bring to class one business letter that you believe is well written and one that is poorly written. Be prepared to explain your reasons for thinking that one is better than the other. If you are working full- or part-time, you may be able to find letters in your office. Alternatively, obtain letters from friends or relatives, or find examples among the correspondence you receive in the mail.

2. Rewrite the following statement to make it more positive and less blunt.

   I will not pay you because you have not sent the double-jointed widget. If you do not send the right one right away, I will not pay you at all.

3. Rewrite the following passage to make it less unfriendly.

   I wrote for the record you advertised on television, and not only did it take six weeks to get here, but it was the wrong record. Can't you get anything right? I'm canceling payment on my check and sending this record back!

4. Revise the following passage to make it clearer and less pretentious.

   With reference to and in connection with your recent automobile accident, I have been unable to contact you due to the fact that I have been in Chicago on work-related business. I should be back in the office in the neighborhood of the 15th or so. In the unforeseen and unlikely event that I should be delayed, you can utilize Mr. Strawman, of my office, who will also endeavor in your behalf.

5. Find a letter containing bad news that you believe is unnecessarily blunt. Rewrite the letter to protect the goodwill of the organization that sent it. Attach your revision to the original, and submit both to your instructor.

6. Summarize an article on the "you" viewpoint or goodwill from either the *Journal of Business Communication* or the American Business Communication Association *Bulletin*. Limit the summary to 150–250 words. Submit it to your instructor, and (if your instructor so directs) prepare an oral summary for class discussion.

7. Find an example of overdone goodwill. (Mass-produced sales letters, for example, may be useful.) Rewrite the letter or message, retaining goodwill while eliminating poor style.

7

Types of Business Letters

Almost as many types of letters exist as there are reasons for writing. That is why it is important to study the principles discussed in the preceding chapter and apply them to both the situation and your reader's needs. A number of types of letters are so common that standard approaches have been developed to meet specific situations. This chapter is devoted to such letters: primarily the order letter, the inquiry letter, the response to an inquiry, the transmittal (or "cover") letter, the acknowledgment letter, the complaint letter, the adjustment letter, the refusal letter, the collection letter series, and the sales letter.

Because the most important business letter that most people write is the job-application letter, it is discussed separately in Chapter 15, along with other strategies for finding a job.

THE ORDER LETTER

One of the most common reasons for writing a letter, especially if you work for a small organization or are self-employed, is the need to order supplies or equipment. The equipment may be anything from company letterhead stationery to x-ray film. Obviously, an order letter must be specific and complete if you are to receive the exact item you want. But be careful not to clutter the letter with unnecessary details, such as why you need the items or who will use them. Above all, be accurate. Since a misspelled word or misplaced decimal point could cause a staggering error, proofread carefully and double-check all price calculations.

Make sure that the order letter contains the following information, as it applies to the item or items you are purchasing.

1. The exact name and part number (if appropriate) of the item.
2. Any useful description of the item: size, style, color, and so on.
3. The quantity needed of each item.
4. The price of the item, both unit price and total price, if appropriate.
5. The shipping method: mail, air, express, or, perhaps, simply the "best route."
6. The date of the order and the date by which you need the item (indicate "rush" or other instructions).
7. The place to which the material is to be shipped (make sure you provide the exact and full shipping address).
8. The method of payment: for example, indicate that you have enclosed a check or money order, that you will pay c.o.d. (usually more expensive), or that you have enclosed a purchase order number and the seller is to bill your company.

If you order several items, list them. A list will make your order easier to read.

The example shown in Figure 7–1 is a typical order letter.

If you receive no response to an order letter you may need to send a follow-up letter. If you do send such a letter, be courteous and avoid showing irritation. Identify the order by referring to the date of the original letter, and preferably include a copy of that letter. The example shown in Figure 7–2 is a typical follow-up letter.

THE INQUIRY LETTER

Another frequently sent business letter is the inquiry letter, in which the writer requests information from the recipient. Such a letter may be as simple as a note asking the Far 'N' Wide Travel Bureau for a copy of the free brochure "Inexpensive Fly and Drive Vacations" that was offered in a recent issue of your local newspaper; it may be as complex as a letter asking a financial consultant to define the specific requirements for floating a multimillion-dollar bond issue.

There are two broad categories of inquiry letters. The first kind is of obvious benefit to the recipient—you may be asking, for instance, for information about a product that a company has recently advertised. The second kind of inquiry letter primarily benefits the writer;

HOLT TOOL COMPANY
1012 Clarke Street
Phoenix, AZ 85019

(602) 297-3100

September 5, 19--

Downtown Parts Company
109 South State Street
Chicago, IL 60650

Attention: Sales Department

Please send the following items listed in
your current parts catalog by October 1.

    2 Tempered steel cylinders,
      2" diameter and 5" long,
      part number C5789S,
      @ $12.75 each $25.50

    4 Aluminum castings with
      corrosion-resistant coating,
      part number S312A,
      @ $4.89 each $19.56

    12 Special tempered sheet
       metal screws, 1 1/4" long
       with hexagonal heads,
       @ $.57 each $ 6.84

                      TOTAL $51.90

The enclosed check for $56.31 covers the
price, sales tax, and parcel post charges.

Sincerely,

James Siemer

James Siemer
Parts Manager

JS:tb
Enclosure: Check

FIGURE 7–1. Order letter.

HOLT TOOL COMPANY
1012 Clarke Street
Phoenix, AZ 85019

(602) 297-3100

October 12, 19--

Downtown Parts Company
109 South State Street
Chicago, IL 60650

Attention: Sales Department

On September 5, I sent you a letter in which
I placed an order for a number of parts
listed in your current catalog. I also sent a
check for $56.31.

I have enclosed a copy of that letter, and I
request that you please rush this material to
me. If for some reason you cannot send the
material, please cancel my order and return
the check. Thank you.

Sincerely,

James Siemer

James Siemer
Parts Manager

JS:tb
Enclosure: Copy of order letter

FIGURE 7-2. Order follow-up letter.

an example would be a request to a nonprofit religious organization to send information on the number of worshippers in a geographic area. If the letter of inquiry you are writing is of the second type, it is particularly important to be considerate of your reader's needs. Your objective in writing the letter will probably be to obtain, within a reasonable period of time, answers to specific questions. You will be more likely to receive a prompt, helpful reply if you follow two guidelines: keep the number of questions to a minimum, so that you do not intrude unduly on the reader's time; and phrase your questions in such a way that the reader will know immediately what type of information you are seeking, why you are seeking it, and what use you will make of it. Be sure, as you write your questions, that you are asking the ones that you had intended to ask. It will be a waste of the reader's time, and a source of frustration to you later on, if you word your questions in such a way that your reader misinterprets them. And your reader will probably find it easiest to answer your questions one by one if you present them in a numbered list.

Your reader may also appreciate it if you offer to send a copy of material (a proposal for a project, for example) that you plan to prepare based, in part, on the information that you are requesting. As a courtesy, too, you should promise to keep confidential any personal information you may receive. And at the end of your letter, express your thanks to the reader for taking the time and trouble to respond. Do not forget, also, to include the address to which the material is to be sent. (This is most important, of course, if the information will be sent to an address other than the one in your heading.) It is sometimes a good idea to enclose a stamped, self-addressed return envelope, especially if you are writing to someone who is self-employed. A typical inquiry letter appears in Figure 7–3.

RESPONSE TO AN INQUIRY LETTER

Sometimes, of course, you may be on the receiving end of a letter of inquiry. When you do receive such a letter, first read it quickly to determine whether you are the right person in your organization to answer it—whether, that is, you are the one who possesses both the information and the authority to respond. If you are in a position to answer, do so as promptly as you can, and be sure to answer every question the writer has included. How long your responses should be, and how much technical language you should use, depend, of course, on the nature of the question and on what information the writer has provided about himself or herself. Even if the writer has asked a question that sounds obvious or unimportant to you, be polite. You

P.O. Box 113
University of Dayton
Dayton, OH 45409
March 11, 19--

Ms. Jane Metcalf
Engineering Services
Miami Valley Power Company
P.O. Box 1444
Miamitown, OH 45733

Dear Ms. Metcalf:

Could you please send me some information on heating systems for an all-electric, energy-efficient, middle-priced house that our systems design class at the University of Dayton is designing. The house, which contains 2,000 square feet of living space (17,600 cubic feet), meets all the requirements stipulated in your brochure "Insulating for Efficiency." We need the following information:

1. The proper size heat pump to use in this climate for such a home;

2. The wattage of the supplemental electrical furnace that would be required for this climate; and

3. The estimated power consumption, and current rates, of these units for one year.

We will be happy to send you a copy of our preliminary design report. Thank you very much.

Sincerely yours,

Kathryn J. Parsons

Kathryn J. Parsons

FIGURE 7–3. Inquiry letter.

may point out that the reader has omitted or misunderstood a particular piece of information or has in some other way introduced an error, but be tactful in your correction, so that the reader won't feel foolish or ignorant. If, on the other hand, you see an opportunity to give your reader praise or encouragement, do so. And at the end of the letter, offer to answer any further questions the writer may have.

Sometimes a letter of inquiry sent to a large company arrives at the desk of a staff member who realizes that he or she is not the employee best able to answer the letter. If you have received a letter that you feel you can't answer (because you lack the information or the authority or both), you should do two things. First, find out (if you don't know offhand) who in the company *is* best equipped to answer the letter. Second, forward the letter to the co-worker. The co-worker's letter answering the inquiry should state in the first paragraph that although the letter was addressed to you, it is being answered by someone else in the firm, because he or she is better qualified to respond to the inquiry. Figure 7–4 shows a letter indicating to an inquirer that her letter has been forwarded; Figure 7–5 shows a typical response to the inquiry.

THE TRANSMITTAL LETTER

When you send a formal report, proposal, brochure, or other type of material, you should include with it a short letter called a transmittal (or cover) letter, which identifies what you are sending and why you are sending it. A transmittal letter that accompanies a report may contain the title of the report, a brief description of the report, an acknowledgment of any help received during its preparation, and the authorization or reason for the report. The transmittal letter provides the writer with a record of when and to whom the material was sent.

Written in the form of a standard business letter, the transmittal letter most often opens with a brief paragraph (one or two sentences) explaining what is being sent and why. The next paragraph contains a brief summary of the material or stresses some feature that would be important to the reader. A letter accompanying a proposal, for example, might briefly present convincing evidence that your firm is the best one to do the job. The letter may go on to point out specific sections in the proposal that would be of particular interest to the reader. You might also want to mention any special conditions under which the material was prepared (limitations in time or money, for instance). The closing paragraph should acknowledge any help re-

MIAMI VALLEY POWER COMPANY
P.O. BOX 1444
MIAMITOWN, OH 45733

(513) 264-4800

March 15, 19--

Ms. Kathryn J. Parsons
P.O. Box 113
University of Dayton
Dayton, OH 45409

Dear Ms. Parsons:

Thank you for inquiring about the heating
system we would recommend for use in homes
designed according to the specifications outlined in our brochure "Insulating for Efficiency."

Since I cannot answer your specific questions, I have forwarded your letter to Mr.
Michael Stott, Engineering Assistant in our
development group. He should be able to answer the questions you have raised.

Sincerely,

Jane E. Metcalf

Jane E. Metcalf
Director of Public Information

JEM/mk
cc: Michael Stott

FIGURE 7-4. Letter indicating that an inquiry has been forwarded.

████ MIAMI VALLEY POWER COMPANY ████
P.O. BOX 1444
MIAMITOWN, OH 45733

(513) 264-4800

March 24, 19--

Ms. Kathryn Parsons
P.O. Box 113
University of Dayton
Dayton, OH 45409

Dear Ms. Parsons:

Jane Metcalf has forwarded your letter of
March 11 about the house that your systems
design class is designing. I can estimate the
insulation requirements of a typical home of
17,600 cubic feet, as follows:

1. We would generally recommend, for such a
   home, a heat pump capable of delivering
   40,000 BTUs. Our model AL-42 (17 kilowatts)
   meets this requirement.

2. With the efficiency of the AL-42, you would
   not need a supplemental electrical furnace.

3. Depending on usage, the AL-42 unit averages
   between 1,000 and 1,500 kilowatt hours from
   December through March. To determine the
   current rate for such usage, check with the
   Dayton Power and Light Company.

I can give you an answer that would apply
specifically to your house only with information about its particular design (such as
number of stories, windows, and entrances).
If you would send me more details, I would be
happy to provide more precise figures--your
project sounds interesting.

Sincerely,

Michael Stott

Michael Stott
Engineering Assistant

FIGURE 7-5. Response to an inquiry letter.

ceived in the preparation of the material, offer additional assistance, or express the hope that the material will fulfill its purpose.

These elements are basic to many transmittal letters. Keep additional remarks brief. The report, pamphlet, or whatever should speak for itself. A transmittal letter should not run beyond a few short paragraphs; it should never exceed one page. Figure 7–6 is a typical letter of transmittal.

Some letters of transmittal are not as detailed as this one—they say essentially "here it is." Figure 7–7 is typical of short transmittal letters.

THE ACKNOWLEDGMENT LETTER

One of the ways to build goodwill in any business is to let customers or clients know that something they sent has arrived. A letter that serves such a function is called an acknowledgment letter. It is usually a short, polite note. The examples shown in Figures 7–8 and 7–9 are typical.

THE COMPLAINT LETTER

The best complaint letters do not sound complaining. That statement may sound contradictory, but it's not.

By the time it becomes necessary for you to write a complaint letter (sometimes called a *claim letter*), you may be irritated and angry. If you write a letter that reflects *only* your annoyance and anger, however, you may not be taken seriously—you may simply appear petty and irrational. Remember, too, that the person who receives your letter may not be the one who was directly responsible for the situation about which you are complaining. Venting your anger at someone who was not at fault is neither fair nor useful.

An effective complaint letter—a letter that accomplishes its purpose—should be both firm and well thought out. It should assume, first, that the recipient will be conscientious in correcting the problem. Second, it should indicate that the writer is capable of handling the situation calmly. Finally, the letter should convey that you expect the situation to be corrected.

Although the circumstances and the severity of the problem may vary, effective complaint letters should generally follow the same pattern. They should:

WATERFORD PAPER PRODUCTS
P.O. BOX 413
WATERFORD, WI 53474

(414) 738-2191

January 16, 19--

Mr. Roger Hammersmith
Ecology Systems, Inc.
1015 Clarke Street
Chicago, IL 60615

Dear Mr. Hammersmith:

Enclosed is the report estimating our power
consumption for the year as requested by John
Brenan, Vice President, on September 4.

The report is a result of several meetings
with the Manager of Plant Operations and her
staff and an extensive survey of all our employees. The survey was delayed by the temporary layoff of key personnel in Building "A"
from October 1 to December 5. We believe,
however, that the report will provide the information you need to furnish us with a cost
estimate for the installation of your Mark II
Energy Saving System.

We would like to thank Diana Biel of ESI for
her assistance in preparing the survey. If
you need any more information, please let me
know.

Sincerely,

James G. Evans

James G. Evans
New Projects Office

JGE/fst
Enclosure

FIGURE 7–6. Long transmittal letter.

WATERFORD PAPER PRODUCTS
P.O. BOX 413
WATERFORD, WI 53474

(414) 738-2191

November 12, 19--

Ms. Nancy Melcher
2021 State Street
Racine, WI 53307

Dear Ms. Melcher:

Thank you for your interest in Waterford Paper Products. The enclosed brochure describes
our product line and our current prices.

If I can be of further help, please let me
know.

Sincerely,

Lawrence Smith

Lawrence Smith
Customer Relations

LS:ik
Enclosure

FIGURE 7-7. Short transmittal letter.

Ecology Systems, Inc.
1015 Clarke Street
Chicago, IL 60615

(312) 719-6620

January 21, 19--

Mr. James G. Evans
New Projects Office
Waterford Paper Products
P.O. Box 413
Waterford, WI 53474

Dear Mr. Evans:

I received your report today; it appears to
be complete and well done.

When I finish studying it thoroughly, I will
send you our cost estimate for the installation of the Mark II Energy Saving System.

Again, thanks for your effort.

Sincerely,

Roger Hammersmith

Roger Hammersmith
Sales Manager

RLH/rlt

FIGURE 7–8. Acknowledgment letter.

ECADS, INCORPORATED

501 BEACH STREET
MIAMI, FL 33167

(305) 834-7200

January 18, 19--

Mr. Joel Baker
3078 Terrace Boulevard
Miami, FL 33117

Dear Mr. Baker:

I received in today's mail the defective part
that we talked about last week on the phone.

As soon as one of our engineers can examine
it, I will phone you.

Sincerely,

Marylin Sanches

Marylin Sanches

MS/bk

FIGURE 7-9. Acknowledgment letter.

1. Identify the faulty item, including invoice numbers, part names, dates, and so forth. (Often it is a good idea to include a photocopy of the bill or contract.)
2. Explain logically, clearly, and specifically what went wrong. (Avoid expressing an opinion of why you *think* some problem occurred if you have no way of knowing.)
3. State what you expect the reader to do to solve the problem to your satisfaction.

Large organizations often have special departments, with such names as "Customer Relations," "Consumer Affairs," or "Adjustment," to handle complaints. If you address your letter to one of these departments, it should reach someone in the company who can be of help to you. In smaller organizations, you might write to a vice president in charge of sales or of service. For very small businesses, write directly to the owner. As a last resort, you may find that a complaint letter photocopied and sent to more than one person in a company will get fast results. Each employee receiving the letter knows (because of the carbon-copy notation) that others, possibly higher in the organization, have received the letter and will notice whether the problem has been solved.

Figure 7–10 shows a sample complaint letter.

THE ADJUSTMENT LETTER

If you, as the manager of the Customer Relations Department of the television company, receive the letter of complaint from Paul Denlinger, you should take it—and any letter like it—seriously. What is at stake is more than nine tuners. Regardless of how trivial the incident may seem to you, your employer's reputation is on the line. And if the writer, Mr. Denlinger, is satisfied with the way you handle his complaint, he may decide that when the hospital next orders television sets, he'll place the order with your company. What is at stake, then, are both the good name of your company and potential orders of several dozen television sets worth thousands of dollars.

An appropriate response to Mr. Denlinger's letter would be an adjustment letter—a letter that explains to the reader how a complaint he or she has made will be settled. To prepare an adjustment letter, you must first investigate what happened and what you can do to satisfy the customer. After you have obtained the facts, you should organize your letter into three basic parts.

1. Refer to the letter of complaint and identify the item or service in question. If your company is responsible for the error, offer

BAKER MEMORIAL HOSPITAL
Television Services
501 Main Street
Springfield, OH 45321

(513) 683-8100

September 23, 19--

Manager, Customer Relations
General Television, Inc.
5521 West 23rd Street
New York, NY 10062

On July 9th I ordered nine TV tuners for your
model MX-15 color receiver. The tuner part
number is TR-5771-3.

On August 2nd I received from your Newark,
New Jersey, parts warehouse seven tuners, labeled TR-413-7. I immediately returned these
tuners with a note indicating the mistake
that had been made. However, not only have I
failed to receive the tuners I ordered, but I
have also been billed repeatedly.

Would you please either send me the tuners I
ordered or cancel my order. I have enclosed a
copy of my original order letter and the most
recent bill.

Sincerely,

Paul Denlinger

Paul Denlinger
Manager

PD:sj
Enclosures

FIGURE 7-10. Complaint letter.

an apology early in the letter. Doing so will help you to regain the customer's goodwill.

2. Explain clearly why the error occurred or outline the company policy related to the problem, or do both. This is especially important if you are not able to do everything the customer asks.

3. State specifically what you intend to do or have done to solve the problem. If you are not able to do exactly what the customer asks, give a partial adjustment if possible.

Figures 7–11 and 7–12 show two cirumstances: in the letter shown in Figure 7–11, the company was at fault; in the letter shown in Figure 7–12, the customer was at fault.

THE REFUSAL LETTER

When you receive a complaint letter or an inquiry letter to which you must give a negative reply, you may need to write a refusal letter. Such a letter is difficult to write because it contains bad news. However, you can convey the news tactfully and courteously.

In your letter you should lead up to the refusal. To state the bad news in your opening would certainly affect your reader negatively, as discussed in Chapter 6. The ideal refusal letter says no in such a way that you not only avoid antagonizing your reader but keep his goodwill. To achieve such an objective, you must convince your reader of the justness of your refusal *before refusing*. The following pattern is an effective way to deal with this problem:

1. A buffer that establishes a positive tone
2. The bad news, based on the facts
3. A goodwill closing

The primary purpose of a buffer beginning is to establish a pleasant and positive tone. You want to convince your reader that you are a reasonable person. One approach is to indicate some form of agreement with, or approval of, the reader or the project. If your refusal is in response to a complaint letter, do not begin by bringing up the reader's disappointment ("We regret your dissatisfaction . . ."). Keep your buffer paragraph positive and pleasant. You can express appreciation for your reader's time and effort, if appropriate. Stating such appreciation will soften the disappointment and pave the way for future good relations.

Next you should analyze the circumstances of the situation sympathetically. Place yourself in your reader's position and try to see things from his or her point of view. Establish very clearly the reasons you

General Television, Inc.
5521 West 23rd Street
New York, NY 10062

Customer Relations
(212) 574-3894

September 28, 19--

Mr. Paul Denlinger, Manager
Baker Memorial Hospital
Television Services
501 Main Street
Springfield, OH 45321

Dear Mr. Denlinger:

Thank you for your letter regarding your order for nine TR-5771-3 tuners. We have
shipped the correct tuners by United Parcel;
you should receive them shortly after you receive this letter. I have also canceled your
original order so that you will not be sent
overdue notices and so that we can charge you
at our preferred-customer rate.

Please accept our apologies. Evidently a dock
worker failed to see your letter in the package, and it was sent to our Rebuilt Parts Department. That is why your note did not come
to the attention of our Parts Manager.

To prevent further inconvenience, please send
any future packages directly to Mr. Gene
Smith, Parts Manager at our Newark facility.

If I can be of any further help, please let
me know.

Sincerely,

Susan Siegel

Susan Siegel
Assistant Director

SS/mr

FIGURE 7-11. Adjustment letter—company at fault.

General Television, Inc.
5521 West 23rd Street
New York, NY 10062

Customer Relations
(212) 574-3894

September 28, 19--

Mr. Fred J. Swesky
7811 Ranchero Drive
Tucson, AZ 85761

Dear Mr. Swesky:

Thank you for your letter regarding the replacement of your KL-71 television set.

You said in your letter that you used the set
on an uncovered patio. As our local service
representative pointed out, this model is not
designed to operate in extreme heat conditions. As the instruction manual accompanying
your new set states and our engineers confirm, such exposure can produce irreparable
damage to this model. Since your set was used
in such extreme heat conditions, therefore,
we cannot honor the two-year replacement warranty.

However, we are enclosing a certificate enti-
tling you to a trade-in allowance equal to
your local GTI dealer's markup for the set.
This means you can purchase a new set from
the dealer at wholesale, provided you return
your original set to the local dealer.

Sincerely yours,

Susan Siegel

Susan Siegel
Assistant Director

SS/mr
Enclosure

FIGURE 7-12. Adjustment letter—customer at fault.

cannot do what the reader wants—even though you have not yet said you cannot do it. A good explanation of the reasons should so thoroughly justify your refusal that the reader will accept your refusal as a logical conclusion. Then state your refusal quickly, clearly, and as positively as possible.

Close your letter with a friendly remark, whether to assure the reader of your high opinion of his product or merely to wish him success in the future. Figure 7–13 shows a refusal letter sent to a supplier whose product was not selected.

THE COLLECTION LETTER SERIES

With the expansion of credit in recent decades, many companies now need to send collection letters. These letters serve a twofold purpose of (1) helping to collect the overdue bill, and (2) preserving the customer's goodwill.

Most companies send a series of collection letters that become increasingly demanding and urgent, though the number and frequency of letters sent vary from one company to another. Although many firms rely on form letters, a short, personal note will usually motivate a customer to pay a bill faster than will a form letter. Collection letters should be polite; you can demonstrate insistence with the letters' frequency as well as with their tone. The intervals between letters should be long enough for the customer to respond, however. Generally, you should be more patient with a steady, long-time customer than with a new or unknown customer.

The collection process may vary from one business to another. A furrier, for example, might give customers a longer time to pay than would a discount hardware store. Competition is also a factor: if your major competitors gave customers eight months before starting legal action, you should not take action after only two months.

A series of collection letters usually proceeds in three stages, each of which may include several letters. All letters, even form messages, must be courteous and should show genuine concern for whatever problems are preventing prompt payment.

The first stage of collection letters consists of reminders stamped on the invoice, form letters, or brief personal notes. These early reminders should be written in a friendly tone that emphasizes the customer's good credit record until now. You should remind him of the debt and indicate that you are sure that payment has merely been overlooked. You may even solicit additional business by including promotion for new sales items, as is done in Figure 7–14.

MARTINI REALTY COMPANY
251 West 57th Street
New York, New York 10019

11 February 19--

Mr. Henry Bliss
Abbott Office Products, Inc.
P.O. Box 544
Detroit, MI 48206

Dear Mr. Bliss;

Thank you for your cooperation and your patience with us as we struggled to reach a decision. We believe our long involvement with your company indicates our confidence in your products.

However, the Winton Check Sorter has all the features that your sorter offers and, in fact, has two additional features that your sorter does not. The more important one is a back-up feature that retains totals in its memory, even if the power fails, so that sorting doesn't have to start again from scratch following a power failure. The second additional feature is stacked pockets, which are less space-consuming than the linear pockets on your sorter. After much deliberation, therefore, we have decided to purchase the Winton Check Sorter.

Although we did not select your sorter, we were very favorably impressed with your system and your people. Perhaps we will be able to use other Abbott products in the future.

Sincerely,

Muriel Johansen

Muriel Johansen
Business Manager

MJ:ct

FIGURE 7–13. Refusal letter.

ABBOTT OFFICE PRODUCTS, INC.
P.O. Box 544
Detroit, Michigan 48206

30 August 19--

Mr. Thomas Holland
Walk Softly Shoes
1661 East Madison Boulevard
Garfield, AL 36613

Dear Mr. Holland:

With the new school year about to begin, your
shoe store must be busier than ever as students purchase their back-to-school footwear.
Perhaps in the rush of business you've overlooked paying your account of $742, which is
now 60 days overdue.

Enclosed is our fall sales list. When you
send in your check for your outstanding account, why not send in your next order and
take advantage of these special prices.

Sincerely,

Henry Bliss

Henry Bliss
Sales Manager

HB:ew

FIGURE 7–14. Collection letter—first stage.

At the second stage, the collection letters are more than just reminders. You now assume that some circumstances are preventing payment. Ask directly for payment, and inquire about possible problems, perhaps inviting the customer to discuss the matter with you. If you have a standard optional payment plan, you might suggest it to him. Mention the importance of good credit, appealing to his pride and self-esteem as well as to his sense of fair play. Remind him that he has always received good value from you. Make it easy to respond by enclosing a return envelope or offering a toll-free telephone number. At this stage, your tone should be firmer and more direct than in the earlier stage, but you should never sound rude, sarcastic, or threatening. Notice how the letter in Figure 7–15 is more direct than the first letter, but no less polite.

The third stage of collection letters reflects a sense of urgency, for the customer has not responded to your previous letters. Although your tone should remain courteous, make your demand for payment explicit. Point out how reasonable you have been, and urge the customer to pay at once to avoid legal action. Again, make it easy to respond by providing a return envelope and a toll-free telephone number, as is done in Figure 7–16.

The effectiveness of a series of collection letters is based on the psychological pressure exerted by frequent requests for payment that become increasingly demanding in tone. Throughout the correspondence, however, you should emphasize your company's willingness to work with the customer to arrange payment. Whenever possible, you want to avoid turning the account over to an attorney or collection agency.

THE SALES LETTER

A sales letter, or letter that promotes a product, service, or store, is a difficult letter to write because it requires both a thorough knowledge of the product or service and a keen awareness of the potential customer's needs. For this reason, many businesses (such as department stores) employ specialists to compose their sales letters. However, if you are employed in a small business or are self-employed, you will probably have to write your sales letters yourself.

Whether you write sales letters for a small company or a large one, your first task is to determine who they should be sent to. One good source of names is a list of past and recent customers; those who have, at some time, purchased a product or service from you may become users again. Other sources are lists of people who may

ABBOTT OFFICE PRODUCTS, INC.
P.O. Box 544
Detroit, Michigan 48206

1 December 19--

Mr. Thomas Holland
Walk Softly Shoes
1661 East Madison Boulevard
Garfield, AL 36613

Dear Mr. Holland:

We are concerned that we have not heard from
you about your overdue account of $742, even
though we have written 3 times in the past 90
days. Since you have always been one of our
best customers, we have to wonder if some
special circumstances have caused the delay.
If so, please feel free to discuss the matter
with us.

By sending us a check today, you can preserve
your excellent credit record. Because you
have always paid your account promptly in the
past, we are sure that you will want to settle this balance now. If your balance is more
than you can pay at present, we will be happy
to work out satisfactory payment arrangements.

Please use the enclosed envelope to send in
your check, or call (800) 526-1945, toll-
free, to discuss your account.

Sincerely,

Henry Bliss

Henry Bliss
Sales Manager

HB:ew

FIGURE 7–15. Collection letter—second stage.

ABBOTT OFFICE PRODUCTS, INC.
P.O. Box 544
Detroit, Michigan 48206

1 March 19--

Mr. Thomas Holland
Walk Softly Shoes
1661 East Madison Boulevard
Garfield, AL 36613

Dear Mr. Holland:

Your account in the amount of $742 is now 180 days overdue. You have already received a generous extension of time, and in fairness to our other customers, we cannot permit a longer delay in payment.

Because you have not responded to any of our letters, we will be forced to turn your account over to our attorney for collection if we do not receive payment immediately. Such action, of course, will damage your previously fine credit rating.

Why not avoid this unpleasant situation by sending your check in the enclosed return envelope within 10 days or by calling (800) 526-1945 to discuss payment.

Sincerely,

Henry Bliss

Henry Bliss
Sales Manager

HB:ew

FIGURE 7-16. Collection letter—third stage.

be interested in certain products or services. Such lists, which are often compiled by companies that specialize in marketing techniques, · are drawn from the membership rolls of clubs, fraternal and religious organizations, professional societies, and the like. Because these lists tend to be expensive, they should be selected with care.

After you decide who your mailing list will include, you should prepare your letter carefully. As you do, keep the following points in mind.

1. The opening should attract the reader's attention and arouse his or her interest. Start out, for example, by describing a feature of the product or service that you believe would appeal strongly to your reader's needs. A representative of a company that installs home insulation might use the following opening, addressed to "Dear Homeowner":

   ```
       If you've thought that home insulation is a
   good idea but too expensive, think again. We
   can fully insulate your home at no cost to you.
   Impossible? With the new Federal Energy Tax
   Credit and the money that we guarantee you'll
   save . . . .
   ```

   Be careful, of course, that any claim you make in a sales letter is valid. Mail fraud carries heavy legal penalties.
2. Continue to emphasize the benefits of the product to the reader. Don't exaggerate; you will lose the reader's confidence if your claims sound unreasonable. And don't downgrade a competitor—it smacks of unfair tactics.
3. Make it easy and worthwhile for the customer to respond. You might include a local street map showing how to get to your store, a discount coupon, or instructions for convenient phone-in orders and free delivery.
4. Suggest ways that the reader can make immediate use of the product or service. A sales letter from a fabric store might give instructions for making pillows, bags, and other home-sewn items.

The sales letter in Figure 7–17 is typical. Notice that it is written in a light, friendly tone—sales letters from small, local businesses frequently are, since their purpose is to make the reader feel comfortable about coming to the shop or office. Note that such sales letters are sometimes "signed" not by an individual but by the shop itself, as is the case in Figure 7–17.

```
                    Janice's Cycle Shop
                     775 First Avenue
                    Ottumwa, Iowa 52501
                      (515) 273-5111


        April 3, 19--

        Mr. Raymond Sommers
        350 College Place
        Sharpsville, Iowa 52156

        Dear Mr. Sommers:

        Are you ready to go bike riding this Spring--
        but your bike isn't?

        Janice's Cycle Shop is ready to get your bike
        in shape for the beautiful days ahead. We
        will lubricate all moving parts; check the
        tires, brakes, chain, lights, horn, and all
        other accessories; and make any minor repairs
        all for only $10 and the coupon enclosed with
        this letter.

        Just stop in any day, Monday through Satur-
        day, between 8:00 a.m. and 9 p.m. We are con-
        veniently located at the corner of First and
        Walker. You can pay with cash, check, or bank
        credit card.

        If you bring your bike in before 10 a.m., you
        can be enjoying a spring bike ride that eve-
        ning.

        Happy riding!


        Janice's Cycle Shop
```

FIGURE 7–17. Sales letter.

CHAPTER SUMMARY

There are a number of different types of business letters that follow established forms. Some of the most frequently written kinds include the following.

- An *order letter* is written by a person who wishes to make a purchase. The letter should be specific, accurate, and complete, but not cluttered with unrelated details.
- An *inquiry letter* is a request for information. It should state clearly and concisely what information is wanted, who wants it, and what use will be made of it.
- A *response to an inquiry letter* should answer all questions that have been raised and should be phrased politely and tactfully.
- A *transmittal letter* accompanies material that is being sent to the recipient. The main purpose of the letter is to identify what is being sent and why it is being sent. The length of the letter varies with the circumstances.
- An *acknowledgment letter,* which reports that something has been received, is sometimes sent as a courtesy.
- A *complaint letter* should be businesslike and logical; it should not sound "complaining." The letter should reflect the fact that the writer is registering the complaint calmly—but it should also indicate that he or she expects the situation to be corrected.
- An *adjustment letter,* often a response to a complaint letter, should explain what caused the problem, specify what is being done to correct it, and, if the company for which the writer works was at fault, apologize for the incident.
- A *refusal letter* should maintain goodwill even though the refusal is clear. It is advisable to use an indirect pattern in which the bad news is preceded by a buffer and followed by a goodwill closing.
- In a *collection letter series,* three stages of letters occur that become increasingly demanding in tone. Throughout the correspondence, however, it should be emphasized that the company is willing to arrange a payment plan, and efforts should be made to retain the customer's goodwill.
- A *sales letter* should catch the reader's attention, arouse the reader's interest, emphasize the benefits of the product or service, and invite the reader to respond.

EXERCISES

1. Prepare a letter of transmittal for either a report or a term paper that you are preparing for a course. Address the letter to the appropriate instructor.

2. The following exercises present situations in which you are asked to respond with different types of correspondence. On the basis of the events described in Exercises *a–e,* write the letters or memos assigned by your instructor. In all exercises, follow the proper format for business letters. Your instructor may ask you to type your letters and envelopes.

   a. Assume that you are writing a letter requesting a free booklet that explains how to clean window-unit air conditioners to achieve better energy efficiency. You must write to an organization called the Energy Conservation Society, located in New York City at 1012 Third Avenue (zip code 10021). You are writing to Nancy Reibold, who is the executive director. You learned about this booklet in an article in *Time* magazine (May 25, 1983). You don't remember the precise title of the booklet.

   b. Assume that you are Nancy Reibold in Exercise *a.* You have received the inquiry letter asking for the booklet. You are out of copies at the moment, however, because you have received more requests for the booklet than you had anticipated. You expect to receive more copies of the booklet within two weeks. Write a response to the inquiry letter explaining the circumstances and telling the reader that you will send the booklet, entitled "Reducing the Cost of Operating Your Window Air Conditioner," as soon as you can.

   c. You are Nancy Reibold's assistant at the Energy Conservation Society (see Exercises *a* and *b*). You have just received 1,000 copies of the booklet from the Jones Printing Company, 105 East Summit Street, New Brunswick, New Jersey (zip code 08910). Both you and Nancy Reibold are very angry. When you opened the box containing the booklets, you discovered that several pages of each booklet had been left unprinted. This is the second printing mistake made by Jones Printing, and the shipment is late as well. Robert Mason, the sales representative for Jones Printing, promised that you would have no problems this time. Nancy Reibold asks you to write a complaint letter to Robert Mason to "get this problem corrected immediately." Write the letter for Ms. Reibold to sign.

d. Assume that you are Robert Mason (see Exercise *c*). You have received the complaint letter about the printing mistake. After checking, you discover that the booklets sent to the Energy Conservation Society had been subcontracted to another printing firm (ILM Printing Company) because of the backlog of printing jobs at Jones. You know that Jones Printing will not be billed for the booklets if you return them to ILM Printing within five working days. You decide that you must write an adjustment letter to Ms. Reibold quickly. You will need to ask her to return the incorrectly printed booklets.

e. Assume that you are Robert Mason (see Exercise *d*). Send a memo to J. R. Jones, your boss and president of Jones Printing, recommending that ILM Printing Company not be used for future subcontracting work. Use the details from the previous exercises to make the memo convincing.

3. As a class, and with the help of your instructor, create a made-up situation similar to the one in Exercises 2*a–e*. From the events and details you have developed, assign various types of letters to be completed as your instructor requires.

4. Find a catalog for parts or equipment with which you are familiar—for example, stereo components, office supplies, or automobile accessories. Photocopy the pages that give you enough information to order items you need (or would like to have). Write an order letter, address an envelope, and submit the letter, envelope, and photocopies of the pertinent pages to your instructor.

5. Assume that eight weeks have passed since you sent the order letter in Exercise 4. Write an order follow-up letter.

6. You have been designated to write a memorandum to Mark Heller, the head of your engineering department, asking for an extension of the deadline originally set for the completion of your engineering group's current project. Your reasons for asking for the extension are that a vendor delivered needed material seven days late and that one of the key draftsmen in your group missed two weeks of work because of illness.

7. You are the manager of Sunny River Resort. Charles James, director of the State Self-Help Society, has written you requesting the use of your lodge for a two-day meeting of his staff. His letter is as follows:

```
Dear ----------:

The Self-Help Society will hold its annual staff
meeting on June 15 of this year. We would like to
use your lodge for this two-day meeting, which
will include about 50 staff members.

We would need to use your meeting hall from 9 a.m.
to 4 p.m. each day. We would also need an overhead
projector, a 16mm projector, a flip chart, and a
podium for the various speakers who will address
our group.

Since some of the staff members will stay at the
lodge for two days or more and we will be paying
for meals in your dining room, we would like to
use your meeting room free of charge. I'm sure the
exposure your lodge will receive during the two
days will more than pay for the facilities in your
meeting hall.

Please let me know by December 10 if we can use
your lodge.

Sincerely,
```

You will need to write to Mr. James, and you'd like his highly respected charitable organization to use your meeting room. But you have a problem: you charge $250 per day to *any* group that uses the meeting room. The room has a number of fixed and variable costs—you can't afford to give it away. (Hint: Does it cost money to clean the room, pay for lighting and air conditioning, supply and repair equipment? What might happen if others knew you had given the room free?) Write a letter to Mr. James selling him on the idea of using your lodge while holding to the position that the $250 fee would apply. Use tact, a positive tone, and persuasive details to write the letter.

8. You are the manager of a store called Hamon's Fine Clothing. Dr. Raymond Warden has purchased two suits (total $575) from you—and is six months overdue in paying for them. You've already sent several standard-form notices about the late payment. You'll now need to start a series of collection letters, but you want to make the pace slow. You understood, when you gave Dr. Raymond a credit line, that he was a well-respected physician in the community. Write a series of collection letters, spacing them appropriately (date the first letter January 2).

9. You are the manager of BT Discount Auto Parts. Jeff Price, a 23-year-old friend of your nephew, owes $325 for parts. You allowed him to charge his purchase because your nephew said Jeff was reliable and promised to cover Jeff's bill if he didn't pay. It's been two months, Jeff has moved across town, and your nephew says he hasn't seen Jeff for a month. Your nephew has given you a check, but you'd like to return it by collecting the money from Jeff. Write a collection letter series to Jeff Price, starting with July 1. (You understand Jeff will be enlisting in the army within five months.)

8

Writing Strategies

In Chapter 2 you learned that writers must sequence, or organize, their material to make it clear and readable: information that is not arranged in a meaningful order will leave the reader more confused than informed. But planning the organization of your material is not the only preparation you must make before you begin to write. As noted earlier, you must also establish a *purpose* in writing. Depending on what kind of material you wish to present and on who your reader will be—and on how familiar he or she is with your subject—you can determine what your purpose is and then decide on the most effective way to present your material.

In this chapter, we'll consider a variety of on-the-job writing objectives. You may want to tell your reader how to perform a certain task, or you may need to explain how something works. You may want to describe something, or compare it with something else. Sometimes your subject will be easier for your reader to grasp if it is first divided into logical parts, or if key terms pertaining to the subject are defined. Or you may want to examine the cause of some event. Finally, your writing goal may be to persuade your reader to accept a particular viewpoint.

The techniques discussed in this chapter should help you, first, to establish your purpose, and then to present your information in a way that will be clear and convincing to your reader.

INSTRUCTIONS

When you tell someone how to do something—how to perform a specific task—you are giving instructions. If your instructions are based on clear thinking and careful planning, they should enable your reader to carry the task out successfully.

To write accurate and easily understood instructions, you must thoroughly understand the task you are describing. Otherwise, your instructions could prove embarrassing or even dangerous. For example, the container of a brand-name drain cleaner carried the following warning:

Use Only as Directed

The instructions then directed the user to

Fill sink with one to two inches of cold water, then close off drain opening.

Users would certainly find it difficult to raise the water level in the sink *before* they closed the drain! Because most users simply ignored the instructions and performed the task according to common sense, no real harm resulted. But suppose such confusing information were to appear on a bottle of intravenous fluid or in the instructions for assembling a piece of high-voltage electrical equipment. The results of inaccurate wording could be both costly and dangerous.

The writer of the drain-cleaning instructions was probably just being careless. Sometimes, though, a writer may not understand an operation well enough to write clear, accurate directions. If you are unfamiliar with a task for which you are writing instructions, watch someone who is familiar with it go through each step. As you watch, ask questions about any step that is not clear to you. Direct observation should help you to write instructions that are exact, complete, and easy to follow.

In writing instructions, as in all job-related writing, you should be aware of your reader's level of knowledge and experience. Is the reader skilled in the kind of task for which you are writing instructions? If you know that your reader has a good deal of technical background, you might feel free to use fairly specialized, technical vocabulary. If, on the other hand, your reader has little or no technical knowledge of the subject, it would be more appropriate to use simple, everyday language—to avoid specialized or technical terms as much as possible.

To test the accuracy and clarity of your instructions, it's a good idea to ask someone who is not familiar with the operation to follow the directions you've written. A first-time user can spot missing steps or point out passages that should be worded more clearly. You may find it helpful, as you observe your tester, to note down any steps that seem especially puzzling or confusing.

To make your instructions easy to follow, divide them into short, simple steps. Be sure to arrange the steps in the proper sequence. (Review the information on step-by-step organization.) Steps can be organized in one of two ways. (1) You can label each step with a sequential number.

1. Connect each black cable wire to a brass terminal . . . .
2. Attach one 4-inch green jumper wire to the back . . . .
3. Connect both jumper wires to the bare cable wires . . . .

(2) Or you can use words that indicate time or sequence.

First, determine what the problem is that the customer is reporting to you. *Next,* observe and test the system in operation. *At that time,* question the operator until you believe that the problem has been explained completely.

Keeping the steps in the proper order is not always easy. Sometimes two operations must be performed at the same time. You should either state this fact in an introduction to the instructions or include both operations in the appropriate step.

WRONG   4. Hold the CONTROL key down.
             5. Press the BELL key before releasing the CONTROL key.

RIGHT   4. While holding the CONTROL key down, press the BELL key.

You may find that the clearest, simplest instructions are those whose steps are phrased as "commands." Your instructions will be less wordy, and easier to follow, if you address each sentence directly to your reader.

INDIRECT   The operator should raise the access lid.
DIRECT   Raise the access lid.

Make instructions concise, but do not phrase them as if they were telegrams. You can write shorter sentences by leaving out articles (*a, an the*) and some pronouns (*you, this, these*) and verbs, but sentences that have been shortened in this way often have to be read more than once to be understood. The following instruction for cleaning a computer punch card assembly, for example, is not easily understood at first reading.

Pass card through punch area for debris.

The meaning of the phrase *for debris* needs to be made clearer. Revised, the instruction is understandable at once.

Pass *a* card through *the* punch area *to clear away* any debris.

Since many people fail to read a set of instructions completely through before beginning a project, you should be aware of this tendency and plan ahead for your reader. If a process in Step 9 is affected by instructions in Step 2, say so in Step 2. Otherwise your reader may reach Step 9 before discovering that an important piece of information that should have been given in advance was not.

If any special tools or materials are needed for the project, tell your reader so at the beginning of the instructions. List any essential equipment at the beginning, in a section labeled "Tools Required" or "Materials Required." The reader should not get three-fourths of the way through a project only to discover that a special wrench is necessary for the final steps. The following list of materials appeared at the beginning of a set of instructions for developing film at home.

Materials Required

Exposed film	Towel (paper or cloth)
Developing tank and reel	Scissors
Photographic thermometer	Glassine negative sleeves
Timer (clock or watch)	D-76 developer solution
Funnel (glass or plastic)	Fixing solution (hypo)
Measuring cup (glass or plastic)	Water
Viscose sponge	Storage containers for D-76 and
String	fixing solution (plastic, glass, or
Clothespins	stainless steel)

The instructions, which were written for beginners, continued with a discussion of those terms likely to confuse inexperienced film developers: *developing tank and reel, developer solution,* and *fixing solution.*

In any operation, certain steps must be performed with more exactness than others. Anyone who has boiled a three-minute egg for four minutes understands this principle. Alert your reader to steps that require precise timing or measurement.

You also must warn readers of potentially hazardous steps or materials before the steps are taken or the materials are handled. The conditions that require such warnings are numerous: electrical, chemical, mechanical, biological, and radioactive work, for example, all require some caution. Those handling hazardous materials need to be cautioned about requirements for special clothing, tools, equipment, or other measures they must take to safely complete their task.

When you write instructions, bring warnings, cautions, and precautions to the reader's attention by special devices that make them stand out from the surrounding text. Warning notices can be presented in a box, for instance. Other attention-getting devices include all-capital letters, distinctive typefaces, and the use of colored type. Professional printers and graphic designers can recommend such devices. If you do not have professional printing and design help available, use typefaces available on a standard office typewriter. Many typewriters have changeable type, usually a "golf ball" that contains the letters of the alphabet in **boldface** and *italic,* as well as standard typefaces.

Figure 8–1, instructions written for maintenance and repair crews of heavy industrial equipment, gives general guidelines regarding the steps that must be taken to secure machinery before the crew members begin their work. Note the underlined instructions, separated by rules from the other steps, directing crews to shut off power sources and "bleed" any residual energy from the equipment before they begin work.

Drawings can also be a valuable aid. Clear, well-thought-out illustrations can make instructions for even the most complex operations quickly understandable. Illustrations can simplify instructions by reducing the number of words necessary to explain something. Appropriate pictures and diagrams will enable your reader to identify parts and the relationships between parts more easily than will long explanations. They'll also free you, the writer, to focus on the steps making up the instructions rather than on descriptions of parts. Not all instructions require illustrations, of course. Whether illustrations will be useful depends on your reader's needs and on the nature of the project. Instructions for inexperienced readers should be more heavily illustrated than those for experienced readers. For a full discussion of how to create effective illustrations, see Chapter 13.

Figure 8–2 shows instructions that guide a medical laboratory technician through the steps of "streaking" a saucer-sized disk of material (called *agar*) used to grow bacteria colonies for laboratory examination. The objective is to thin out the original specimen (the inoculum) so that the bacteria will grow in small, isolated colonies. The streaking process makes certain that part of the saucer is inoculated heavily, while its remaining portions are inoculated progressively more lightly. The streaking is done by hand with a thin wire, looped at one end for holding a small sample of the inoculum.

EXPLAINING A PROCESS

When you prepare instructions, your goal is to enable your reader to complete a specific task by following the step-by-step procedure

Follow these steps for a typical lockup before all maintenance and repair work:

Step 1. Alert the operator and floor supervisor that you are ready.

Step 2. Identify all sources of residual
energy on the machinery.

WARNING

Before beginning work, perform these procedures in the following order:

STEP 3. Place padlocks on the switch, lever, or valve to lock the equipment
in the OFF position.

Put tags at this location to indicate that maintenance is in progress.

STEP 4. "Bleed" all hydraulic or pneu-
matic pressure and all electrical
current (capacitance) so that machine components will not accidentally move.

Step 5. Test operator controls.

Step 6. After work is finished, replace all
machine safeguards that were removed. Secure and check them to
make sure they fit properly.

Step 7. Finally, remove padlocks and clear
the machine for operation.

FIGURE 8-1. Set of instructions with precautions made clear.

INSTRUCTIONS

Distribute the inoculum over the surface of
the agar in the following manner:

Step 1. Beginning at one edge of the saucer, thin the inoculum by streaking
back and forth over the same area
several times, sweeping across the
agar surface until approximately
one-quarter of the surface has been
covered.
Sterilize the loop in an open
flame.

Step 2. Streak at right angles to the originally inoculated area, carrying
the inoculum out from the streaked
areas onto the sterile surface with
only the first stroke of the wire.
Cover half of the remaining sterile
agar surface.
Sterilize the loop.

Step 3. Repeat as described in Step 2, covering the remaining sterile agar
surface.

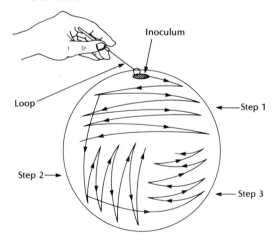

FIGURE 8–2. "Streaking" instructions.

you have outlined. You know that your reader will use your directions to become a *doer*. If you are asked to write an explanation of a process, on the other hand, you will have a different purpose in mind: you will be telling your reader how something works or how something is done—but probably not something that your reader will actually do himself or herself. The process you explain might be an event that occurs in nature (the tidal pull of the moon), a function that requires human effort (rice harvesting), or an activity in which men and women operate machinery to produce goods or services (automobile assembly-line production).

Just as it is essential for you to be familiar with a task before you can write clear instructions for carrying it out, so you must thoroughly understand a process yourself before you can explain it to your reader. And, as in all work-related writing, you must aim your writing at a level appropriate to your reader's background. Beginners, you will probably find, require more basic information, and less technical vocabulary, than do experienced workers.

The explanation of a process has something else in common with written instructions: both kinds of writing are composed of steps. The steps in a process explanation should be as clear, accurate, and complete as those in a set of instructions.

In your opening paragraph, tell your reader why it is important to become familiar with the process you are explaining. Before you explain the steps necessary to form a corporation, for example, you could cite the tax savings that incorporation would permit. To give your reader a framework for the details that will follow, you might present a brief overview of the process. Finally, you might describe how the process works in relation to a larger whole of which it is a part. In explaining the air brake system of a large dump truck, you might note that the braking system is one part of the vehicle's air system, which also controls the throttle and transmission-shifting mechanisms.

A process explanation can be long or short, depending on how much detail is necessary. The following elementary description of the way in which a camera controls light to expose a photographic film, intended for beginning photographers, fits into one paragraph. Note the writer's choice of words and definitions that are designed to communicate the ideas to an audience unfamiliar with the subject. Simple language is used, and specialized terms are defined.

> The camera is the basic tool for recording light images. It is simply a **box** from which all light is excluded except that which passes through a small opening at the front. Cameras are equipped with various devices for controlling the light rays as they enter this

opening. At the press of a button, a mechanical blade or curtain, **called a shutter,** opens and closes automatically. During the fraction of a second that the shutter is open, the light reflected from the subject toward which the camera is aimed passes into the camera through a piece of optical glass **called the lens.** The lens focuses, or projects, the light rays onto the wall at the back of the camera. These light reflections are captured on a sheet of film attached to the back wall.

Many process explanations require more details and will, of course, be longer than a paragraph. The following example, which makes up part of a report intended for environmental decision-makers, discusses several methods of surface mining for coal. The writer begins with an overview of the elements common to all the processes, defines the terms important to the explanation, and then describes each separately. Transitional words and phrases serve to achieve unity within paragraphs, and headings mark the transition from one process to the next.

SURFACE MINING OF COAL

The process of removing the earth, rock, and other strata (called overburden) to uncover an underlying mineral deposit is generally referred to as surface mining. Strip mining is a specific kind of surface mining in which all the overburden is removed in strips, one cut at a time. Three types of strip mining methods are used to mine coal: area, contour, and mountaintop removal. Which method is used depends on the topography of the area to be mined.

Area Strip Mining

Area strip mining is used in regions of flat to gently rolling terrain, like those found in the Midwest and West. Depending on applicable reclamation laws, the topsoil may be removed from the area to be mined, stored, and later reapplied as surface material during reclamation of the mined land. Following removal of the topsoil, a trench is cut through the overburden to expose the upper surface of the coal to be mined. The length of the cut generally corresponds to the length of the property or of the deposit. The overburden from the first cut is placed on unmined land adjacent to the cut. After the first cut is completed, the coal is removed and a second cut is made parallel to the first. The overburden (now referred to as spoil) from each of the succeeding cuts is deposited in the adjacent pit from which the coal was just removed. The final cut leaves an open trench equal in depth to the thickness of the overburden plus the coal bed, bounded on one side by the last spoil pile and on the other side by the undisturbed soil. The final cut may be as far as a mile from the first cut. The overburden from all the cuts, unless graded and leveled, resembles the ridges of a giant washboard.

Contour Strip Mining

In areas of rolling or very steep terrain, such as in the eastern United States, contour strip mining is used. In this method, the overburden is removed from the mineral seam in a pattern that follows the contour line around the hillside. The overburden is then deposited on the downslope side of the cut until the depth of the overburden becomes too great for economical recovery of the coal. This method leaves a bench, or shelf, on the side of the hill, bordered on the inside by a highwall (30 to 100 feet high) and on the outer side by a high ridge of spoil.

A method of mining that is often used in conjunction with contour mining is auger mining. This method is employed when the overburden becomes too thick and renders contour mining uneconomical and when extraction by underground mining would be too costly or unsafe. In auger mining, an instrument bores holes horizontally into the coal seam. The coal can then be removed like the shavings produced by a drill bit. The exposed coal seam in the highwall is left with a continuous series of bore holes from which the coal was removed.

Mountaintop Removal

In areas of rolling or steep terrain, an adaptation of area mining to conventional contour mining is used; it is called the mountaintop removal method. With this method, entire mountaintops are removed down to the coal seam by a series of parallel cuts. This method is economical when the coal lies near the tops of mountains, ridges, or knobs. If there is excess overburden that cannot be stored on the mined land, it may be transported elsewhere.

DESCRIPTION

When you give your reader information about an object's size, shape, color, method of construction, or other feature of its appearance, you are describing it. The kind of descriptions you will write on the job depends, of course, on where you work and on what you do. Office administrators describe office space and layouts. Equipment maintenance workers write parts and equipment descriptions. And police descriptions of accident scenes are routinely used in court cases. The key to effective descriptions is the accurate presentation of details. To select appropriate details, determine what use your reader will make of the description. Will your reader use it to identify something? Will your reader have to assemble or repair the object you are describing? Which details you include, then, will depend on the task the reader will perform.

Descriptions can be brief and simple, or they can be highly complex. Simple descriptions usually require only a simple listing of key features. A purchase order, shown in Figure 8–3, is a typical example of simple descriptive writing. Purchase-order descriptions should be clear and specific. An inaccurate or omitted detail may result in the delivery of the wrong item. Even an order for something as ordinary as trash compactor bags needed, in addition to the part number, four specific descriptive details.

Complex descriptions, of course, require more detail than do simple descriptions. The details you select should accurately and vividly convey what you are describing. If it is useful for your reader to visualize an object, for instance, include details—like color and shape—that appeal to the sense of sight. The example that follows is a description of the leaf abnormalities that occur when trees are planted in soil lacking the necessary minerals. The writer, a forester writing for other

PURCHASE ORDER		
Part No.	Description	Quantity
GL/020	Trash compactor bags, 31″ × 50″ tubular, non-transparent, 5-mil thickness, including 100 tie wraps per carton	5 cartons @ 100 per carton

FIGURE 8–3. Purchase order.

foresters, offers precise details of the changes in color that he has observed.

> Foliage of the black cherry trees showed striking and unusual discolorations in mid-August. Bright red margins extended one half the distance to the midrib and almost to the tip of the leaf. Nearly all leaves were similarly discolored and showed a well-defined line of demarcation between the pigmentation and the normal coloration. By late September, the pigmentation margins had widened and extended to the tips of the leaves. The red deepened in intensity and, in addition, blue and violet hues were apparent for the first time.

The description of leaf abnormalities concentrates on appearance—it tells the reader what the discolored leaves looked like. Sometimes, however, you may want to describe the physical characteristics of an object and at the same time itemize the parts that go into its makeup. If you intended to write a description of a piece of machinery, for example, you would probably find this approach, called the *whole-to-parts* technique, the most useful for your purpose. You would first present a general description of the device, since an overall description would provide your reader with a frame of reference for the more specific details that follow—the physical description of the various parts and the location and function of each in relation to the whole. The description would conclude with an explanation of the way the parts work together to get their particular job done.

The paragraph shown in Figure 8–4 describes the assembly of

```
The Die Block Assembly (Figure 1) consists of
two machined block sections, eight Code Punch
Pins, and a Feed Punch Pin. The larger sec-
tion, called the Die Block, is fashioned of a
hard, non-corrosive beryllium-copper alloy.
It houses the eight Code Punch Pins and the
smaller Feed Punch Pin in nine finely ma-
chined guide holes. The guide holes at the
upper part of the Die Block are made smaller
to conform to the thinner tips of the Punch
Pins. Extending over the top of the Die Block
and secured to it at one end is a smaller,
arm-like block called the Stripper Block. The
Stripper Block is made from hardened tool
steel, and it also has been drilled through
with nine finely machined guide holes. It is
carefully fitted to the Die Block at the fac-
```

tory so that its holes will be precisely above those in the Die Block and so that the space left between the blocks will measure .015″ (plus or minus .003″). This space should be barely wide enough to allow the passage of a tape or edge-card. It is here, as the Punch Pins are driven up through the media and into the Stripper Block, that the actual cutting, or punching, of the code and feed holes takes place. The residue (chad) from the hole punching operation is pushed out through the top of the Stripper Block and guided out of the assembly by means of a plastic Chad Collector and Chad Collector Extender.

Figure 1. Dye block assembly.

FIGURE 8–4. Illustration to aid description.

an electronic typewriter that feeds coded tape or punch cards into the machine. Intended for the typewriter mechanic, this description includes an illustration of the assembly mechanism.

Illustrations can be powerful aids in descriptive writing, especially when they show details too cumbersome to explain in writing. Do not hesitate to use an illustration with a complex description if the illustration creates a clearer image. Detailed instructions on the use of illustrations appear in Chapter 13.

COMPARISON

To explain something on the job, you may have to tell how it is like or unlike something else. When you do, you are making a comparison; you are saying A is like B.

EXAMPLE   A direct-read water meter gives at-a-glance totals of cubic feet used, just as the odometer of a car provides cumulative readings of miles driven.

Comparisons that point out how things differ are also useful.

EXAMPLE   Air-powered filters attract dust, pollen, and pollutants electrostatically; *they differ from electronic filters in using moving air instead of electricity to generate a charge.*

Comparisons come naturally to us. Think of how often you use comparisons yourself. You regularly compare the merits of television shows, athletic teams, candidates for political office, and the like. In deciding which of two or more items is most suitable for a specific purpose, you automatically weigh the advantages and disadvantages of each one. On the job, you may be called upon to select the best product, the least expensive messenger service, or even the applicant most qualified for a position.

To be sure that your choice will be the best one, you must first determine on what basis you will make the comparison. If you were responsible for the purchase of chain saws for a logging company, you would have a number of factors to take into account in order to establish your bases for comparison. Because loggers use the equipment daily, you would have to select durable saws, with the right-size engine for the type of wood most frequently cut. Large hardwood trees require high-horsepower saws with thick chains and long bars. Saws used on softwood trees, or used primarily for cutting limbs rather than trunks, can be smaller and lighter. Since chain saws produce noise and vibration, you would want to compare the quality and cost of the various silencers on the market. In considering the various features of chain saws, you would *not* include in your comparison such irrelevant factors as color or place of manufacture. Taking all of these elements into account, you would establish a number of bases for choosing from among the available chain saws—engine size, chain thickness, bar length, antivibration mountings, and noise mufflers.

Once you have decided on what basis (or bases) you will make the comparison, you can determine the most effective method of organization to use. Comparisons can be organized in several ways, but two methods that present the information in proper balance between likeness and difference appear most frequently. In the *whole-by-whole method,* all the relevant characteristics of one item are discussed before those of the next item are considered. In the *part-by-part method,* the relevant features of each item are compared one by one. The following discussion of typical woodworking glues, organized according to the whole-by-whole method, describes each type of glue and its characteristics before going on to the next type.

COMMON WOODWORKING ADHESIVES

WHITE GLUE is the most useful all-purpose adhesive for light construction, but it should not be used on projects that will be exposed to moisture, high temperature or great stress. Wood that is being joined with white glue must remain in a clamp until the glue dries, which will take about 30 minutes.

ALIPHATIC RESIN GLUE has a stronger and more moisture-resistant bond than white glue. It must be used at temperatures above 50°F. The wood should be clamped for about 30 minutes. . . .

PLASTIC RESIN GLUE is the strongest of the common wood adhesives. It is highly moisture resistant—though not completely waterproof. Sold in powdered form, this glue must be mixed with water and used at temperatures above 70°F. It is slow setting and the joint should be clamped for four to six hours. . . .

CONTACT CEMENT is a very strong adhesive that bonds so quickly it must be used with great care. It is ideal for mounting sheets of plastic laminate on wood. It is also useful for attaching strips of veneer to the edges of plywood. Since this adhesive bonds immediately when two pieces are pressed together, clamping is not necessary, but the parts to be joined must be very carefully aligned before being placed together. Check the label before you work with this adhesive. Most brands are quite flammable and the fumes can be harmful if inhaled. For safety's sake, work in a well-ventilated area, away from flames or heat.[1]

As is often the case when the whole-by-whole method is used, the purpose of this comparison is to weigh advantages and disadvantages of each glue for certain kinds of woodworking. The comparison could be expanded, of course, by the addition of other types of glue. In this kind of comparison, organize the paragraphs so that the sequence in which the information is presented is as consistent as the subject matter permits. The comparison of woodworking adhesives first fo-

---

[1] *Space and Storage* (Alexandria, Va.: Time-Life Books, 1977), p. 61.

cused on the relative strength of the glue, then noted constraints on its use (such as moisture and temperature conditions), and finally discussed clamping.

If, on the other hand, your purpose were to consider, one at a time, the various characteristics of all the glues, the information might be arranged according to the part-by-part method:

CHARACTERISTICS OF WOODWORKING ADHESIVES

Woodworking adhesives are rated primarily according to their bonding strength, moisture resistance, and setting times.

Bonding strengths are categorized as very strong, moderately strong, or adequate for use with little stress. Contact cement and plastic resin glue bond very strongly, while aliphatic resin glue bonds moderately strongly. White glue provides a bond least resistant to stress.

Moisture resistance of woodworking glues is rated as high, moderate, and low. Plastic resin glues are highly moisture-resistant. Aliphatic resin glues are moderately moisture-resistant; white glue is least moisture-resistant.

Setting times for these glues vary from an immediate bond to a four-to-six-hour bond. Contact cement bonds immediately and requires no clamping. Because the bond is immediate, surfaces being joined must be carefully aligned before being placed together. White glue and aliphatic resin glue set in thirty minutes; both require clamping to secure the bond. Plastic resin, the strongest wood glue, sets in four to six hours and also requires clamping.

With the part-by-part method, comparisons might also be made according to temperature ranges, special warnings, common uses, and so on. This approach—making comparisons among a number of possible solutions to a problem based on a set of criteria by which each possible solution is evaluated—is sometimes referred to as the problem-solution pattern.

DIVISION AND CLASSIFICATION

An effective way to approach a complex subject is to divide it into manageable parts and then go on to explain each part separately. Because this technique is especially well suited to subjects that can be readily broken down into units, it can be used as the method of

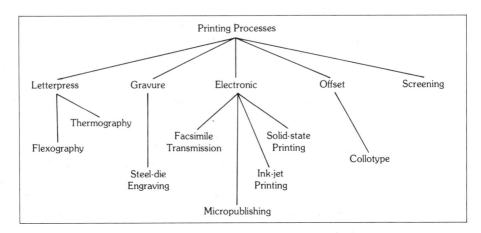

FIGURE 8–5. Division model.

organization in a good deal of job-related writing. You might use this approach, called *division,* to describe a physical object, like a machine; to examine an idea, like the terms of a new labor–management contract; or to explain a process, like the stages of an illness.

To explain the different types of printing processes currently in use, for example, you could divide the field into its major components and, where a fuller explanation is required, subdivide those components (see Figure 8–5). The emphasis in division is on breaking down a complex whole into a number of like units—because it is easier to consider smaller units and to examine the relationship of each to the other.

The process by which a subject is divided is similar to the process by which a subject is classified. While division involves the separation of a whole into its component parts, *classification* is the grouping of a number of units (people, objects, ideas, and so on) into related categories. Consider the following list:

Triangular file	Steel tape ruler
Needle-nose pliers	Vise
Pipe wrench	Keyhole saw
Mallet	Tin snips
C clamps	Rasp
Hacksaw	Plane
Glass cutter	Ball-peen hammer
Steel square	Spring clamp
Claw hammer	Utility knife
Crescent wrench	Folding extension ruler
Slip-joint pliers	Crosscut saw
Tack hammer	Utility scissors

How would you group the items in the list? You would begin by asking what they have in common. The most obvious characteristic they share is that they all belong in a carpenter's tool chest. With that observation as a starting point, you can begin to group the tools into related categories. Pipe wrenches belong with slip-joint pliers because both tools grip objects. The rasp and the plane belong with the triangular file because all three tools smooth rough surfaces. By applying this kind of thinking to all the items in the list, you can group each tool according to function (see Figure 8–6).

When dividing or classifying a subject, you must observe some basic rules of logic. First, divide the subject into its largest number of equal units. The basis for division depends, of course, on your subject and your purpose. If you are describing the *structure* of the Wankel rotating combustion engine, for example, you might begin by dividing the subject into its three major parts—the triangular-shaped rotor, the crankshaft, and the housing that contains them. If a more detailed explanation were needed, each of these parts, in turn, might be subdivided into its components. A discussion of the *function* of the same engine, on the other hand, would require a different logical basis for the division; such a breakdown would focus on the way in which combustion engines function: (1) intake, (2) compression, (3) combustion and expansion, and (4) exhaust.

Once you have established the basis for the division, you must apply it consistently. Put each item in only one category, so that items do not overlap categories. An examination of the structure of the rotary combustion engine that listed the battery as a major part would be illogical. Although it is part of the car's ignition system (which starts the engine), the battery is not a part of the engine itself. And a discussion of the parts of the ignition system in which the battery is not mentioned would be just as illogical.

In the following example, two Canadian park rangers classify typical park users according to four categories; the rangers then go on to discuss how to deal with potential rulebreaking by members of each group. The rangers could have classified the visitors in a variety of other ways, of course: as city and country residents, backpackers and drivers of recreational vehicles, United States and Canadian citizens, and so on. But for law-enforcement agents in public parklands, the size of a group and the relationships among its members were the most significant factors.

DEALING WITH GROUPS

First, recognize the various types of campers. They can be broken down as follows:

A. Family for weekend stay
B. Small groups ("a few of the boys")
C. Large groups or conventions
D. Hostile gangs

Persons in groups A and B can probably be dealt with on a one-to-one basis. For example, suppose a member of the group is picking

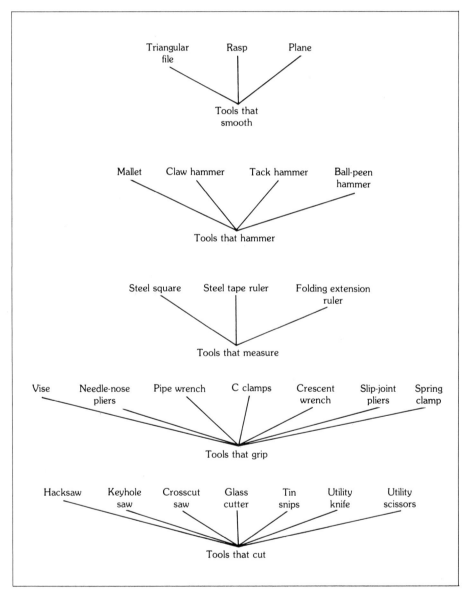

FIGURE 8–6. Classification model.

wild flowers, which is an offense in most park areas. Two courses of action are open. You could either issue a warning or charge the person with the offense. In this situation, a warning is preferable to a charge. First, advise the person that this action is an offense but, more importantly, explain why. Point out that the flowers are for all to enjoy and that most wild flowers are delicate and die quickly when picked.

For large groups, other approaches may be necessary. Every group has a leader. The leader may be official or, in informal or hostile groups, unofficial. If the group is organized, seek the official leader and hold this person responsible for the group's behavior. For informal groups, seek the person who assumes command and try to deal with this person.[2]

DEFINITION

Accurate definitions are crucial to many kinds of writing, especially for readers unfamiliar with your subject. Depending on your reader's needs, your definition can be formal, informal, or extended.

Formal Definitions

A *formal definition* is a form of classification. In it, you place a term in a class of related objects or ideas and show how it differs from other members of the same class.

DEFINITIONS

Term	Class	Difference
spoon	eating utensil	that consists of a small, shallow bowl on the end of a handle
auction	public sale	in which property passes to the highest bidder through successively increased offers
annual	plant	that completes its life cycle, from seed to natural death, in one growing season

Informal Definitions

In an *informal definition,* a familiar word or phrase is used as a synonym for an unfamiliar word or phrase.

[2] A. W. Moore and J. Mitchell, "Vandalism and Law Enforcement in Wildland Areas," in *Proceedings of the Wildland Recreation Conference,* February 28–March 3, 1977, Banff Centre, Alberta, Canada.

EXAMPLES An invoice is a *bill.*

Many states have set aside wildlife habitats (or *living space*).

Plants live in a symbiotic, or *mutually benefiting,* relationship with certain kinds of bacteria.

The system is controlled by a photoelectric (*optical*) sensing device.

Equipment functioning with transverse motion (*motion in a straight, continuous line*) can be hazardous.

The advantage of informal definitions is that they permit you to explain the meaning of a term with a minimum of interruption in the flow of your writing. Informal definitions should not be used, however, if the completeness of a formal definition is needed to make the term easier to understand.

Extended Definitions

When more than a phrase or a sentence or two is needed to explain an idea, use an *extended definition,* which explores a number of qualities of the item being defined. Some extended definitions may take only a few sentences, while others may run for several paragraphs. How long an extended definition ought to be depends on your reader's needs and on the complexity of the subject. A reader familiar with a topic or an area might be able to handle a long, fairly technical definition, whereas a newcomer to a topic would require simpler language and more basic information.

Compare the language and detail provided in the following two definitions, which explain the chemical concept *pH.* The first definition is intended for people in the graphic arts who need a general understanding of the concept but not a detailed explanation of the principles underlying the concept.

> **pH.** A number used for expressing the acidity or alkalinity of solutions. A value of 7 is neutral in a scale ranging from 0 to 14. Solutions of a lower value are considered acid, while those higher are alkaline.[3]

The second definition of pH, from an article about hydrogen ion activity in human blood, is intended for chemistry students and clinical laboratory technicians. The author assumes that his readers are familiar with chemical symbols (H^+), abbreviations (*mol/liter*), and terms (*ions*).

[3] International Paper Company, *Pocket Pal—A Graphic Arts Production Handbook,* 11th ed. (New York: International Paper Company, 1974), p. 179.

About 70 years ago, the pH scale was devised to express hydrogen ion concentration in convenient numbers. The pH value, the exponent of the H^+ concentration in mol/liter with the sign changed from minus to plus, increases as hydrogen ion concentration increases. The normal pH of blood lies between 7.38 and 7.42 and a small change in pH can mean a big change in the H^+ concentration. For example, when pH changes from 7.4 to 7.0, the H^+ concentration increases 2½ fold, from 4×10^{-8} to 10×10^{-8} mol/liter.[4]

Clarifying Definitions

Perhaps the easiest way to define a term is to give specific examples of it. A landscape architect, for example, performed a land-use analysis of a regional park for officials of the Parks Department. Crucial to the analysis were a number of abstract concepts like *form, line,* and *color,* used in precise ways not necessarily corresponding to their everyday use. Without an understanding of these concepts, the officials would be unable to understand the analysis. Specific examples and easy-to-picture details bridge the gap between writer and reader, as in this definition of *form.*

> Form, which is the shape of landscape features, can best be represented by both small-scale features, such as *trees and shrubs,* and by large-scale elements, such as *mountains* and *mountain ranges.*

Another way to define a difficult concept, especially when you are writing for nonspecialists, is to link the unfamiliar to the familiar by means of an analogy (resemblance in some aspects between things that are otherwise not alike). Defining radio waves in terms of their length (long) and frequency (low), a writer develops an analogy to show why a low frequency is advantageous.

> The low frequency makes it relatively easy to produce a wave having virtually all its power concentrated at one frequency. Think, for example, of a group of people lost in a forest. If they hear sounds of a search party in the distance, they all will begin to shout for help in different directions. Not a very efficient process, is it? But suppose that all the energy which went into the production of this noise could be concentrated into a single shout or whistle. Clearly the chances that the group will be found would be much greater.

Some terms are best defined by an explanation of their causes. Writing in a professional journal, a nurse describes an apparatus used

[4] John A. Lott, "Hydrogen Ions in Blood," *Chemistry* 51, May 1978, p. 6.

to monitor blood pressure in severely ill patients. Called an indwelling catheter, the device displays blood-pressure readings on an oscilliscope and on a numbered scale. Users of the device, the writer explains, must understand what a *dampened wave form* is.

> The *dampened wave form*, the smoothing out or flattening of the pressure wave form on the oscilliscope, is *usually caused by an obstruction* that prevents blood pressure from being freely transmitted to the monitor. The obstruction might be *a small clot or bit of fibrin* at the catheter tip. More likely, *the catheter tip has become positioned against the artery wall* and is preventing the blood from flowing freely.

The most significant point about the occurrence of a dampened wave form is that it is usually the result of a potentially dangerous obstruction. The definition, therefore, emphasizes cause and indicates what factors may, in turn, produce the obstruction in blood-pressure transmission.

Some writers make a formal definition easier to understand by breaking a concept into manageable parts.

Formal definition

> Fire is the visible heat energy released from the rapid oxidation of a fuel. A substance is "on fire" when the release of heat energy from the oxidation process reaches visible light levels.

Division into component elements

> The classic fire triangle illustrates the elements necessary to create fire: *oxygen, heat,* and *burnable material* or *fuel.* Air provides sufficient oxygen for combustion; the intensity of the heat needed to start a fire depends on the characteristics of the burnable material or fuel. A burnable substance is one that will sustain combustion after an initial application of heat to start it.

The techniques for dividing the elements of a concept follow the guidelines discussed earlier in this chapter.

Under certain circumstances, the meaning of a term can be clarified and made easier to remember by an exploration of its origin. Scientific and medical terms, because of their sometimes unfamiliar Greek and Latin roots, benefit especially from an explanation of this type. Tracing the derivation of a word can also be useful when you want to explain why a word has favorable or unfavorable associations—particularly if your goal is to influence your reader's attitude toward an idea or an activity.

> Efforts to influence legislation generally fall under the head of *lobbying,* a term that once referred to people who prowl the lobbies of houses of government, buttonholing lawmakers and trying to get them to take certain positions. Lobbying today is all of this, and

much more, too. It is a respected—and necessary—activity. It tells the legislator which way the winds of public opinion are blowing, and it helps inform him of the implications of certain bills, debates, and resolutions he must contend with.[5]

Sometimes it is useful to point out what something is *not* in order to clarify what it *is*. A what-it-is-not definition is effective only when the reader is familiar with the item with which the defined item is contrasted. If you say x is not y, your readers must understand the meaning of y for the explanation to make sense. In a crane operators' manual, for instance, a "negative definition" is used to show that, for safety reasons, a hydraulic crane cannot be operated in the same manner as a lattice boom crane.

> A hydraulic crane is *not* like a lattice boom crane in one very important way. In most cases, the safe lifting capacity of a lattice boom crane is based on the *weight needed to tip the machine*. Therefore, operators of friction machines sometimes depend on signs that the machine might tip to warn them of impending danger.
> This is a very dangerous practice with a hydraulic crane. . . .[6]

Problems in Definition

When you use a definition as a means of presenting your material, you should keep in mind a few "don'ts"—pitfalls that may result in confusing, inaccurate, or incomplete definitions.

Avoid *circular definitions*, which merely restate the term to be defined and therefore fail to clarify it.

CIRCULAR   *Spontaneous combustion* is fire that begins spontaneously.

REVISED   *Spontaneous combustion* is the self-ignition of a flammable material through a chemical reaction like oxidation and temperature buildup.

Avoid "is when" and "is where" definitions; such definitions overlook one of the three elements of formal definition—they do not *classify* the term being defined.

"IS WHEN"   A *contract* is when two or more people agree to something.
DEFINITION

---

[5] Bill Vogt, *How to Build a Better Outdoors* (New York: McKay, 1978), p. 93.
[6] *Operator's Manual* (Model W-180), Hamishfeger Corporation.

REVISED	A *contract* is a binding agreement between two or more people. (*Binding agreement* is the class of which *contract* is a member.)
"IS WHERE" DEFINITION	A *day-care center* is where working parents can leave their preschool children during the day.
REVISED	A *day-care center* is a facility at which working parents can leave their preschool children during the day. (*Facility* is the class of which *day-care center* is a member.)

Do not use definitions made up of terms your readers won't understand. Even informally written material will occasionally require the use of a term in a special sense unfamiliar to your readers; such terms should be defined too.

> In these specifications, the term *safety can* refers to an approved container of not more than five-gallon capacity having a spring-closing spout cover designed to relieve internal pressure when exposed to fire.

CAUSE AND EFFECT

When your purpose is to explain why something happened, or why you think something will happen, cause-and-effect analysis is a useful writing strategy. If you were asked to report on why the accident rate for the company truck fleet rose by 30 percent this year over last year, you would use cause-and-effect analysis. In this case, you would be working from an effect (higher accident rate) to its cause (bad driving weather, inexperienced drivers, poor truck maintenance, and so on). If, on the other hand, your purpose were to report on the possible effects that the switch to a four-day workweek (ten hours per day) would have on the office staff, you would also use cause-and-effect analysis—but this time you would start with cause (the new work schedule) and look for possible effects (changes in morale, in productivity, in absenteeism, and the like).

The goal of cause-and-effect analysis is to make the relationship between a situation and either its cause or its effect as plausible as possible. The conclusions you draw about the relationship will be based on the evidence you have gathered. *Evidence* is any pertinent fact or argument that helps explain the circumstances of an event. Because not all evidence will be of equal value to you as you draw conclusions, it's a good idea to keep some guidelines in mind for evaluating evidence.

Evidence Should Be Pertinent

The facts and arguments that you gather should be pertinent, or relevant, to your topic. That is, even if the evidence you collect is accurate, you should be careful not to draw from it a conclusion that it does not lead to or support. You may have researched some statistics, for example, which show that an increasing number of Americans are licensed to fly small airplanes. But you cannot use this information as evidence that there is a slowdown in interstate highway construction in the United States—the evidence does not lead to that conclusion. Other, more relevant evidence is available to explain the decline in interstate construction—greatly increased construction costs, opposition from environmental groups, new legislation that transfers highway construction funds to mass transportation, and so on. Statistics on the increase in small-plane licensing may be relevant to other conclusions, however. You could argue that the upswing has occurred because small planes save travel time, provide easy access to remote areas, and, once they are purchased, are economical to operate.

Evidence Should Be Sufficient

Incomplete evidence can lead to false conclusions.

> Driver training classes in the schools do not help prevent auto accidents. Two people I know who completed driver training classes were involved in accidents.

Although the evidence cited to support the conclusion may be accurate, there is not enough of it here even to justify making a statement about the driver training program at one school. A thorough investigation of the usefulness of driver training classes in keeping the accident rate down would require many more than two examples. And it would require a comparison of the driving records of those who had completed driver training with the records of those who had not.

Evidence Should Be Representative

If you conduct a survey to obtain your evidence, be sure that you do not solicit responses only from individuals or groups whose views are identical to yours—that is, be sure you obtain a representative sampling. A survey of backpackers in a national park on whether the park ought to be open to off-the-road vehicles would more than likely show them overwhelmingly against the idea. Such a survey should include opinions from more than one interested group.

Evidence Should Be Plausible

Two events that occur close to each other in time or place may or may not be causally related. Thunder and black clouds do not always signal rain, but they do so often enough that if we are outdoors and the sky darkens and we hear thunder, we seek shelter unless we're prepared to get wet. However, if you walk under a ladder and shortly afterward sprain your ankle on a curb, you cannot conclude that walking under a ladder brings bad luck—unless you are superstitious. Although the two events occurred close to each other in time, the first did not cause the second. Merely to say that X caused Y (or will cause Y) is inadequate. You must demonstrate the relationship with pertinent facts and arguments.

For example, a driver lost control of his car one summer day and crashed into a tavern. He told the police that the accident had occurred because his car had been in the sun so long and absorbed so much solar energy that he could no longer control it. The cause the driver gave for the accident cannot be taken as either plausible or objective. A careful examination of the event would probably reveal that the driver had been a patron of the tavern shortly before the crash took place. But even this explanation would have to be demonstrated with convincing facts. The police would have to interview other tavern patrons and test the driver to determine breath and blood alcohol levels. If the patrons identified the driver as a recent customer in the tavern, and if the breath and blood tests showed intoxicating levels of alcohol in his system, the evidence would be sufficient to explain why the car had hit the tavern.

Linking Causes to Effects

To show a true relationship between a cause and an effect, you must demonstrate that the existence of the one *requires* the existence of the other. It is often difficult to establish beyond any doubt that one event was *the* cause of another event. More often, a result will have more than one cause. As you research your subject, your task is to determine which cause or causes are most plausible.

When several probable causes are equally valid, report your findings accordingly, as in the following article on the use of an energy-saving device called a furnace-vent damper. The damper is a metal plate fitted inside the flue or vent pipe of natural-gas or fuel-oil furnaces. When the furnace is on, the damper opens to allow the gases to escape up the flue. When the furnace shuts off, the damper closes, thus preventing warm air from escaping up the flue stack. The dampers are potentially dangerous, however. If the dampers fail to open at the proper time, they could allow poisonous furnace gases to back into the house and asphyxiate anyone in a matter of minutes. Tests run on several dampers showed a number of probable causes for their malfunctioning.

> One damper was sold without proper installation instructions, and another was wired incorrectly. Two of the units had slow-opening dampers (15 seconds) that prevented the [furnace] burner from firing. And one damper jammed when exposed to a simulated fuel temperature of more than 700 degrees.[7]

The investigator located more than one cause of damper malfunctions and reported on them. Without such a thorough account, recommendations to prevent similar malfunctions would be based on incomplete evidence.

PERSUADING YOUR READER

Suppose you and a friend are arguing over whether the capital of Maine is Portland or Augusta. The issue is a simple question of fact that can be easily checked in an almanac or an atlas. (It's Augusta.) But suppose you are trying to convince your company that it ought to adopt flexible working hours for its employees. A quick look in a reference book will not settle the issue. Like Christine Thomas in Chapter 1, you will have to *persuade* managememt that your idea is a good one. And to achieve your goal—to convince your company to accept your suggestions and act on them—you will probably have to put your recommendations in writing.

In all on-the-job writing, it is important to keep your reader's needs, as well as your own, clearly in mind. This is especially true in persuasive writing, where your purpose may often be to ask your reader to change his or her working procedures or habits. You may think, as Christine Thomas did, that most people would automatically accept a recommendation for an improvement in the workplace. But improvement means change, and people tend to resist change. What you see as an improvement others may see as change for the sake

---

[7] Don DeBat, "Save Energy But Save Your Life, Too," *Family Safety*, Fall 1978, p. 27.

of change. ("We've always done it this way. Why change?") The idea you are proposing may be a threat to a staff member's pet project, or it may make the knowledge and experience that a veteran employee has accumulated seem out of date—so both will probably resist your suggestion. To overcome their resistance, you'll have to convince them that your suggestion has merit. You can do this most effectively by establishing the need for your recommendation and by supporting it with convincing, objective evidence.

Keep in mind, as you seek to persuade your reader, that the way you present your ideas is as important as the ideas themselves. Be thoughtful of your reader's needs and feelings by applying some basic manners in your writing. Avoid sarcasm or any other hostile tone that will offend your reader. If anger shows through in your writing, you will quickly turn the reader against your point of view. Also avoid being overly enthusiastic. Your reader may interpret such an attitude as insincere or presumptuous. Of course, you should not conceal genuine enthusiasm; just be careful not to overdo it.

The following memorandum was written by a supervisor to overcome resistance on the part of employees who had done an excellent job but who were now being asked to change their work habits.

MEMORANDUM

```
     TO:  Parts Distribution Section Employees
   FROM:  Bernadine Kovak, Supervisor ßκ
   DATE:  April 8, 19—
SUBJECT:  Plans for Automated Inventory Control
```

As you all know, our workload has jumped by 30 percent in the past month. It has increased because we have begun to centralize parts distribution here at Edgewood Division. We no longer have to get parts from the home plant in Lexington.

For us, centralized parts distribution has meant more work. In the next few months the workload will increase another 30 percent. Even a staff as experienced as you are cannot handle such a workload without help—nor will you be asked to.

In the next few weeks we will be installing electronic equipment for the automation of inventory control. Instead of the present manual system of keeping track of parts storage, a small computer will do the memorizing and searching for us.

The new system, unfortunately, will cause some disruption at first. We will have to move most of our parts stock to the new warehouse. We will also have to reorganize the area once the stock is

moved. And all of us will have to learn to operate
some new equipment.

I would like to put your knowledge and experience to work by having you help the new system get
into operation. Let's meet in my office to discuss
these improvements on Friday, April 12, at 1 p.m.
I'll have details of the plan to discuss with you.
I'm also eager to get your comments, suggestions,
and--most of all--your cooperation.

Notice that not everything in this memorandum is painted a rosy
hue. Change brings disruption, and the writer points out that fact.

Do not overlook opposing points of view. Most issues have more
than one side, and you should acknowledge them. For example, if
you were listing reasons why flexible working hours are a good idea,
it would be a mistake to overlook the added paperwork that might
be required to keep track of separate schedules for all employees. It
would be most effective to admit that the paperwork will increase—
and then go on to show that the added burden would be more than
made up for by improved employee morale and perhaps by greater
productivity. By including differing points of view, you gain several
advantages. First, you show your reader that you are honest enough
to recognize opposite views when they exist. Second, you can demonstrate the advantage of your viewpoint over others. And by bringing
up opposing views *before* your co-workers do, you may be able to blunt
some of their objections.

CHAPTER SUMMARY

Writing on the job is writing with a purpose. The purpose will
always be specific and practical.

When you give someone instructions on how to perform a task,
be sure that you understand the task thoroughly. Then present the
information at a level appropriate to your reader's background in
the subject. Write concisely, addressing yourself directly to the reader.
Divide the task into steps, and present each step in its correct sequence.
Mention any necessary preparations at the beginning, and provide
appropriate warnings where necessary. Use illustrations when they
will add clarity.

Most of the guidelines for writing instructions apply to the writing
of process explanations as well. Introduce the process by giving the
reader pertinent information about its purpose or significance. Then
divide the process into steps and present each step in its proper sequence.

Descriptive writing requires the careful selection of pertinent details. Simple descriptions, like parts lists, should be specific and detailed. Complex descriptions, like those of equipment made up of many interacting components, require greater selectivity of details. The whole-to-parts method may be the most effective one for providing your reader with a framework when you are explaining a large or complex subject. Illustrations can be used to clarify descriptive material.

Comparisons show how two or more things are like or unlike one another. For the comparison to be effective, its basis must be valid and consistently applied. Comparisons can be organized on a whole-by-whole or on a part-by-part basis, depending on your reader's needs. The type of organization chosen should be used consistently to avoid confusing the reader.

A complex subject can be made more understandable if it is divided into its largest number of equal parts. Continue the breakdown until it is sufficiently detailed to explain the subject clearly. Classification can be used to group people, ideas, or objects on the basis of their common characteristics. For subjects that can be divided or classified in more than one way, select the basis for the division or grouping that best represents your writing objective. Dealing with all pertinent parts, apply the basis for the division or classification consistently.

Define terms that may be unfamiliar to your readers. Terms can be defined formally, informally, or by extended definition, depending, again, on your reader's needs. To define a term formally, state which grouping, or class, the term belongs to and show how it differs from all other members of the class. To define a term informally, substitute familiar words and phrases for the unfamiliar term. Difficult or important terms can be explained by a variety of methods that extend the original definition. Terms used in a sense different from their accustomed meaning should also be defined. Avoid circular definitions and "is when" and "is where" definitions.

In cause-and-effect explanations, your goal is to establish a plausible relationship between an event and its cause, or between an event and its likely effect. Such explanations require a careful evaluation of the evidence. Is it pertinent? Is it representative? Is it sufficient? Is it merely coincidental? When your evidence is accurate and applicable, state your conclusions carefully. Overstated conclusions will misrepresent your evidence regardless of how pertinent it is.

In persuasive writing, the way in which ideas are presented is as important as the ideas themselves. Take your reader's feelings into account. Avoid a hostile tone, and appeal instead to the reader's good sense. When writing about controversial issues, acknowledge other points of view. The reader will appreciate your honesty, and you can then demonstrate the advantage of your views over the other views.

EXERCISES

1. Choose one of the following topics to write about. First, decide whether you will develop the topic as a *set of instructions* or as *an explanation of a process*. Then, using the approach you have selected, write a paper, of assigned length, on the topic. Assume that your reader has no knowledge of the topic. Use illustrations where they would be helpful to the reader.

    a. Operation of a photocopy machine
    b. Blood pressure measurement
    c. How automobile-battery terminals are cleaned
    d. Purchase of 10 shares of common stock
    e. Directions from your home to the nearest commercial airport

2. Write a *description* of one of the following items or of an item of your choice. Specify who your reader will be, and write the description in sufficient detail to permit your reader either to visualize or to locate the item without further assistance. Do not illustrate this assignment.

    a. The prominent features (of face, body, clothing, and so on) of a close friend or relative for a "missing persons" bulletin
    b. A small mechanical device with no more than five moving parts (pencil sharpener, can opener, etc.)
    c. A nonmechanical household or recreational device (rolling pin, tennis racquet, etc.)
    d. A piece of land. First give an overview, then establish its location relative to city street or natural boundaries; complete the description with significant details of the land.

3. Write a paper, of assigned length, on one of the following topics by *comparing* the two items cited. Before you begin to write, specify who your reader will be. Make the comparison detailed enough to suit the needs of the reader.

    a. Two career choices
    b. Two job offers
    c. Two products or services with which you are familiar
    d. Two persons who are being considered for promotion to the same position
    e. A comparison of your choice, organized by either the whole-by-whole method or the part-by-part method (for example, a comparison of two products or appliances designed to do the same job)

4. Choose one of the following topics to write about. First, decide whether you will develop the topic through *division* (separation

of a complex whole into several smaller units) or *classification* (grouping of a number of small units into larger, related categories). Then, using the approach you have selected, write a paper, of assigned length, on the topic. Before you begin to write, be sure that you have determined who your reader will be and what your scope will be.

a. Road signs in your area
b. Home-heating methods
c. Hand-held calculators
d. A community service organization in your locality
e. 35-mm cameras
f. Recreational or athletic programs in your community
g. A college library
h. Safety regulations where you work
i. Fire extinguishers
j. The set-up of an office, hospital, or other organization with which you are familiar

5. Write an *extended definition* of a key concept or term related to an occupation or a school subject. Use some or all of the techniques discussed in the chapter for creating extended definitions. Assume that your reader is unfamiliar with the term.

6. Choose one of the following statements to write about. First, decide whether you will develop the topic through *cause and effect* or *persuasion*. Then, using the approach you have selected, write a paper, of assigned length, on the topic. Before you begin to write, be sure that you have determined who your reader will be and what your scope will be.

a. A dangerous practice or condition in your office or school is likely to cause an accident.
b. You ought to be promoted to a job with greater responsibility.
c. Businesses should be encouraged to locate in your community.
d. Setting up job-training programs in connection with a college will lead to higher employment in your community.
e. Some aspects of your present job (such as working conditions, equipment, availability of help, organization of your work area) should be changed.
f. Some aspect of your school (such as the grading system, the library facilities, work programs) should be changed.
g. Smoking should (or should not) be permitted in public places.

9

Informal Reports

Reports make up a large part of on-the-job communication. The successful operation of many firms depends on reports that either circulate within the company or are submitted to customers, clients, and others with whom a company does business. It would be difficult, in fact, to find a job in business or industry that did not require, at least on occasion, the writing of reports.

What is a report? Although the term is used to refer to hundreds of different types of written communication, the word can be defined as an organized presentation of information, serving an immediate and practical purpose by furnishing requested or needed data.

All reports fall into two broad categories: *formal reports* and *informal reports*. Formal reports, which are explained in detail in Chapter 11, are generally the outgrowth of projects that require many months of work and large sums of money, or of projects done on behalf of governmental agencies. Formal reports, which may take several hundred pages, are usually accompanied by a letter of transmittal to the recipient; frequently, such reports have a table of contents and other aids to the reader. Informal reports, on the other hand, normally run from a few paragraphs to a few pages and include only the essential elements of a report (introduction, body, conclusions, recommendations). And informal reports, because of their brevity, are customarily written as a letter (if the report is to be sent outside the company) or as a memorandum (if it is to be distributed within the firm).

WRITING THE REPORT

If you will be writing a report on an activity in which you are participating (a special project, for example), it's a good idea to collect information and keep notes as the activity progresses. You may have trouble obtaining all the information later on, when you prepare to write the report.

In determining what notes to take, include all the information that will meet the objective of your report (for example, whatever information will persuade your boss to adopt the plan of action you are proposing) and the needs of your reader (exactly the information that will enable your boss to understand your proposal and to see its logic and benefits).

The purpose of taking notes is to record, in an abbreviated form, the information that will go into your report. The advantage of taking notes is that you don't have to rely on your memory to recollect every detail at exactly the moment when you need to include it in your report. Be careful, however, not to make a note so brief that you forget what you intended when you wrote it. The critical test of a note is whether, a week later, you will still be able to recall all the information and significance that you had in mind when you made the note. (Note-taking is discussed in more detail in Chapter 10.)

Once you have prepared all your notes, organize your outline as explained in Chapter 2. Then work your notes into the appropriate places in your outline.

An informal report is almost always intended for one specific reader or for a small group of readers. Because you will know, in most cases, who your reader will be and how much technical background he or she has, you should be able to determine just how much specialized or technical language to use. You should also have a good idea of how much background information you will need to provide for your reader.

THE PARTS OF THE REPORT

Most reports that you will be called on to write have at least three, and sometimes four, main parts: the introduction, the body, conclusions, and recommendations. The *introduction* serves several key functions: it announces the subject of the report, gives the purpose, and, when appropriate, gives essential background information. The introduction should also concisely summarize any conclusions, findings, and/or recommendations made in the report. Managers, supervisors, and clients find a concise summary useful because it gives them the essential information at a glance and helps focus their thinking as they read the rest of the report. The *body* of the report should present a clearly organized account of the report's subject—the results of a test carried out, the status of a construction project, and so on. The amount of detail to include in the body depends on the complexity of the subject and on your reader's familiarity with the subject. In the *conclusion* of the report, you should summarize your findings and tell the reader what you think their significance may be. In some reports there is a final section giving *recommendations*. (Sometimes the conclusions and recommendations may be combined.) In this section, you would make suggestions based on the data you have presented—suggestions, say, for instituting new work procedures, for setting up new departmental responsibilities, or for hiring new employees.

TYPES OF REPORTS

Because there are so many different types of informal reports, and because the categories sometimes overlap (a trip report, for example, might also be a progress report), it would be unrealistic to attempt to study every type. But it is possible to become familiar with report writing in general and to examine some of the most frequently written kinds of reports. In this chapter we will examine the trouble (or accident) report, the investigative report, the progress (and periodic) report, the trip report, and the test report. If you master the techniques of writing these kinds of informal reports, you should be able to prepare other kinds as well.

Trouble Report

In many kinds of work you may do, accidents, equipment failures, and work stoppages will occur. Every such incident must be reported, so that its cause can be determined and any necessary steps taken to prevent a recurrence. The record of an accident or a breakdown—a *trouble report*, or *accident report* as it is also called—may even be used by the police or by a court of law in establishing guilt or liability. Because it can be vital in preventing further injury or disruption in service, and because it may become legal evidence, a trouble report should be prepared as accurately, objectively, and promptly as possible.

The trouble report should normally be in the form of a memorandum written by the person in charge of the site where the incident occurred and addressed to his or her superior. (Some companies have printed forms for specific types of trouble reports, but even form reports include a section in which the writer must explain in detail what happened.) On the subject line of the memorandum, briefly state the nature of the incident you are reporting.

SUBJECT: Personal-Injury   Accident   in   Section   A-40, October 10, 19- -

Then, after a brief introductory summary, state exactly when and where the accident or breakdown took place. Describe any physical injury or any property damage—no matter how slight—that occurred. Itemize any expenses that resulted from the incident (for example, an injured employee may have missed a number of workdays, or an equipment failure may have caused a disruption in service to the company's customers). Since insurance claims, worker's compensation awards, and, in some instances, lawsuits may hinge on the information in a trouble report, be sure to include precise data on times, dates, locations, treatment of injuries, the names of any witnesses, and any other crucial information. Include in the report a detailed analysis of what you believe caused the trouble. Avoid any tone of condemnation or blame. Be thorough, exact, and objective, and support any opinion you offer with facts. Mention what has been or will be done to correct the conditions that may have led to the incident. Finally, present your recommendations for the prevention of a recurrence of the trouble (such as increased safety precautions, improved equipment, or the establishment of training programs). If you are speculating on the cause of the accident, make sure that this is clear to the reader; your guess is no doubt an educated one, but it still should be labeled as a guess.

Figure 9–1 shows a trouble report written by the foreman of a group of punch-press operators and addressed to the plant's safety officer, at the request of the safety officer. No witnesses were present, so the foreman obtained the information for the report by talking to the plant nurse, to hospital personnel, and to the victim—and by inspecting the equipment being used by the victim at the time of the accident.

Investigative Report

Although an *investigative report* may be written for a variety of reasons, it is most often produced in response to a request for information. You might be asked, for instance, to check the range of prices that companies charge for a particular item, to conduct an opinion survey among customers, to study a number of different procedures for performing a specific operation, to review a recently published

MEMORANDUM

To: James K. Arburg, Safety Officer
From: Lawrence T. Baker, Foreman of Section *LTB*
      A-40
Date: November 30, 19--

Subject: Personal-Injury Accident in Section
         A-40, October 10, 19--

Introduction

On October 10, 19--, while Jim Hollander was
operating a punch press, he severed his left
thumb. A safety device on the press should
have prevented this, but Mr. Hollander had
inactivated it. To prevent further such accidents, I have explained the cause of this accident to all punch-press operators.

Accident Description

On October 10, 19--, at 10:15 p.m., Jim Hollander, operating punch press #16, accidentally brushed the knee switch of his punch
press with his right knee as he swung a metal
sheet over the punching surface. The switch
activated the punching unit, which severed
Hollander's left thumb between the first and
second joints as his hand passed through the
punch station. While an ambulance was being
summoned, Margaret Wilson, R.N., administered
first aid at the plant dispensary. There were
no witnesses to the accident.

The ambulance arrived from Mercy Hospital at
10:45 p.m., and Hollander was admitted to the
emergency room at the hospital at 11 p.m. He
was treated and kept overnight for observation, then released the next morning.

Hollander returned to work one week later, on
October 17. He has been given temporary duties in the tool room until his injury heals.

Conclusions About the Cause of the Accident

The Maxwell punch press on which Hollander
was working has two switches, a hand switch

FIGURE 9-1. Trouble report.

and a knee switch, and <u>both</u> must be pressed
to activate the punch mechanism. The hand
switch must be pressed first, and then the
knee switch, to trip the punch mechanism. The
purpose of the knee switch is to leave the
operator's hands free to hold the panel being
punched. The hand switch, in contrast, is a
safety feature. Because the knee switch cannot activate the press until the hand switch
has been pressed, the operator cannot trip
the punching mechanism by touching the knee
switch accidentally.

Inspection of the punch press that Hollander
was operating at the time of the accident
made it clear that Hollander had taped the
hand switch of his machine in the ON position, effectively eliminating its safety
function. He could then pick up a panel,
swing it onto the machine's punching surface,
press the knee switch, stack the newly
punched panel, and grab the next unpunched
panel, all in one continuous motion--elimi-
nating the need to let go of the panel, after
placing it on the punching surface, in order
to press the hand switch.

To prevent a recurrence of this accident, I
have conducted a brief safety session with
all punch-press operators, at which I described Hollander's experience and cautioned
them against tampering with the safety features of their machines.

FIGURE 9–1, *continued.*

work, and so on. You would then present your findings in an investigative report.

An investigative report is usually prepared as a memorandum.
Open with a brief introductory summary that includes a statement
of the information you were seeking. Then define the extent of your
investigation. Finally, state your findings and any recommendations
you may have.

In the example shown in Figure 9–2, an industrial training manager has asked the senior instructor to investigate and report on a
method of preparing repair manuals that eliminates the need to translate the manuals into foreign languages. The report explains how
the new method works and offers alternative ways in which it might
be adopted by the report writer's company.

MEMORANDUM

To: Noreen Rinaldo, Training Manager
From: Charles Lapinski, Senior Instructor
Date: February 14, 19--   *CL*

Subject: The Addison Corporation's Basic
         English Program

Introduction

As you requested, I have investigated the Addison Corporation's Basic English Program to
determine whether we might also adopt such a
program. The program does not teach the English language as a whole, but only recognition of the 800 basic words used in the company's repair manuals. For us, this program
would probably be most beneficial if limited
to preparation of student manuals for the international students in our service school.
However, since our product lines are broader
than Addison's, we would need to create more
illustrated manuals. One for each product
line should be adequate.

Program Description

The purpose of the Addison Basic English
course is to teach foreign mechanics who do
not speak or read English to understand repair manuals written in a special 800-word
vocabulary called "Basic English," and thus
eliminate the need for Addison to translate
its manuals into a number of different languages. The Basic English Program does not
attempt to teach the mechanics to be fluent
in English, but rather teaches them to recognize the 800 basic words that appear in the
repair manuals.

The course does not train mechanics. Students
must know, in their own language, what a word
like torque means; the course simply teaches
them the English term for it. As prerequisites for the course, students must have a
basic knowledge of their trade, must be able
to identify a part in an illustrated parts

FIGURE 9-2. Investigative report.

book, and must be able to read and write in
their own language.

Students are given the specially prepared instruction manual, an illustrated book of
parts with their English names, and a pocket
reference containing all 800 words of the Basic English vocabulary plus the English names
of parts. (Students can write the corresponding words in their language beside the English words and then use the pocket reference
as a bilingual dictionary.) The course consists of 30 two-hour lessons, each lesson introducing approximately 27 words. No effort
is made to teach pronunciation; the course
teaches only recognition of the 800 words,
which include 450 nouns, 70 verbs, 180 adjectives and adverbs, and 100 articles, prepositions, conjunctions, and pronouns.

The 800-word vocabulary enables the writers
of the manuals to provide mechanics with any
information that might be required, because
the area of communication is strictly limited
to maintenance, inspection, troubleshooting,
safety, and the operation of Addison equipment. All nonessential words (such as apple,
father, mountain, and so on) have been eliminated, as have most synonyms (for example,
under appears, but beneath does not).

Conclusions and Recommendations

I see three possible ways in which we might
be able to use some or all of the elements of
the Basic English Program: (1) in the preparation of all our student manuals, (2) in the
preparation of manuals for the international
students in our service school, or (3) as Addison uses the program.

I think it would be unnecessary to use the
Basic English methods in the preparation of
student manuals for all our students. Most of
our students are English-speaking people to
whom an unrestricted vocabulary presents no
problem.

In conjunction with the preparation of manuals for international students, the program

FIGURE 9–2, *continued.*

```
might have more appeal. Students would take
the Basic English course either before coming
to this country to attend school or after ar-
riving but before beginning their technical
training.

As for our initiating a Basic English Program
similar to Addison's, we could create our own
version of the Basic English vocabulary and
write our service manuals in it. Since our
product lines are much broader than Addi-
son's, however, we would need to create il-
lustrated parts books for each of the differ-
ent product lines.
```

FIGURE 9–2, *continued.*

Progress and Periodic Reports

Progress Reports. The purpose of a progress report is to keep an individual or a group—usually management—informed of the status of a project. In answering various questions (Is the project on schedule? Is it staying within its budget? Is the staff running into any unexpected snags?), the report lets the reader know precisely what work has been completed and what work remains to be done. Often the report will include recommendations for changes in procedure or will propose new courses of action. Progress reports are generally prepared when a particular stage of a project is reached.

Projects that are most likely to generate progress reports are those that last for a considerable period of time and are fairly complex. The construction of a building, the development of a new product, and the opening of a branch office in another part of town are examples of such projects. Sometimes, too, a progress report is a specified requirement in the contract for a project.

The chief value of a progress report is that it allows management not only to check on the status of a project but to make any necessary adjustments in assignments, schedules, and budget allocations while the project is under way. Progress reports can make it easier for management to schedule the arrival of equipment and supplies so that they will be available when they are needed. And such reports can, on occasion, avert crises. If a hospital had planned to open a new wing in February, for instance, but a shortage of wallboard caused a two-month lag in construction, a progress report would alert hospital managers to the delay—in time for them to prepare alternate plans.

Many projects, of course, require more than one progress report. In general, the more complicated the project, the more frequently management will want to review it. All reports issued during the life of a project should be of the same format. Project reports to be sent outside the company are normally prepared as letters (see Figure 9–3); otherwise, they can be written as memorandums. The first in a series of reports should identify the project in detail and specify what materials will be used and what procedures will be followed throughout the project. Later reports will contain only a transitional introduction that briefly reviews the work discussed in the previous reports. The body of the reports should describe in detail the current status of the project. And every report should end with any conclusions or recommendations—for instance, alterations in schedule, materials, or procedures.

In the example shown in Figure 9–3, a contractor reports to the city manager on his progress in rewiring a city-owned arena. Notice that the emphasis is on meeting specified costs and schedules.

Periodic Reports.   Periodic reports perform most of the functions performed by progress reports; the difference between the two is that periodic reports are issued at regular intervals—daily, weekly, monthly, quarterly, annually—rather than at particular stages in a project.

Quarterly and annual reports, because of their length, are usually organized as formal reports (see Chapter 11). Most other kinds of periodic reports seldom run longer than a page or two. Like progress reports, these shorter reports are most often written as memorandums within an organization and as letters when sent to clients and customers outside an organization.

Many kinds of routine information that must be reported periodically—and that do not require a narrative explanation—can be either recorded on forms or entered into computers. Examples are personnel, accounting, and inventory records, production and distribution figures, and travel and task logs.

Preprinted forms have established formats (see Chapter 12), as do formal reports (see Chapter 11). One- and two-page periodical reports, however, can be organized in a variety of ways. The standard format of *introduction, body,* and *conclusion/recommendations* may serve your needs. Otherwise, modify the organizational pattern to suit your reader's reporting requirements. The sample periodic report shown in Figure 9–4 is organized as follows:

- Introduction
- Work performed during this period
- Problems encountered
- Project plans

HOBARD CONSTRUCTION COMPANY
9032 Salem Avenue
Lubbock, Texas 79409

(806) 769-0823

August 17, 19--

John H. Mambert,
City Manager
109 Main Street
Lubbock, Texas 79416

Subject: Rewiring the Sports Arena

Dear Mr. Mambert:

The rewiring program at the Sports Arena is
progressing on schedule and within budget.
Although the cost of certain equipment is
higher than our original bid had indicated,
we expect to complete the project without exceeding the estimated costs, because the
speed with which the project is being completed will reduce overall labor expenses.

Equipment used up to now has cost $10,800,
and labor costs have been $31,500 (including
some subcontracted plumbing). Our estimate
for the remainder of the equipment, based on
discussions with your lighting consultant, is
$11,500; remaining labor costs should not be
in excess of $25,500.

As of August 15, we had finished the installation of the circuit breaker panels and meters, of level-one service outlets, and of
all subfloor wiring. The upgrading of stage-
lighting equipment, the installation of
level-two service outlets, and the replacement of lighting fixtures are in the preliminary stages (the wiring has been completed,
but installation of the fixtures has not yet
begun).

We have scheduled the upgrading of stage-
lighting equipment to take place from August
16 to October 5, the installation of level-
two service outlets from October 6 to November 12, and the replacement of lighting fix-

FIGURE 9–3. Progress report.

tures from November 15 to December 17. We see
no difficulty in having the arena finished
for the December 23 Christmas program, as
specified in our contract.

                    Sincerely yours,

                    William L. Hobard

                    William L. Hobard

WLH/jsi

FIGURE 9–3, *continued.*

It could just as well have been ordered as:

- Introduction
- Accomplishments
- Concerns
- Plans

The sample periodic report shown in Figure 9–4 is one of several
monthly reports that keep the project manager of a computerized
document-retrieval system (the Document Control System) up to date
on how the training staff is progressing with its work.

                    MEMORANDUM

To: James R. Lundy, Project Officer
From: Diana F. Talbot, Training Coordinator DFT
Date: May 3, 19--

Subject: User Training and Assistance for
         April 19--

Introduction

The training staff held one advanced and two
basic training courses in April. In May, we

FIGURE 9–4. Periodic report.

have scheduled two advanced courses and one
basic course. Until enrollment increases, we
will consolidate scheduled classes. The "Document Control System User's Manual" will be
ready for distribution by May 15.

Work Performed During This Period

Three training sessions were held in April:
an advanced course on April 3 and two basic
courses on April 13 and 20. To date, 200
staff members have participated in 31 user
training sessions since training was started
in June 19--.

Problems Encountered

Scheduled training sessions are not being attended in sufficient numbers to fill all
classes. Until enrollment increases, we will
consolidate the number of scheduled classes
to ensure adequate class size. We encourage
potential system users to participate in
scheduled training sessions. These sessions
provide the best systematic approach for users to learn about the advantages that the
system offers them as a review and research
tool.

Project Plans

The following classes are scheduled for May:

    May 15 Advanced Course
        (Materials Staff)

    May 22 Advanced Course
        (Records Control Staff)

    May 29 Basic Course
        (Open to All)

Final editorial changes are being made in the
"Document Control System User's Manual." The
cover, spine, section dividers, and final
artwork for several drawings are nearing completion. The manual will be ready by May 15,
at which time copies will be distributed for
each system terminal.

FIGURE 9–4, *continued.*

Trip Report

Many companies require or encourage reports on the business trips their employees take. A *trip report* not only provides a permanent record of a business trip and its accomplishments but also enables many employees to benefit from the information that one employee has gained.

A trip report should be in memorandum format, addressed to your immediate superior. On the subject line give the destination (or purpose) and dates of the trip. After a brief introductory summary, explain why you made the trip, who you visited, and what you accomplished. The report should devote a brief section to each major event and may include a heading for each section (you needn't give equal space to each event but, instead, elaborate on the more important events). Follow the body of the report with any appropriate conclusions and recommendations.

A sample trip report appears in Figure 9–5.

```
                       MEMORANDUM

     To: Manuel Cruz, Manager, Customer Relations
     From: Isoroku Somoto, Field Service Engineer  IS
     Date: May 31, 19--

     Subject: Trip to Inspect New Power Unit
              Installations, May 26-30


     Introduction

     Between May 26 and May 30, I inspected our
     installations at five hospitals. I checked
     the equipment, conducted trial runs, and held
     training sessions. In every case, our equip-
     ment functioned properly. Also, the staff at
     each hospital was pleased with our sales and
     installation staffs.

     Hospitals Visited

     The purpose of this trip was to inspect the
     installation of Taylor Auxiliary Power Units
     in five hospitals and to train the mainte-
     nance staffs at those hospitals to operate
     the units during a commercial power failure.
     I visited the New Orleans General Hospital on
```

FIGURE 9–5. Trip report.

the 26th, Our Lady of Mercy Hospital in San
Antonio on the 27th, Dallas Presbyterian Hos-
pital on the 28th, St. Elizabeth Hospital in
Oklahoma City on the 29th, and the Jefferson
Davis Memorial Hospital in Atlanta on the
30th.

Testing Results

At each site, I found that the equipment had
been installed properly. After inspecting the
equipment and its installation, I held a
brief training session with the maintenance
staff. The training consisted of instruction
in starting the unit's engine, in operating
the generator's controls to produce 220 volts
of electricity at 60 Hertz, and in activating
the operating unit in the event of a commercial power failure.

I then made arrangements in each hospital
with the administrative office and placed the
hospital on auxiliary power for one hour as a
trial run. In every location, the transfer
from commercial to auxiliary power was made
without problems.

Conclusion

In all five hospitals, both the administrative and maintenance staffs appeared to have
a favorable opinion of the Taylor Power
Equipment Company, its product, and its field
personnel. Our sales staff and installers
seem to be doing a good job.

FIGURE 9–5, *continued.*

Test Report

The *test report,* also called the *laboratory report,* records the results of tests and experiments. Normally, those who write test reports
do so as a routine part of their work. Tests that form the bases of
reports are not limited to any particular occupation; they commonly
occur in many fields, from chemistry to fire science, from physics to
home economics, from metallurgy to medical technology, and include
studies on cars, blood, mercury thermometers, pudding mixes, smoke

detectors—the list is endless. Information collected in testing may be used to upgrade products or to streamline procedures.

Because the accuracy of a test report is essential, be sure to take careful notes while you are performing the test. When you prepare the report, state your findings in clear, straightforward language. Since a test report should be as objective as possible, it is one of the few writing formats in which the passive voice is usually more suitable than the active voice (see Chapter 4). A test report may be either a letter or a memorandum.

On the subject line, identify the test you are reporting on. If the purpose of the test is not obvious to your reader, explain it in the body of the report. Then, if it is helpful to your reader, outline the testing procedures. You needn't give a detailed explanation of how the test was performed; rather, provide just enough information for your reader to have a general idea of the testing methods. Next, present the data—the results of the test. If an interpretation of the results would be useful to your reader, furnish such an analysis in your conclusion. Close the report with any recommendations you are making as a result of the test.

Figure 9–6 shows one example of a test report. This report does not explain how the test was conducted, because such an explanation is unnecessary. Compare this report with the one shown in Figure 9–7, which does explain how the tests were performed.

Biospherics, Inc.
4928 Wyaconda Road
Rockville, MD 20852

March 14, 19--

Mr. John Sebastiani, General Manager
Midtown Development Corporation
114 West Jefferson Street
Milwaukee, WI 53201

Subject: Results of Analysis of Soil Samples
        for Arsenic

Dear Mr. Sebastiani:

The results of our analysis of your soil samples for arsenic showed considerable varia-

FIGURE 9–6. Test report.

tion; a high iron content in some of the samples may account for these differences.

Following are the results of the analysis of 22 soil samples. The arsenic values listed are based on a wet-weight determination. The moisture content of the soil is also given to allow conversion of the results to a dry-weight basis if desired.

Hole Number	Depth	Percent of Moisture	Arsenic Total as ppm
1	12"	19.0	312.0
2	Surface	11.2	737.0
3	12"	12.7	9.5
4	12"	10.8	865.0
5	12"	17.1	4.1
6	12"	14.2	6.1
7	12"	24.2	2540.0
8	Surface	13.6	460.0

I noticed that some of the samples contained large amounts of metallic iron coated with rust. Arsenic tends to be absorbed into soils high in iron, aluminum, and calcium oxides. The large amount of iron present in some of these soil samples is probably responsible for retaining high levels of arsenic. The soils highest in iron, aluminum, and calcium oxides should also show the highest levels of arsenic, provided the soils have had approximately equal levels of arsenic exposure.

If I can be of further assistance, please do not hesitate to contact me.

Yours truly,

Gunther Gottfried

Gunther Gottfried
Chemist

GG/jrm

FIGURE 9–6, *continued.*

≣ Biospherics, Inc.
4928 Wyaconda Road
Rockville, MD 20852

September 9, 19--

Mr. Leon Hite, Administrator
The Angle Company, Inc.
1869 Slauson Boulevard
Waynesville, VA 23927

Dear Mr. Hite:

On Tuesday, August 30, Biospherics, Inc.,
performed asbestos-in-air monitoring at your
Route 66 construction site, near Front Royal,
Virginia. Six persons and three construction
areas were monitored. In every case, exposure
was well below the standards set by the National Institute for Occupational Safety and
Health (NIOSH) in 1972.

All monitoring and analyses were performed in
accordance with "Occupational Exposure to Asbestos," U.S. Department of Health, Education, and Welfare, Public Health Service, National Institute for Occupational Safety and
Health, 1972. Each worker or area was fitted
with a battery-powered personal sampler pump
operating at a flow rate of approximately one
liter per minute. The airborne asbestos was
collected on a 37-mm Millipore type AA filter
mounted in an open-face filter holder. Samples were collected over an 8-hour period.

A wedge-shaped piece of each filter was
mounted on a microscope slide with a drop of
1:1 solution of dimethyl phthalate and di-
ethyl oxalate and then covered with a cover
slip. Samples were counted within 24 hours
after mounting, using a microscope with phase
contrast option.

In all cases, the workers and areas monitored
were exposed to levels of asbestos fibers
well below the NIOSH standard. The highest
exposure found was that of a driller who was
exposed to 0.21 fibers per cubic centimeter.

FIGURE 9–7. Test report.

The driller's sample was analyzed by scanning
electron microscopy followed by energy dis-
persive X-ray techniques which identify the
chemical nature of each fiber, thereby veri-
fying the fibers as asbestos or identifying
them as other fiber types. Results from these
analyses show that the fibers present are
tremolite asbestos. No nonasbestos fibers
were found.

Yours truly,

Gary Willis

Gary Willis
Chemist

GW/jrm
Enclosures

FIGURE 9–7, *continued.*

CHAPTER SUMMARY

Much on-the-job writing consists of various kinds of reports. Informal reports, normally no longer than a few pages, may take the form
of a memorandum that circulates within an organization or be prepared as a letter to be sent to someone outside the organization.

The *introduction* of an informal report should state the report's
subject and its purpose. In addition, the introduction may summarize
the writer's conclusions and recommendations. The *body* of an informal report should present a detailed account of the work or activity
being reported on. Any *conclusions* and *recommendations* the writer
wishes to offer should close the report.

A *trouble report,* the record of an accident, breakdown, or work
stoppage, is usually written as a memorandum. The writer should
identify the precise time and place of the trouble, any injury or property damage involved, and any expenses that resulted from the incident. The report should continue with a detailed analysis of the likely
cause of the accident or breakdown and should conclude with a statement of what is being done or what will be done to prevent a recurrence
of the incident.

An *investigative report* is, in most cases, the presentation of data
that the writer has gathered. The report, ordinarily in memorandum

format, opens with a statement of the information the writer has sought and goes on to define the extent of the investigation. The report then presents the writer's findings and an interpretation of them if such an analysis is appropriate. The report ends with conclusions and possibly recommendations.

A *progress report* informs the reader of the status of an ongoing project, frequently one that lasts a fairly long period of time. Progress reports issued at regular intervals are called *periodic reports*. By stating precisely what work has been done and what work remains to be completed, these reports can alert the reader to any necessary adjustments in scheduling, budgeting, and work assignments.

A *trip report,* generally a memorandum submitted to the writer's immediate superior following a business trip, includes the destination and the dates of the trip in the subject line. The body of the report explains why the trip was made, who was visited, and what was accomplished. Any conclusions and recommendations that the writer wishes to present would come at the end of the report.

A *test report* gives the results of a test or experiment. The test reported on is identified in the subject line. The body of the report states the purpose of the test and, if appropriate, explains the procedures used to conduct the test. The results of the test, and any interpretations that the writer considers helpful to the reader, appear in the body. The report closes with any recommendations the writer may be making as a result of the test.

EXERCISES

1. Write a *trouble report* in the form of a memo to your instructor on a recent incident or accident with which you are familiar. Be specific and detailed. If appropriate, make recommendations about how similar incidents can be prevented. Your instructor will specify report length.

2. Write one of the following *trouble reports* in the form of a memo.

   a. You are the traffic manager of a trucking company that has had four highway accidents within a one-week period. Using the following facts, write a *trouble report* to your company president, Millard Spangler.

      • Your company operates intrastate (your state).
      • The four accidents occurred in different parts of the state and on different dates (specify the date and location of each).

- Each accident has resulted in damage not only to the truck (specify the dollar amount of the damage) but to the cargo as well (specify the type of cargo and the dollar amount of the damage).
- Only one of the accidents involved another vehicle (truck swerved into a parked car when a tire blew out). Give the make and year of the damaged car and its owner's name.
- Only one of the accidents involved injury to a company driver (give the name).
- Your maintenance division traced the accidents to faulty tires, all the same brand (identify the brand), and all purchased at the same time and place (identify the place and date).
- The tires have now been replaced and your insurance company, Acme Underwriters, has brought suit against the tire manufacturer to recover damages, including lost business while the four trucks are being repaired (specify the dollar amount of the lost business).

b. You are the dietitian at a hospital. A fire has occurred in the cafeteria, which is under your supervision. Using the following information, write a *trouble report* to the hospital's administrator, Mildred Garnett.

- The chief cook, Pincus Berkowitz, came to work at 5:30 A.M. (specify the date).
- He turned on the gas jets under the grill. The pilot light had gone out, and the jets did not light.
- The cook went to find a match, neglecting to turn off the gas jets.
- He found matches, returned, and lit a match, thus igniting the accumulated gas under the grill.
- The resulting explosion destroyed the grill (estimate the damage) and injured the cook.
- The fire was put out by the security force, but the fire department was called as a precaution.
- The cook was treated by the emergency room physician, then admitted to the hospital's burn unit as a patient, with second-degree burns on his hands, face, and neck.
- He was hospitalized for three days and will be off work for four weeks.

3. You have been asked to provide information on *one* of the following topics. Gather the information pertinent to the topic and present the information in an *investigative report*. Your instructor will specify the length of the assignment.

    a. Your energy-consumption habits at home

    b. Your recommendations on the best hotel or motel in your area for out-of-town guests

    c. Which of two local garages that have serviced your car you would recommend to a friend

    d. Which of two local charities you think more worthy of support (specify from among charities in your area)

    e. Which of two or more products or services you use at home or on the job you would recommend to someone and why

4. As the medical staff secretary at a hospital, you must write a *progress report* to the director of the hospital outlining the current status of the annual reappointment of committees. Using the following facts, write the report.

    • A total of 19 committees must be staffed.

    • The Chief of Staff has telephoned each person selected to chair a committee, and you have sent each of them a follow-up letter of thanks from the Chief of Staff.

    • You have written letters to all physicians who are currently on committees but are not being reappointed, informing them of this fact.

    • You have written letters to all physicians being asked to serve on committees.

    • You expect to receive replies from those physicians declining the appointment by the 15th of the following month.

    • Once committee assignments have been completed, you will type up the membership of all committees and distribute the membership lists to the complete medical staff.

5. Write a *trip report* for a trip you have recently taken. The trip may have been a class trip, a job-related trip, or a personal trip.

6. Submit a laboratory *test report,* written in memo form, from a laboratory class that you are taking or have taken.

10

Researching Your Subject

When Tom Cabines, the production manager, received a memo from Alice Enkend, chief of the Purchasing Department, asking him how many copies of its holiday calendar a customer had commissioned the firm to print, Tom probably had the answer at his fingertips or would be able to find it after a quick look in his production-scheduling book. The *research*—or tracking down of information on the topic—that Tom might have to do would be minimal. Suppose, though, that Tom was asked to review current literature on new developments in printing or marketing techniques and to write a report on the subject. How would he go about obtaining the necessary information? For these tasks he *would* have to do some research. He'd probably go first to the library—either the company library, if the firm had one, or the public library.

This chapter will discuss the research facilities most libraries provide, and then go on to consider several other sources of information for a research report: the personal interview, the questionnaire, first-hand observation, and free or inexpensive materials from private and governmental bodies. The chapter will also discuss techniques for systematically recording your research findings (note-taking) and for furnishing proper credit to your sources.

The skills discussed in this chapter are admittedly used more in college than on the job. Nonetheless, mastery of research techniques in a general sense is valuable: you can apply the methods, if not the specifics, discussed here to a variety of situations throughout your career.

IN THE LIBRARY

The key tools of library research are reference works, such as encyclopedias, specialized dictionaries, and handbooks and manuals; the *card catalog*, which represents a listing of every book the library owns; *periodical indexes*, which furnish the names of articles in journals, magazines, and newspapers; and published *bibliographies*, which contain the names of books and other materials available. In addition, *computer retrieval facilities*, through which a researcher can compile a very specialized bibliography in seconds, are increasingly common in libraries.

Reference Works

Reference works—encyclopedias, dictionaries devoted to special subjects (such as music or medicine), handbooks, manuals, statistical sources, and atlases—are often good places to begin your research, particularly if you know little about your subject. Reference books can provide you with a brief but reliable overview of your subject, and they can also direct you to more specialized sources. Most libraries have a reference librarian who can recommend suitable reference works and assist you in locating them.

Encyclopedias are comprehensive, multivolume collections of articles, usually arranged alphabetically and often illustrated. Some encyclopedias cover a wide range of general subjects, while others specialize in a particular subject. *General encyclopedias* provide the researcher with an overview of a particular subject that can be helpful to someone new to the topic. As a source of background information, the articles in general encyclopedias usually include the terminology essential to an understanding of the subject. Some articles contain bibliographies that can lead the researcher to additional information. The two best-known general encyclopedias are:

Encyclopedia Americana. 30 vols. New York: Grolier, 1972.
Encyclopaedia Britannica. 24 vols. Chicago: Encyclopaedia Britannica, Inc., 1974.

Subject encyclopedias provide detailed information on all aspects of a particular field of knowledge. Their treatment of a subject is sufficiently thorough to make it desirable that the researcher have some background information on the subject in order to use the information to full advantage. There are many more specialized encyclopedias than there are general encyclopedias. The following list indicates the range available.

Encyclopedia of Chemical Technology. 3rd ed. New York: Interscience Publishers, 1980.

Heyel, Carl, ed. *The Encyclopedia of Management.* 3rd ed. New York: Van Nostrand Reinhold, 1982.

Hopke, William, ed. *The Encyclopedia of Careers and Vocational Guidance.* 5th ed. 2 vols. New York: Doubleday, 1982.

International Encyclopedia of the Social Sciences. 2 vols. New York: Crowell Collier and Macmillan, 1968.

McGraw-Hill Encyclopedia of Science and Technology. 4th ed. 15 vols. New York: McGraw-Hill, 1977.

Dictionaries contain definitions, arranged in alphabetical order, of a selection of the words in a language or subject. They also contain information on how words are spelled and pronounced, how they are divided into syllables, and where they originated. *General English-language dictionaries* will provide the meanings of terms from numerous fields of knowledge. For the meanings of words too specialized for a general dictionary, a subject dictionary is useful. *Subject dictionaries* define the terms used in a particular field, such as business, geography, architecture, and consumer affairs. Definitions in subject dictionaries are generally more current and complete than those found in general dictionaries.

The vocabulary section of the Writer's Guide lists a selection of desk-size English-language dictionaries. Unabridged dictionaries, which are larger and more comprehensive in their coverage, often contain basic terms from many specialized subjects. The three major up-to-date, unabridged English-language dictionaries are:

Funk & Wagnalls Standard Dictionary. New York: Funk & Wagnalls, 1980.

The Random House Dictionary of the English Language. New York: Random House, 1966.

Webster's New International Dictionary of the English Language. 3rd ed. Springfield, Mass.: Merriam, 1971.

Following is a selection of subject dictionaries.

Dictionary of the Environmental Sciences. Palo Alto, Calif.: National Press Books, 1973.

A Dictionary of Paper. 3rd ed. New York: American Pulp and Paper Association, 1965.

Dorland's Illustrated Medical Dictionary. 26th ed. Philadelphia: Saunders, 1980.

Harris, C. M., ed. *Dictionary of Architecture and Construction.* New York: McGraw-Hill, 1975.

McGraw-Hill Dictionary of Scientific and Technical Terms. 2nd ed. New York: McGraw-Hill, 1978.

Monkhouse, F. J., ed. *A Dictionary of Geography.* 2nd ed. Chicago: Aldine, 1970.

University Dictionary of Business and Finance. New York: Thomas Y. Crowell, 1972.

Handbooks and *manuals* are usually one-volume compilations of frequently used information in a particular field of knowledge. The information can include brief definitions of terms or concepts, explanations of how certain organizations function, graphs and tables that display basic numerical data, maps, and the like. Handbooks and manuals are a ready source of fundamental information about a subject, although they are usually intended for the researcher with a basic knowledge of the subject, particularly in scientific or technical fields. Every field has its own handbook or manual; the following listing shows some typical examples.

Becker, Ester, and Evelyn Anders. *The Successful Secretary's Handbook.* New York: Harper & Row, 1971.

CRC Handbook of Chemistry and Physics. Cleveland, Ohio: Chemical Rubber Company. Annual.

Environment Regulation Handbook. New York: Special Studies Division of Environment Information Center, 1973.

Merritt, F. S., ed. *Building Construction Handbook.* 4th ed. New York: McGraw-Hill, 1981.

Russell, M. M. *The Blue Book of Occupational Education.* New York: CCM Information Corp., 1971.

U.S. Government Manual. Washington, D.C.: Government Printing Office. Annual.

Statistical sources are collections of numerical data. They are the best source for such information as the height of the Washington Monument; the population of Boise, Idaho; the cost-of-living in Aspen, Colorado; and the annual number of motorcycle fatalities in the United States. The answers to many statistical reference questions can be found in almanacs and encyclopedias. However, for answers to more difficult or comprehensive questions, you may need to consult works devoted exclusively to statistical data, a selection of which follows:

American Statistics Index. Washington, D.C.: Congressional Information Service, 1978 to date. Monthly, quarterly, and annual supplements.

The *Statistics Index* lists all statistical publications issued by agencies of the United States government. The publications cited include periodicals, reports, special surveys, and pamphlets.

> Bureau of the Census. *County and City Data Book.* Washington, D.C.: Government Printing Office, 1952 to date. Issued at irregular intervals.

The *Data Book* includes a variety of data from cities, counties, congressional districts, metropolitan areas, and the like. The information, arranged by geographic and political areas, covers such topics as climate, dwellings, population characteristics, school districts, employment, and city finances.

> Bureau of the Census. *Statistical Abstract of the United States.* Washington, D.C.: Government Printing Office, 1879 to date. Annual.

The *Statistical Abstract* includes statistics on social, political, and economic conditions in the United States. Compiled by the Bureau of the Census, the data include vital statistics and cover broad topics like population, education, and public land. Some state and regional data are given.

An *atlas* is a collection of maps. Atlases are classified into two broad categories based on the type of information they present—general maps that represent physical and political boundaries, and thematic maps that represent a special subject, such as climate, population, natural resources, or agricultural products. Listed below are several well-known general atlases.

> *Hammond Medallion World Atlas.* New Census ed. Maplewood, N.J.: C. S. Hammond, 1971.
> *National Geographic Atlas of the World.* 5th ed. Washington, D.C.: National Geographic Society, 1981.
> *Rand McNally Cosmopolitan World Atlas.* Census ed. Chicago: Rand McNally, 1981.
> *The Times Atlas of the World.* Revised ed. Boston: Houghton Mifflin, 1980.

The following are thematic atlases.

> Department of Agriculture. *Atlas of United States Trees.* Washington, D.C.: Government Printing Office, 1971.

Environmental Science Services Administration. *Climatic Atlas of the United States.* Washington, D.C.: Government Printing Office, 1968.

Card Catalog

A *card catalog* is a listing of all the books a library owns. A card catalog can furnish the answers to some questions that are vital to you as a researcher: Does the library own a particular book by a particular author? What books, if any, on a specific subject does the library own? Where in the library is a given book located?

For most books, there are three cards on file in the catalog: an *author card* (Figure 10–1), a *title card* (Figure 10–2), and a *subject card* (Figure 10–3). Every card is arranged in the catalog alphabetically. Thus, an author card appears under the author's last name; a title card is alphabetized by the first important word in the title (*A, An,* and *The* at the beginning of a title are ignored in alphabetizing); and a subject card is filed alphabetically by the first word of the subject heading. All three types of cards contain the book's "vital statistics": author's name; title; date and place of publication; publisher's name; number of pages; the term *illus., bibliography,* or *index* if the book has illustrations, bibliography, or index; the size of the book in centimeters; the major subjects the book covers; and, sometimes, additional information.

If you want to locate a book whose title or author you know, you can look in the card catalog for the book under either its title or its author's name. If, on the other hand, you are trying to find a book on a particular subject and do not have a title or an author in

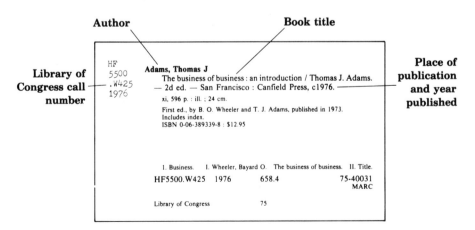

FIGURE 10–1. Author card.

Title

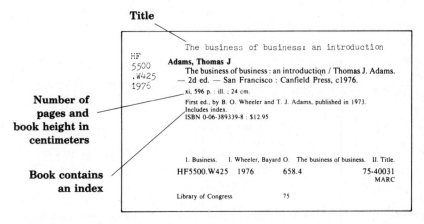

FIGURE 10–2. Title card.

mind, you can look through the card catalog for the subject card or
cards that correspond to the topic you are researching. For example,
if you were trying to locate information on the plant nursery business,
you would look at the cards in back of the letter *N* in the card catalog
and go alphabetically through the *N*'s until you reached the subject
cards under the heading *Nurseries.* Included under that broad heading
would be a number of specific topics. The books under one subject
heading are arranged alphabetically by authors' last names. The sample card in Figure 10–3 refers to a report on the nursery business in
Texas.

Some subject cards do not list a particular book but, instead, provide "see also" subject headings that the researcher may want to consult in tracking down additional books (Figure 10–4).

FIGURE 10–3. Subject card.

```
      Florida.  State Board of Conservation.
      Marine Laboratory, St. Petersburg.

      see also

      Florida Board of Conservation Marine Research
      Laboratory.
```

FIGURE 10–4. "See also" subject card.

A *call number,* which indicates where on the shelves (or stacks) a book can be found, is located in the upper-left-hand corner of all three cards. The same call number normally appears on the lower portion of the spine of the book itself. Libraries use one or both of two systems of *classification*—that is, the system under which every book is assigned an identifying call number: the older system is the Dewey Decimal System; the newer system is the Library of Congress System. Check with the librarian about which system or systems your library uses.

You can frequently tell from a book's title what the book is about. Another factor to take into account as you decide whether to include a particular book in your research is the author's reputation: Is the writer considered an authority in the field? Has the author written other, well-thought-of books in the field or in a related field? You might check in the card catalog under the author's name to see what other books, if any, the author has written. And you might ask a librarian, an instructor, or someone you know who is familiar with the subject area whether the author has an established reputation in the field. Still another guide in determining whether the book will be useful to you in your research is the book itself (if necessary, you can examine the book in the library before deciding whether to use it). Does the book have an index? Indexes are indispensable in tracking down specific topics within a book. Does the book have informative diagrams, charts, tables, and so on? Does the book have a comprehensive bibliography that you can use in locating additional material

QA
76.5
.K382

Kemeny, John G.

Man and the Computer
N.Y. : Scribner, 1972

FIGURE 10–5. Bibliography card—book.

for your research? Is the book reasonably up to date? Timeliness is especially important in a fast-changing field like computer technology.

For any book that you decide to include in your research, prepare a three- by five-inch note card, with the following information on it: the call number (having the call number handy will enable you to locate the book on the shelves); the author (if the "author" is an organization, indicate that fact); the city of publication; the publisher's name; and the year of publication. When you are ready to prepare a bibliography for your research report, you can do so easily from the information you have recorded on these cards (known as *bibliography cards*). See Figure 10–5 for a bibliography card for a book and Figure 10–6 for a bibliography card for an article in a periodical. Having the author's

Arcuri, A. F.

"Police, Lawyers, and Judges:
Implacable Allies — Survey of
New Jersey Policemen,"
Intellect, 104 (April 1976), 517-519

FIGURE 10–6. Bibliography card—periodical.

last name near the upper-left-hand corner of the card will assist you in preparing the bibliography, in which the titles of the books and articles you used are arranged alphabetically according to the authors' last names.

Periodical Indexes and Bibliographies

Periodical indexes and bibliographies are lists of journal articles and books. *Periodical indexes* are devoted specifically to journal, magazine, and newspaper articles (the term *periodical* is applied to publications that are issued at regular intervals—daily, weekly, monthly, and so on). *Bibliographies* list books, periodicals, and other research materials published in a particular subject area, such as business, engineering, medicine, the humanities, or the social sciences.

After you have selected the periodical indexes and bibliographies that deal with your subject, consult the instructions in the front of the volume or in the first volume of a series (see Figure 10–7). There you will find a key to the abbreviations and symbols used in the volume and an explanation of the way information is arranged in the books, as well as a listing of the specific subjects covered and, for periodical indexes, a listing of the newspapers, magazines, and journals that have been included in the work.

Some of the bibliographies and indexes that you are likely to find useful are the following.

Applied Science & Technology Index (formerly *Industrial Arts Index*), 1913——. (Alphabetical subject listing of articles from 50,000 periodicals; issued monthly)

Bibliographic Index: A Cumulative Bibliography of Bibliographies, 1937——. (Subject list of bibliographies that appear separately or in books; issued three times a year)

Bibliography of Agriculture, 1942——. (Listing of literature covering agriculture and allied subjects; issued monthly)

Bibliography and Index to Geology, 1969——. (Bibliography of world literature dealing with the earth sciences; entries are arranged within 29 subject areas; issued monthly)

Biological and Agricultural Index, 1964——. (Alphabetical subject listing of biological and agricultural periodicals; issued monthly)

Business Periodicals Index, 1958——. (Alphabetically arranged by subject and title; issued monthly)

Cumulative Index of the National Industrial Conference Board Publications, 1962——. (Subject index of publications of interest to commerce and industrial managers; issued annually)

Cumulative Index to Nursing Literature, 1965——. (Subject and author index to nursing journals)

Engineering Index, 1906——. (Alphabetically arranged by subject; issued monthly)

Essay and General Literature Index, 1900——. (Semiannual index to information on all subjects in collections of articles; organized by subject, but sometimes by title)

Government Reports Index (formerly *U.S. Government Research and Development Reports*), 1965——. (A semimonthly index of reports arranged by subject, author, and report number)

Index of Labor Union Periodicals, 1960——. (Monthly index of articles from labor union periodicals)

Index of Supermarket Articles, 1963——. (Subject index of articles on supermarkets and the food industry)

Monthly Catalog of U.S. Government Publications, 1895——. (Lists unclassified publications of all federal agencies by subject, author, and report number)

New York Times Index, 1851——. (Alphabetically arranged listing of subjects covered in *New York Times* articles; issued bimonthly)

Readers' Guide to Periodical Literature, 1900——. (Monthly index of general U.S. periodicals, arranged alphabetically by subject)

Social Sciences Index, 1974——. (Alphabetical subject and author listing of social science periodicals; issued quarterly)

Wall Street Journal Index, 1958——. (Monthly index of business and financial news covered in the *Journal*)

Typical of specialized indexes is the *Applied Science & Technology Index*. This index lists, by subject, articles in the fields of aeronautics and space science, chemistry, computer technology and applications, the construction industry, energy resources and research, engineering, fire and fire prevention, food and the food industry, geology, machinery, mathematics, metallurgy, minerology, oceanography, petroleum and gas research, physics, plastics technology, the textile industry, transportation, and other industrial and mechanical arts. In addition, the index covers several branches of engineering—chemical, civil, electrical and telecommunication, environmental, industrial, mechanical, mining, and nuclear. Figure 10–7 shows the explanation that appears at the front of the index (following that page are a key to the abbreviations of journal titles and a listing of all periodicals indexed). Figure

PREFATORY NOTE

The APPLIED SCIENCE & TECHNOLOGY INDEX is a cumulative index to English language periodicals. The main body of the Index consists of subject entries to periodical articles arranged in one alphabet. In addition there is an author listing of citations to book reviews, following the main body of the Index.

Subject fields indexed include aeronautics and space science, chemistry, computer technology and applications, construction industry, energy resources and research, engineering, fire and fire prevention, food and food industry, geology, machinery, mathematics, metallurgy, mineralogy, oceanography, petroleum and gas, physics, plastics, textile industry and fabrics, transportation and other industrial and mechanical arts.

The following engineering disciplines are covered: chemical, civil, electric and telecommunications, environmental, industrial, mining, mechanical, and nuclear.

The Committee on Wilson Indexes of the American Library Association's Reference and Adult Services Division advises the publisher on indexing and editorial policy by means of in-depth contents studies conducted at intervals of several years. The Committee as part of its study prepares a list of periodicals, representative of all subject areas included in the Index, for consideration by the subscribers.

Selection of periodicals for indexing from this list is accomplished by subscriber vote. In voting their preferences subscribers are asked to place primary emphasis on the reference value of the periodicals under consideration. They are also asked to give particular consideration to subject balance in order to insure that no important field be overlooked in proportion to overall index coverage.

While the responsibility for all indexing and editorial decisions rests with The H. W. Wilson Company, every effort is made by the Company to follow the recommendations of the Committee and the subscribers to a given periodical index.

Suggestions for addition or deletion of titles should be brought to the attention of The H. W. Wilson Company, 950 University Avenue, Bronx, N. Y. 10452.

May 1983. Vol. 71. No. 5.

APPLIED SCIENCE & TECHNOLOGY INDEX (ISSN 0003-6986) is published monthly except July, with a bound cumulation each year. Sold only on the service basis; apply to publisher for rates. Copyright © 1983 by The H. W. Wilson Company, 950 University Avenue, Bronx, N.Y. 10452. All rights reserved. No part of this work may be reproduced or copied in any form or by any means, including but not restricted to graphic, electronic, or mechanical—for example, photocopying, recording, taping, or information and retrieval systems—without the express written permission of the Publisher. Second-class postage paid at Bronx, N.Y. Printed in U.S.A.

FIGURE 10–7. Prefatory note to the *Applied Science & Technology Index.*

ACADEMIC freedom
    Academe and industry debate partnership. B. J.
    Culliton. Science 219:150-1 Ja 14 '83
    Academic freedom and the classified information
    system. R. A. Rosenbaum and others. Science
    219:257-9 Ja 21 '83
ACCELERATORS (Particles)
    CERN reports first vector boson evidence. A. L.
    Robinson. Science 219:480 F 4 '83
    Laser-driven electron-positron colliders. diags
    Phys Today 36:19-21 F '83
    Proposing the office of Pan American collabora-
    tion [guest editorial] L. M. Lederman. Phys
    Today 35:9+ Ag '82; Discussion. 36:107-8 F '83

                Numerical control
    Surface structure of silicon carbide irradiated
    with helium ions with monoenergy and contin-
    uous energy distributions. S. Miyagawa and
    others. bibl il diag J Appl Phys 53:8697-705 D
    '82
ACCIDENTS
    See also
    Automobile accidents
    Burns and scalds
    Safety education
ACCIDENTS, Industrial
    See also
    Burns and scalds
    Safety education

FIGURE 10–8. Sample column from the *Applied Science & Technology Index*.

10–8 shows part of a column in the index proper. In the first entry, for example, the index refers to a special report on food packaging that appeared in Volume 28 of the periodical *Package Engineering* on pages 63 through 79. The issue was published in January 1983; the report is illustrated with diagrams. If this article seemed useful to your research, you would prepare a three- by five-inch note card recording this information.

    After completing your search for periodical articles, locate the necessary periodical volumes in the stacks. Many libraries shelve periodicals alphabetically by title in a separate section of the library. If the periodicals you need are not in your library, you can submit an interlibrary loan request. This service permits you to borrow books and photocopied periodical articles from other libraries that have the materials you need in their collections. Consult your librarian for specific details of the system.

Computerized Information Retrieval

    Many libraries—particularly those at large universities—now offer a computer service for the compilation of bibliographies. Computer information retrieval makes use of one or more of the several hundred data bases that can be drawn on in searches for pertinent articles on a given subject. Libraries lease the data base, a file that can be read by a computer, and communicate with the file through a terminal. The search is conducted by entering key words and phrases on the terminal to establish the boundaries of the search. Libraries that provide this service employ a librarian skilled in the strategies that selecting key words involves: the researcher goes to the librarian and explains his or her problem, the librarian determines the key words that will best represent the researcher's area of study and enters them on the terminal, and the screen indicates how many items are available. If the researcher wishes to expand or limit the number of available items, a different arrangement of key words is entered.

Suppose, for example, that you were researching the role of supertankers in the American merchant fleet. Your librarian might begin the search with the key words "cargo ships," and read on the terminal screen that 874 articles pertain to that broad subject. You do not wish to wade through this many articles, so the librarian limits the search by entering the key words "American" and "oil." The revised number is pared down to 211 articles—still too many for your purposes. You decide that you are really only interested in articles published during the past year. When this limitation is entered, the number of pertinent articles is reduced to a manageable 14. You then request a printout of a bibliography of the 14 items.

Most libraries that provide computerized information retrieval charge for the service. Nonetheless, the speed, accuracy, and timeliness of computerized retrieval make it a valuable tool. In time, virtually all libraries should have access to at least one, if not several, data bases. In view of the profusion of material being written, computerized retrieval is becoming by far the most practical means for keeping track of bibliographic information.

TAKING NOTES

The purpose of taking notes is to condense and record information from the books and articles you have chosen for your research. The notes you take will furnish much of the material for your outline and final written work.

For your notes, you may use either three- by five-inch or four- by six-inch cards—but whichever you choose, stick to that size, because when you arrange the cards by topic later on, you may have trouble handling cards of two different sizes. You may well find that the larger-size card is handier: it provides more room for the information and is readily distinguishable from the three- by five-inch bibliography cards. Make one note per card, on one side of the card only; use ink, since pencil tends to smudge. Near the bottom of each card, identify the source of the information: put in the author's last name (include first name or initials if you have two authors with the same last name) and the page number or numbers on which the material appears in the original source. If you have consulted more than one book or article by an author, include the title as well; for long titles, you may use a shortened form to save space on the card. And be sure to put information from only one source on each card.

As you are taking notes, it's a good idea to make a list of the topics that you will be covering in your research. Then, on the upper-left-hand corner of each note card, enter the appropriate identifying topic (these are sometimes called "slugs"). When you arrange the cards by topic in preparation for working up an outline, you can use the "slugs" as a guide in organizing your material.

Notes can be gathered in one of three ways. The information can be quoted word for word from the original source, as a *direct quotation;* it can be *paraphrased,* or restated in the researcher's own words; or it can be *summarized,* or stated by the researcher in a highly condensed form.

Quoting Directly

A *direct quotation* is an exact, word-for-word copy of an original source. Such quotations, which can be of a word, of a phrase, of a sentence, or, occasionally, of a paragraph, should be used sparingly and chosen carefully. A direct quotation is appropriate when the wording of the original source will support a point you are making, or when you feel that your reader will gain some insight from a particularly well-expressed passage. In both instances, the quoted material should be fairly brief. In addition, such material as policy statements, laws, and mathematical and scientific formulas should ordinarily be quoted exactly. Figure 10–9 shows a note card with a direct quotation on it.

There are two ways of presenting direct quotations. If the quotation you have chosen occupies more than four lines of typed copy, it should be set off from your text. Set-off quotations are usually separated from the text by a double-space; every line of the quotation is indented ten spaces from the left margin; the quotation is single-spaced; and quotation marks are not needed. It is a good idea to introduce the quotation smoothly—that is, to tell the reader, in your own words, what significance the quotation has for your report.

```
The county Motor Vehicles Department has strict
rules that govern driving during snow emergencies:
```

Snow emergency is declared when snow or ice
creates a road hazard. Under such circumstances driving is prohibited on all roads
designated "emergency snow route" except
when vehicles are equipped with snow tires
or chains. Parking on these designated road-
ways is prohibited.[1]

Motorists who get stuck on a snow emergency route
without chains are subject to a $50 fine.

File Units

"File units represent a class of components
which should be viewed in terms of more
than one operation, since they generally
provide the capability not only of input
and output, but of some degree of
indexing."
Kemeny, Man and the Computer, p. 52.

FIGURE 10–9. Note card—direct quotation.

The following note, either at the bottom of the page or at the end of
the paper, would identify the source of the quotation (see the discussion
of documentation):

[1]Citizen's Guide to Public Services in Mont-
gomery County, Maryland. (Rockville, Md.: Mont-
gomery County, 1971), p. 12.

The second kind of direct quotation, which takes up four lines
of typed copy or less, is run-in with the text—it is not set off. It is
enclosed in quotation marks.

When you are planning your remodeling project,
don't forget that residential construction requires a building permit. To obtain a building
permit in our area, contact the Department of In-

```
spections and Licenses. "An applicant must submit
an application in duplicate, two sets of blue-
prints, three plot plans drawn to scale, and an
application for a driveway apron."² Once the ap-
plication has been obtained, it must be posted at
the project site.
```

Again, a note would identify the source.

```
²Citizen's Guide to Public Services, p. 15.
```

There may be times when you want to quote directly from only part of a passage. Suppose, for example, you saw a sentence like the following in a company house organ.

```
SpeedMail, Incorporated, just hired two junior-
level copywriters, who will report to the adver-
tising manager, and a direct-mail assistant, who
will be working closely with the director of pro-
motion.
```

If you wanted to quote only the portion of the sentence that pertains to the direct-mail assistant, you would omit the text relating to the copywriters. When you omit material that falls *within a quoted passage,* you insert *three spaced dots* (called *ellipses*) to indicate where the omission occurs.

```
SpeedMail, Incorporated, just hired . . . a di-
rect-mail assistant, who will be working closely
with the director of promotion.
```

If, on the other hand, you intended to quote the portion of the sentence that deals with the copywriters, you would delete the reference to the direct-mail aide. To indicate the omission of material that comes *at the end of a quoted passage,* you place *a period followed by three spaced dots* after the last quoted word.

```
SpeedMail, Incorporated, just hired two junior-
level copywriters, who will report to the adver-
tising manager. . . .
```

Paraphrasing

A *paraphrase* of a written passage is a restatement of the essential ideas of the passage in the researcher's own words. Because a paraphrase does not quote the source word for word, quotation marks are not necessary. When you use paraphrased material in your own work, however, you must credit the source in a footnote.

As you are getting ready to write a paraphrase, you may find it helpful, after you've read the passage, to put it aside for a moment while you decide how to word the paraphrase; this brief period of reflection will give you a chance both to make sure that you understand the writer's message and to prepare your own version of it. When you start to write, pick up the original and refer to it. Check to be certain that you include every important point in the original that is relevant to your topic.

The passage should be paraphrased, of course, according to your topic and the scope of your written work; if the source contains more information than is pertinent to your subject, paraphrase only the material that relates to your purpose in writing. As an example, consider the following passage and the two paraphrases of it.

> Another industrial application of computers lies in the numerical control of machine tools. A great many parts of machines are produced by either milling or routing, processes in which a cutting tool moves so as to cut some contoured shape out of sheet metal or heavier stock. In conventional methods this demands the constant attention of a skilled machine operator, particularly if the contour to be formed is irregularly curved. Under the control of a computer the cutter can be made to move in any desired path, and it is in principle no more difficult to produce "sculptured" shapes bounded by complex curved surfaces than it is to produce objects with flat faces. The numerical control of machine tools has enjoyed an extraordinary success because it guarantees the reliability and reproducibility of even the most elaborate shapes. The spoilage due to human error is reduced to the vanishing point, and many parts are now practicable that would be prohibitively expensive to produce if a human operator had to monitor the settings of the machine.[1]

If your purpose in writing were to compare human efficiency on the job with that of a machine, you might paraphrase the passage as in Figure 10–10. If your purpose in writing were to examine the industrial application of computers, your paraphrase might read as in Figure 10–11.

[1] Steven Anson Coons, "The Uses of Computers in Technology," in *Information, A Scientific American Book* (San Francisco: W. H. Freeman, 1966), p. 134.

Computer adjusts machines

A skilled machinist must continually monitor machine tools, especially when contoured or sculptured parts are made. Computer-controlled machines produce the same parts without waste. For complex-shaped parts, the computer adjusts machines more cheaply than a machinist can.

Coons, p. 134.

FIGURE 10-10. Note card—paraphrase I.

Summarizing

A *summary* is a highly condensed version, in the researcher's own words, of an original passage. Summary notes present only the essential ideas or conclusions of the original. As such, they are considerably shorter than paraphrases of the same passage. As with directly quoted and paraphrased material, the source of summarized information must be credited in a footnote.

Machined parts

Computers direct machine tools to cut complex shapes from metals and other materials. Contoured objects are as easily produced as flat objects, and with greater efficiency and less expense than those produced by a skilled machinist. Computer-controlled machines now produce complex parts that were too expensive to produce before.

Coons, p. 134.

FIGURE 10-11. Note card—paraphrase II.

Why fuels burn

The chemical makeup of a substance determines whether it's flammable. Carbon and hydrogen are highly flammable elements, so material made up largely of these elements, called hydrocarbons, are good fuels. Substances made up of carbon, hydrogen, and oxygen, with hydrogen and oxygen in the same proportion as they are in water, are also flammable; they're called carbohydrates. Heat is required before any fuel will burn.

Meidl, pp. 8-9.

FIGURE 10–12. Note card—summary.

Figure 10–12 shows a note card summary of the following passage.

Now that we have learned something about the nature of elements and molecules, what are fuels? Fuels are those substances that will burn when heat is applied to them. Some elements, in themselves, are fuels. Carbon, hydrogen, sulfur, magnesium, titanium and some other metals are examples of elements that can burn. Coal, charcoal, and coke, for example, are almost pure carbon; hydrogen, another element, is a highly flammable gas. But the most familiar combustible materials are not pure elements; they are compounds and mixtures.

Wood, paper and grass are principally composed of molecules of cellulose, a flammable substance. If we examine the chemical makeup of this compound, we will discover what elements form the basic fuels in most solid materials. The cellulose molecule contains twenty-one atoms: six carbons, ten hydrogens and five oxygen atoms: $C_6H_{10}O_5$. Since oxygen is not flammable (see Oxygen, below), it follows that the carbon and hydrogen found in most common combustible solids are the elements that burn. This conclusion becomes even stronger when we look at common flammable liquids. Gasoline, kerosene, fuel oils and other petroleum compounds are composed of only carbon and hydrogen atoms, in varying amounts. These compounds, called Hydrocarbons (hydrogen + carbon), will all burn.

Other flammable compounds are composed of carbon, hydrogen, and oxygen atoms in a fixed ratio, making it appear as if there is a water molecule attached to each carbon atom. A good example is glucose, a common sugar, which has the formula $C_6H_{12}O_6$. Chemists call this type of molecule a "hydrated (watered) carbon," or carbohydrate. Carbohydrates also burn, but are not to be confused with hydrocarbons.

Carbon and hydrogen are only two of the elements which will burn. But, since most common flammable materials contain a combination of carbon and hydrogen fuels, we will limit our discussion of combustion to them at this point.

Fuel, as we have seen, is only one side of the fire triangle. Before it will burn, any fuel requires the addition of heat, another side of the triangle.[2]

Take summary notes to remind yourself of the substance of a research source. Summarized information can also be useful to your reader, because it condenses passages that give more details than the reader needs.

PLAGIARISM

To use someone else's exact words or original ideas in your writing without giving credit in a footnote reference is known as *plagiarism.* Plagiarism is illegal; in class or on the job it may be grounds for dismissal. Whether the words and ideas come from a published source, or from a fellow student's work, plagiarism is a form of theft for which you can be held accountable.

You may present the words and ideas of another person as long as you give appropriate credit by footnoting the passage. Ideas and facts considered "common knowledge" need not be cited in a footnote. The dates and names of historical events, and many kinds of scientific and statistical information, are common knowledge. Specific examples of common knowledge include the temperature at which water boils, the year the Constitution was ratified, the number of passengers a 747 jetliner can hold, and the area in square miles that Dallas, Texas, occupies.

INTERVIEWING

If you need information that is not readily available in print, you may be able to do some of your research by interviewing someone who is an expert on the subject. If, for instance, your subject is nursing-home care in your community, the logical experts to interview would

[2] James H. Meidl, *Flammable Hazardous Materials* (Beverly Hills, Calif.: Glencoe Press, 1970), pp. 8–9.

be the directors of several local nursing homes. Sources that can help you decide whom to interview—and how to get in touch with them—include membership lists of professional societies (the membership rolls of large professional organizations are available in many libraries), the yellow pages of the local telephone book, and a firm or organization in the area whose staff includes experts on your subject.

Once you have selected the person or persons you would like to interview, use the following guidelines to help you to obtain the information you need with a minimum of time and trouble for your interviewee and for yourself.

Before the Interview

Always request an interview in advance and make an appointment. You can do so either by telephone or by letter, although a letter may sometimes take too long to permit you to meet a deadline. When you request the interview, explain who you are, what kind of information you are seeking, and why you have chosen to interview this particular expert. Also state that you will schedule the interview at the convenience of the interviewee. Gather some background information about the person and his or her occupation before the interview. You need not exhaust all information sources, of course; let common sense be your guide. How much time will you have before the interview? Is the information difficult to obtain? Be aware, however, that the more preparation you put into an interview, the more you will get out of it.

Your first contact with the interviewee is important because it gives you the opportunity to tell the expert exactly what kind of information you are seeking and allows the interviewee time to prepare for the interview. Some people are made nervous by a tape recorder, so if you would like to use one during the interview, request permission at this point. If the interviewee refuses permission, plan to bring a note pad instead. If you intend to bring a tape recorder, check to see that it's in good working order. However, even a tape recorder that works well can malfunction unexpectedly. Prepare for the worst; bring a writing pad and several pens or pencils to the interview as a backup.

After you have made the appointment, prepare a list of specific questions, based on your writing purpose, that you will ask. Avoid the tendency of the beginning interviewer to ask general rather than specific questions. Analyze your questions to be certain that they are direct and to the point. "Tell me about the kinds of people admitted to Hillcrest Nursing Home" is too broad a request. You will probably get a rambling, general answer in reply. Productive questions would be "What is the average age of persons who come to Hillcrest?" "Are the majority from this vicinity?" "What's the ratio of men to women?" Such queries are much easier to answer than general questions.

Conducting the Interview

Because an interview represents an imposition on someone's time—usually someone who is busy—arrive promptly at the appointed time.

After you arrive and introduce yourself, a few minutes of informal conversation will help both you and the interviewee to relax. But don't drag this period out; an interview is largely straightforward question and response.

During the interview, use the following guidelines.

1. Be pleasant but purposeful. The interviewee knows you are there to get information, so don't be timid about asking your questions. And don't confuse an elementary question on a subject with an ignorant question. If you are too timid, you will go away empty-handed.

2. Refer to the list of questions you prepared in advance, and follow them—don't let yourself become sidetracked. Avoid being rigid, however; if you realize that a prepared question is no longer suitable, go on to the next question.

3. Let the interviewee do most of the talking. Don't try to impress the interviewee with your knowledge of the subject on which he or she is the expert. And don't rebut every point the interviewee makes; after all, you are there to get information, not to debate.

4. Some answers prompt follow-up questions; ask them. "Mr. Bolchalk, has the automated mail-handling system been as efficient as originally planned?" If the answer is no, you can follow up with "Why?" or "In what specific areas has the system failed?" If the answer is yes, ask details about the differences between the old and the new systems.

5. If the interviewee gets off the subject, be ready with a specific question to direct the conversation back on the track. Your prepared list of questions will help.

6. Take only the notes you really need. Obviously, you cannot write down every word of the interview, so concentrate on the important ideas and the key facts and figures. You will be the best judge of how pertinent an idea or a statistic is. If the interviewee is talking too fast, ask him or her to speak more

slowly. Anyone who wants to be quoted accurately will be glad to. And if you need a clarification of the facts, politely ask the speaker to explain a point.

7. As the interview is reaching a close, take a few minutes to skim your notes. If you feel there is time, ask for a clarification of anything that is still ambiguous. But be careful not to overstay your welcome.

8. If you use a tape recorder, do not be lulled into a feeling that all your work is being done for you and thereby neglect to ask crucial questions.

After the Interview

As soon as possible after the interview, go over your notes again and fill in any material that is obviously missing. This is the time to summarize the speaker's remarks. Then type or write out the notes in complete sentences. After writing out your notes, select the important information you need and transfer it to your note cards. Observe the same guidelines for creating interview note cards that you used for creating library-research cards. Provide a topic "slug" for each card.

USING A QUESTIONNAIRE

A *questionnaire*—a series of questions on a particular topic, sent out to a number of people—is a sort of interview on paper. It has several advantages over the personal interview, and several disadvantages. A questionnaire allows you to test the thinking of many more people than personal interviews would. It enables you to obtain responses from people in different parts of the country. Even people who live near you may be easier to reach by mail than in person. Those responding to a questionnaire do not face the constant pressure posed by someone jotting down their every word—a fact that could result in more thoughtful answers from questionnaire respondents. And the questionnaire reduces the possibility that the interviewer might influence an answer by tone of voice or facial expression. Finally, the cost of a questionnaire is lower than the cost of numerous personal interviews.

Questionnaires have drawbacks too. People who have strong opinions on a subject are more likely to respond to a questionnaire than those who do not. This factor could slant the results. An interviewer can follow up on an answer with a pertinent question; at best, a questionnaire can be designed to let one question lead logically to another. Furthermore, mailing a batch of questionnaires and waiting for replies take considerably longer than a personal interview does.

The advantages of a questionnaire will work in your favor only if the questionnaire is properly designed. Your goal should be to obtain as much information as possible from your recipients with as little effort on their part as possible. The first rule to follow is to keep the questionnaire brief. The longer the questionnaire is, the less likely the recipient will be to complete and return it. Next, the questions should be easy to understand. A confusing question will yield confusing results, whereas a carefully worded question will be easy to answer. Ideally, questions should be answerable with a "yes" or "no."

```
Would you be willing to work a four-day workweek,
ten hours a day, with every Friday off?

    Yes _____

    No _____

    No opinion _____
```

When it is not possible to phrase questions in such a straightforward style, provide an appropriate range of answers.

```
How many hours of overtime would you be willing to
work each week?

    4 hours _____      10 hours _____

    6 hours _____      More than 10 hours _____

    8 hours _____      No overtime _____
```

And questions should be neutral; they shouldn't be worded in such a way as to lead the respondent to give a particular response.

When preparing your questions, remember that you must eventually tabulate the answers; therefore, try to formulate questions whose answers can be readily computed. The easiest questions to tabulate are those for which the recipient does not have to compose an answer. And questions that require a comment for an answer take time to think about and write. As a result, they lessen your chances of obtaining a response. They are also difficult to interpret. Questionnaires should include a section for additional comments, though, where recipients may clarify their overall attitude toward the subject. If the information will be of value in interpreting the answers, include questions about the recipient's age, education, occupation, and so on. Include your name, your address, the purpose of the questionnaire, and the date by which an answer is needed.

A questionnaire sent by mail must be accompanied by a letter explaining who you are, what purpose the questionnaire will serve, how the questionnaire will be used, and the date by which you would like to receive a reply. If the information provided will be kept confidential, say so in the letter. If the recipient's identity will not be disclosed, state this in the letter too.

Selecting the proper recipients for your questionnaire may be easy or difficult, depending on your needs. If you want to survey the opinions of all the employees in a small shop or a laboratory, you simply send each worker a questionnaire. To survey the members of a club or a professional society, you would mail questionnaires to those who are on a membership list. But to survey the opinions of large groups in the general population—for example, all medical technologists working in private laboratories, or all independent garage owners—is not so easy. Since you cannot include everybody in your survey, you would have to choose a representative cross-section. How would you go about selecting such a cross-section, and how large should such a sample be? Methods of large-scale sampling are beyond the scope of this text. The best sources of information on sampling techniques are research and statistics texts.

The sample questionnaire in Figure 10–13 was sent to employees

October 18, 19--

To: All Company Employees

From: Nelson Barrett, Director *NB*
       Personnel Department

Subject: Review of Flexible Working Hours
          Program

Please complete and return the attached questionnaire regarding Luxwear Corporation's trial program of flexible working hours. Your answers will help my staff and me to decide whether the program is worthwhile enough to continue permanently.

Return the completed questionnaire to Ken Rose, Mail Code 12B, by October 28. Your sig-

FIGURE 10–13. Sample questionnaire.

nature on the questionnaire is not necessary.
Feel free to raise additional issues pertaining to the program. All responses will be
given consideration.

If you want to discuss any item in the questionnaire, call Pam Peters in the Personnel
Department at extension 8812.

1. What kind of position do you occupy?

      Supervisory _____

      Nonsupervisory _____

2. Indicate to the nearest quarter of an hour
   your starting time under flexitime.

    7 A.M. _____   8:15 A.M. _____

    7:15 A.M. _____   8:30 A.M. _____

    7:30 A.M. _____   8:45 A.M. _____

    7:45 A.M. _____   9 A.M. _____

    8 A.M. _____   Other, specify _____

3. Where do you live?

    Talbot County _____ Greene County _____

    Montgomery
    County _____   Other, specify _____

4. How do you usually travel to work?

    Drive alone _____   Walk _____

    Taxi _____   Bus _____

    Train _____   Motorcycle _____

    Car pool _____   Other, specify _____

    Bicycle _____

5. Has flexitime affected your commuting
   time?

FIGURE 10–13, *continued.*

Increase: Approx. number of minutes _____ .

Decrease: Approx. number of minutes _____ .

No change _____

6. If you drive alone or in a car pool, has
flexitime increased or decreased the
amount of time it takes you to find a
parking space?

Increased _____   Decreased _____

No change _____

7. Has flexitime had an effect on your productivity?

a. Quality of work

Increase _____   Decrease _____

No change _____

b. Accuracy of work

Increase _____   Decrease _____

No change _____

c. Quiet time for uninterrupted work

Increase _____   Decrease _____

No change _____

8. Have you had difficulty getting in touch
with employees who are on different work
schedules from yours?

Yes _____   No _____

9. Have you had trouble scheduling meetings
within flexible starting and quitting
times?

Yes _____   No _____

FIGURE 10–13, *continued.*

10. Has flexitime affected the way you feel about your job?

Feel better about   Feel worse about
job   job

Slightly _____   Slightly _____

Considerably _____   Considerably _____

No change _____

11. How important is it for you to have flexi- bility in your working hours?

Very _____   Not very _____

Somewhat _____   Not at all _____

12. Has flexitime allowed you more time to be with your family?

Yes _____   No _____

13. If you are responsible for the care of a young child or children, has flexitime made it easier or more difficult for you to obtain babysitting or day-care ser- vices?

Easier _____   More difficult _____

No change _____

14. Do you recommend that the flexitime pro- gram be made permanent?

Yes _____   No _____

15. Do you have suggestions for major changes in the program?

Yes (please specify)   No _____

THANK YOU FOR YOUR ASSISTANCE

FIGURE 10–13, *continued.*

in a large organization who had participated in a six-month program of flexible working hours. Under the program, employees worked a forty-hour, five-day week, with flexible starting and quitting times. Employees could start the work day between 7 and 9 A.M. and leave between 3:30 and 6:30 P.M., provided that they worked a total of eight hours each day and took a one-half-hour lunch period midway through the day.

OTHER SOURCES OF INFORMATION

Two additional sources of information may prove fruitful in providing you with materials for your research: first-hand observation and experience, and free or inexpensive materials from private and governmental agencies and organizations.

First-Hand Observation and Experience

Why not interview yourself? If your topic deals with something you know well (a hobby or an area of interest, for example), or relates to an occupation you are in or hope to be in, you may already have enough information to get started. Check your home or office for any materials you have acquired on the subject. From your knowledge of the topic, make a rough outline—it will tell you how much you know about the topic, which areas you are strong in, and which areas you are weak in. When your flow of ideas turns to a trickle and then stops, you can expand your knowledge from the other sources discussed in this chapter. For topics that involve a great deal of factual data, you should, in addition, check the accuracy of any facts and figures that you aren't certain about.

Free or Inexpensive Materials from Private and Governmental Agencies and Organizations

In your search for materials on your topic, do not overlook the field of private and governmental agencies and organizations. These include corporations, business and professional associations, nonprofit organizations, and the numerous bureaus and offices of the federal, state, and local governments. Most of these sources distribute free or inexpensive material on virtually any subject. A reference librarian can show you how to go about obtaining material from the agencies and organizations.

When you request information from governmental or private organizations, you must be specific in describing the material or materials you are seeking. If you know the title of a pamphlet or a booklet you want, refer to the title, and to any other information that will serve to identify the pamphlet, in your letter requesting the item. If you are aware that there is a charge for the material, send a check or money order with the request. Doing so will save time for both you and the recipient, because it won't be necessary for the organization to write to you asking for payment before it can send you the materials. One final note: requests for information from private and governmental agencies are usually handled by mail, and postal deliveries can be slow. Therefore, do not rely too heavily on such materials for your research, because the deadline for your written work may arrive before the requested material does.

DOCUMENTATION

The final version of a research paper should give complete, accurate credit to your sources of information, in notes either at the bottom of the page or at the end of the report, and should provide an alphabetical listing of all the sources you used in doing your research—that is, a bibliography. Together, footnotes (or endnotes) and bibliography are referred to as *documentation.*

The data to include in footnote references and in the bibliography will come from your bibliography note cards. The following pages provide examples of standard forms for documentation. It is essential to follow a standard form so that your reader will be able to identify and locate the source materials you have used. The details given for traditional footnotes and bibliographies are based on the *MLA Handbook for Writers of Research Papers, Theses, and Dissertations* (New York: The Modern Language Association of America, 1977). Although this kind of footnote is not used in most on-the-job writing, it is the most comprehensive system used, and it is standard in the humanities. Furthermore, many colleges prefer traditional footnotes to the systems discussed later in the chapter.

Traditional Footnotes

In nonscientific writing, credits for sources of information ordinarily go in one of two places: credits that are placed at the bottom, or foot, of the page on which quoted, paraphrased, or summarized material appears are called *footnotes;* when all the credits for a chapter, report, or entire book appear at the end of the chapter, report, or book, they are called *endnotes* or, simply, *notes*.[3] The term *footnotes* will be used here to indicate both bottom-of-page and end-of-work credits.

In your own work, you may find it easier to use endnotes than footnotes, because the latter require you to fit the credits on the bottom of the pages as you type. If your instructor or employer prefers footnotes or endnotes, follow that preference. Otherwise follow the style you are more comfortable with, but be consistent throughout a work.

Footnotes are numbered consecutively, in the order in which the quoted, paraphrased, or summarized material occurs in the text of your report. Footnote numbers in the text are normally raised slightly above the typewritten line of copy. You can position a footnote number correctly by moving the platen (roller) of the typewriter toward you, by hand, about half a turn. In scientific writing, footnote numbers are not usually raised above the line and are enclosed in parentheses. Footnote numbers for direct quotations should follow the closing quotation mark for material that is run in with the text, or the end punctuation mark for material that is set off from the text. For paraphrased or summarized material, the footnote number should normally be placed at the end of the paraphrased passage or the summary, following the end punctuation mark.

The footnote number in the text identifies the numbered note (either at the foot of the page or in the "Notes" section) in which the information source appears. According to *MLA* style, the first line of a footnote is indented, like a paragraph, five spaces from the left margin; any additional lines of the footnote are typed flush with the left margin. Following *MLA* style for published works, single space footnotes that are longer than one line and double space between footnotes.

In some types of writing, a distinction is made between *source notes* (those citing a book, article, or other publication) and *explanatory footnotes* (those adding a fact, opinion, or definition to clarify a point in the text). When such a system is used, the footnote numbers appearing in the text refer only to the numbered source notes, which fall together at the end of the written piece. Explanatory footnotes appear at the bottoms of pages and are usually indicated by an asterisk (*).

An alternative system is to number both source notes and explanatory footnotes together, in a continuing sequence (the approach used in this chapter). Such notes may appear at the bottoms of pages or may be given together at the end of the article or chapter.

---

[3] In some publications, footnote references are given at the end of each chapter; other books list all credits, usually arranged by chapter, at the end of the publication.

First-reference Footnotes.   In your report, you may have occasion to credit a research source—book, article, interview, and so on—
just once or more than once. The first footnote (it may be the only
one) referring to a source must give the author's full name (or the
names of the authors if the work has more than one); the full title
of a book or article; the name and location of the publisher of a book
or the name of the periodical in which an article appeared; the date
of publication (the year for a book; the day, month, and year for a
daily or weekly periodical; the month and year for articles from
monthly magazines; the volume number and year for journal articles);
and the page number on which the footnoted material occurred in
the original source.

The following list shows the *MLA* preferred style for first-reference footnotes. Information on handling second-and-later footnotes
follows.

Book, One Author

[1]Wayne Hanley, Natural History in America
(New York: Quadrangle Press/New York Times Books,
1977), p. 183.

Book, Two Authors

[2]Herbert M. Jelley and Robert O. Herrmann,
The American Consumer: Issues and Decisions
(New York: McGraw-Hill, 1973), p. 65.

Book, Three or More Authors

[3]Hugo Young, Bryan Silcock, and Peter Dunn,
Journey to Tranquility (Garden City, N.Y.: Doubleday, 1970), pp. 8-9.

Book Edition, If Not the First

[4]Wesley E. Woodson and Donald W. Conover, Human Engineering: Guide for Equipment Designers,
2nd ed. (Berkeley: Univ. of California Press,
1964), pp. 2-7.

Multivolume Work

[5]John Bartholemew, ed., Times Atlas of the
World (London: Times Publishing, 1955), I, 27.

The information given in the footnote indicates that the researcher
used only one volume, the first, of a multivolume work. The page

number, 27, follows the volume number. For other forms of footnotes for multivolume works, consult the *MLA* handbook or another style guide.

Corporate Author

⁶Commission on Vocational Education, Job Se-lection in the 1980's (Washington, D.C.: American Vocational Institute, 1973), p. 12.

Journal Article

⁷Keith D. Gardels, "A Controlled Experiment to Assess Centralized Word Processing," Technical Communication 24 (1977), 5.

The number *before* the year is the volume number; if a journal uses Roman numerals as its volume number, the figure is often converted to Arabic numerals in footnotes and bibliographies. The number *after* the year is the page number. Note that the abbreviation for *page* is ordinarily not used in journal article footnotes where a volume number is given.

Magazine Article, with Author's Name Given

⁸Susan Renner-Smith, "Satellite-to-You TV," Popular Science, March 1978, p. 69.

General-circulation magazines, as opposed to specialized professional or technical journals, are identified by date. The abbreviation for *page* or *pages* is used.

Magazine Article, with No Author's Name Given

⁹"The New American Farmer," Time, 6 Nov. 1978, p. 92.

Note that the date precedes the month, and no comma is used between the month and the year.

Newspaper Article

¹⁰John H. Allan, "Fixed-Income Securities Ease," New York Times, Late City Ed., 15 June 1979, Sec. D, p. 7.

Encyclopedia Article

¹¹"Electricity." Encyclopaedia Britannica 14th ed.

Because encyclopedia articles are arranged alphabetically, page and volume numbers are unnecessary. If the encyclopedia article is signed, begin the footnote with the author's first and last names.

Pamphlet or Booklet

[12]U.S. Bureau of the Census, Our Cities and Suburbs (Washington, D.C.: Government Printing Office, 1973), p. 14.

Personal Interview

[13]Personal interview with Virgil Denlinger, Assistant Chief of Police, Milwaukee, Wisconsin, 15 March 1979.

Second-and-later References. Second-and-later footnote references to a source are usually shorter than first references, since it is not necessary to repeat all the data furnished in the first footnote. In second-and-later references, it is ordinarily sufficient to give the author's last name and the appropriate page number or numbers. Keep in mind that a second footnote reference to a particular source may have a different page number; as long as the author, title, and other publication data are the same, it is still considered a second reference. (Often second-and-later references switch to the author/date system; see p. 267.)

[14]Evans, p. 32.

If you have footnoted more than one work by an author, second-and-later references should include the author's last name, a shortened version of the title of the work, and the page number or numbers.

[15]Evans, Erosion, p. 41.

For a second-and-later reference to a work that has more than one author, give the last name of each author and the appropriate page number.

[16]Woodson and Conover, p. 128.

To credit a work that appears in the immediately preceding footnote as well, simply repeat the information, inserting the new page number, or repeat the number if the page number is the same.

^{17}Gardels, p. 9.

^{18}Gardels, p. 12.

^{19}Gardels, p. 12.

Numbered References. In much scientific and technical writing, the form used to give credit to your information sources differs from the form used in other fields. Information sources are listed in a separate section called "References." The entries in the reference section frequently are arranged according to the order in which they are first referred to in the text. In this system, number 1 in parentheses (1) after a quotation or a reference to a book or an article refers the reader to the information in the first entry in the reference section; number 2 in parentheses (2) refers the reader to the second entry in the reference section; and so on. A second number in parentheses, separated from the first by a colon, indicates the page number in the report or book from which the information was taken—for example, the notation "(3:27)" in the text indicates that the material is found on page 27 of entry 3 in the reference section.

The reference section for relatively short reports appears at the end of the report. For reports with a number of major sections or chapters, the reference section appears at the end of the section or the chapter. See Chapter 11 for information on the placement of a reference section in a formal report.

The details of reference systems in the sciences vary widely from field to field. Although the following examples are common in scientific and technical publications, consult publications in your field for precise details.

Book

    1. Ying, R. Introductory laboratory manual
of soil science. Iowa State University
Press, Ames, ed. 2. 1977.

Note that the last name appears first, followed by one or two initials. In the title of the work, only the first word and proper nouns are capitalized, and underlining is not used.

Journal Article

    2. Hirst, E. N., and Carney, J. Effects of
federal residential energy conservation programs in California and Nevada. Science,
1978, 199: 845–851.

Only the first word and proper nouns in the article title are capitalized, and no quotation marks are used. The journal name is not underlined.

The Author/Date System. An increasingly popular notation system used in both the natural and the social sciences is known as "author/date." Like the numbered references system, the author/date system refers readers to a list of references by giving, after the cited material, the surname of the author and the publication date of the material in question. This information is enclosed in parentheses.

> A recent article on magnetic fluids ex-
> plains that they are made by crushing magne-
> tite, an iron oxide, into tiny particles
> that are mixed with an oil-like substance
> called a diester (Free 1979).

Should the reader wish to know more about the article by Free, the reference section would provide complete bibliographic data. When the author/date system is used, references are arranged alphabetically by author and by date.

When you must identify a specific page in this system, follow the date with a comma and the page number:

> . . . substance called a diester (Free
> 1979, 57).

The advantages of this system are economy and flexibility. By including the author's name, you tell your reader a little more about your source than you would with just a number. Also, by identifying your source within the text, you spare your reader the inconvenience of going to the bottom of the page or the end of the chapter or article.

The author/date system varies among the different disciplines that have adopted it. The style described here is that suggested by the *Chicago Manual of Style,* 13th Edition, 1982.

A Final Word About Footnotes. Be alert to the forms used by your employer or the publication for which you are writing. Also, once you have adopted a form, be consistent.

Bibliography

A *bibliography* is a list of books or articles arranged alphabetically at the end of a report or research paper. The purpose of a bibliography is to present the sources of the writer's information in a convenient, standardized form that will be useful to a reader who would like to locate any of the research materials the writer has included.

A bibliography may consist of all the material used in the preparation of a research paper (a *full* bibliography), or it may list only the material specifically referred to in the text (a *selected* bibliography). An *annotated* bibliography includes a brief description, by the writer, of some or all of the works listed.

Use a full bibliography when you have conducted a comprehensive literature search of all pertinent information sources for your topic; otherwise, use a selected bibliography. Use an annotated bibliography if you want to provide your readers with a convenient means of determining which of your information sources are useful to their needs.

When typing a bibliography, single-space within an entry and double-space between entries. Indent the second and subsequent lines of an entry five spaces from the left margin, so that the author's name will stand out.

The details of bibliographic systems vary from one field of study to another, but all bibliographic entries, no matter how complex the work being credited, should contain the author or corporate author's name, the full title of the work, and the facts of publication.

Alphabetizing.   Since bibliographic entries are arranged alphabetically, give the author's last name first, followed by the first name. For an entry that has more than one author, give the first author's name in reverse order and then list the other name or names in normal order. *Doe, Jane Q., and John R. Roe* is the form for a two-author work. The form for a work with three authors or more is *Doe, Jane Q., John R. Roe, and June P. Low.*

Alphabetize all works by the same author according to their titles if you have used traditional notes. When listing multiple works by the same author, replace the author's name in all entries except the first with a line made by typing ten hyphens, followed by a period.

```
Grahm, Frank, Jr. Disaster by Default: Politics
     and Water Pollution. New York: M. Evans,
     1966.
----------. Since Silent Spring. Boston: Houghton
     Mifflin, 1970.
```

When no author, editor, or compiler is listed for a work, alphabetize the entry according to the first major word in the title. (In the following example alphabetize under *E.*)

```
The Encyclopedia of Associations. 9th ed. 3 vols.
     Detroit: Gale Research, 1975.
```

Bibliographic Forms.   The following list shows the *MLA* preferred style for bibliographic entries for nonscientific works. Because the bibliography repeats information provided in the footnotes, a bibliography is not always necessary in this system. If you refer only to a few sources, footnotes alone will suffice; if you refer to a large number of sources, an alphabetically arranged bibliography is a necessary convenience for your reader.

Book, One Author

> Hanley, Wayne. Natural History in America. New York: Quadrangle Press/New York Times Books, 1977.

Note that in a bibliographic entry, page numbers are not ordinarily given for books, because the researcher may have read and made note cards for a good deal of the book. *Inclusive* page numbers are given for articles from periodicals (that is, for the first and last pages of the article).

Book, Two Authors

> Jelley, Herbert M., and Robert O. Herrmann. The American Consumer: Issues and Decisions. New York: McGraw-Hill, 1973.

Book, Three or More Authors

> Young, Hugo, Bryan Silcock, and Peter Dunn. Journey to Tranquility. Garden City, N.Y.: Doubleday, 1970.

Book Edition, If Not the First

> Woodson, Wesley E., and Donald W. Conover. Human Engineering: Guide for Equipment Designers. 2nd ed. Berkeley: Univ. of California Press, 1964.

Multivolume Work

> Bartholemew, John, ed. Times Atlas of the World. London: Times Publishing, 1955. Vol. I.

Corporate Author

> Commission on Vocational Education. Job Selection in the 1980's. Washington, D.C.: American Vocational Institute, 1973.

Journal Article

> Gardels, Keith D. "A Controlled Experiment to Assess Centralized Word Processing." Technical Communication 24 (1977), 2–6.

The number before the year is the volume number; the numbers following the year are the *inclusive* page numbers.

Magazine Article, with Author's Name Given

> Renner-Smith, Susan. "Satellite-to-You TV." Popular Science, March 1978, pp. 66–69.

Magazine Article, with No Author's Name Given

> "The New American Farmer." Time, 6 Nov. 1978, pp. 92–102.

Newspaper Article

> Allan, John H. "Fixed-Income Securities Ease." New York Times, Late City Ed., 15 June 1979, Sec. D, p. 7.

Encyclopedia Article

> "Electricity," Encyclopaedia Britannica. 14th ed.

If the encyclopedia article is signed, begin the entry with the author's last name and alphabetize by the name.

Pamphlet or Booklet

> U.S. Bureau of the Census. Our Cities and Suburbs. Washington, D.C.: Government Printing Office, 1973.

Personal Interview

> Denlinger, Virgil. Assistant Chief of Police, Milwaukee, Wisconsin. Personal interview. 15 March 1979.

Sample Bibliography. The bibliography in Figure 10–14 is intended to serve as a guide for alphabetization and *MLA* entry style. It is not intended, of course, to serve as the bibliography for any specific work.

If you follow the numbered references or author/date system, bibliographic style is somewhat different. The basic form of these styles, whether numbered or not, is author, date, title, place of publica-

BIBLIOGRAPHY

Allan, John H. "Fixed-Income Securities
    Ease." New York Times, Late City Ed., 15
    June 1979, Sec. D, p. 7.
Bartholemew, John, ed. Times Atlas of the
    World. London: Times Publishing, 1955.
    Vol. I.
Commission on Vocational Education. Job Se-
    lection in the 1980's. Washington, D.C.:
    American Vocational Institute, 1973.
Denlinger, Virgil. Assistant Chief of Police,
    Milwaukee, Wisconsin. Personal interview.
    15 March 1979.
"Electricity." Encyclopaedia Britannica. 14th
    ed.
Gardels, Keith D. "A Controlled Experiment to
    Assess Centralized Word Processing."
    Technical Communication 24 (1977), 2-6.
Grahm, Frank, Jr. Disaster by Default: Poli-
    tics and Water Pollution. New York: M.
    Evans, 1966.
----------. Since Silent Spring. Boston:
    Houghton Mifflin, 1970.
Hanley, Wayne. Natural History in America.
    New York: Quadrangle Press/New York Times
    Books, 1977.
Jelley, Herbert M., and Robert O. Herrmann.
    The American Consumer: Issues and Deci-
    sions. New York: McGraw-Hill, 1973.
"The New American Farmer." Time, 6 Nov. 1978,
    pp. 92-102.
Renner-Smith, Susan. "Satellite-to-You TV."
    Popular Science, March 1978, pp. 66-69.
U.S. Bureau of the Census. Our Cities and
    Suburbs. Washington, D.C.: Government
    Printing Office, 1973.
Woodson, Wesley E., and Donald W. Conover.
    Human Engineering: Guide for Equipment
    Designers. 2nd ed. Berkeley: Univ. of
    California Press. 1964.
Young, Hugo, Bryan Silcock, and Peter Dunn.
    Journey to Tranquility. Garden City,
    N.Y.: Doubleday, 1970.

FIGURE 10-14. Sample bibliography.

tion, and publisher. Title capitalization and the use of quotation marks are also different. Further, initials rather than full first names are generally used. The following versions of the first three entries in Figure 10–14 illustrate these differences.

```
Allan, J. H. 1979. Fixed income securities ease.
    New York Times. Late city ed. 15 June: Sec.
    D, p. 7.
Bartholemew, J., ed. 1955. Times atlas of the
    world. Vol. 1. London: Times Publishing.
Commission on Vocational Education. 1973. Job se-
    lection in the 1980's. Washington, D.C.:
    American Vocational Institute.
```

Naturally, if you were following the numbered references system, you would number and list your sources in the order in which you first referred to them. In the author/date system, the references are arranged alphabetically. When listing several works by the same author, substitute ten hyphens for the author's name in all entries after the first and arrange these entries chronologically.

CHAPTER SUMMARY

Many information sources are available to you as you research job-related topics. Libraries provide the most complete, systematically arranged body of information. Other sources include the personal interview, the questionnaire, knowledge gained from personal experience, and materials available to you from private and governmental organizations.

The *library* provides the tools for you to find books, articles, reference works, and other materials for your research. Once you have located the materials available in the library, take careful notes and record the sources of your information.

A personal interview with an expert can provide you with up-to-date information not readily available in printed material. Select the person to interview, and obtain some background information on the interviewee. Prepare a list of specific questions to ask; take brief, memory-jogging notes of the answers; and summarize the notes in writing after the interview.

A questionnaire permits you to obtain the views of a group of people without having to go to the time and expense necessary for numerous personal interviews. Take full advantage of the increased number of views a questionnaire provides, and design the questionnaire to produce as much information as you will need without its being a burden to answer. Keep the number of questions brief, and word each one carefully so that the answers marked can be summarized conveniently for your purposes. In a letter accompanying the questionnaire, inform the recipient of who you are, the purpose of the questionnaire, the use to which the answers will be put, and the date by which you would like the information returned.

Other sources of information include your own knowledge and experience, and the pamphlets, booklets, reports, and other materials provided by companies, professional or trade associations, public-interest groups, and various governmental agencies. To tap your own resources, jot down what you know about a topic and supplement this information with any materials you have available at home or at work. Organize your notes into a rough outline. On the basis of this outline, you can determine particular areas where additional information is needed. You can also pinpoint areas that need to be double-checked for accuracy. A reference librarian can help you to identify the types of information available from private organizations and governmental agencies. Be as specific as possible when you write for this type of material, and enclose any fees that may be required. Allow time for mail handling so that the information will arrive when you need it.

Give complete and accurate credit to all of your information sources. Failure to do so will make you guilty of *plagiarism*. Information you quote, paraphrase, or summarize in your text must be credited in footnotes that appear either at the bottoms of text pages or in a separate section at the end of a chapter or section. In scientific and technical writing, if the numbered reference system is used, source notes are listed consecutively in a "Reference" section in the order in which they first appeared in the text. If the author/date system is used, references are arranged alphabetically.

To provide readers with a convenient place to review your information sources, arrange your sources alphabetically in a *bibliography*. A *full bibliography* lists all the information sources examined in your research; a *selected bibliography* lists only the material actually referred to in the text. An *annotated bibliography* includes a brief description of some or all of your information sources. The type of bibliography you provide will depend on how much information about your research would be useful to your reader.

EXERCISES

Note: The exercises in this chapter may be used as the basis for the preparation of a formal report according to the guidelines presented in Chapter 11.

1. Select a topic from your career field or other area of interest. Using the card catalog in your library, locate five books on your topic.

Prepare a separate three- by five-inch bibliography card for each book. (If you prefer, you may use, instead of a note card, a sheet of paper ruled into three- by five-inch segments.) Follow the instructions on pages 239–240 for preparing a bibliography card for a book.

2. Using the periodical index or indexes in your library, locate five articles, from magazines, newspapers, or journals, on the topic you chose for Exercise 1. Prepare a separate three- by five-inch bibliography card for each item (or use a ruled sheet of paper as described in Exercise 1). Follow the instructions on pages 239–240 for preparing a bibliography card for an article.

3. *Paraphrase* each of the two following paragraphs on a four- by six-inch note card (or use a sheet of paper ruled into four- by six-inch segments). Then, on a separate note card, *summarize* the information from each paragraph. Identify each card with a "slug" line and indicate the source from which the information was obtained.

   a.   To keep pipes from freezing, wrap the pipes in insulation made especially for water pipes, or in layers of old newspaper, lapping the ends and tying them around the pipes. Cover the newspapers with plastic to keep out moisture. When it is extremely cold and there is real danger of freezing, let the faucets drip a little. Although this wastes water, it may prevent freezing damage. Know where the valve for shutting off the water coming into the house or apartment is located. You may as a last resort have to shut off this main valve and drain all the pipes to keep them from freezing and bursting.[4]

   b.   The Federal Energy Administration (FEA) estimated in 1976 that annual energy use in the United States was about 75 quadrillion BTUs (or 75 quads), and that use by 1985 would be 98.9 quads. The agency also estimated that even under the most favorable conditions the U.S. cannot expect to gain more than 6 quads from emerging technology by 1990. A more realistic figure, it indicated, might be 2 quads.

   The emerging technologies evaluated by FEA included solar, geothermal, and synthetic fuels, but evidently excluded forest biomass. Energy currently obtained from wood is estimated at 1.1 to 1.7 quads. Members of the task force are confident that wood use for energy is increasing greatly, but we have no way of knowing the extent.[5]

4. Using the topic you chose in Exercise 1, complete one or both of the following assignments, depending on your instructor's require-

[4] Department of Energy, *Winter Survival: A Consumer's Guide to Winter Preparedness* (Washington, D.C.: Government Printing Office, 1978), p. 3.

[5] "Forest Biomass as an Energy Source: Study Report of a Task Force of the Society of American Foresters," *Journal of Forestry* 77, 1979, p. 3.

ments: (1) create a ten-item sample questionnaire that you could use to gather information on the subject, or (2) interview someone knowledgeable about the subject and submit your rewritten and organized notes of the interview to your instructor. Also submit one of the following with your assignment, as appropriate: a letter to accompany your questionnaire or a letter requesting an interview.

5. Prepare a footnote for each of the following reference items, using the guidelines provided in this chapter.

   a. A magazine article on page 42 of the August 1979 issue of *Studio Photography,* by Lou Jones, entitled "The Key to Location Photography."
   b. The unsigned "New Products" column of the same issue of *Studio Photography.* The column appears on page 13.
   c. The fourth edition of a 1976 book entitled *Environmental Conservation,* by Raymond F. Dassmann. The book is published by John Wiley, in New York City. Your reference is on page 365.
   d. An article entitled "Ensuring Safer Stomach Suctioning with the Salem Sump Tube," by Edwina A. McConnell, that appears on page 56 of the September 1977 issue of the journal *Nursing.*
   e. An article in the *Washington Post* entitled "Futuristic Autos— Prize-Winning Canadians Get 60 Miles Per Gallon," by William M. Adler. The article appears on page 8 of Section A in the August 19, 1979, issue.
   f. A booklet entitled *Controlling Fleas,* by the United States Department of Agriculture and published in Washington, D.C., by the Government Printing Office in 1978. Your reference is on page 5.
   g. Your interview of the Vice President of Ridgeway Electronics of Leesburg, Virginia, on April 14, 1979. Her name is Josetta Jameson.
   h. A book entitled *A Walk in the Forest: The Woodlands of North America* and written by Albert List, Jr., and Ilka List. The book was published in New York by Thomas Y. Crowell in 1977. Your reference is on page 11.
   i. Hallie Black's book *Dirt Cheap: The Evolution of Renewable Resources,* published by William Morrow in New York in 1979. Your reference is on page 91.
   j. An article from the 1977 edition of the *McGraw-Hill Encyclopedia of Science and Technology,* entitled "Lubricant."

6. Prepare an author/date bibliography entry for each item given in Exercise 5. Inclusive page numbers for items *a* and *d* are pages 41–42 and pages 54–62, respectively.

11

Formal Reports

Formal reports are the written accounts of major projects. Projects that are likely to generate a formal report include research into new developments in a field, explorations of the advisability of launching a new product or an expanded service, or an end-of-year review of developments within an organization. The scope and complexity of the project will determine how long and how complex the report will be. Most formal reports—certainly those that are long and complex—require a carefully planned structure that provides the reader with an easy-to-recognize guide to the material in the report. Such aids to the reader as a table of contents, a list of illustrations, and an abstract (brief summary of the report) serve to make the information in the report more accessible. Making a formal topic outline, which lists the major facts and ideas in the report and indicates their relationship to one another, should help you to write a well-organized report.

Most formal reports are divided into three major parts—front matter, body, and back matter—each of which, in turn, contains a number of elements. Just how many elements are needed for a particular report depends on the subject, the length of the report, and the kinds of material covered.

ORDER OF ELEMENTS IN A FORMAL REPORT

The arrangement of the elements in a formal report may vary. Many companies and governmental and other institutions have a preferred style for formal reports and furnish guidelines that staff members must follow. If your employer has prepared a set of style guidelines, follow it; if not, use the format recommended in this chapter. The following list includes most of the elements a formal report might contain.

Front Matter

> Title page
> Abstract
> Table of contents
> List of figures
> List of tables
> Preface
> List of abbreviations and symbols

Body

> Summary
> Introduction
> Text (including headings)
> Conclusions
> Recommendations
> Explanatory footnotes
> References

Back Matter

> Bibliography
> Appendixes
> Glossary

FRONT MATTER

The *front matter*, which includes all the elements that precede the body of the report, serves several purposes: it gives the reader a general idea of the author's purpose in writing the report; it indicates whether the report contains the kind of information that the reader is looking for; and it lists where in the report the reader can find specific chapters, headings, illustrations, and tables. Not all formal reports require every element of front matter. A title page and table of contents are usually mandatory, but whether an abstract, a preface, and lists of figures, tables, abbreviations, and symbols are included will depend on the scope of the report and its intended audience. The front matter pages are numbered with lower-case Roman numerals.

Throughout the report, page numbers should be centered near the bottom of each page.

Title Page

The formats of title pages for formal reports vary, but the page should include the following information.

1. Full title of the report. The title should indicate the topic and announce the scope and objective of the report. Titles often provide the only basis on which readers can decide whether or not to read a report. Titles too vague or too long not only hinder readers but can prevent efficient filing and information retrieval by librarians and other information specialists. Follow these guidelines when creating the title:
   - Do not use "Report on . . ." or "Technical Report on . . ." in the title, since the fact that the information appears in a report will be self-evident to your reader.
   - Do not use abbreviations in the title. Use acronyms only when the report is intended for an audience familiar enough with the topic that the acronym will not confuse them.
   - Do not include the period covered by a report in the title; include that information in a subtitle:

   EFFECTS OF PROPOSED HIGHWAY
   CONSTRUCTION ON PROPERTY VALUES

   Annual Report, 19--

2. Name of the writer, principal investigator, or compiler. Frequently contributors simply list their names. Sometimes they identify themselves by their job title in the organization (Jane R. Doe, Cost Analyst; Jack T. Doe, Head, Research and Development). Sometimes contributors identify themselves by their tasks in contributing to the report (Jane R. Doe, Compiler; Jack T. Doe, Principal Investigator).
3. Date or dates of the report. For one-time reports, you should list the date when the report is to be distributed. For periodic reports, which may be issued monthly or quarterly, list the time period that the present report covers, as well as the date when the report is to be distributed.
4. Name of the organization *for* which the writer works.
5. Name of the organization *to* which the report is being submitted, if the work is being done for a customer or client.

These categories are standard on most title pages. Some organizations may require additional information. A sample title page appears in Figure 11–1.

The title page, although unnumbered, is considered page i (small Roman numeral 1). The subsequent pages of the front matter are numbered beginning with page ii.

Abstract

An *abstract* is a condensed version of a longer piece of writing that summarizes and highlights the major points, enabling the prospective reader to decide whether the report in full will be worthwhile to read. Usually 200 words or less, abstracts must make sense independently of the works they summarize. Depending on the kind of information they contain, abstracts are usually classified as either *descriptive* or *informative*.

A *descriptive abstract* includes information about the purpose, scope, and/or methodology of a report (see Figure 11–2). An *informative abstract*, unlike the descriptive abstract, contains some information from the report. In addition to information about the purpose, scope, and methods, the informative abstract includes the results, conclusions, and recommendations, if any. Figure 11–3 shows an informative abstract, which is an expanded version of the descriptive abstract shown in Figure 11–2.

Writing abstracts is a skill that improves with practice. However, the following tips may prove useful:

1. Write the abstract after writing the report.
2. Begin with a topic sentence.
3. Condense the information, but do not delete articles (*a, an, the*) and needed transitional words (*however, therefore, for example, in summary*).
4. Avoid overloading your abstract with technical terms or unnecessary jargon, since not all your readers may be as familiar as you are with the subject matter.
5. Do not include illustrations, tables, or bibliographic references in the abstract.

An abstract normally follows the title page and is numbered page ii.

Table of Contents

A table of contents lists all the headings or sections of the report in their order of appearance, along with their page numbers. It includes

EFFECTS OF NUCLEAR POWER PLANTS ON
COMMUNITY GROWTH AND RESIDENTIAL PROPERTY
VALUES

Manuscript Published: April 1979

Prepared by
H. B. Gamble, R. H. Downing, and
O. H. Sauerlender

The Pennsylvania State University Institute
for Research on Land and Water Resources
University Park, PA 16802

Prepared for
Division of Health, Siting, and
Waste Management
Office of Nuclear Regulatory Research
U.S. Nuclear Regulatory Commission
Washington, DC 20555

FIGURE 11-1. Sample title page.

                    ABSTRACT

        This study tested the hypothesis that nu-
    clear power plants adversely affect community
    growth and residential property values in
    nearby municipalities. Total assessed real
    property values from 1960 to 1976 for 64 mu-
    nicipalities and market sales data from 1975
    to 1977 on 540 single-family dwellings formed
    the data base. The data were for residential
    property within 20 miles of 4 nuclear power
    plants in the northeastern United States:
    Pilgrim in Massachusetts, Millstone in Con-
    necticut, Oyster Creek in New Jersey, and
    R. E. Ginna in New York.

Purpose

Method and scope

ii

FIGURE 11–2. Descriptive abstract.

ABSTRACT

Purpose

This study tested the hypothesis that nuclear power plants adversely affect community growth and residential property values in nearby municipalities. Total assessed real property values from 1960 to 1976 for 64 municipalities and market sales data from 1975 to 1977 on 540 single-family dwellings formed the data base. The data were for residential property within 20 miles of 4 nuclear power plants in the northeastern United States: Pilgrim in Massachusetts, Millstone in Connecticut, Oyster Creek in New Jersey, and R. E. Ginna in New York.

Method and scope

Analysis of the time series data showed that the average annual growth rates of total assessed values, in real terms, were inversely related to distances from the plants, and that growth in sales for the years following plant construction were higher than for the years before plant construction, with the largest growth rate observed in the host municipalities. Multiple regression analysis of the cross-section data explained about 80% of the variation in housing prices. The plants exerted no influence on the price of housing, so the original hypothesis is rejected. Most people in the areas studied apparently have little fear over plant-related health and safety factors, and the presence of a plant does not in itself influence residential location decisions. Lower tax rates in host municipalities may even encourage development.

Expanded methodology discussion

Conclusions (recommendations are not appropriate for this study)

ii

FIGURE 11–3. Informative abstract.

a listing of all front matter and back matter except the title page and the table of contents itself. The table of contents begins on a new page. Note that in Figure 11–4 the table of contents is numbered page iii because it follows the title page (page i) and the abstract (page ii). By convention, the table of contents itself is not listed in the body of the table of contents page.

Along with the abstract, a table of contents permits the reader to preview the contents of a report and to assess its value. It also aids a reader who may want to look only at certain sections of the report. For this reason, the wording of chapter and section titles in the table of contents should be identical to those in the text.

Sometimes, the table of contents is followed by lists of the figures and tables contained in the report. These lists should always be presented separately, and a page number should be given for each item (see Figure 11–4).

Preface

The preface is an optional introductory statement that announces the purpose, background, or scope of the report. Sometimes a preface specifies the audience for whom the report is intended, and it may also highlight the relationship of the report to a given project or program. A preface may contain acknowledgments of help received during the course of the project or in the preparation of the report, and, finally, it may cite permission obtained for the use of copyrighted works. If a preface is not included, place this type of information, if it is essential, in the introduction (discussed later in this chapter).

The preface follows the table of contents (and the lists of figures or tables, if these are present); it begins on a separate page titled "Preface." The preface shown in Figure 11–5 precedes the body of the report.

List of Abbreviations and Symbols

When the abbreviations and symbols used in a report are numerous, and when there is a chance that the reader will not be able to interpret them, the front matter should include a list of all abbreviations and symbols and what they stand for in the report. Such a list, which follows the preface, is particularly appropriate for technical reports whose audience is not restricted to technicians.

Figure 11–6 shows a list of symbols that appear in a report as part of equations that calculate the transfer of heat and water vapor

TABLE OF CONTENTS

ABSTRACT ii
LIST OF FIGURES iv
LIST OF TABLES v
PREFACE vii
1 SUMMARY 1
2 INTRODUCTION 6
3 METHODOLOGY 10
   3.1 Selection of Study Areas 10
   3.2 Descriptions of Study Sites 11
       3.2.1 Pilgrim 1 12
       3.2.2 Millstone 1 12
       3.2.3 Oyster Creek 13
       3.2.4 R. E. Ginna 14
   3.3 Time Series Analysis 14
   3.4 Cross-Section Analysis 17
       3.4.1 Real Selling Price 17
       3.4.2 House Characteristics 18
       3.4.3 Lot Characteristics 19
       3.4.4 Accessibility
             Characteristics 19
       3.4.5 Locational
             Characteristics 20
   3.5 Collection of Data 22
       3.5.1 Time Series Data 23
       3.5.2 Cross-Section Data 24
4 DATA ANALYSIS AND INTERPRETATION 27
   4.1 Time Series Studies 27
       4.1.1 Data Analysis 28
       4.1.2 Interpretation of
             Results 28
   4.2 Cross-Section Studies 30
       4.2.1 Functional Forms of
             the Model 31
       4.2.2 Statistical Package 33
       4.2.3 Regression Results:
             Individual Study Areas . . . 35
       4.2.4 Regression Results:
             Pooled Data 37
             4.2.4.1 Linear Model 37
             4.2.4.2 Log-Log Model 39
   4.3 References 41
5 CONCLUSIONS 43
APPENDIX A-1

iii

FIGURE 11-4. Table of contents.

PREFACE

Background of study

Over the past decade, it has become increasingly difficult for electric utilities to receive timely approval of new nuclear generating facilities. In part, siting difficulties arise because of strong opposition to nuclear plants by some citizens who perceive that such plants pose threats to health and safety. If many people hold such views, it seems logical to expect that people would not choose to live in communities near such plants and that, as a consequence, residential property values would decline and economic growth would be adversely affected.

Intended audience

Information about the extent to which society holds such fears about health and safety would enable utilities and government agencies to make better-informed siting decisions. This study aims to supply some of this information.

Purpose of study

No economically sound research has been conducted to examine the effects of nuclear generating plants on surrounding property values. Accordingly, the objectives of this research are twofold:

1. To ascertain whether, over time, nuclear generating plants have adversely affected the growth of the towns or communities in which they are located.

2. To determine the effects of nuclear generating plants on the market values of residential properties.

Acknowledgment of help

The authors wish to acknowledge the assistance provided by the many local tax assessors and other local and state officials who cooperated so generously with us in providing the data. We also wish to thank the Plymouth County, Massachusetts, multiple-listing service for making their files available. We are grateful to Howard Hester, Daniel Huegel, and Kathy Phillips of the Institute of Land and Water Resources for the time they spent collecting, processing, and coding the data.

FIGURE 11–5. Preface.

SYMBOLS

A	Pond surface area, ft^2 or acres
A_0	One-half the daily insulation, Btu/ft^2
A_n	Surface area of nth segment of the plugflow model, ft^2
C	Cloud cover in tenths of the total sky obscured
C_1	Bowen's ratio, 0.26 mm Hg/°F
C_p	Heat capacity of water, Btu/lb/°F
E_1, E_2	Estimation of equilibrium temperatures using data from offsite and onsite records, respectively,°F
$E(\bar{x})$	Estimation of equilibrium temperature using monthly average meteorologic data,°F
e_a	Saturation pressure of air above pond surface, mm Hg
e_s	Saturation pressure of air at surface temperature, T_s, mm Hg
g	Skew coefficient
H	Heat content, Btu

vi

FIGURE 11–6. List of symbols.

from the surface of cooling ponds. The list is made up of symbols unique to this report. The author assumes that the report readers have a technical education, however, because Btu (British thermal unit), Hg (chemical symbol for mercury), and similar abbreviations are not identified.

BODY

The *body* of a formal report is the text as well as any accompanying footnotes, headings, tables, illustrations, and references. The first page of the body is numbered page 1 (Arabic rather than Roman numerals are used).

Summary

A summary provides a more complete overview of a report than either a descriptive or an informative abstract. The summary states the purpose and nature of the investigation and gives major findings, conclusions, and, if any are to be made, recommendations. It also provides an account of the procedures used to conduct the study. Although more complete than an abstract, the summary should not contain a detailed description of the work upon which the findings, conclusions, and recommendations were based. Summaries typically run from 500 to 1,000 words.

Some summaries are written to follow the organization of the report, dealing briefly with the information in each chapter (or section), in order. Others highlight the findings, conclusions, and recommendations by summarizing them first, before going on to discuss procedures or methodology.

A summary enables people who may not have time to read a lengthy report to scan its primary points quickly and then decide whether they need to read the report in full. Because they are often intended for busy managers, summaries are sometimes called "executive summaries." Addressed primarily to this audience, summaries often appear as the first section of the body of a report. Figure 11–7

---

1. SUMMARY

Purpose of report   Electric utilities are experiencing increased resistance from the public with regard to the siting of new nuclear generating facilities. This resistance supposedly reflects fears for health and safety. The extent to which such fears are held by the general public is unknown. If people's perceptions of possible health and safety effects are real and strong, these perceptions should be reflected in their locational choices for housing. In turn, growth rates in communities near nuclear plants should be lessened, and the local real estate market, all else being equal, should show lower housing prices compared with prices in areas away from nuclear power plants. The hypotheses to be tested in this study are: (1) that growth in communities near nuclear generating plants is less than growth in more distant communi-

FIGURE 11–7. Summary.

ties; and (2) that nuclear generating plants have an adverse effect on residential property values--that is, that property values are directly related to distance from such plants.

Methodology used to conduct study

Four nuclear plants in the northeastern United States were selected for this study: Pilgrim (Mass.), Millstone (Conn.), Oyster Creek (N.J.), and R. E. Ginna (N.Y.). Total assessed real property values, equalized from 1960 to 1976 for 64 municipalities within 20 miles of the four plants, were assumed to adequately reflect community growth trends, and were used as the data base for the time series analysis. The cross-section analyses employed multiple regression using linear and log-log forms to statistically analyze data on 540 single-family houses, located within about 20 miles of the plants, that were sold between 1975 and 1977. Market sales price (corrected for inflation) formed the dependent variable, while the independent variables included approximately 70 descriptors of house, lot, community, environment, and accessibility characteristics. "Distance from house to nuclear plant" and "nuclear plant visible from the house" were the two key independent variables that were used to reflect the effects of the plant on selling price. Regression runs were made for each study area separately, and then the data from the four study areas were combined and regressions were run on the pooled data.

Findings

The assessed values for all property classes were equalized for the years of the study to full 1976 market values for all municipalities in all study areas. Average annual compound growth rates were determined from the increases in assessed values. The results for the pooled data show that, following plant construction, the rates of growth were inversely related to distance from the plant. Between 1970 and 1976, host communities had the highest annual growth rate (7.5%); other communities within 10 miles of the plant had a growth rate of 7.1%, while communities 10 to 20 miles from the plant had a 5.7% growth rate. This order was reversed between 1960 and 1970, which were basically the years preceding the time when the plants became operational. For that period, the host towns had the lowest growth

FIGURE 11-7, *continued.*

rate (4.4%), while the communities 10 to 20 miles away had the highest (5.3%). In all four regions, growth rates after the plants became operational exceeded the growth rates between 1960 and 1970.

Discussion of methodology relative to findings

Both forms of the regression equations (linear and log-log) for the pooled data in the cross-section analysis were significant at the 1% level, as were the equations for each study area examined separately. The pooled data equations explained about 80% of the variation in housing prices, and contained about 25 variables significant at the 1% level. The predicted signs of the regression coefficients turned out as expected, and the magnitudes of most of the coefficients were very reasonable.

Of most significance, however, is the fact that neither of the two independent variables intended to reflect the possible effects of the nuclear plant on housing prices ("distance to plant" and "plant visible") were significant. When the "plant visible" variable was calculated, it was significant at the 5% level, but it was positive rather than negative, as hypothesized.

In the log-log form of the model, a dummy variable for a low tax rate town was significant at the 5% level. This, coupled with the results of the time series analysis, lends strong credence to the supposition that the low tax rates in the host municipalities, resulting from the large local tax payments by the utilities, initially attract residential and subsequently other development. The issue of local tax impacts from nuclear plants is a fruitful area for future research.

Conclusions

The conclusions that can be drawn from this research are quite clear. The presence of the nuclear power plants had no adverse effects on the growth rates of the host or nearby communities, nor did they have any significant effects on the price of single-family housing within 15 miles of the plants between 1975 and 1977. Therefore, the hypotheses stated earlier must be rejected. The fears for health and safety associated with nuclear power plants, as expressed by some individuals and groups in society, apparently are not shared by the majority of people.

FIGURE 11–7, *continued*:

shows the summary of the report on the effects of nuclear power plants on community growth and property values. Like abstracts, summaries should not contain tables, illustrations, or bibliographic citations. The summary is considered part of the body of the report.

Introduction

The purpose of an introduction is to provide your readers with any general information they must have in order to understand the detailed information in the rest of the report. An introduction sets the stage for the report. In this respect, it resembles the first act of a play in which the audience learns about the characters, their backgrounds, and where the action takes place so it can appreciate what happens from then on. The introduction does not, like the informative abstract or the summary, include the findings, conclusions, and recommendations of the report. In writing the introduction, you need to state the subject, the purpose, the scope, and the way you plan to develop the topic. You may also describe how the report will be organized. Figure 11–8 shows the introduction to the nuclear power plant report. Note that there is some overlap between the contents of the introduction and the contents of the preface (Figure 11–5), but this is not always the case.

Stating the Subject. In stating the subject, help your reader by including general background information on the history or theory of the subject. You may need to define the topic if it is one that some of your readers will be unfamiliar with.

```
2.  INTRODUCTION

    Over the past decade, it has become in-
creasingly difficult for electric utilities
to receive timely approval of new nuclear
generating facilities. Lengthy delays not
only are very costly to the utility, but may
become costly to the utility's consumers as
well. Because of higher construction costs,
utility rates are higher, and there are more
frequent interruptions of power as generating
```

FIGURE 11–8. Introduction.

capacity fails to keep pace with power demand.

Background of subject

In part, siting difficulties arise because of strong opposition to nuclear plants by some citizens who perceive that such plants pose threats to health and safety. The extent to which such views are held by society at large is very difficult to ascertain, however. If many people hold such views, it seems logical to expect that people would not choose to live in communities near such plants and that, as a consequence, residential property values would decline and economic growth would be adversely affected.

Information about the extent to which society holds fears about health and safety would enable utilities and government agencies to make better-informed siting decisions. This study aims to supply some of this information.

Economists and others have recognized for many years that land values reflect the beneficial impacts arising from public and private investment expenditures. Numerous studies have documented the dramatic increase in land values following the introduction in rural areas of interstate highways and large water impoundments for recreation.

History of subject

In recent years, economists have begun to study how land values may reflect the negative influences of developmental activities. Adverse effects such as noise and air pollutants from highways and airports have received the most attention, and a number of studies have empirically verified the negative effects of these influences on nearby property values. Another study examined the effect of a sanitary landfill solid waste disposal site on nearby land values.

Place of this study in history of subject

To the best of our knowledge, there has been no economically sound research conducted to directly examine the effects of nuclear generating plants on surrounding property values. If a sizable proportion of the population holds genuine fears about the health and safety aspects of a nuclear power generating facility, then they certainly would not choose to own residential property near one.

Purpose

The specific objectives of this research are as follows:

FIGURE 11-8, *continued.*

1. To ascertain whether, over time, nuclear generating plants have had an effect on the growth of the towns or communities in which they are located as compared to the growth of towns or communities more distantly located (control areas). Such growth would be evidenced by changes in equalized real property assessments.

2. To determine the effects of nuclear generating plants on the market values of residential properties.

Development of topic

The specific hypotheses to be tested in the research are:

1. That growth in communities near nuclear generating plants is less than growth in more distant communities.

2. That nuclear generating plants have an adverse effect on residential property values--that is, property values are directly related to distance from the nuclear plant (the closer to the plant, the lower the value).

Scope

To achieve the above objectives, four nuclear power generating plants were chosen for study:

1. Pilgrim, in Plymouth, Massachusetts
2. Millstone, in Waterford, Connecticut
3. Oyster Creek, near Toms River, New Jersey
4. R. E. Ginna, near Rochester, New York.

Organization of report

The remainder of this report is divided into three chapters and an appendix. Chapter 3 discusses the selection of study sites and briefly describes them, presents the methodologies employed in the time series (longitudinal) and cross-section analyses, and describes the collection of data. Chapter 4 describes the analyses of the time series and cross-section data and provides an interpretation of the results. Chapter 5 presents the conclusions. The appendix contains a more detailed description of the regression models and how they were used, as well as more detailed data on the time series analysis.

FIGURE 11-8, *continued.*

Stating the Purpose.   The statement of purpose in your introduction should function as a topic sentence does in a paragraph. It should make your readers aware of your goal as they read your supporting statements and examples. It should also tell them why you are writing about the subject and whether your material provides a new perspective or clarifies an existing perspective.

Stating the Scope.   This information tells the reader how much or how little detail to expect. Does your report present a broad survey of the topic, or does it concentrate on one part of the topic? Once you state your scope, stop. Save the details for the main body of the report.

Stating How the Topic Will Be Developed.   In a long report, help your reader by stating how you plan to develop or organize your topic. Is the report an analysis of the component parts of some whole? Is it an analysis of selected parts (or samples) of a whole? Is the material presented in chronological order? Does it move from details to general conclusions, or from a general statement to the details that verify the statement? Does it set out to show whether a hypothesis is correct or incorrect? Providing such information allows your readers to anticipate how the subject will be presented and gives them a basis for evaluating how you arrived at your conclusions or recommendations.

Text

Generally the longest section of the report, the text (or body) presents the details of how the topic was investigated, how the problem was solved, how the best choice from among alternatives was selected, or whatever else the report covers. This information is often clarified and further developed by the use of illustrations and tables and may be supported by references to other studies.

Most formal reports have no single best organization. How the text is organized will depend on the topic and on how you have investigated it. The text is ordinarily divided into several major sections, comparable to the chapters in a book. These sections are then subdivided to reflect logical divisions in your main sections. The main portion of the text usually ends with a conclusions and recommendations section, depending on the type of information reported. See the sample table of contents (Figure 11–4) for an example of how the text for the nuclear power study was organized.

Heads.   In formal reports, it is advisable to use *heads* (also called *headings*). These are titles or subtitles within the body of a report that serve as guideposts for the reader. They divide the work into manageable segments, call attention to the main topics, and signal changes of topic.

In long and complicated reports, you may need several levels of heads to indicate major divisions and subdivisions of the topic. There is no one "correct" format for heads, but the following two systems are most widely used.

The decimal numbering system uses a combination of numbers and decimal points to subordinate levels of heads in a report. It is the system used in the sample table of contents in Figure 11–4. The outline below shows the correspondence between different levels of headings and the decimal numbers used.

1.   FIRST–LEVEL HEAD

1.1   Second–Level Head

1.2   Second–Level Head

1.2.1   Third–Level Head

1.2.2   Third–Level Head

1.2.2.1   Fourth–Level Head

1.2.2.2   Fourth–Level Head

1.3   Second–Level Head

1.3.1   Third–Level Head

1.3.2   Third–Level Head

2.   FIRST–LEVEL HEAD

Although the second-, third-, and fourth-level heads are indented in an outline or table of contents, as headings they are flush with the left margin in the body of the report. For an example of how the heads help organize a portion of text, see Figure 11–9 or the Writer's Guide at the end of this book.

Note that the first-level heads are typed in all-capital letters; the second-level heads and all subsequent levels of heads are typed in capital and lower-case letters. That is, the first letter of the first word and of every important word is capitalized; prepositions and conjunctions of five letters or more are also capitalized. Every head is typed on a separate line, with an extra line of space above and below the head.

The unnumbered heading system makes use of the typewriter to differentiate visually among levels of headings. Various systems exist,

3. METHODOLOGY

3.1 Selection of Study Areas

The selection of nuclear power generating
sites was restricted to those in the northeastern United States in order to keep travel
costs and time to a minimum. The Nuclear Regulatory Commission supplied the researchers
with a list of eleven northeastern plants
that had been in operation for three or more
years, together with data on host county population growth in 1965-1975, host county per
capita income, and population within five
miles of each plant. From this list, seven
plants were identified as possible candidates. For the four plants excluded from initial selection, the Indian Point plant in New
York exhibited high population within five
miles but very little growth (2.2% in ten
years), indicating the possibility of a
rather stagnant real estate market. The other
three plants (Vermont Yankee, Yankee Rowe,
and Maine Yankee) were in areas of low population, again reflecting a thinness to the
real estate market.
    Criteria were established for selecting the
four study sites out of the seven potentially
identified. There had to be a population of
about 10,000 within five miles of the plant
in order to provide sufficient data on residential property transactions; the local tax
assessment offices had to have their data in
a form that would readily provide information
(descriptors) on individual properties; the
county courthouses had to be able to provide
information on property sales; and the local
planning commissions or township governments
had to be able to provide maps and other information on land use.
    All seven potential sites were visited, and
contact was made with local planning officials, tax assessors, and recorders of deeds
in the courthouses. On the basis of these
site visits, the Peach Bottom plant in Penn-

FIGURE 11-9. Section from text of report.

sylvania, the Connecticut Yankee, and the
Nine Mile Point plant in New York were eliminated, primarily because of sparsity of data
on residential property sales during the past
few years.

The four plants finally selected and ap-
proved by the Nuclear Regulatory Commission
were: Pilgrim 1 in Plymouth, Massachusetts;
Millstone 1 in Waterford, Connecticut; Oyster
Creek in Lacey Township, New Jersey; and
R. E. Ginna in the town of Ontario, New York.
Figure 3.1 shows the general location of each
plant in the Northeast.

Because these plants were not randomly selected, the findings of this study are applicable only to these plants or to plants that
would be similar in all locational attributes, including the socioeconomic variables

Figure 3.1.Location of four plant sites in
Northeastern United States.

FIGURE 11-9, *continued.*

associated with the surrounding communities.
The results should not be used in a pre-
dictive way for existing or potential sites
elsewhere.

3.2 Descriptions of Study Sites   Table 3.1
summarizes general information about each of
the four study sites. Site visits were made
to each of the four plants, and those portions of the following discussion that deal
with land use are based on field observations.

3.2.1 Pilgrim 1

The Pilgrim plant, owned by the Boston Edison Company, is located in the southeastern
part of Massachusetts about 3.5 miles from
the town of Plymouth. It is located on Cape
Cod Bay about 36 miles south of Boston and 44
miles east of Providence, Rhode Island.
Pilgrim 1 has a 670 MWe generating capacity
and is a boiling water reactor. Cooling is
accomplished by drawing water from Cape Cod
Bay, which is returned through a discharge
channel. The plant was constructed between
1968 and 1972 and became operational in December 1972.
The site occupies 517 acres on a bluff
overlooking the bay. The structure is about
180 feet tall, but a forested portion of the
tract forms an effective sight barrier to ob-
servers from the land side. Approximately 60
percent of the area within a 50-mile radius
of the plant is open water. Within two miles
of the plant, development is sparse, with the
exception of seasonal home developments along
the bay shore south of the plant.

3.2.2 Millstone 1

The Millstone plant, owned and operated by
Northeast Utilities, is located on the north
shore of Long Island Sound in the town of Waterford, Connecticut. It is about four miles
southwest of New London, 40 miles east of New
Haven, and 60 miles southwest of Providence,
Rhode Island.
The Millstone 1 plant has a rated capacity
of 652 MWe and is a boiling water reactor.

FIGURE 11–9, *continued.*

TABLE 3.1

General information on the four nuclear power plant study areas

| Plant Name | Year | | 1975 Population | | | Distance To Nearest City of 50,000 | Host County Per Capita Income Change | |
	Construction Began	Plant Operational	Within 5 Miles	Host County	Host County Change 1965-1975		1975	1965-1975
					(%)	(miles)	($)	(%)
Pilgrim 1	1968	1972	14,401	379,800	+24.1	36	5,555	+117
Millstone 1	1966	1970	46,550	240,600	+11.2	40	6,079	+121
Oyster Creek	1964	1969	9,835	296,800	+81.3	60	6,259	+112
R. E. Ginna	1966	1970	10,800	708,400	+ 7.9	20	7,009	+ 98

SOURCE: U.S. Nuclear Regulatory Commission.

FIGURE 11-9, *continued.*

Millstone 2 generates 830 MWe and is a pressurized water reactor. The once-through cooling system draws water directly from Niantic Bay, and discharges it back to the bay via an old quarry. Construction began on unit 1 in May 1966 and on unit 2 in November 1969. Units 1 and 2 became operational in December 1970 and December 1975, respectively.

The plant site occupies about 500 acres of land on Millstone Point, which juts into Long Island Sound. The areas along the shore of the sound are quite heavily developed for residential use, including many seasonal homes. The plant, about 160 feet tall with a ventilating stack 375 feet high, is very visible to the heavily developed areas across Niantic Bay from Millstone Point. The flat terrain and lack of forest cover make it difficult to blend the plant into the environs. Inland a few miles from the shore, land use is mostly agriculture and open space.

3.2.3 Oyster Creek

The Oyster Creek plant is operated by the Jersey Central Power and Light Company. It is located in Ocean County, New Jersey, 2 miles inland from Barnegat Bay and is mostly in Lacey Township. A small portion of the site is in Ocean Township. The site is about 60 miles south of Newark and 35 miles north of Atlantic City.

Oyster Creek plant has a rated capacity of 640 MWe and uses a boiling water reactor. Coolant water is taken from a series of canals from Barnegat Bay, South Branch Forked River, and Oyster Creek, and from deep wells. Discharge water goes into a canal feeding into the bay. Construction of the plant began in 1964, and it became operational in December 1969.

The site occupies 1,416 acres. The reactor building is 140 feet tall with a 368-foot-tall stack. The plant is very visible from nearby areas and particularly from the bay area. Vegetative cover renders the plant much less visible from inland areas.

Between 1960 and 1970, New Jersey's population increased by 18.2%, while that of Ocean County increased by 92.6% and that of Lacey

FIGURE 11–9, *continued.*

and Ocean Townships increased by 138% and
141%, respectively. The bay area is one of
the state's most rapidly growing areas and is
used heavily for water-based recreation. Many
of the developments in the area are seasonal
homes.

3.2.4 R. E. Ginna

The Ginna plant is owned and operated by
the Rochester Gas and Electric Company and is
located in the town of Ontario in Wayne
County, New York. It is on the shore of Lake
Ontario about 20 miles east of Rochester.
Construction of the plant began in 1966, and
it became operational in 1970.

The Ginna plant has a design power level of
490 MWe, and uses a pressurized-water reactor. Coolant water (400,000 gpm) is drawn
from Lake Ontario and is returned to the lake
by underground conduits. The Rochester Gas
and Electric Company owns 338 acres at the
site, of which about 30 acres are occupied by
the reactor and auxiliary buildings.

FIGURE 11-9, *continued.*

but the method described in the following guidelines is serviceable
and simple.

1. The first-level head is in all-capital letters, is underscored, and
   is typed flush with the left margin on a line by itself. There
   is an extra line of space above and below the head.
2. The second-level head is in capital and lower-case letters (that
   is, the first letter of the first word and of every important word
   is capitalized; prepositions and conjunctions of five letters or
   more also begin with a capital). Like the first-level head, this
   head is underscored, is typed flush with the left margin on a
   line by itself, and has an extra line of space above and below
   it.
3. The third-level head is also in capital and lower-case letters.
   (Follow the same capitalization guidelines as for second-level
   heads.) This head is typed flush with the left margin, with
   an extra line of space above and below, and is not underlined.
4. The fourth-level head is underlined and is indented as a paragraph. The first word of the head is capitalized; the remaining

words are not (unless they are proper nouns). The head is typed on the same line as the first sentence of the material it introduces. Therefore, a period generally appears after the head to set it apart from the text that follows. There should be an extra line of space above the head.

The four levels are arranged as follows:

FIRST-LEVEL HEAD

      Begin text here.

Second-Level Head

      Begin text here.

Third-Level Head

      Begin text here.

      Fourth-level head. Begin text here.

As you write your report, keep in mind the following guidelines.

1. A new head should signal a shift to a new topic. Lower-level heads should signal shifts to new subtopics within a major topic.
2. Within a topic, all heads at one level should be parallel in their relationship to the topic. Note in the sample table of contents (Figure 11–4) that "METHODOLOGY" (a first-level head) is followed by five parallel second-level heads, all bearing the same relation to the first-level head—they are all facets of the method by which the subject was investigated. (The word "References" is considered a second-level head when it occurs within a section or chapter, as it does in Figure 11–4. If the "References" section appears at the end of a report, it is listed in the table of contents as a separate section of the report; that is, it is identified as a first-level head.)
3. Too many heads on too many levels can be as bad as too few. They can make the report look cluttered, subdividing the topic too often for your reader to be able to sort out major from subordinate ideas.

Conclusions

The conclusion section pulls together the results of your study in one place. Here you inform the reader about what you have learned and about its implications. You show how the results follow from the study objectives and methodology. You should also point out any unexpected results.

The conclusion section in Figure 11–10 comes from the report on how real estate values in four specific areas were affected by nearby nuclear power plants.

---

5. CONCLUSIONS

Brief statement of purpose

This study was undertaken to test the hypotheses that nuclear power plants have an adverse effect on (1) community growth, and (2) residential property values. Implicit in the second hypothesis is the idea that prices paid for residential properties reflect people's perceptions of house and lot quality, community services and attributes, and environmental characteristics, and that if people in general perceive nuclear plants as a possible threat to health and safety, they will tend to avoid living close to them. Such actions should be reflected in the real estate market for residential properties and, everything else being equal, the closer to the plant the lower the price for housing.

Findings

The following conclusions are apparent from an analysis of time series data on total assessed real property values from 1960 to 1976 and from a regression analysis of 540 single-family house sales in 1975, 1976, and 1977 in the vicinity of four nuclear power generating plants in the Northeast:

1. Assuming that the real (deflated) increase in total assessed property values is a good indicator of growth, the presence of the nuclear plants has had no adverse effects on the growth rates of communities in close proximity to such plants.
2. In light of the fact that (a) growth rates were inversely related to distance from the plant, and (b) annual growth

FIGURE 11–10. Conclusions.

rates for the years following plant construction were higher than for the years
before plant construction, with the increase in the growth rate for the host
communities being higher than the increase for the region as a whole, the
presence of the nuclear plant may actually serve as a stimulus to growth. The
likely explanation for this is the lower
tax rates in the host municipalities,
which are made possible by the large tax
assessments levied on the plants.

3. The presence of the nuclear power
   plants, at least in 1975, 1976, and
   1977, exerted no influence on the price
   of single-family housing within 20 miles
   of these plants. Therefore, our hypothesis that residential property values are
   directly related to distance from the
   nuclear power plants must be rejected
   and the null hypothesis accepted.

4. For most people in these study areas,
   the proximity of a nuclear power plant
   does not appear as a factor in residential location choice. The fears for
   health and safety expressed by some individuals and groups in society are not
   reflected in the housing decisions of
   residents in communities near the nuclear plants studied.

**Restatement
of scope
and its
implications**

These conclusions are applicable only to
the four areas studied. Since the plants were
preselected and do not represent a random
sample of all nuclear plants, the findings
cannot be used to predict influences on
growth and property values at other plant
sites. Moreover, society's perceptions and
values change over time, and what may have
been true in the mid-1970s may not hold true
in the future.

FIGURE 11–10, *continued.*

Recommendations

Recommendations, which are sometimes combined with the conclusions section, state what course of action should be taken based

on the results of the study. Of the three possible locations for a new warehouse, which is the best? Which make of delivery van should be purchased to replace the existing fleet? Which contractor has submitted the best proposal for remodeling the company cafeteria? Which type of word processing equipment should the office buy? Should the equipment be leased rather than purchased? The recommendations section says, in effect, "I think we should purchase this, or do that, or hire them."

The emphasis is on the verb *should*. Recommendations advise the reader on the best course of action based on the researcher's findings. Generally someone up the organizational ladder, or a customer or client, makes the final decision about whether or not to accept the recommendations. The example in Figure 11–11 is from a research report, and it combines conclusions and recommendations. The report evaluated two garments designed to help workers at power plants overcome heat stress problems in harsh environments.

CONCLUSIONS AND RECOMMENDATIONS

Objective

    The primary objective of this project was to assess two approaches to unrestricted (portable) cooling of power plant workers. To this end, a prototype frozen water garment and a prototype liquid cooling garment were developed and subjected to a series of controlled laboratory tests. Testing was con-

Methodology

ducted in a climatic chamber calibrated to simulate extreme environmental conditions found in a power plant. Results of these

Results

tests indicated that more effective cooling was provided by the frozen water garment. Criteria for effective cooling were maximum

Criteria for evaluating results

stay time in the hot environment (as determined by the test subject's voluntary withdrawal from the test chamber or by his core temperature or heart rate or both reaching predetermined limits) and the rate of change of physiological indicants of heat stress. The frozen water garment was observed to provide longer stay times and a less rapid rise in core temperature and heart rate in comparison to both the prototype circulating liquid garment developed especially for this study (System A) and a commercially available circulating liquid garment (System B) loaned to

FIGURE 11–11. Conclusions and recommendations section.

the project by a utility company. Moreover,
the effective cooling of the frozen water
garment was observed under conditions in
which test subjects were and were not heat-
acclimated.

The preceding results can be explained in
part by the garment design factors that affect cooling. The main factors involved in
the personal cooling systems of this study
were the amount of cooling material and the
surface area (SA) of the body that was exposed to the cooling. The Cool Head and the
Cool Suit involved cooled circulating liquid
that transfers the body heat only by temperature gradient. Thus, the potential of cooling
is 1 Kcal per 1°C gradient for each liter of
circulating water. The body's surface area
covered and the rate of heat flow define the
rates of cooling by these two systems. Both
systems seemed to have kept the body temperature below that of the control. However, the
rate of rise, particularly in core body temperature, was as fast as that for the control. Although the systems of circulating
liquid did cool, the cooling rate was not
sufficient for the ambient and clothing conditions employed in our laboratory studies.

Other Criteria

While garment durability, ease of decon-
tamination, ease of cleaning, and ease of
freezing the heat sink are important criteria, the project team has no specific experience to report in these areas. Appendix A,
however, does address these issues.

RECOMMENDATIONS REGARDING GARMENT USE
AND IMPLEMENTATION

Primary recommendation   Results of this study indicate that under
extreme environmental conditions where the
onset of heat stress may occur rapidly and
work duration may be shortened, use of a frozen water garment offers potential for improving worker safety and productivity. This
conclusion is based primarily on the results
of controlled laboratory studies, and for
that reason it should be considered preliminary. Data from the field use of the garment,
while encouraging, are insufficient to draw a
strong conclusion.

FIGURE 11–11, *continued.*

Secondary
recommendation Prior to implementing a program of personal cooling, each utility should evaluate its site-specific needs and assess the potential benefits of various cooling approaches. Material contained in this report should be useful in that evaluation process.

  If the results of these analyses point to implementation of a personal cooling program, we recommend an initial period of trial implementation involving only a few units of the cooling system selected for application at the site. The trial-use period allows a more measured assessment of the degree to which any system meets site-specific requirements.

Additional
recommendations The management of manual work under heat stress conditions and the use of cooling systems to mitigate heat stress should always be approached with a great deal of caution. Stay times observed in the laboratory and field studies that are cited in this report should not be used to set standards, either formal or informal, at other sites. Workers in a hot environment, whether cooled or not, should be encouraged to leave the hot area when they feel either dizzy or nauseated. Further, when using the frozen water garment, workers should follow the procedures outlined in Appendix C. If these simple cautions are observed, a program of personal cooling can lead to more effective and productive work.

FIGURE 11–11, *continued.*

Explanatory Footnotes

  Occasionally, you will need to offer an explanatory comment to suggest an idea mentioned in the main body of the text. As discussed on page 262, this type of footnote is generally placed at the foot of the page on which the comment occurs. Mark the first such footnote on a page with an asterisk (*), the second with a dagger (†), the third with a double dagger (‡), and the fourth with a section mark (§).

  A description of the 76 variables identified for inclusion in the regression equations, together with their method of construction, data, source, means, and ranges, is given in Appendix A. The

following discussion elaborates on those variables
that proved most important in explaining housing
price variations.*

_____

*The number in parentheses refers to the var-
iable number as used in the regression equation.

References

If, in your report, you refer to material in or quote directly from
a published work or other research source, you must provide a list
of references in a separate section called "References." If your employer has a preferred reference style, follow it; otherwise, use the
guidelines that were provided in Chapter 10 for the author/date system.

For a relatively short report, the references should go at the end
of the report. For a report with a number of sections or chapters,
the reference section should fall at the end of each major section or
chapter. In either case, every reference section should be labeled as
such and should start on a new page. If a particular reference appears
in more than one section or chapter, it should be repeated in full in
each appropriate reference section.

BACK MATTER

The *back matter* of a formal report is composed of supplemental
information—material that is not absolutely necessary for your reader
to know but that may shed some additional light on the topic.

Bibliography

If you have quoted from or referred to any research sources, you
must include in your report a bibliography as well as a reference
section. The bibliography, which usually appears in the back matter,
is the listing, in alphabetical order, of all the sources of information
you consulted to prepare the report. Accordingly, the bibliography
may be longer than the reference section, and because it is arranged
alphabetically, it enables a reader interested in seeing whether you
consulted a particular source to discover as much at a glance. To
prepare a bibliography, follow the guidelines provided in Chapter 10.
Like other elements in the front and back matter, the bibliography
starts on a new page and is labeled by name.

Appendixes

Material typically placed in an *appendix* includes long charts and supplementary graphs or tables; copies of questionnaires and other material used in gathering information; texts of interviews; pertinent correspondence; and explanations too long for explanatory footnotes but helpful to the reader who is seeking further assistance or clarification. A report may have one or more appendixes; generally, each appendix contains one type of material.

Place the first appendix on a new page directly after the bibliography. Additional appendixes also begin on a new page. Identify each with a title and a heading. Appendixes are ordinarily labeled Appendix A, Appendix B, and so on. If your report has only one appendix, simply label it "Appendix," followed by the title. To call it Appendix A would imply that an Appendix B will follow.

```
Appendix A

Sample Questionnaire
```

If there is only one appendix, the pages are generally numbered A-1, A-2, A-3, and so forth. If there is more than one appendix, the pages are double-numbered according to the letter of each appendix (for example, the first page of Appendix B would be numbered B-1).

Glossary

A *glossary* is a list of selected terms, on a particular subject, that are defined and explained. Include a glossary only if your report contains many words and expressions that will be unfamiliar to your intended audience. Arrange the terms alphabetically, with each entry beginning on a new line. Definitions then follow each term, dictionary style. The glossary, labeled as such, appears directly after the appendix and begins on a new page.

GRAPHIC AND TABULAR MATTER

Formal reports often contain illustrations and tables that clarify and support the text. These materials may be numbered and sequenced in varying ways. The following guidelines show one conventional system for integrating such materials smoothly into the text. For a full discussion of the creation and use of illustrations and tables, see Chapter 13.

Figures

Identify each figure with a title and a number, in Arabic numerals, above or below the figure. For fairly short reports, number figures sequentially throughout the report (Figure 1, Figure 2, and so forth). For long reports, number figures by chapter or by section. According to the latter system, the first figure in Chapter 1 would be Figure 1.1 (or Figure 1–1), and the second figure would be Figure 1.2 (or Figure 1–2). In Chapter 2, the first figure would be Figure 2.1, and so on. See the map that appears in Figure 11–9. In the long report in which the map appeared, this illustration was the first in the third section, and therefore was numbered 3.1.

In the text, refer to figures by number rather than by location ("Figure 2.1" rather than "the figure below"). When the report is typed, the figures may not fall exactly where you originally expected.

Tables

Identify each table with a title and a number, centering both of these lines above the table. For fairly short reports, number the tables sequentially throughout the report (Table 2, Table 3, and so on). For long reports, number tables by chapter or by section according to the system described for figure numbering. See the sample table in Figure 11–9. As with figures, refer to tables in the text by number rather than by location ("Table 4.1" rather than "the above table").

CHAPTER SUMMARY

Formal reports, which are the written accounts of major projects, normally contain three major parts: front matter, body, and back matter. The *front matter* of a formal report may include a title page, an abstract, a table of contents, a list of figures, a list of tables, a preface, and a section for abbreviations and symbols. The *body* of a formal report includes the text of the report, complete with footnotes, headings, tables, illustrations, and references. The text may open with a summary and an introduction and may end with a conclusions and recommendations section. The *back matter* of a formal report may include a bibliography, appendixes, and a glossary.

EXERCISES

1. Come to class prepared to discuss the following questions.

    a. Why should a formal report contain a table of contents?

    b. What is the function of a preface in a formal report?

    c. What is the function of explanatory footnotes in a formal report?

    d. What function do heads perform in a formal report?

    e. What is the difference between *conclusions* and *recommendations*?

    f. What determines when a new head is to be used?

    g. What is the difference between a *reference section* and a *bibliography*?

    h. What types of material should appear in an *appendix*?

    i. What is the function of a *glossary* in a formal report?

2. Select a feature article from the current issue of *Scientific American* or from a journal chosen by your instructor. Using the article as your starting point, do the following:

    a. Create a formal topic outline, using the guidelines in Chapter 2.

    b. Convert the outline to a descriptive and an informative abstract, and label each accordingly.

    c. Using the outline, create a table of contents for the article as though it were a formal report, using the elements discussed in this chapter that are appropriate.

3. Write a formal report on a topic from your career field or other area of interest. You may want to use the topic you selected and the information you gathered in doing the exercises for Chapter 10. Prepare a topic outline for the report, and submit it for your instructor's review. Include at least the following elements in the report (plus any additional elements your paper may require): title page, descriptive abstract, table of contents, preface, summary, heads, conclusions and/or recommendations, references, and bibliography.

12

Proposals and Other Kinds of On-the-Job Communication

Much on-the-job writing—for example, proposals, minutes of meetings, and job descriptions—cannot be classified either as correspondence or as reports. Yet such types of communication can be just as important as the letters, routine memos, and reports that you write. Another kind of communication—the printed form—frequently requires only a minimum of writing and yet can in some circumstances be the most effective and efficient way to communicate. This chapter deals with several of the less-recognized kinds of on-the-job communication: proposals, minutes of meetings, job descriptions, and printed forms.

PROPOSALS

The general purpose of any proposal is to persuade the reader to do something, whether it is (1) to persuade a potential customer to purchase your products and services or (2) to persuade your boss to fund a project you would like to launch. You would write a sales proposal to accomplish the first objective; you would write an internal proposal to accomplish the second. (These types of proposals will be discussed shortly.) Any proposal offers a plan to fill a need, and your reader will evaluate your plan according to how well your written presentation answers his questions about *what* you are proposing to do, *how* you plan to do it, *when* you plan to do it, and *how much* it is going to cost.

To answer these questions effectively for your reader, you must be certain that your proposal is written at your reader's level of knowledge. If you have more than one level of audience—a fairly common occurrence, since proposals often require more than one level of management approval—you must take all your readers into account. For example, if your immediate reader is an expert on your subject but the next higher level of management (which must also approve the proposal) is not, you would provide an executive summary written in language that is as nontechnical as possible. You might also include a glossary that explains the technical terms used in the body of the proposal, or appendixes that explain the technical information in nontechnical language. On the other hand, if your immediate reader is not an expert but the person at the next level is, you would write the proposal with the layman in mind and might include appendixes that contain the technical details of your proposal.

Proposals that are short or of medium length basically consist of an introduction, a body, and a conclusion. (Long proposals, as will be discussed, generally contain more elements.) The *introduction* should summarize the problem you are proposing to solve and your solution to the problem; it may also indicate the benefits that your reader will receive from your solution and the total cost of that solution. The *body* should explain in complete detail exactly (1) how the job will be done, (2) what methods will be used to do it (and, if applicable, the specific materials to be used and any other pertinent information), (3) when work will begin, (4) when the job will be completed, and (5) the detailed cost breakdown for the entire job. The *conclusion* should emphasize the benefits that the reader will realize from your solution to the problem and should urge the reader to action. Your conclusion should have an encouraging, confident, and reasonably assertive tone.

Persuasive Writing

Proposals, by definition, are persuasive writing, since you are attempting to convince someone to do something. Your goal is to prove to your reader that he or she needs what you are proposing to do, that it is practical, and that it is appropriate. For an unsolicited proposal, you may even need to convince your reader that he or she *has* a problem and that the problem is serious enough for a solution to be necessary. You would then offer your solution in such a way as to build a persuasive case for the logic of the approach you are proposing. Your facts must lead logically, even inevitably, to your conclusions and your solution.

Give your evidence in descending order of importance; that is, begin with the most important evidence and end with the least important. Anticipate and answer any objections your reader may have to your approach to the problem and your solution to it. Consider any alternative solutions that might be offered and show how yours is superior to them—but be very careful about the tone you use in doing so. For example, the use of sarcasm in describing opposing points of view could very likely backfire.

The tone of your proposal should be positive, confident, and tactful. The following example demonstrates a tone that is arrogant and therefore inappropriate in a proposal.

> The Qualtron Corporation has obviously not considered the potential problem of not having backup equipment available when a commercial power failure occurs. The corporation would also be wise indeed to give a great deal more consideration to the volume of output expected per machine.

The following version of the same passage is timid and therefore equally inappropriate.

> There could perhaps be a possibility of a problem with not having backup equipment available when commercial power fails. Also, it might be advisable to perhaps reconsider the volume of output expected per machine.

The following version of the same passage is positive, confident, and tactful.

> The system should be designed in such a way as to provide backup equipment in the event of a commercial power failure. Also, the system should be based on realistic expectations concerning the output of each machine.

Internal Proposals

An *internal proposal* is normally prepared as a memorandum by an employee and is sent to a higher-ranking person in the same organization for approval. An internal proposal can serve any of three purposes:

1. It can recommend a change in the way something is being done.

2. It can recommend that something be done that is not presently being done.
3. It can recommend a capital appropriation for a large purchase.

As an example of the first kind, a proposal might recommend that the management of multiple manufacturing operations be decentralized. Typical of the second kind might be a proposal to initiate assigned parking places. The third kind might be a proposal to replace an outdated computer system (Christine Thomas in Chapter 1 wrote just such a proposal).

Writing the Introduction. The function of the introduction to an internal proposal is to establish that a problem exists for which a solution is urgently needed. The problem, and the negative results it is causing, must be very clearly presented, even if you think the reader is probably already aware of it—don't rely on assumptions. If the person who must approve your proposal is not convinced that a serious problem exists, approval of your solution is unlikely.

After identifying the problem, the introduction should summarize your proposed solution. You might indicate the benefits to be realized from the adoption of your proposal and its total cost, although these features are more common in sales proposals than in internal proposals. Notice how the following introduction states the problem and then summarizes the writer's proposed solution.

```
    TO:    Marge Dundas, Director
           Personnel Resources

    FROM:  Leslie Galusha, Manager
           Administrative Support Services

SUBJECT:   Upgrading from Typewriters to Word Pro-
           cessors
```

```
We are receiving an increasing number of requests
to prepare direct mailings that involve sending
each recipient an original copy, especially from
the Advertising, Public Relations, and Employee
Relations Departments. The cost of calling in
temporary help to get the typing done is very
high, and an abnormal workload results from our
efforts to get the extra work done. In addition,
the pressure causes much confusion and many frayed
nerves.
```

```
I propose that we purchase a word processor to
enable us to handle the increased workload without
the cost and disruption of bringing in temporary
```

help. The following details show the savings and
efficiency of the Toshiba EW-100 Word Processor as
compared with our present method of dealing with
the problem.

Writing the Body.   The body of an internal proposal should provide a detailed description of your solution to the problem. The key word here is *detailed*. Try to put yourself in your reader's position and ask yourself what information *you* would need if you had to make the decision you are asking your reader to make. Then be sure to include all the necessary information. Your presentation of your solution should grow naturally out of your statement of the problem. When applicable, include the following information:

1. A breakdown of costs
2. The methods to be used in achieving the proposed solution to the problem, as well as the equipment, material, and personnel that would be required
3. A detailed schedule for completing the project, possibly broken down into separate tasks

The following sample body is a continuation of the preceding introduction.

Efficiency

The Toshiba EW-100 Word Processor has a merge
feature that permits the operator to type the basic letter as one file, substituting a special
character for any word or words that will change
from one letter to the next (such as name and address), and to type the word or words to be substituted for the special character (such as name
and address) as a separate file. Then the operator
simply sets up the printer for merge printing and
presses the MERGE key. The system automatically
types all the letters, substituting the indicated
word or words from the second file in each consecutive letter. This operation is many times
faster than the best human typist, and it is entirely error-free, once programmed.

Keyboard entry on the Toshiba EW-100 Word Processor is much more efficient than it is with a
typewriter. Instead of having to "paint out" an
error or use typewriter correction paper, the operator simply strikes over the error. (The system
automatically corrects the error on the diskette.)
Because correcting an error is so easy, statistics
show that the operator's typing speed increases.

An additional advantage of upgrading from typewriter to word processor is file storage. Rather
than using bulky filing cabinets for 8 1/2- by 11-
inch paper, we can store over 600 pages on a single 8-inch diskette. One single 1 1/2-inch diskette container holds ten diskettes, or more than
6,000 pages (double-spaced), thereby reducing our
storage requirements dramatically.

Having a Toshiba EW-100 Word Processor and one
trained operator would eliminate the need for
temporary typists and the confusion caused by our
training these typists while attempting to meet
our own deadlines. In short, we could carry on
with our normal office routine. A normal routine
not only would improve our employees' morale but
would increase their efficiency.

Cost Savings

Purchase of the Toshiba EW-100 Word Processor--
with a Ricoh 45-characters-per-second daisy-wheel
printer--would result in a savings of over $3,500
in the first year, as shown below.

Purchase price of Toshiba EW-100 with Ricoh printer	$5,000
Cost of temporary typists from Wilson Secretarial Agency last year	$7,400
Typewriter rental from World Office Machines last year	$1,120
Savings the first year ($7,400 + $1,120 − $5,000 = $3,520)	$3,520

Since purchase of the Toshiba EW-100 Word Processor is a one-time cost, the savings would be
substantially greater after the first year.

Writing the Conclusion. The function of the conclusion of an
internal proposal is to tie everything together, possibly restate your
recommendation, and close with a spirit of cooperation (offering to
set up a meeting, supply additional information, or provide any other
assistance that might be needed). Your conclusion should be brief.
Notice how the following continuation of the sample proposal concludes.

On the basis of these facts, I recommend that we
purchase a Toshiba EW-100 Word Processor. Enclosed
is a brochure that describes the Toshiba EW-100
Word Processor in detail. I will be happy to provide any additional details about the system, as I
understand it, at your request.

Figure 12–1 shows a typical internal proposal. The proposal was
written by a plant safety officer to the plant superintendent and recommends changes in the way things are presently being done.

Proposals for Capital Appropriations. For any purchase cost-
ing more than a certain amount (a typical figure is $25,000), companies
often require a formal internal proposal called a capital appropriations
request. This is a proposal to commit company funds to buy or build
equipment or to buy property.

The introduction to such a proposal should provide any background information your reader might need in order to make the
decision in question. The introduction should also briefly describe any
feasibility study you may have conducted, the conclusions the study
led you to reach, and the decision you made on the basis of those
conclusions.

The body of the proposal should identify all the equipment or
property you are asking to acquire and should state the economic
justification for the expenditure involved. If you need to purchase

---

MEMORANDUM

TO: Harold Clurman,
         Plant Superintendent

FROM: Fred Nelson, Safety Officer *FN*

DATE: August 4, 19--

SUBJECT: Safety Practices for Group 333

Many accidents and near-accidents have occurred in Group 333 because of the hazardous
working conditions in this area. This memorandum identifies those hazardous conditions
and makes recommendations for their elimination.

FIGURE 12–1. Internal proposal.

Hazardous Conditions

Employees inside the factory must operate the walk-along crane through aisles that are frequently congested with scrap metal, discarded lumber, and other refuse from the shearing area. Many surfaces in the area are oil-coated.

The containers for holding raw stock and scrap metal are also unsafe. On many of the racks, the hooks are bent inward so far that the crane cannot fit into them properly unless it is banged and jiggled in a dangerous manner. To add to the hazard, employees in the press group do not always balance the load in the racks. As a result, the danger of falling metal is great as the unbalanced racks swing practically out of control overhead. These hazards endanger employees in Group 333 and also employees in the raw-stock and shearing areas, because the crane passes over these areas.

Hazards also exist in the yard and in the chemical building. The present method of dumping strip metal into the scrap bins is the most dangerous practice of all. To dump this metal, the tow-motor operator picks up a rack, with the rack straddling the tow-motor forks, and raises it over the edge of the scrap-metal bin. The operator then rotates the forks to permit the scrap metal to fall from one end of the rack. As the weight shifts, the upright frame at the other end of the rack slams into one of the tow-motor forks (now raised 12 feet above the ground, inside the scrap tub). This method of operation has resulted in two tow-motor tip-overs in the past month. In neither incident was the driver injured, but the odds are great that someone will be seriously harmed if the practice continues.

Group 333 employees must also dump tubs full of scrap metal from the tow motor into the 10-foot-high scrap bins. In order to dump the metal on the tow-motor forks, the operator must raise the tubs high above his head. Because of the unpredictable way in which the

FIGURE 12–1, *continued.*

metal falls from the tubs, many facial cuts
and body bruises have resulted. Employees who
work in the yard are also subject to danger
in winter weather: all employees have been
cut and bruised in falls that occurred as
they were climbing up on scrap bins covered
with snow and ice to dump scrap from pallets
that had not been banded.

Finally, nearly all Group 333 employees who
must handle the caustic chemicals in the
chemical building report damaged clothing and
ruined shoes. Poor lighting in the building
(the lights are nearly 20 feet above the
floor), storage racks positioned less than
two feet apart, and container caps incorrectly fastened have made these accidents impossible to prevent.

Recommendations

To eliminate these hazards as quickly as possible, I recommend that the following actions
be taken:

1. That Group 333 supervisors rigorously
   initiate and enforce a policy to free
   aisles of obstructions.
2. That all dangerous racks be repaired and
   replaced.
3. That the Engineering Group develop a
   safe rack dumper.
4. That heavy wire mesh screens be mounted
   on the front of all tow motors.
5. That Group 333 employees not accept
   scrap in containers that have not been
   properly banded.
6. That illumination be increased in the
   chemical building and that a compulsory
   training program for the safe handling
   of caustic chemicals be scheduled.

I would like to meet with you and the supervisor of Group 333 before the end of the
month, as your schedule permits. You will
have my complete cooperation in working out
all of the details of the proposed recommendations.

Copy: Jim Hanchett, Supervisor, Group 333

FIGURE 12–1, *continued.*

equipment, be sure to identify *all* the equipment you need so that you don't find yourself preparing another proposal for the rest of it later. Include an economic justification of either the calculated return on investment or the internal rate of return. Your proposal should include all the following items that are applicable to your particular capital appropriations request.

1. A brief description of the item to be purchased
2. The alternative choices you considered before deciding on the one you are recommending
3. The specific products or projects to be supported by the item
4. The volume of usage that the item would receive over a specified period, such as the next two years
5. If the company already has some of the item, an explanation of the volume of usage that necessitates an additional purchase
6. The life expectancy of the item and the life expectancy of the current product or project it is to support
7. Any future products or projects the item could be used to support
8. Whether a leasing arrangement is available and more economical than purchasing the item
9. The impact on the company if the item is not acquired
10. The latest feasible date of acquisition, including the impact that a 90-day delay would have
11. The calculated return on investment, or the internal rate of return

With your capital appropriations request, you should submit a cover memo. The memo, which should be no more than one page long, should give a brief description of the item and the essential reason it is needed.

Sales Proposals

The *sales proposal* (or *external proposal*), which is one of the major marketing tools in use in business and industry today, is one company's offer to provide specific goods or services to a potential buyer within a specified period of time and for a specified price. The primary purpose of a sales proposal is to demonstrate that the prospective customer's purchase of the seller's products or services would be a wise investment.

Sales proposals vary greatly in size and relative sophistication. Some may run a page or two and be written by one person; others may be many pages long and be written by several people; still others may take hundreds of pages and be written by a team of professional proposal writers. A short sales proposal might bid for the construction of a single home; a sales proposal of moderate length might bid for the installation of a network of computer systems; and a very long sales proposal might be used to bid for the construction of a multibillion-dollar aircraft carrier.

Your first task in writing a sales proposal is to find out exactly what your potential customer wants. If you can obtain this information from the customer, in writing, you have an advantage. Often, however, you will need to determine what the customer wants on the basis of your experience. You must then determine whether your organization can satisfy the customer's needs. Before preparing a sales proposal, you should also try to find out who your primary competitors are. Then compare your company's strengths with the strengths of the competing firms, determine where you have advantages over your competitors, and emphasize those advantages in your proposal. For example, a small software company bidding for an Air Force contract at a local base would be familiar with its competitors. If the proposal writer believed that his company had better-qualified personnel than its competitors, he might include the resumes of the key people who would be involved in the project as a way of emphasizing that advantage.

Solicited and Unsolicited Sales Proposals. Sales proposals may be either solicited or unsolicited. The latter are not so unusual as they may sound: companies often operate for years with a problem they have never recognized (unnecessarily high maintenance costs, for example, or poor inventory-control methods). You might prepare an unsolicited proposal for such a company if you were convinced that the potential customer could realize substantial benefits by adopting your solution to the problem. You would, of course, need to persuade the customer of the excellence of your idea and of the need for what you are proposing.

To ensure that you don't waste a lot of time and effort, you might precede an unsolicited proposal with an inquiry to determine any potential interest. If you receive a positive response, you might then need to conduct a detailed study of the prospective customer's needs and requirements in order to determine whether you can be of help at all and, if so, exactly how you can help the customer. You would then prepare your proposal on the basis of your study.

An unsolicited proposal must clearly identify the potential customer's problem but at the same time should be careful not to overstate it. Further, the proposal must convince the customer that the problem needs to be solved. One way to do this is to emphasize the benefits that the customer will realize from the solution being proposed.

The other type of sales proposal—the solicited sales proposal—is a response to a request for goods or services. Procuring organizations that would like competing companies to bid for a job commonly issue a *Request for Proposals.* The Request for Proposals is the means used by many companies and government agencies to find the best method of doing a job and the most qualified company to do it. A Request for Proposals may be rigid in its specifications governing how the proposal should be organized and what it should contain, but it is normally quite flexible about the approaches that bidding firms may propose. Normally, the Request for Proposals simply defines the basic work that is to be accomplished.

The procuring organization generally publishes its Request for Proposals in one or more journals, in addition to sending it to certain selected companies that have good reputations for doing the kind of work needed. Some companies and government agencies even hold a conference for the competing firms at which they provide all pertinent information about the job being bid for.

Managers interested in responding to Requests for Proposals scan the appropriate publications regularly. Upon finding a project of interest, an executive in the sales department of such a company obtains all available information from the procuring company or agency. The data are then presented to management for a decision on whether the company is interested in the project. If the decision is positive, the technical staff is assigned the task of developing an approach to the work described in the Request for Proposals. The technical staff normally considers several alternatives, selecting one that combines feasibility and a price that will yield sufficient profit. The staff's concept is presented to higher management for a decision on whether the company wishes to present a proposal to the requesting organization. Assuming that the decision is to proceed, preparation of the proposal is the next step.

When you respond to a Request for Proposals, pay close attention to any specifications in the request governing the preparation of the proposal. Follow the specifications to the letter, even if you don't like them.

Writing a Simple Sales Proposal. Even a short and uncomplicated sales proposal should be carefully planned. The introduction should state the purpose and scope of the proposal. It should indicate the date on which you propose to begin work on the project, the date on which you expect to complete work, any special benefits of your proposed approach, and the total cost of the project. The introduction could also refer to any previous association your company may have had with the potential customer, assuming of course that the association was positive and mutually beneficial.

The body of a sales proposal should itemize the products and services you are proposing to furnish. It should include, if applicable, a discussion of the procedures you would use to perform the work and any specific materials to be used. It should also present a time schedule indicating when each stage of the project would be completed. Finally, the body should include a precise breakdown of the costs of the project.

The conclusion should express your appreciation for the opportunity to submit the proposal, as well as your confidence in your company's ability to do the job to the customer's satisfaction. You might add in the conclusion that you look forward to establishing good working relations with the customer and that you would be glad to provide any additional information that might be needed. Your conclusion could also review any advantages your company may have over its competitors. It should specify the time period during which your proposal can still be considered a valid offer. If any supplemental materials, such as blueprints or price sheets, accompany the proposal, include a list of them at the end of the proposal. Figure 12–2 shows a typical short sales proposal.

PROPOSAL

To Landscape the New Corporate Headquarters
of the
Watford Valve Corporation

Submitted to: Ms. Tricia Olivera,
               Vice President
Submitted by: Jerwalted Nursery, Inc.
Date submitted: February 1, 19--

Jerwalted Nursery, Inc., proposes to landscape the new corporate headquarters of the Watford Valve Corporation, on 1600 Swason Avenue, at a total cost of $8,000. Landscaping would begin no later than April 30, 19--, and would be completed by May 31.

The lot to be landscaped is approximately 600 feet wide and 700 feet deep. The following trees and plants would be planted in the quantities and sizes given and at the prices specified. They would be positioned as indicated in the enclosed drawing.

FIGURE 12–2. Short sales proposal.

```
4 maple trees (not less than 7
   ft.) $40 each                    $   160
41 birch trees (not less than 7
   ft.) $65 each                      2,665
2 spruce trees (not less than 7
   ft.) $105 each                       210
20 juniper plants (not less than
   18 in.) $15 each                     300
60 hedges (not less than 18 in.)
   $7 each                              420
200 potted plants (various
   kinds) $2 each                       400

           Total cost of plants  $4,155
                        Labor     3,845
                   Total cost    $8,000
```

All trees and plants would be guaranteed
against defect or disease for a period of 90
days, with the warranty period to begin June
1, 19--.
The prices quoted in this proposal will be
valid until June 30, 19--.
Thank you for the opportunity to submit
this proposal. Jerwalted Nursery, Inc., has
been in the landscaping and nursery business
in the Providence area for thirty years, and
our landscaping has won several awards and
commendations, including a citation from the
National Association of Architects. We are
eager to put our skills and knowledge to work
for you, and we are confident that you will
be pleased with our work. If we can provide
any additional information or assistance,
please call.

Writing a Long Sales Proposal. A long sales proposal begins
with a *cover letter,* which expresses your appreciation for the opportunity to submit your proposal and for any assistance you may have
received in studying the customer's requirements. The letter should
acknowledge any previous association with the customer, assuming
that it was a positive experience. Then it should summarize the recommendations offered in the proposal and express your confidence that
they will satisfy the customer's needs. Figure 12–3 shows the cover
letter for the proposal illustrated in Figures 12–4 through 12–11—a
proposal that the Waters Corporation of Tampa provide a computer
system for the Cookson chain of retail stores.

The Waters Corporation
17 North Waterloo Blvd.
Tampa, Florida 33607

September 1, 19--

Mr. John Yeung, General Manager
Cookson's Retail Stores, Inc.
101 Longuer Street
Savannah, Georgia 31499

Dear Mr. Yeung:

The Waters Corporation appreciates the opportunity to respond to Cookson's Request for
Proposals dated July 26, 19--. We would like
to thank Mr. Becklight, Director of your Management Information Systems Department, for
his invaluable contributions to the study of
your operations that we conducted before preparing our proposal.

It has been Waters's privilege to provide
Cookson's with retail systems and equipment
since your first store opened many years ago.
Therefore, we have become very familiar with
your requirements as they have evolved during
the expansion you have experienced since that
time. Waters's close working relationship
with Cookson's has resulted in a clear understanding of Cookson's philosophy and needs.

Our proposal describes a Waters Interactive
Terminal/Retail Processor System designed to
meet Cookson's network and processing needs.
It will provide all of your required capabilities, from the point-of-sale operational requirements at the store terminals to the host
processor. The system uses the proven Retail
III modular software, with its point-of-sale
applications, and the superior Interactive
Terminal with its advanced capabilities and
design. This system is easily installed without massive customer reprogramming.

FIGURE 12-3. Cover letter.

Mr. J. Yeung
Page 2
September 1, 19--

The Waters Interactive Terminal/Retail Processor System, which is compatible with much
of Cookson's present equipment, not only will
answer your present requirements but will
provide the flexibility to add new features
and products in the future. The system's
unique hardware modularity, efficient microprocessor design, and flexible programming
capability greatly reduce the risk of obso-
lescence.

Thank you for the opportunity to present this
proposal. You may be sure that we will use
all the resources available to the Waters
Corporation to ensure the successful implementation of the new system.

Sincerely yours,

Janet A. Curtain

Janet A. Curtain
Executive Account Manager
General Merchandise Systems

FIGURE 12–3, *continued.*

EXECUTIVE SUMMARY

The Waters 319 Interactive Terminal/615 Retail Processor System will provide your management with the tools necessary to manage
people and equipment more profitably with
procedures that will yield more cost-effective business controls for Cookson's.

The equipment and applications proposed for
Cookson's were selected through the combined
effort of Waters and Cookson's Management Information Systems Director, Mr. Becklight.
The architecture of the system will respond
to your current requirements and allow for a
logical expansion in the future.

The features and hardware in the system were
determined from data acquired through the
comprehensive survey we conducted at your
stores in February of this year. The total of
71 Interactive Terminals proposed to service
your four store locations is based on the
number of terminals currently in use and on
the average number of transactions processed
during normal and peak periods. The planned
remodeling of all four stores was also considered, and the suggested terminal placement
has been incorporated into the working floor
plan. The proposed equipment configuration
and software applications have been simulated
to determine system performance based on the
volumes and anticipated growth rates of the
Cookson stores.

The information from the survey was also used
in the cost justification, which was checked
and verified by your controller, Mr. Deiter-
ing. The cost-effectiveness of the Waters Interactive Terminal/Retail Processor System is
apparent. Expected savings, such as the projected 46% reduction in sales audit expenses,
are realistic projections based on Waters's
experience with other installations of this
type.

FIGURE 12–4. Executive summary.

An *executive summary* follows the cover letter. Addressed to the executive who will ultimately accept or reject the proposal, it should summarize in nontechnical language how you plan to approach the work. Figure 12–4 shows the executive summary of the Waters Corporation proposal. If your proposal offers products as well as services, it should also include a *general description* of the products. Figure 12–5 shows a typical general description.

GENERAL SYSTEM DESCRIPTION

The point-of-sale system that Waters is proposing for Cookson's includes two primary Waters products. These are the 319 Interactive Terminal and the 615 Retail Processor.

Waters 319 Interactive Terminal

The primary component in the proposed retail system is the Interactive Terminal. It contains a full microprocessor, which gives it the flexibility that Cookson's has been looking for.

The 319 Interactive Terminal provides you with freedom in sequencing a transaction. You are not limited to a preset list of available steps or transactions. The terminal program can be adapted to provide unique transaction sets, each designed with a logical sequence of entry and processing to accomplish required tasks. In addition to sales transactions recorded on the selling floor, specialized transactions such as theater tickets sales and payments can be designed for your customer service area.

The 319 Interactive Terminal also functions as a credit authorization device, either by using its own floor limits or by transmitting a credit inquiry to the 615 Retail Processor for authorization.

Data-collection formats have been simplified so that transaction editing and formatting are much more easily accomplished. Mr. Sier

FIGURE 12–5. General description of products.

has already been provided with documentation
on these formats and has outlined all data-
processing efforts that will be necessary to
interface the data to your current systems.
These projections have been considered in the
cost justification.

Waters 615 Retail Processor

The Waters 615 Retail Processor is a minicomputer system designed to support the Waters
family of retail terminals. The processor
will reside in the computer room in your data
center in Buffalo. Operators already on your
staff will be trained to initiate and monitor
its activities.

The 615 will collect data transmitted from
the retail terminals, process credit, check
authorization inquiries, maintain files to be
accessed by the retail terminals, accumulate
totals, maintain a message-routing network,
and control the printing of various reports.
The functions and level of control performed
at the processor depend on the peripherals
and software selected.

Software

The Retail III software used with the system
has been thoroughly tested and is operational
in many Waters customer installations.

The software provides the complete processing
of the transaction, from the interaction with
the operator on the sales floor through the
data capture on cassette or disk in stores
and your data center.

Retail III provides a menu of modular applications for your selection. Parameters condition each of them to your hardware environment and operating requirements. The
selection of hardware will be closely related
to the selection of the software applications.

FIGURE 12–5, *continued.*

PAYROLL APPLICATION

Current Procedure

Your current system of reporting time requires each hourly employee to sign a time
sheet; the time sheet is reviewed by the department manager and sent to the Payroll Department on Friday evening. Since the week
ends on Saturday, the employee must show the
scheduled hours for Saturday and not the actual hours; therefore, the department manager
must adjust the reported hours on the time
sheet for employees who do not report on the
scheduled Saturday or who do not work the
number of hours scheduled.

The Payroll Department employs a supervisor
and three full-time clerks. To meet deadlines
caused by an unbalanced work flow, an additional part-time clerk is used for 20 to 30
hours per week. The average wage for this
clerk is $4.25 per hour.

Advantage of Waters's System

The 319 Interactive Terminal can be programmed for entry of payroll data for each
employee on Monday mornings by department
managers, with the data reflecting actual
hours worked. This system would eliminate the
need for manual batching, controlling, and
keypunching. The Payroll Department estimates
conservatively that this work consumes 40
hours per week.

Hours per week	40
Average wage	×4.25
Weekly payroll cost	$170.00
Annual savings	$8,840.00

Elimination of the manual tasks of tabulat-
ing, batching, and controlling can save .25
units. Improved work flow resulting from
timely data in the system without keypunch

FIGURE 12–6. Detailed solution.

processing will allow more efficient use of
clerical hours. This would reduce payroll by
the .50 units currently required to meet
weekly check disbursement.

Eliminate manual tasks	.25
Improve work flow	.75
40-hour unit reduction	1.00
Hours per week	40
Average wage	4.75
Savings per week	$190.00
Annual savings	$9,880.00

TOTAL SAVINGS: $18,720.00

FIGURE 12–6, *continued.*

Following the executive summary and the general description,
you explain in detail exactly how you plan to do what you are proposing. This detailed section will be read by specialists who can understand and evaluate your plan, and you can feel free to use technical
language and discuss complicated concepts. Figure 12–6 shows one
part of the detailed solution appearing in the Waters Corporation
proposal, which included several other applications in addition to the
payroll application. Notice that this discussion, like that found in an
unsolicited sales proposal, begins with a statement of the customer's
problem, follows with a statement of the solution, and concludes with
a statement of the benefits to the customer.

Essential to any sales proposal are a *cost analysis* and a *delivery
schedule.* The cost analysis itemizes the cost of all the products and
services that you are offering; the delivery schedule commits you to
a specific timetable for providing those products and services. Figure
12–7 shows the cost analysis and delivery schedule of the Waters Corporation proposal. Also essential if your recommendations involve modifying the customer's physical plant is a *site preparation description*
that details the modifications required. Further, if the products you
are proposing to sell require training of the customer's personnel,
your proposal should specify the *required training* and its cost. Figure
12–8 shows the site preparation section and Figure 12–9 the training
section of the Waters proposal.

COST ANALYSIS

This section of our proposal provides detailed cost information for the Waters 319 Interactive Terminal and the 615 Waters Retail Processor. It then extends these major elements by the quantities required at each of your four locations.

319 Interactive Terminal

	Price	Maint. (1 yr)
Terminal	$2,895	$167
Journal Printer	425	38
Receipt Printer	425	38
Forms Printer	525	38
Software	220	--
TOTALS	$4,490	$281

615 Retail Processor

	Price	Maint. (1 Yr)
Processor	$57,115	$5,787
CRT I/O Writer	2,000	324
Matrix Printer	4,245	568
Software	12,480	---
TOTALS	$75,840	$6,679

The following breakdown itemizes the cost per store.

Store No. 1

Description	Qty	Price	Maint.
Terminals	16	$68,400	$4,496
Digital Cassette	1	1,300	147
Thermal Printer	1	2,490	332
Software	16	3,520	---
TOTALS		$75,710	$4,975

FIGURE 12–7. Cost analysis and delivery schedule.

Store No. 2

Description	Qty	Price	Maint.
Terminals	20	$85,400	$5,620
Digital Cassette	1	1,300	147
Thermal Printer	1	2,490	332
Software	20	4,400	---
TOTALS		$93,590	$6,099

Store No. 3

Description	Qty	Price	Maint.
Terminals	17	$72,590	$4,777
Digital Cassette	1	1,300	147
Thermal Printer	1	2,490	332
Software	17	3,740	---
TOTALS		$80,120	$5,256

Store No. 4

Description	Qty	Price	Maint.
Terminals	18	$76,860	$5,058
Digital Cassette	1	1,300	147
Thermal Printer	1	2,490	332
Software	18	3,960	---
TOTALS		$84,610	$5,537

Data Center at Buffalo

Description	Qty	Price	Maint.
Processor	1	$57,115	$5,787
CRT I/O Writer	1	2,000	324
Matrix Printer	1	4,245	568
Software	1	12,480	---
TOTALS		$75,840	$6,679

The following summarizes all costs.

Location	Hardware	Maint.	Software
Store No. 1	$72,190	$4,975	$3,520
Store No. 2	89,190	6,099	4,400
Store No. 3	76,380	5,256	3,740
Store No. 4	80,650	5,537	3,960
Data Center	63,360	6,679	12,480
Subtotals	$381,770	$28,546	$28,100

TOTAL $438,416

FIGURE 12–7, *continued.*

DELIVERY SCHEDULE

```
Waters is normally able to deliver 319 Inter-
active Terminals and 615 Retail Processors
within 120 days from the date of the con-
tract. This can vary depending on the rate
and size of incoming orders.

All the software recommended in this proposal
is available for immediate delivery. We do
not anticipate any difficulty in meeting your
tentative delivery schedule.
```

FIGURE 12–7, *continued.*

To prevent misunderstandings about what your responsibilities will be and what the customer's responsibilities will be, you should draw up a *statement of responsibilities.* The statement of responsibilities, such as the one shown in Figure 12–10, usually appears toward the end of the proposal. Also toward the end of the proposal is a *description of the vendor.* This section should give a factual description of your company, its background, and its present position in the industry. Following this description, many proposals add what is known as an *institutional sales pitch.* Up to this point, the proposal has attempted to sell specific goods and services. The sales pitch strikes a somewhat different chord and is designed to sell the company and its general capability in the field. Less matter-of-fact than the vendor description, the sales pitch unabashedly sings the company's praises and always concludes the proposal on an upbeat note. Figure 12–11 shows the vendor description and sales pitch sections of the Waters proposal.

SITE PREPARATION

Waters will work closely with Cookson's to ensure that each site is properly prepared prior to system installation. You will receive a copy of Waters's installation and wiring procedures manual, which lists the physical dimensions, service clearance, and weight of the system components in addition to the power, logic, communication-cable, and environmental requirements. Cookson's is responsible for all building alterations and electrical facility changes, including the purchase and installation of communication cables, connecting blocks, and receptacles.

Wiring

For the purpose of future site considerations, Waters's in-house wiring specifications for the system call for two twisted pair wires and twenty-two shielded gauges. The length of communications wires must not exceed 2,500 feet.

As a guide for the power supply, we suggest that Cookson's consider the following.

1. The branch circuit (limited to 20 amps) should service no equipment other than 319 Interactive Terminals.
2. Each 20-amp branch circuit should support a maximum of three Interactive Terminals.
3. Each branch circuit must have three equal-size conductors--one hot leg, one neutral, and one insulated isolated ground.
4. Hubbell IG 5362 duplex outlets or the equivalent should be used to supply power to each terminal.
5. Computer room wiring will have to be upgraded to support the 615 Retail Processor.

FIGURE 12–8. Site preparation section.

TRAINING

To ensure a successful installation, Waters offers the following training course for your operators.

Interactive Terminal/Retail Processor Operations

Course number: 8256
Length: three days
Tuition: $500.00

This course provides the student with the skills, knowledge, and practice required to operate an Interactive Terminal/Retail Processor System. On-line, clustered, and stand-alone environments are covered.

We recommend that students have department store background and that they have some knowledge of the system configuration with which they will be working.

FIGURE 12–9. Training section.

RESPONSIBILITIES

On the basis of its years of experience in installing information-processing systems, Waters believes that a successful installation requires a clear understanding of certain responsibilities.

Generally, it is Waters's responsibility to provide its users with needed assistance during the installation so that live processing can begin as soon thereafter as is practical.

Waters's Responsibilities

--Provide operations documentation for each application that you acquire from Waters.

--Provide forms and other supplies as ordered.

--Provide specifications and technical guidance for proper site planning and installation.

--Provide advisory assistance in the conversion from your present system to the new system.

Customer's Responsibilities

--Identify an installation coordinator and system operator.

--Provide supervisors and clerical personnel to perform conversion to the system.

--Establish reasonable time schedules for implementation.

--Ensure that the physical site requirements are met.

--Provide competent personnel to be trained as operators and ensure that other employees are trained as necessary.

--Assume the responsibility for implementing and operating the system.

FIGURE 12–10. Statement of responsibilities.

DESCRIPTION OF VENDOR

The Waters Corporation develops, manufac-
tures, markets, installs, and services total
business information-processing systems for
selected markets. These markets are primarily
in the retail, financial, commercial, industrial, health-care, education, and government
sectors.

The Waters total system concept encompasses
one of the broadest hardware and software
product lines in the industry. Waters computers range from small business systems to powerful general-purpose processors. Waters computers are supported by a complete spectrum
of terminals, peripherals, data-communication
networks, and an extensive library of software products. Supplemental services and
products include data centers, field service,
systems engineering, and educational centers.

The Waters Corporation was founded in 1934
and presently has approximately 26,500 employees. The Waters headquarters is located
at 17 North Waterloo Boulevard, Tampa, Florida, with district offices throughout the
United States and Canada.

WHY WATERS?

Corporate Commitment to the Retail Industry

Waters's commitment to the retail industry is
stronger than ever. We are continually striv-
ing to provide leadership in the design and
implementation of new retail systems and applications that will ensure our users of a
logical growth pattern.

Research and Development

Over the years, Waters has spent increasingly
large sums on research and development ef-

FIGURE 12-11. Description of vendor and institutional sales pitch.

```
forts to assure the availability of products
and systems for the future. In 19--, our re-
search and development expenditure for ad-
vanced systems design and technological inno-
vations reached the $70 million level.

Leading Point-of-Sale Vendor

Waters is a leading point-of-sale vendor,
having installed over 150,000 units. The
knowledge and experience that Waters has
gained over the years from these installa-
tions ensure well-coordinated and effective
systems implementations.
```

FIGURE 12–11, *continued.*

MINUTES OF MEETINGS

Organizations and committees keep official records of their meetings; such records are known as *minutes*. If, in the course of your work, you attend many business-related meetings, you may be asked to serve as *recording secretary* at some of them. The duties of the secretary are to write down and distribute the minutes of a meeting. Usually, at the beginning of each meeting the minutes of the preceding meeting are read aloud if printed copies of the minutes were not distributed to the members beforehand. The group then votes to accept the minutes as prepared or to revise or clarify specific items.

The minutes of meetings should include the following information.

1. Name of the group or committee that is holding the meeting.
2. The place, time, and date of the meeting.
3. The kind of meeting being held (a regular meeting or a special meeting called to discuss a specific subject or problem).
4. The number of members present. If the committee or board is small (ten or fewer), members' names should be given.
5. A statement that the chairperson and the secretary were present, or the name of the substitute if either one was absent.
6. A statement that the minutes of the previous meeting were approved or revised, or a statement that the reading of the minutes was dispensed with.
7. A list of the reports that were read and approved. It is seldom necessary to give a detailed account of the substance of the reports submitted.

8. All the main motions that were made, with statements as to whether they were carried, defeated, or tabled (vote postponed). Do not include motions that were withdrawn. It is also customary to include the names of those who made and seconded the motions.
9. Resolutions that were adopted, written out in full. If a resolution was rejected, make a simple statement to that effect.
10. A record of all ballots, complete with the number of votes cast "for" and "against."
11. The time that the meeting was adjourned (officially ended) and the place, time, and the date of the next meeting.
12. The recording secretary's signature (and typed name) and, if desired, the signature of the chairperson.

Since minutes are often used to settle disputes, they must be accurate, complete, and clear. When approved, minutes of meetings are official and can be used as evidence in legal proceedings.

Keep your minutes brief and to the point. Give complete information on each topic, but do not ramble—conclude the topic and go on to the next one. Following a set format will help you to keep the minutes concise. You might, for example, use the heading TOPIC, followed by the subheadings *Discussion* and *Action Taken,* for each major point that is discussed, as in this extract:

```
              NORTH TAMPA MEDICAL CENTER

           Minutes of the Regular Meeting of the
                 Medical Audit Committee

    DATE: July 26, 19--

    PRESENT: G. Miller (Chairperson), C. Bloom, J.
             Dades, K. Gilley, D. Ingoglia (Secre-
             tary), S. Ramirez, D. Rowan, C. Tsien, C.
             Voronski.
    ABSENT: R. Fautier, R. Wolf

    Dr. Gail Miller called the meeting to order at
    12:45 p.m. Dr. David Ingoglia made a motion that
    the June 1, 19--, minutes be approved as distrib-
    uted. Dr. Carole Tsien seconded the motion, which
    was passed.

        The committee discussed and took action on the
    following topics.

    (1) TOPIC: Meeting Time
```

<u>Discussion:</u> A discussion was held on the most convenient time for the committee to meet.

<u>Action Taken:</u> The committee decided to meet on the fourth Tuesday of every month, at 12:30 p.m.

Keep abstractions and generalities to a minimum and, most important, be specific. If you are referring to a nursing station on the second floor of a hospital, say "the nursing station on the second floor" or "the second-floor nursing station," not "the second floor."

Keep in mind the possibility that the minutes you are preparing may be used, at some time in the future, by a lawyer, a judge, or jury members who probably won't be familiar with the situation you are describing—and that you may not be reachable to explain what you wrote. (Even if you are available, you may not remember any of the details of the situation.) After all, the reason for taking minutes is to create a permanent record that will be available if it should be needed—at any time and for any reason.

Be specific, too, when you refer to people. Avoid using titles ("the chief of the Word Processing Unit") in favor of names and titles ("Ms. Florence Johnson, head of the Word Processing Unit"). And be consistent in the way you refer to people. Do not call one person *Mr.* Jarrell and another *Janet* Wilson. It may be unintentional, but a lack of consistency in titles or names may reveal a deference to one person at the expense of another. Avoid adjectives and adverbs that suggest either good or bad qualities, as in "Mr. Sturgess's *capable* assistant read the *extremely comprehensive* report of the subcommittee." Minutes should always be objective and impartial.

If a member of the committee is to follow up on something and report back to the committee at its next meeting, state clearly the member's name and the responsibility he or she has accepted. There should be no uncertainty as to what task the member will be performing for the committee.

When you have been assigned to take the minutes at a meeting, go adequately prepared. Bring more than one pen and plenty of paper. If it is convenient, you may bring a tape recorder as backup to your notes. Have ready the minutes of the previous meeting and any other material that you may need. If you do not know shorthand, take memory-jogging notes during the meeting and then expand them with the appropriate details immediately after the meeting. Remember that minutes are primarily a record of specific actions taken, although you may sometimes need to summarize what was said or state the essential ideas in your own words. Figure 12–12 shows a sample set of minutes that uses a less rigid format than the preceding extract.

WARETON MEDICAL CENTER
DEPARTMENT OF MEDICINE

Minutes of the Regular Meeting of the
Credentials Committee

DATE: April 18, 19--

PRESENT: M. Valden (Chairperson), R. Baron, M.
Frank, J. Guern, L. Kingson, L. Kins-
low (Secretary), S. Perry, B. Roman,
J. Sorder, F. Sugihana

Dr. Mary Valden called the meeting to order
at 8:40 p.m. The minutes of the previous
meeting were unanimously approved, with the
following correction: the secretary of the
Department of Medicine is to be changed from
Dr. Juanita Alvarez to Dr. Barbara Golden.

Old Business

None.

New Business

The request by Dr. Henry Russell for staff
privileges in the Department of Medicine was
discussed. Dr. James Guern made a motion that
Dr. Russell be granted staff privileges. Dr.
Martin Frank seconded the motion, which was
passed unanimously.
Similar requests by Dr. Ernest Hiram and
Dr. Helen Redlands were discussed. Dr. Fred
Sugihana made a motion that both physicians
be granted all staff privileges except respiratory-care privileges, because the two physicians had not had a sufficient number of
respiratory cases. Dr. Steven Perry seconded
the motion, which was passed unanimously.
Dr. John Sorder and Dr. Barry Roman asked
for a clarification of general duties for active staff members with respiratory-care

FIGURE 12–12. Minutes.

privileges. Dr. Richard Baron stated that he would present a clarification at the next scheduled staff meeting, on May 15.

Dr. Baron asked for a volunteer to fill the existing vacancy for Emergency Room duty. Dr. Guern volunteered. He and Dr. Baron will arrange a duty schedule.

There being no further business, the meeting was adjourned at 9:15 p.m. The next regular meeting is scheduled for May 15, at 8:40 p.m.

Respectfully submitted,

Leslie Kinslow
Medical Staff Secretary

Mary Valden, M.D.
Chairperson

JOB DESCRIPTIONS

To ensure an efficiently functioning organization, most large companies and many small ones find it necessary to specify, in a formal *job description,* the duties of and requirements for many of the jobs in the firm. Job descriptions fulfill several important functions: they provide information on which equitable salary scales can be based; they help management determine whether all responsibilities within a company are adequately covered; they let both prospective and currently working employees know exactly what is expected of them; and, together, a firm's job descriptions present a picture of the organization's structure.

Sometimes plant or office supervisors are given the task of writing the job descriptions of the employees assigned to them. In many organizations, though, an employee may draft his or her own job description, which is then checked over and approved by the immediate superior.

Format for Writing Job Descriptions

Although job description formats vary from organization to organization, the following headings are typical.

- *Accountability.* This section identifies, by title, the person or persons to whom the employee reports.

- *Scope of responsibilities.* This section provides an overview of the primary and secondary functions of the job and states, if it is applicable, who reports to the employee.
- *Specific duties.* This section gives a detailed account of the specific duties of the job, as concisely as possible.
- *Personal requirements.* This section lists the education, training, experience, and licensing required or desired for the job.

Tips for Writing Job Descriptions

If you have been asked to prepare a job description for your position, the following guidelines should be of help to you.

1. Before attempting to write your job description, keep a list of all the different tasks you do in a week or a month. Otherwise, you will almost certainly leave out some of your duties.
2. Focus on content. Remember that you are writing a description of your job, not of yourself.
3. List your duties in decreasing order of importance. Knowing how your various duties rank in importance makes it easier to set valid job qualifications.
4. Begin each statement of a duty with a verb, and be specific about what the duty is. Write "Answer and route incoming telephone calls" rather than "Handle telephone calls."
5. Review existing job descriptions that you know have been successful.

The typical job description shown in Figure 12–13 never mentions the person holding the job described. It focuses, instead, on the job and on the qualifications any person must possess to fill the position.

CREATING BUSINESS FORMS

Because they provide a time-saving, efficient, and uniform way to record data, *business forms* are used for countless purposes in almost all occupations. It is easier and quicker to supply information by filling out a well-designed form than by writing a detailed memorandum, letter, or report. Another advantage the form has over other types of written communication is that on every copy of a form, each particular piece of information appears in the same place—a fact that is especially important when many people are furnishing similar information. If each person providing information sent in an individually written letter, every sheet of paper submitted would be different and would require time-consuming reading and interpretation. In contrast,

JOB TITLE: Welding Supervisor

ACCOUNTABILITY: Reports directly to the Plant
Manager

SCOPE OF RESPONSIBILITIES: Is responsible for
supervising the work of fifteen welders, for
preparing production reports, for maintaining
and replacing equipment, and for carrying out
such duties as the Plant Manager may specify.

SPECIFIC DUTIES:

Supervises the work of fifteen welders. Eval-
uates, every six months, the performances of
the welders assigned to him or to her. Instructs new employees in safe working habits.
Prepares a monthly attendance report. Periodically checks the quality of work by examining tubes and balls for weld splatters and by
reviewing the inspector's quality reports.
Prepares production reports. Prepares a
monthly memorandum itemizing production for
the preceding month, including reasons for
any failure to meet the production schedule.
Maintains and replaces equipment. Maintains
accurate logs for each machine. Makes sure
that all equipment is in good operating condition and ready for the start of the next
shift. Makes sure that all safety devices
function properly.
Carries out such duties as the Plant Manager
may specify. Meets each week with the Plant
Manager and attends special meetings as requested. Attends in-service training programs
and keeps up to date on the latest welding
techniques.

PERSONAL REQUIREMENTS: Trade or technical
college certification or degree in welding.
Six years of welding experience. Ability to
interact well with employees and management.
Desire to stay up to date in the field.

FIGURE 12–13. Job description.

when the information is supplied on a form, the person filling out the form will have spent less time and effort in furnishing the data, and the person using the information from the form will have a much easier task retrieving and evaluating the data.

Preparing the Form

To be effective, a form should make it easy for one person to supply information and for another person to retrieve and interpret the information. Ideally, a form should be self-explanatory, even to a person who has never seen it before. If you are preparing a form, plan it carefully first. Determine what kind of information you will be seeking and arrange the requests for information in a logical order— logical from the point of view of both the person supplying the data and the person receiving it.

Make a draft of the form, putting in all the requests for information you've decided to include and arranging the items in the order you consider the most logical. If any co-workers will be using the form, show the draft to them—you'll be rewarded for the extra time this step takes by the helpful criticism and suggestions you are likely to receive. Once you're satisfied with the draft, you can then prepare a final copy of the form.

Instructions and Captions.   To make certain that information will be easy to enter on your form, be sure that you give the proper instructions in the proper place. You've probably had the experience, at some time or another, of starting to fill out a form only to realize too late that you've put your name on the line intended for your street address. When the instructions are clear and properly placed, the person filling out the form will not be confused about which information goes where.

Instructions, which are used primarily for long, complicated forms, should go at the beginning of the form; they are often preceded by a heading designed to attract the reader's attention.

INSTRUCTIONS FOR COMPLETING THIS FORM

1. Complete the applicable blue-shaded portions on the front of pages 1, 2, and 3.
2. Mail page 1 to the Securi-Med Insurance Company at the address shown above.
3. Give page 2 to your doctor.
4. If services were rendered in a hospital, give page 3 to the hospital.
5. Use the back of page 1 to itemize bills that are to go toward your major medical deduction.

Instructions for distributing the various copies of multiple-copy forms are normally placed at the bottom of the form. These instructions are repeated on every copy of the form.

On the form itself, requests for information are normally worded as captions. Keep captions brief and to the point; avoid unnecessary repetition by combining requests for related pieces of information under an explanatory heading.

CHANGE   What make of car do you drive? _____

What year was it manufactured? _____

What model is it? _____

What is the body style? _____

TO   Vehicle Information

Make _____   Year _____

Model _____   Body style _____

Planning for Responses.   In preparing a form, it is important to provide questions that can be answered simply and briefly. The best responses are check marks, circles, or underlining; next best are numbers, single words, or brief phrases. Sentence responses are the least effective, since they take the most time to write and to read.

Make captions as specific as possible. For example, if a requested date is a date other than that on which the form is being filled out, make the caption read "Effective date," "Date issued," or whatever it may be, rather than simply "Date." As in all job-related writing, put yourself in your reader's place and try to imagine what sorts of requests would be clear to you.

Sequencing of Data.   In designing a form, try to arrange your requests for information in an order that will be most helpful to the person filling out the form. At the top of the form, include *preliminary information,* such as the name of your organization, the title of your form, and any file number or reference number. In the *main portion* of the form, include the entries you need in order to obtain the necessary data. At the *end* of the form, include space for the signature of the person filling out the form and the date.

Within the main portion of your form, the arrangement of the entries should depend on several factors. First, the subject matter of the entries will frequently determine the most logical order. A form requesting reimbursement for travel expenses, for instance, would logically begin with the first day of the week (or month) and end with the last day of the appropriate period. Second, if the response to one item is based on the response to another item, be sure that the items appear in the correct order. Third, whenever possible, group requests for related information together. Fourth, if a form is to move from one individual or one department to another, to be partly filled out by each in turn, put the data to be supplied by the first individual or department at the top of the form, the data to be supplied by the second next, and so on (and each section of the form should state clearly who is responsible for its completion). Finally, entries should, in general, be arranged on the form from left to right and from top to bottom, since that is the way we are accustomed to reading.

In many cases, you'll want to title your form. The title of the form should describe its use and application. A title should be no more than a few words long and should normally be positioned at the top center of your form. If space is critical, the title can be placed at the top left-hand corner of the form.

Designing Forms

When you sit down to prepare the final version of a form, you should pay particular attention to details of design—the arrangement on the page of the entry lines (where the responses will be filled in), and the amount of space provided for the responses.

Entry Lines. The form can be laid out so that the person filling out the form supplies information on a writing line, in a writing block, or in square boxes.

The *writing line* is simply a caption.

_____   _____
                (Name)   (Telephone)

_____
                        (Street Address)

_____   _____   _____
        (City)   (State)   (Zip Code)

_____   _____   _____   _____
  (Age)   (Weight)   (Height)   (Sex)

The *writing block* is essentially the same except that each entry is enclosed in a ruled block, making it impossible for the person filling out the form to associate a caption with the wrong line.

Name		Telephone	
Street Address			
City		State	Zip Code
Age	Weight	Height	Sex

When all the possible responses to any one question can be anticipated, you can save the person filling out the form time and effort by writing the question on the form, supplying a labeled *square box* for each possible answer, and instructing the person filling out the form to put an X in the box that corresponds to the correct answer. Such a plan will also save you time and effort in retrieving the data. Be sure that your questions are both simple and specific.

EXAMPLE   Would you buy another Whapo? ☐ Yes   ☐ No

The boxes may either precede or follow the question. Be sure, however, that the boxes and their labels are close enough together that they will be unmistakably associated.

REVISE   red ☐   blue ☐   green ☐   yellow ☐

TO   red ☐   blue ☐   green ☐   yellow ☐

Spacing.   Be sure to provide enough space for the person filling out the form to enter the data. Everyone has filled out a form on which the address, signature, or other item could not possibly fit in the space allowed for it. Insufficient writing space or uneven lines are guaranteed to irritate the person filling out the form and make the information supplied hard to read. In a long form that is poorly designed, errors occur with increasing frequency as the person filling out the form becomes more and more frustrated. And if you have trouble reading responses that are too tightly spaced or that snake around the side of the form, you may introduce additional errors as you retrieve the data.

Forms may be filled out either in longhand or on a typewriter. Always allow sufficient space to accommodate both typewritten and handwritten responses. If you think that at least some people filling it out will use longhand, provide adequate space for a relatively large handwriting. And if you expect that some will reply by typewriter, take their needs into account as well. It is especially important to plan for typewritten responses if you intend to have your form *typeset* (composed on a machine that sets copy for books, newspapers, and other materials). If you do not inform the typesetter that the printed form must be easy to use on a typewriter, those who use a typewriter may have difficulty aligning the form vertically in their machines. The reason is simple: a typewriter types 6 lines to the inch, but the typeset equivalent (the regular text of this book, for example) is 6.0386 lines to the inch. Because of this slight difference in spacing, any typewriter will be off the writing line by the time it nears the bottom of a page-long typeset form. Be sure, then, to remind the typesetter to set *exactly* 6 lines to the inch.

If the form will contain more than one response per line, align the column entries vertically whenever possible, so that the person filling out the form can set tabs on the typewriter (when the tab is pressed, the platen, or roller, automatically moves to a previously set point along the line). As for horizontal spacing, there are two kinds of typewriters: the *elite*, which has twelve characters (both letters and spaces) to the inch, and the *pica*, which has ten characters to the inch. Allow adequate space for responses typed on a pica typewriter.

CHAPTER SUMMARY

Proposals, job descriptions, and minutes of meetings—although not required as frequently as letters, memos, and reports—are nonetheless very important kinds of on-the-job writing. The use of well-designed forms is another form of communication that can sometimes, under the right circumstances, be more effective and efficient than writing.

Two kinds of proposals are commonly written in the business world: internal and external. An *internal proposal*, which is written to someone higher in the management structure of an organization, recommends a change or an improvement within an organization. A *sales proposal* (or external proposal) is a document that offers to provide a potential customer with a product or service, or both, at a specific price within a specified period of time. Sales proposals may be unsolicited or solicited; long proposals provide greater detail than short ones and may include such items as an executive summary, a general description of products, a cost analysis, a delivery schedule, a site preparation section, a training section, a statement of responsibilities, a description of the vendor, and an institutional sales pitch.

Minutes are the official records of business meetings. Written by the designated secretary of the committee or group, they are used to settle disputes and sometimes are even offered as evidence in lawsuits.

Job descriptions specify the duties and requirements for specific jobs. They help management to establish equitable salary scales and determine whether all responsibilities within a company are adequately covered. They also help employees to know exactly what is expected of them in their jobs.

Well-designed *business forms* provide a time-saving, efficient, and uniform way to record routine data. Filling in such a form is quicker and easier than writing detailed letters or reports.

EXERCISES

1. Write a proposal in which you recommend a change in a procedure. The procedure should be one with which you are familiar, either at school or at work. The proposal should state the nature of the problem and explain how the new procedure would be put into effect. Give at least three reasons for the change, and support your reasons with facts that show the advantages of your proposal. Address the proposal to a dean or other school official (if the proposal is school-related) or to your immediate supervisor (if the proposal is work-related).

2. Assume that you are a landscaping contractor and would like to respond to the following Request for Proposals, which appears in your local newspaper:

    > Lawn-mowing agreement for the Town of Augusta, Oregon. Weekly mowing of 5 miles of Route 24 median and sidings, 10 acres in Willoughby Park, and 23 acres at Augusta Memorial Golf Course, May 30 through September 30. Proposals are due April 30.

    Indicate in your proposal the number of man-hours that you estimate the contract would require, what you would charge, the ability of your personnel and equipment to do the job, your firm's experience and qualifications, and the weekly schedule that you propose to follow.

3. Attend a meeting of an organization. Go to the meeting prepared to take careful, complete notes of the proceedings. From the notes you have taken, write up the minutes of the meeting.

4. Interview someone who holds a job in a field that interests you. On the basis of the information you obtain about the job from the interview, prepare a job description of the position.

5. If you are currently employed, write a description of your job according to the guidelines presented in this chapter. If you are not employed, describe your most recent job (what you did last summer, for example). Try to reconstruct a typical day at that job, recalling as many particulars as possible.

6. Design a weekly time card for factory employees at United Agricultural Products. Employees work Mondays through Fridays, 8 A.M. to noon, 12:30 to 3:30 P.M., and have a half hour for lunch. Include on the time card a column listing the days of the week (vertical column) and columns labeled "Time In," "Time Out" (morning), "Lunch," "Time In," "Time Out" (afternoon), and "Overtime" (horizontal columns). Supervisors are to fill in the times that employees actually arrive at work and leave for the day and the times of their lunch breaks. They are also to fill in the number of hours of overtime (if any) that employees work each day. Include columns for the total hours worked each day and a final box or space for total hours worked for the week. Be sure to leave spaces for the dates that the time card covers and for the signatures of both the employee and the supervisor.

13

Creating Tables and
Illustrations

The primary purpose of including tables and illustrations in your writing is to increase your reader's understanding of what you are saying. Tables, graphs, photographs, drawings, charts, and maps—often collectively called *visuals* or *visual aids*—can often express ideas or convey information in ways that words alone cannot. Tables allow easy comparison between large numbers of statistics that would be difficult to understand if they appeared in sentence form. Graphs make trends and mathematical relationships immediately evident to the reader. And drawings, photographs, and maps can frequently indicate shapes and relationships in space more concisely and efficiently than text can.

Make tables and illustrations functional parts of your writing. If they will not contribute directly to your reader's understanding, do not use them. And when they are necessary, consider your purpose and your reader carefully. For example, the drawing of an x-ray machine for a high school science class would be different from an illustration provided for the technician who repairs such machines.

Many of the qualities of good writing—simplicity, clarity, conciseness, directness—are just as important in the creation and use of tables and illustrations. The following general guidelines apply to most visual materials. Detailed guidelines for specific kinds of illustrations are given in the discussion of each type.

1. Keep the information the illustration is presenting as brief and as simple as possible.

2. Try to present only one or two types of information in each illustration.
3. Label or caption each illustration clearly.
4. When necessary, include a key that identifies any symbols and abbreviations you use in the illustration.
5. When appropriate, specify the proportions used, or include a scale of relative distances.
6. To make the illustration easier to read, whenever possible use lettering that goes from left to right rather than from top to bottom. (The diagonal compromise in Figure 13–12 is sometimes effective.)
7. Keep terminology consistent. Do not, for instance, refer to something as a "proportion" in the text and as a "percentage" in the illustration.
8. Leave enough space around and within the illustration for easy viewing.
9. Position the illustration as close as possible to the text that refers to it. Unless it is simply impossible, the textual reference should precede the figure or table.
10. Be certain that the significance of each illustration is clear from the text.
11. If several tables or illustrations are used, number the illustrations or tables consecutively. Number tables separately from illustrations. In a short report or paper, label tables as Table 1, Table 2, and so on; label all illustrative matter (drawings, photographs, maps, and graphs) as Figure 1, Figure 2, and so on.[1]
12. In a formal report, if more than five illustrations or tables appear, list them, together with figure and page numbers, under a separate heading following the table of contents, labeled "List of Figures" or "List of Tables."

Presented with clarity and consistency, visuals can help your reader focus on key portions of your report. Be aware, though, that even the best illustration only supplements, or supports, the text. Your writing must carry the burden of providing context for the illustration and pointing out its significance.

A discussion of tables and illustrations that are commonly used in on-the-job writing follows. Your topic will ordinarily determine the best type or types of visual material to use when your text needs illustration.

[1] In longer works, such as this book, figures and tables may be double-numbered by chapter or section (for example, the second figure in Chapter 5 would be Figure 5–2).

TABLES

A table is useful for showing large numbers of specific, related data in a brief space. Because a table displays its information in rows and columns, the reader can easily compare data in one column with data in another. If such data were presented in the text, the reader would read through groups of numbers and possibly not recognize their significance. Tables typically include the following elements (see Figure 13–1):

- *Table number.* If you are using several tables, assign each a number; center the number and title above the table. Table numerals are usually Arabic, and they should be assigned sequentially to the tables throughout the text. Tables should be

Table Number ————————— Table 1

Table Title ——— Monthly Average Solar Energy*

	Month	Solar energy available, Btu/ft^2 (a)	Solar energy collectible, Btu/ft^2 (b)
Column headings			
	January	53,500	5,307
	February	57,000	6,139
	March	71,500	14,054
	April	71,000	14,314
Stub (left-hand column)	May	70,000	17,115
	June	70,000	18,635
	July	72,000	21,468
	August	71,200	18,231
	September	66,500	16,971
	October	62,000	12,595
	November	51,000	8,823
	December	47,200	6,012

Source note —— SOURCE: NASA Langley Research Center.

*Latitude 37° N, Hampton, Virginia

Footnotes ⟍ [a]Maximum values at 35° collector tilt angle on a clear day.

[b]Average value where percentage of cloud cover, collector efficiency, and so forth are taken into consideration.

FIGURE 13–1. Sample table.

referred to in the text by table number rather than by location ("Table 4" rather than "the above table"). If your report or paper has more than five tables, list table titles, table numbers, and page numbers on a separate page immediately after the table of contents, labeled "List of Tables."

- *Table title.* The title, which is placed just above the table, should describe concisely what the table represents.
- *Column headings.* Headings should be kept brief but descriptive. Units of measurement, where necessary, should either be specified as part of the heading or enclosed in parentheses beneath the heading. Standard abbreviations are acceptable. Avoid vertical lettering whenever possible.
- *Stub.* The left-hand vertical column of a table is the stub. It lists the items about which information is given in the body of the table.
- *Body.* The body comprises the data below the column headings and to the right of the stub. Within the body, columns should be arranged so that the terms to be compared appear in adjacent rows and columns. Where no information exists for a specific item, substitute a row of dots or a dash to acknowledge the gap.
- *Rules.* These are the lines that separate the table into its various parts. Horizontal rules are placed below the title, below the body of the table, and between the column headings and the body of the table. They should not be closed at the sides. The columns within the table may be separated by vertical rules if such lines aid clarity.
- *Source line.* The source line, which identifies where the data were obtained, appears below the table (when a source line is appropriate). (Many organizations place the source line below the footnotes.)
- *Footnotes.* Footnotes are used for explanations of individual items in the table. Symbols (*, †) or lower-case letters (sometimes in parentheses) rather than numbers are ordinarily used to key table footnotes because numbers might be mistaken for numerical data.
- *Continuing tables.* When a table must be divided so that it can be continued on another page, repeat the column headings and give the table number at the head of each new page with a "continued" label ("Table 3, continued").

GRAPHS

Graphs, like tables, present numerical data in visual form. Graphs have several advantages over tables. Trends, movements, distributions, and cycles are more readily apparent in graphs than they are in tables. By providing a means for ready comparisons, a graph often shows a significance in the data not otherwise immediately evident. Be aware, however, that although graphs present statistics in a more interesting and comprehensible form than tables do, they are less accurate. For this reason, they are often accompanied by tables that give exact figures. (See Figure 13–2.) If the graph remains uncluttered, the exact data can be added to each column, thereby giving the reader both a quick overview of the data and accurate figures. (See Figures 13–11 and 13–12.) There are many different kinds of graphs, most notably line graphs, bar graphs, pie graphs, and picture graphs.

Line Graphs

The line graph, which is the most widely used of all graphs, shows the relationship between two sets of figures. The graph is composed

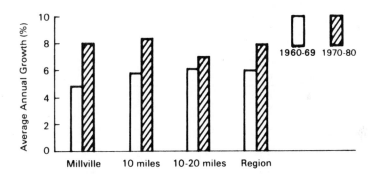

Average annual growth rate for four zones around Millville (based on assessed market value).

Average annual growth rate for four zones around Millville.

Area	Growth (%)*	
	1960–1969	1970–1980
Millville	4.4	7.5
10 miles	5.0	7.2
10–20 miles	5.3	5.7
Region	5.2	6.4

* Data based on assessed market value.

FIGURE 13–2. Figure and table showing the same data.

of a vertical axis and a horizontal axis that intersect at right angles. Each axis represents one set of figures. The relationship between the two sets is indicated by points plotted along appropriate intersections of the two axes. Once plotted, the points are connected to one another to form a continuous line, and the relationship between the two sets of data becomes readily visible.

The line graph's vertical axis usually represents amounts (the vertical axis in Figure 13–3 represents numbers of children), and its horizontal axis usually represents increments of time (the horizontal axis in Figure 13–3 represents ten-year increases).

Line graphs with more than one plotted line are common because they allow for comparisons between two sets of statistics. In creating such graphs, be certain to identify each plotted line with a label or a legend, as shown in Figure 13–4. You can emphasize the difference between the two lines by shading the space that separates them. The following guidelines apply to most line graphs:

1. Give the graph a title that describes the data clearly and concisely.

Fertility ratio: 1890–1970

FIGURE 13–3. Single-line graph.

Truck sales for 1981 and 1982

FIGURE 13–4. Double-line graph with difference shaded.

2. If your report includes several illustrations, assign a figure number to each one.
3. Indicate the *zero point* of the graph (the point where the two axes meet). If the range of data shown makes it inconvenient to begin at zero, insert a break in the scale, as in Figure 13–5.
4. Divide the vertical axis into equal portions, from the least amount at the bottom to the greatest amount at the top. Ordinarily, the caption for this scale is placed at the upper left. Lengthy captions can be placed vertically along the vertical axis, as in Figure 13–4.
5. Divide the horizontal axis into equal units from left to right, and label them to show what values each represents.

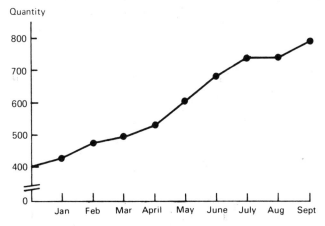

Widget sales for January–September 1979

FIGURE 13–5. Line graph with vertical axis broken.

FIGURE 13–6. Distorted curve (left) and distortion-free curve.

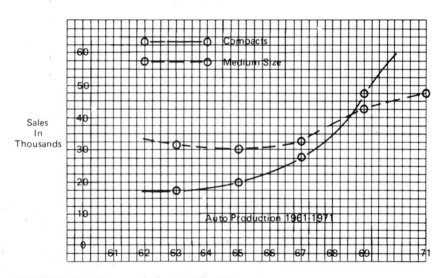

FIGURE 13–7. A line graph that is difficult to read.

6. The angle at which the curved line rises and falls is determined by the scales of the two axes—that is, by the units into which each axis is divided. Therefore, divide the vertical and horizontal scales so that they give an accurate visual impression of the data. The curve can be kept free of distortion if the ratio between the scales is kept constant. See Figure 13–6.

FIGURE 13–8. A more legible version of Figure 13–7.

FIGURE 13–9. A clear version of Figure 13–7.

7. Hold grid lines to a minimum so that the curved lines stand out. Since precise values are usually shown in a table of data accompanying a graph, detailed grid lines are unnecessary. Note the increasing clarity of the three graphs in Figures 13–7, 13–8, and 13–9.
8. Include a key when necessary, as in Figure 13–8. Sometimes a label will do just as well, as in Figure 13–9.

9. If the information comes from another source, include a source line under the graph at the lower left, as in Figure 13–16.
10. Place explanatory footnotes directly below the figure caption. See Figure 13–13.
11. Make all lettering read horizontally if possible.

Bar Graphs

Bar graphs consist of horizontal or vertical bars of equal width but scaled in length or height to represent some quantity. They are commonly used to show the following proportional relations:

1. Varying quantities of the same item during a fixed period of time (Figure 13–10)
2. Quantities of the same item at different points in time (Figure 13–11)
3. Quantities of different items during a fixed period of time (Figure 13–12)
4. Quantities of the different parts that make up a whole (Figure 13–13)

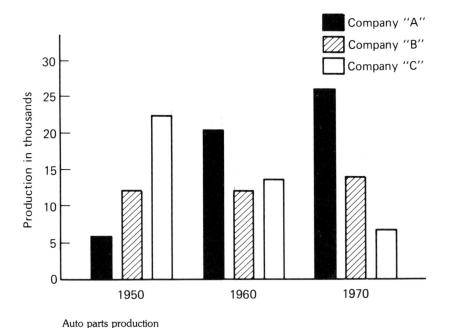

Auto parts production

FIGURE 13–10. Bar graph showing quantities of the same item during a fixed period.

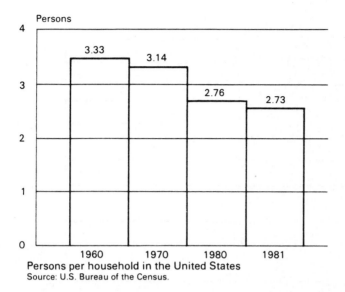

Persons

Persons per household in the United States
Source: U.S. Bureau of the Census.

FIGURE 13–11. Bar graph showing quantities of the same item at different points in time.

Note that in Figure 13–12, showing refined petroleum prices, the exact price appears at the top of each bar. This eliminates the need to have a table giving the price data accompany the graph. If the bars are not labeled, as they are not in Figures 13–10 and 13–14, the different portions must be clearly indicated by shading, crosshatching, or other devices. Include a key that represents the various subdivisions.

Bar graphs can also indicate what proportion of a whole the various component parts represent. In such a graph the bar, which is theoretically equivalent to 100 percent, is divided according to the proportion of the whole that each item sampled represents. (Compare the displays of the same data in Figures 13–13 and 13–15.) In some bar graphs, the completed bar does not represent 100 percent because all the parts of the whole have not been included in the sample (see Figure 13–14).

Pie Graphs

A pie graph presents data as wedge-shaped sections of a circle. The circle equals 100 percent, or the whole, of some quantity (a tax dollar, a bus fare, the hours of a working day), with the wedges representing the various parts into which the whole can be divided. In Figure 13–15, for example, the circle stands for a city tax dollar and

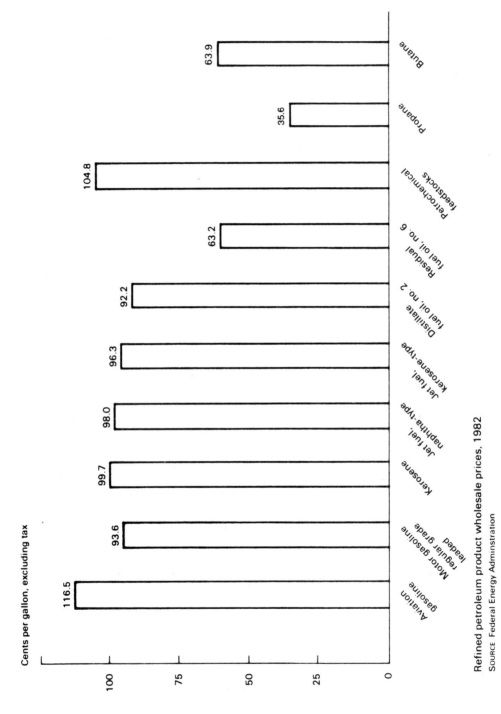

Refined petroleum product wholesale prices, 1982

SOURCE Federal Energy Adminstration

FIGURE 13–12. Bar graph showing varying quantities of different items during a fixed period (1982).

Your municipal tax dollar

* These figures do not include salaries.

FIGURE 13–13. Bar graph showing quantities of different parts making up a whole.

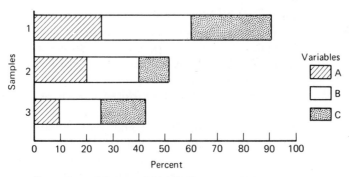

Proportions of three variables in three samples.

FIGURE 13–14. Bar graph in which not all parts of the whole have been included.

is divided into units equivalent to the percentages of the tax dollar spent on various city services.

The relationships among the various statistics presented in a pie graph are easy to grasp, but the information is often rather general. For this reason, a pie graph is often accompanied by a table that

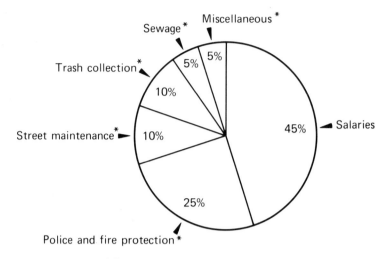

Your municipal tax dollar
* These figures do not include salaries.

FIGURE 13–15. Pie graph.

presents the actual figures on which the percentages in the graph are based.

When you construct a pie graph, keep the following points in mind.

1. The complete 360° circle is equivalent to 100 percent; therefore, each percentage point is equivalent to 3.6°.
2. To make the relative percentages as clear as possible, begin at the 12 o'clock position and sequence the wedges clockwise, from largest to smallest.
3. If you shade the wedges, do so clockwise and from light to dark.
4. Keep all labels horizontal and, most important, give the percentage values of each wedge.
5. Finally, check to see that all wedges, as well as the percentage values given for them, add up to 100 percent.

Although pie graphs have strong visual impact, they also have drawbacks. If more than five or six items of information are presented, the graph looks cluttered. And, unless percentages are labeled on each section, the reader cannot compare the values of the sections as accurately as on a bar graph.

Picture Graphs

Picture graphs are modified bar graphs that use picture symbols to represent the item for which data are presented. Each symbol corre-

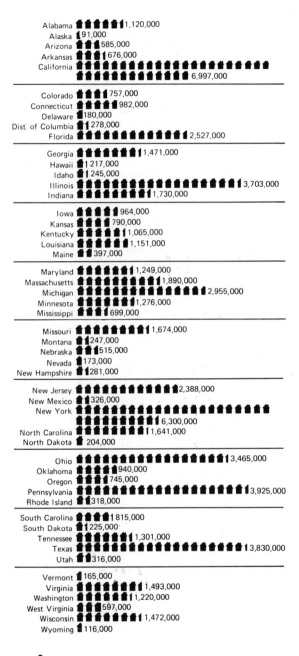

Each 🏠 = 200,000 units

Number of housing units, by states
SOURCE: U.S. Bureau of the Census

FIGURE 13–16. Picture graph.

sponds to a specified quantity of the item. See Figure 13–16. Note that precise figures are also included, since the picture symbol can indicate only approximate figures.

Some tips on preparing picture graphs are:

1. Make the symbol self-explanatory.
2. Have each symbol represent a single item.

FIGURE 13–17. Drawing showing relationships among hand signals for crane operation.

SOURCE: Harnischfeger Corporation.

3. Show larger quantities by increasing the number of symbols rather than by creating a larger symbol, because if the latter is done it is difficult to judge relative size accurately.

DRAWINGS

A drawing is useful when you wish to focus on details or relationships that a photograph cannot capture (see Figures 13–17 and 13–18). It can emphasize the significant piece of mechanism, or its func-

FIGURE 13–18. Cutaway drawing of a collector.
SOURCE: Harnischfeger Corporation.

tion, and omit what is not significant. However, if the precise details of the actual appearance of an object are necessary to your report or document, a photograph is essential.

To show the proper sequence in which parts fit together, or when it is essential to show the details of each individual part, use an *exploded-view drawing*. See Figure 13–19.

1. Wheel Nut	22. Spacer
2. Water Seal	23. Torsion Bar
3. Felt Seal	23A. Pin
4. Snap Ring	24. Valve Spool
5. Washer	24A. Housing Assembly
6. Brass Washer	25. 5/16″ Steel Ball
7. Teflon Washer	26. Ball Retaining Spring
8. Seal	27. 13/16″ Steel Ball
9. Upper Cover	28. Seal (2)
9A. Upper Cover Screw	29. Spacer
10. Seal Ring	30. Drive Link
11. Needle Bearing	31. Metering Element
12. Shims	31A. Stator
13. Snap Ring	31B. Rotor
14. Thrust Washer	32. Manifold
15. Thrust Bearing	33. Commutator Ring
16. Thrust Washer	33A. Commutator
17. Wave Spring Washer	34. Seal Retainer
18. Spacer	35. Washer
19. Input Shaft	36. End Cover Assembly
20. Pin	36A. End Cover Screw (7)
21. Drive Ring	

FIGURE 13–19. Exploded-view drawing of power steering valve.

SOURCE: Harnischfeger Corporation.

Many organizations have their own format specifications for drawings. In the absence of such specifications, the following tips should be helpful:

1. Give the drawing a clear title and a figure number, both of which should be centered below the drawing.
2. Place the source line, if there is one, aligned beneath the title.
3. Show the equipment from the point of view of the person who will use it.
4. When illustrating a subsystem, show its relationship to the larger system of which it is a part.
5. Draw the different parts of an object in proportion to one another, unless you indicate that certain parts are enlarged.
6. Where a sequence of drawings is used to illustrate a process, arrange them from left to right and from top to bottom.
7. Label parts in the drawing so that text references to them are clear.
8. Depending on the complexity of what is shown, labels may be placed on the parts themselves, or the parts may be given letter or number symbols, with an accompanying key. (See Figure 13–19.)

PHOTOGRAPHS

Photographs are vital to many publications. Pictures are the best way to show the surface appearance of an object or to record an event or the development of a phenomenon over a period of time. Not all representations, however, call for photographs. They cannot depict the internal workings of a mechanism or below-the-surface details of objects or structures. Such details are better shown in drawings or diagrams.

Highlighting Photographic Subjects

Stand close enough to the object so that it fills your picture frame. To get precise and clear photographs, choose camera angles carefully. A camera will photograph only what it is aimed at; accordingly, select important details and the camera angles that will record these details. To show the relative size of an unfamiliar object, place a familiar object—such as a ruler, a book, or a person—near the object being photographed.

Tips for Using Photographs

Like all illustrative materials, photographs must be handled carefully. When preparing photographs for a report, observe these guidelines.

1. Mount photographs on white bond paper with rubber cement or another adhesive, and allow ample margins.
2. If the photograph is the same size as the paper, type the caption, the figure number, the page number near which the photograph is to appear, and any other important information on a label and fasten it with rubber cement or another adhesive to the back of the photograph. (Photographs are often given figure numbers in sequence with other illustrations in a publication; see Figure 13–20.)

FIGURE 13–20. Photograph (cash register).

3. Position the figure number and caption so that the reader can view them and the photograph from the same orientation.
4. Do not draw crop marks (lines showing where the photo should be trimmed for reproduction) directly across a photograph. Draw them at the very edges of the photograph.
5. Do not write on a photograph, front or back. Tape a tissue-paper overlay over the face of the photograph, and then write very lightly on the overlay with a soft-lead pencil. Never write on the overlay with a ball-point pen.
6. Do not use paper clips or staples on photographs.
7. Do not fold or crease photographs.

FLOWCHARTS

A flowchart is a diagram of a process that involves stages, with the sequence of stages shown from beginning to end. The flowchart presents an overview of the process that allows the reader to grasp the essential steps of the process quickly and easily. The process being illustrated could range from the steps involved in assembling a bicycle to the stages by which bauxite ore is refined into aluminum ingots for fabrication.

Flowcharts can take several forms to represent the steps in a process. They can consist of labeled blocks (Figure 13–21), pictorial representations (Figure 13–22), or standardized symbols (Figure 13–23). The items in any flowchart are always connected according to the sequence in which the steps occur. The normal direction of flow in a chart is left to right or top to bottom. When the flow is otherwise, be sure to indicate it with arrows.

Flowcharts that document computer programs and other informa-tion-processing procedures use standardized symbols. The standards are set forth in *U.S.A. Standard Flowchart Symbols and Their Usage in Information Processing,* published by the American National Stan-dards Institute, publication X3.5. When creating a flowchart, follow these guidelines:

1. Label the flowchart clearly and concisely.
2. Assign the chart a figure number if it is being used in a docu-ment that contains five or more illustrations.

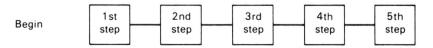

FIGURE 13–21. Simple block flowchart.

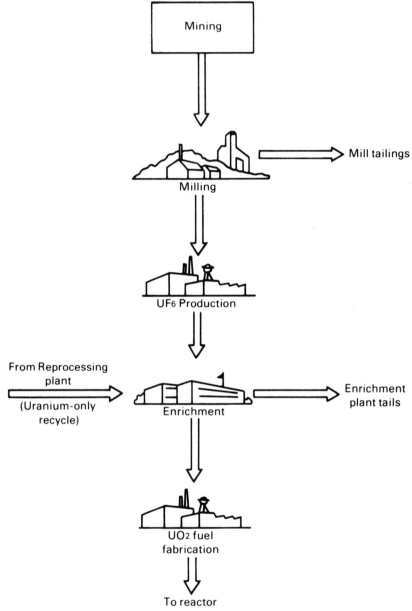

Light-Water Reactor Uranium Fuel Cycle Front-End Operations

FIGURE 13–22. Flowchart using pictorial symbols.

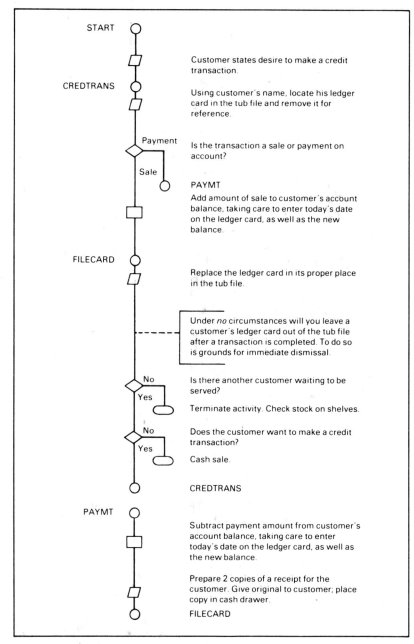

Flowchart of a Credit Transaction

FIGURE 13–23. Flowchart using standard symbols.

3. With labeled blocks and standardized symbols, use arrows to show the direction of flow only if the flow is opposite to the normal direction. With pictorial representations, use arrows to show the direction of all flow.
4. Label each step in the process, or identify it with a conventional symbol. Steps can also be represented pictorially or by captioned blocks.
5. Include a key if the flowchart contains symbols that your reader may not understand.
6. Leave adequate white space on the page. Do not crowd your steps and directional arrows too close together.
7. As with other illustrations, place the flowchart as near as possible to that portion of the text that refers to it.

ORGANIZATIONAL CHARTS

An organizational chart shows how the various components of an organization are related to one another. Such an illustration is useful when you want to give readers an overview of an organization

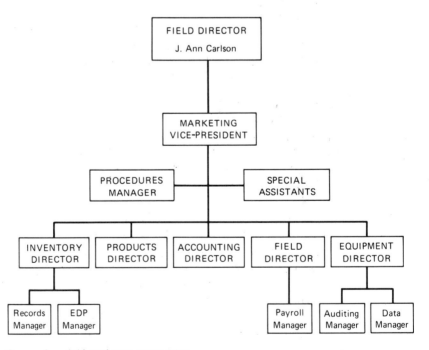

Cramer, Inc., field marketing organization

FIGURE 13–24. Organizational chart.

or indicate the lines of authority within the organization. See Figure 13–24.

The title of each organizational component (office, section, division) is placed in a separate box. These boxes are then linked to a central authority. If your readers need the information, include the name of the person occupying the position identified in each box.

As with all illustrations, place the organizational chart as close as possible to the text that refers to it.

MAPS

Maps can be used to show the specific geographic features of the area represented (roads, mountains, rivers) or to show information according to geographic distribution (population, housing, manufacturing centers, and so forth).

Bear these points in mind as you create maps for use with your text (see Figure 13–25):

1. Label the map clearly.
2. Assign the map a figure number if you are using enough illustrations (usually five) to justify the use of figure numbers.
3. Make sure all boundaries within the map are clearly identified. Eliminate unnecessary boundaries.
4. Eliminate unnecessary information from your map. For example, if population is important, do not include mountains, roads, rivers, and so on.
5. Include a scale of miles or feet to give your reader an indication of the map's proportions.
6. Indicate which direction is north.
7. Emphasize key features by using shading, dots, crosshatching, or appropriate symbols.
8. Include a key telling what the different colors, shadings, or symbols represent.
9. Place maps as close as possible to the portion of the text that refers to them.

CHAPTER SUMMARY

Tables and illustrations—graphs, drawings, photographs, charts, and maps—can increase the reader's understanding of what you are saying; they can express ideas or convey information in ways that words alone cannot. To be effective, illustrations and tables must be appropriate to your purpose and suitable to your reader's needs.

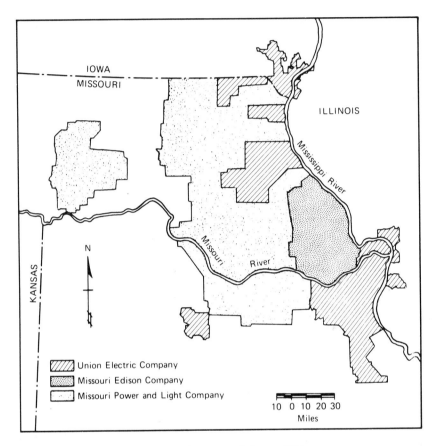

FIGURE 13–25. Map showing service areas of three utilities.

SOURCE: U.S. Nuclear Regulatory Commission.

A *table* is useful for listing large numbers of specific, related figures in a brief space. A table makes comparisons between figures easy
because the figures are arranged in rows and columns.

There are several kinds of graphs. *Line graphs* are used to show
the relationship between two or more sets of figures. *Bar graphs* are
used to show varying quantities of the same item during a fixed period
of time, quantities of the same item at different points in time, quantities of different items during a fixed period of time, or quantities of
the different parts that make up a whole. The circle of a *pie graph*
equals 100 percent, or the whole, of an element. The wedge-shaped
sections into which the circle is divided indicate the percentage of
the whole that each division represents. *Picture graphs* are modified
bar graphs that use picture symbols to represent the item for which
information is given; each symbol corresponds to a specified quantity
of the item.

Drawings are invaluable for depicting details of an object or the relationship between objects. Frequently, a drawing is of the outside of an object. When, however, it is necessary to reveal the internal parts of a machine or other object, a *cutaway drawing* is appropriate. An *exploded-view drawing* is used to illustrate the way in which parts fit together or to present the details of each separate part.

Photographs are useful for showing "things as they are" at a moment in time, or for depicting the development of some condition over time.

When you want to present a visual depiction of various stages of a process, choose a *flowchart*. When, on the other hand, your purpose is to show how the various jobs in an organization relate to one another, or to indicate lines of authority within an organization, an *organizational chart* is appropriate. Material on geographical location or distribution can be displayed on a *map*.

EXERCISES

1. Create a table that shows the features of a seasonal maintenance task that you perform over the period of a year. Lawn and automobile care are among the kinds of tasks you may perform on a routine schedule.

2. Create a graph that shows what percentages of the population of the United States owned homes for the periods discussed in the following passage.

   > For a growing army of people, realizing the American dream of the good life is closely associated with owning a home. Of 63.4 million occupied housing units counted in the 1970 census, nearly 63 percent (about 40 million) were lived in by their owners. More than 7 million home-owners were added to the U.S. total between 1960 and 1970.
   >
   > The proportion of owner-occupied homes was 62 percent in 1960 and 55 percent in 1950. In 1940, the first complete housing census found that the owner-occupied proportion was less than 44 percent.[2]

   Are the data more effectively presented as written or as they are presented in your graph?

3. Prepare a pie graph showing 1979 ownership of commercial forest land in the United States. Ownership percentages by group are

[2] U.S. Bureau of the Census.

as follows: state and community, 6 percent; forest industries, 13 percent; federal lands, 21 percent; farms, 34 percent; other private ownership, 26 percent.

4. Prepare a bar graph showing how you budget your present income for a typical month.

5. Create a bar graph that plots student enrollments over the past twenty years at the school you are presently attending. Present the same information in a table.

6. Create a graph that compares sales in thousands of dollars among the various truck parts divisions of the ABC Corporation for 1978, 1982, and 1983. Sales for each division are as follows: axles—1983 ($225), 1982 ($200), 1978 ($75); universal joints—1983 ($125), 1982 ($100), 1978 ($35); frames—1983 ($125), 1982 ($100), 1978 ($50); transmissions—1983 ($75), 1982 ($65), 1978 ($50); clutches—1983 ($35), 1982 ($30), 1978 ($15); and gaskets and seals—1983 ($28), 1982 ($25), 1978 ($20).

7. Modify the following graph so that it can be understood more easily than it can in its present form.

8. Select five drawings from reports, articles, or textbooks. Explain whether or not you think the illustrations make the text more meaningful or easier to follow. Take into consideration how well the illustrations support the ideas presented in the text and

whether the illustrations have been correctly placed in relation to the text.

9. Explain whether a photograph or a line drawing would better illustrate features of the following subjects: a dry cell battery (for an article in a general encyclopedia); a flower arrangement (in a florist's brochure); an electrical outlet box (in a wiring instructions booklet); an automobile accident (for an insurance claims adjuster); the procedure for wrapping a sprained ankle (for a first aid handbook); and a tick (in a backpacker's handbook).

10. Draw a flowchart that traces the path you followed in locating and obtaining books from your library as outlined in Chapter 10.

11. Create an organizational chart of a club or group to which you belong.

14

Making an Oral Presentation

Nearly everyone must, at one time or another, make an oral presentation on the job. You may be asked, for example, to report orally on what you learned at a workshop you attended, on the progress of a special project, or on the results of an evaluation program. You may need to present a product or service to potential customers or give cost estimates to a committee. Or a part of your job may be to demonstrate devices to co-workers, give patients instructions for using medical equipment, or show customers how to operate machinery safely. Regardless of the type of job you have, you will very likely need to know how to make an effective oral presentation.

Basically, there are three types of oral presentations: the read speech, the impromptu speech, and the extemporaneous speech.

A *read speech* is delivered by a speaker reading directly from a carefully prepared manuscript. Traditionally, papers were presented as read speeches at meetings held by professional societies. The current trend, however, is for papers to be distributed to the audience beforehand and then summarized by the speaker. The basic weakness of a read speech is that it tends to bore the audience because it does not require the speaker to establish two-way communication with the audience.

An *impromptu speech* is given without advance preparation by the speaker. The impromptu speech is used primarily during a meeting in which the speaker is asked "to say a few words" about something with which he is familiar (often a project with which he is involved). The speaker must then organize his ideas either while he is speaking or in a very short time before he speaks. The only way to prepare for an impromptu speech is to anticipate that you might be asked to report to a group.

By far the most common method of oral presentation is an *extemporaneous speech*. Here, the speaker prepares outlined notes well ahead of the presentation. He then uses his outline only to remind him of what to discuss and in what order to present his material; he does not read from the outline. A goal of extemporaneous speaking is to sound conversational and spontaneous, yet also well-organized.

Since it is the most common and appropriate method for most of the speaking you will do, the extemporaneous method is the basis for the following discussion of oral presentations. However, many of the suggestions for delivery apply to the read speech and the impromptu speech as well.

PREPARING AN ORAL PRESENTATION

Preparing an oral presentation is much like preparing to write. You must analyze your audience, determine your purpose, and then organize your ideas and prepare an outline.

Your Listeners

You cannot hope to communicate with your listeners effectively unless you know who they are. Are they co-workers, customers, clients, management, or fellow members of a professional organization? The answer to this question will help you to determine how much knowledge of your subject your listeners already possess. If you are speaking to those in your own occupational field, you know that they understand the terminology of that field—so you can use it freely. However, if you are speaking to those outside your field, you should carefully define any special terms.

Knowing who your audience is will also help you recognize other factors that might improve your communication with your listeners. An audience composed of management is likely to be interested in the practical aspects of the material you are presenting: costs, scheduling, staff needs, and so on. If you are speaking to technicians, on the other hand, they are likely to be concerned with the technical details of your presentation.

In preparing an oral presentation, you should pay particular attention to the size of your audience. Facial expressions and gestures that would be effective if you were speaking to half a dozen people sitting around a conference table would be lost on an audience of a hundred workers watching you demonstrate cardiopulmonary resuscitation. With the larger audience, you probably could not rely at all on facial expressions to convey an idea; and instead of pointing with your finger at a chart, you'd have to use a pointer. The size of your audience can also influence the approach you take to your presentation. For a small group of listeners, for instance, you might plan a presentation that is mainly discussion, composed of a short talk and a long question-and-answer period. For a large audience, on the other hand, you would be more likely to prepare a longer, more formally organized presentation with only a brief question-and-answer period.

Your Purpose

Determine the purpose of your presentation by asking, "What do I want my listeners to know, to be able to do, or to believe after I am finished?" Without a clear purpose, you will not know what to include in your presentation to make it effective, and you will either confuse your listeners or lose their interest.

One way to ensure that you have a specific, clear objective is to write out a statement of your purpose before you develop your presentation. Suppose, for example, that you are the assistant manager of the supply room at Westdale Medical Center. You must present an overview of how the supply room sterilizers, called "autoclaves," work. Your audience will be the new professional employees of the medical center. You might use the following statement of purpose for your presentation: "My purpose in speaking is to explain the function and operation of the autoclave so that new hospital employees will understand it and appreciate its value to the hospital." After preparing such a statement, your next step is to develop an outline.

Your Outline

Speaking requires an approach to the development of your subject that differs slightly from the preparation a written report requires. Any audience has a limited attention span. A presentation crammed with difficult ideas or numerous statistics is sure either to confuse your listeners or to put them to sleep. Cite facts and figures sparingly, and insert them in such a way that they directly support the major points you wish to make. Put your most important ideas into your opening and closing, where your listeners are more likely to remember them. Unless your presentation is short (under ten minutes), your conclusion should summarize the information presented in the rest of the talk.

There are as many ways to develop a topic in speaking as there are in writing. Several methods are especially good for oral presentations. The particular method of development you choose is less important than the fact that your subject is logically developed.

- *Increasing order of importance* develops your topic from the least important point to the most important point. This leaves the audience with the most important points fresh in their minds at the end.
- *The problem-solution pattern* first describes and analyzes the problem, then presents the criteria for evaluating possible solutions, and finally explains the advantages and disadvantages of each possible solution. Make sure that you are being clear when you define the problem and present the recommended solution.
- *Cause-and-effect,* by stressing the connection between a result and a preceding event, explains why something happened or why you predict that something will happen. This approach can be used effectively in a speech because it holds the interest of the audience much as a detective story does.
- *Specific-to-general* begins with such specific details as statistics, expert opinions, and examples and then goes on to make a general statement that stems logically from the details.
- *General-to-specific* presents a general statement and then follows it with supporting details—statistics, expert opinions, and examples.

When you have determined the best method of development for your subject, create an outline for your presentation. The following example shows how the assistant manager of the supply room at Westdale Medical Center might structure his presentation regarding autoclaves. You will notice that oral presentation outlines are less rigidly logical than outlines for written material (see Chapter 2): the oral presentation outline is not only a map of your method of development but also your cue card or prompter as you speak. Accordingly, you need to tailor it to your own speaking requirements.

OUTLINE

Background Information About the
Autoclave (Sterilizer)

I. Opening
    A. I am Steve Philisandro, Assistant Manager of the Supply Department.
    B. Ms. Cynthia Lipanski has given you an overview of the department—now I would

like to give you some background about
our autoclave sterilizer units.
C. The points I will cover are explained in
greater detail in our department manual,
which each of our employees uses.

II. Definitions

A. Sterilizing kills all living organisms,
unlike disinfecting, which merely inhib-
its the growth of organisms (especially
pathogens).
B. Sterilization kills multiplying organisms (including spores) with steam, under high temperature and pressure, or
with gases.
C. Briefly explain differences between
steam autoclaves and ethylene oxide
sterilizer (point to units).

III. Materials

A. Materials that are sterilized include
cloth, metal, glass, liquid, rubber, and
plastic.
B. Items that are sensitive to steam must
be sterilized with the ethylene oxide
unit: rubber goods, electric cords,
telescopic lenses, and delicate instruments, for example.
C. The materials, other than liquids, are
wrapped in muslin or placed in peel
packages and heat sealed (show instrument and "peel" packages).
D. Liquids, such as saline, are placed in
pyrex bottles with closures that allow
steam to penetrate.
E. Each type of material requires precise
settings for time, pressure, and temperature (show operators' manual).

IV. Procedure

A. Operator checks that items are properly
wrapped and spaced on the sterilizer
cart (point to cart).
B. Chemical indicators are placed inside
the packages, and heat-sensitive tape is
used on the outsides.
C. The operator loads the cart (cooled to
prevent condensation) into the sterilizer units.
D. Although settings are usually pre-set,
the operator checks time, temperature,
and pressure (show gauges).

E. The operator closes the door, then
    pushes the "lock" button; the operation
    proceeds automatically from that point.
F. Lights on the front of the door will in-
    dicate the completion of cycle.
G. The operator removes the sterilizer
    cart, using asbestos gloves.
H. The packages are allowed to cool before
    they are placed on the storage shelves
    in the next room.
I. Westdale's process is more automated
    than those at smaller hospitals.

V. Closing

A. I hope I've given you some idea of how
    our sterilizer units work.
B. Are there any questions?
C. Thank you!
D. Mrs. Sanches will now demonstrate Unit
    #2.

The amount of detail you should include in such an outline will
depend on both your confidence in front of a group and your familiarity
with the subject. Obviously, the more confident and familiar with the
subject you are, the less detail you will need. However, you may need
to write out and read verbatim those portions that you feel need precise
wording, such as important policy statements.

You will also need to decide what physical form of the outline
you wish to use as notes for your presentation. Some speakers find
that placing the outline in a three-ring binder keeps the pages in
order. Other speakers prefer using 4" × 6" note cards because they
are compact. Use whatever form you find most convenient.

Be careful not to cram the cards with too many notes. You should
be able to grasp the information on a card at a glance so that you
can maintain eye contact with your listeners. Number the cards so
you don't get lost during your presentation.

Using Visual Aids

An important decision to make as you prepare your oral presentation is whether to use visual aids and, if so, what kind. (See Chapter
13.) You can choose graphs, drawings, tables, photographs, or models;
you can present them by means of chalkboards, posters, flip charts,
or overhead or slide projectors. Well-planned visual aids can add interest and emphasis to your presentation. They can also clarify and simplify your message by reinforcing its key points.

Visual aids can be overdone, of course. Do not attempt to use visual aids to flesh out a skimpy presentation or to form the focal point of a disorganized one. Use aids only if they clarify a point or make your presentation more vivid and concise. If they are necessary, be certain to check the physical arrangement and facilities of the room where you will speak. Does it have a chalkboard? a projector screen? a flip chart? Will a slide or overhead projector be available? Also consider room size. If you plan to use a chalkboard, will the writing be visible to those seated in the back? Everything you use must be tailored to scale. Check to see that nothing obstructs the view of any member of your audience. Keep in mind the following points as you prepare and use your visual aid:

1. Keep the amount of information on each visual aid to a mimi-num. It is usually a good idea to present only one point on each visual aid. Keep figures and equations to a minimum.
2. Do not write out sentences; use only words and phrases.
3. During your presentation, emphasize a visual aid by pointing to it—with a physical gesture *and* with your text.
4. As you discuss the material on the visual aid, be sure that you don't block it with your body.
5. Be careful to talk to your listeners, not to the visual aid.
6. Do not simply read from the visual aid; after all, your audience can read. It is sometimes helpful, though, to list major points (usually in key words) on the visual aid to help your listeners keep them in mind as you discuss each in turn.

A complete range of visual aids is available. Each has advantages; your choice will depend on the size of the audience and the flexibility that your subject requires.

- A *chalkboard* is easy to use and easy to control; it gives you complete flexibility because you decide what goes on, what comes off, and when. It adds animation to your presentation because you must physically put the information on the board. If your information is too long to put on the board conveniently while you speak, put part or all of your message on ahead of time. A disadvantage of the chalkboard is that it slows you down if you must interrupt your presentation to write on the board as your listeners watch. Chalkboards are good with small and medium-sized audiences (up to 40 people).
- A *poster* is good if it is large enough for your audience to see. Posters can be used for medium-sized and large audiences (40 to 100 people). A common poster size is 2' × 3'. Prepare the poster ahead of time, and make your lettering large enough

to be seen comfortably from the back of the room (check this yourself, ahead of time). Felt-tip markers are good writing instruments for posters. Put the poster on the easel only when you are ready to use it; otherwise, it will be distracting to your audience. A disadvantage of posters is that the material on them cannot easily be changed.

- A *flip chart* provides you with good control of what you want the audience to see—you flip it over only when you need to make the next point. You can draw your illustration ahead of time with light pencil lines and fill the lines in with the bold lines of a felt-tip pen during your presentation (sketching it during the presentation helps hold the audience's attention). Flip charts are good for the same size audiences as chalkboards.
- *Slide* and *overhead projectors* can be easy to use if you take the time to learn how to handle them. Do not put a slide or transparency on the screen until you need it. As you prepare your presentation, decide which slides you will use and where each one will go. Have them made up far enough in advance so that you will be able to rehearse with them. Slides and transparencies may be used for audiences of various sizes (for large audiences, a larger screen is necessary).

DELIVERING AN ORAL PRESENTATION

Your oral presentation is most likely to be on a job-related topic. Therefore, you should be able to speak with knowledge and conviction about your subject. This is important because your listeners will have greater confidence in what you say if you speak with conviction.

The key to delivering your presentation well is to practice. Rehearse with your outline and with your visual aids until you know exactly how you want to move from one idea to another. If you practice, you will have no problem with the words you want to use; they will come naturally, and you will have the confidence you need to face your listeners.

Generating Confidence and Enthusiasm

Speaking is like selling. If you believe in your topic, you will be enthusiastic about it, and your audience will find themselves thinking, "Hey, I didn't know that!" or nodding their heads in agreement as if to say, "I know exactly what you mean!"

You can expect to be nervous. But if you know what you are

going to say and how you are going to say it—as you will if you have developed your subject and created a good outline—you can simply relax and talk. Your nervousness won't cause an all-out attack of stage fright. You can strengthen your confidence by being well prepared, by rehearsing, and by speaking in a strong and clear voice. A neat appearance can also add to your self-confidence.

You will have an advantage in delivering your presentation if you can project an image of friendliness; most people react favorably to a friendly approach. Friendliness cannot be faked—it must be honest to be effective. If your are naturally friendly, you can make that quality work to your advantage.

Another aspect of the image you project to your audience is your posture. Stand poised and erect, but not stiff. A slouching posture can harm your credibility with your listeners because they may assume that you lack confidence or don't care how you look or how you come across to others.

Getting and Holding Your Audience

The opening of a presentation can be crucial. It should arouse interest, stimulate curiosity, or impress your listeners with the importance of your subject. You can begin your presentation in a number of ways that will catch the attention of your listeners.

Statement of a Problem.   One way to catch the attention of your listeners is to describe a problem that directly affects them and then suggest a solution to it.

In the past three months the accident rate in the Press Room has increased by 37%. We've experienced a number of minor accidents and half a dozen serious ones. I've done a thorough investigation of the press area, along with members of Security, and realize that we must set up some new procedures . . . .

Definition.   Although the definition of a word can make a catchy opening, such a beginning should never be contrived—it should be used only if it provides insight into what follows.

Diastrophism comes from the Greek word *diastrophe,* meaning "distortion," and it is applied to the distortion of the earth's crust that created oceans and mountains. It is not surprising, therefore, that geologists regard . . . .

Interesting Fact.   Often an interesting bit of information can be used to stimulate the attention of your listeners.

A recent survey among retailers in our area revealed that the best way to sell a product is to *give it away.* Does that sound ridiculous? It isn't! And here's why . . . .

You may also be able to use an interesting statistic as an opening.

Approximately 15,000 requisitions, each containing from one to fourteen separate items, are processed each year by the Purchasing Department. Every item or service that is purchased . . . .

Background Information.   The background or history of a subject may be quite interesting and can put the topic in perspective for your listeners.

The Chinese used bamboo poles to drill for oil; certainly today's giant rigs drilling in a hundred feet of water represent an immense technical advance in the search for oil. But whether four thousand years ago or today, in ancient China or in a modern city, in twenty fathoms of water or on top of a mountain, the object of drilling is and has always been the same—to manufacture a hole in the ground, inch by inch. The hole may be either for a development well . . . .

This type of opening can easily be overdone, however. Use it only if the background information is of some value to your listeners. Never use it just to get started.

Quotations.   Occasionally, you can use a quotation to stimulate interest in your subject. To be effective, however, the quotation must be pertinent—not just a loosely related remark taken from a book of quotations simply because the item was listed under the subject heading of your topic. Often an effective quotation is one from a respected authority that points to a new trend or development.

Richard Smith, president of the P. R. Smith Corporation, recently said, "I believe that the Photon projector will revolutionize our industry." His statement represents a growing feeling among corporate . . . .

Objective.   In reporting on a project or an activity of some kind, you may wish to open with a statement about the objective of the project. Such an opening gives your listeners a basis for judging the actual results of the project as you present them.

Measuring heat transfer has been a costly, time-consuming, and all-too-often inexact procedure. The primary objective of this project was to develop new techniques for measuring heat transfer in a three-phase system. Our first step was to investigate . . . .

Forecast. Sometimes you can use the forecast of a new development or trend to arouse the interest of your listeners.

> In the very near future, we may be able to call our local library and have a videotape of *Hamlet* or of last year's Super Bowl replayed on our wall television. This project and others are now being developed at Wincom Industries . . . .

Delivery Techniques

In order to deliver an effective oral presentation, observe the following basic "do's and don'ts."

First, when you stand up to speak, *don't rush your opening.* Begin by taking a good look at your listeners, and let them take a good look at you. Then begin your planned opening firmly and authoritatively. Never apologize for inconvenient conditions or tell your listeners how nervous you are (your audience probably won't notice your nervousness—so why call attention to it?).

Try to talk to your listeners about your subject just as you would talk to a friend about it. Be sure to *maintain eye contact* with most of your listeners, not just with one person. Eye contact not only can establish directness of communication with your listeners but can provide you with feedback from them. That is, when you are looking at your listeners, you will probably be able to notice if they begin to look puzzled or confused. Such feedback can serve as a cue that you need to clarify the point you are making.

Be careful not to talk too fast. If you are even a little nervous, speaking too quickly is a real danger. *Do not talk in a monotone;* if you do, you will bore and finally lose your listeners. *Enunciate carefully;* say "going" instead of "gonna," and "don't you think?" instead of "dontchathink?" Try to eliminate fillers like "ah," "like," and "ya-know?" Although such fillers are so common that it may be impossible to eliminate them altogether, make a serious effort to do so. Also, learn to *suppress nervous mannerisms,* such as adjusting your clothing or smoothing your hair.

To emphasize a point, say it—then pause to let its significance register with your listeners—and then repeat the point. You can also achieve emphasis by varying the pitch of your voice, by varying the volume of your voice, and by varying the pace of your presentation. Gestures, too, can create emphasis. A closed fist, for example, can stress an idea dramatically. You can highlight a plea with a palms-up gesture, or indicate the large size of something by making a broad, semicircular motion with one hand. Be sure, though, to use gestures only when they come naturally; in other words, use the same gestures you would in ordinary conversation.

Refer to your notes openly, whether they are on 4″ × 6″ cards or 8½″ × 11″ paper. When you need to look at your notes, do so. Your listeners won't be impatient; they are human too. They won't expect you to be a spellbinding speaker, but they will expect you to be knowledgeable, prepared, and organized.

Rehearse your presentation until you can do it comfortably, in the allotted time, and with no major hesitations. Once you are ready, relax and don't worry about forgetting something. At this point you are not likely to forget a major point, and the sky won't fall if you overlook a minor point.

Concluding

When you are finished, conclude promptly but not abruptly. Don't end as though you were beating a hasty retreat. Plan the ending of your presentation the way you planned your opening. It's your last chance to get your message across, so don't waste it. You may find that it is most effective to conclude with a summary of your main points—so that your listeners will be more likely to remember them. Or, depending on your topic, you might end by making a recommendation, by asking a question, or by using any of the other techniques suggested for written closings in Chapter 3.

Question-and-Answer Period

Depending on the occasion and on your subject, you may want to provide for a question-and-answer session at the end of your presentation. If so, answer questions as completely as time allows or as the question deserves. Be sure that your answers are accurate. Don't be afraid to respond with "I don't know." Be polite and objective in responding to a hostile question, but be prepared to go on to the next question if it becomes evident that the questioner simply wants to argue. Don't play for laughs at a questioner's expense. You'll offend not only the questioner but the rest of your listeners as well.

EFFECTIVE LISTENING

Although you may spend only a small part of your time on the job making oral presentations, you probably spend a great deal of your time listening to other people. You may receive oral instructions, attend workshops sponsored by your employer, or take courses as a part of your continuing education. Whatever the activity may be, it is important to develop effective listening skills.

Tips for Becoming an Effective Listener

You must be motivated to listen—either by an interest in the subject or by a desire to succeed on the job. The following guidelines can help you improve your listening skills.

- Develop a positive attitude toward the speaker. Good listeners assume, for example, that even though the subject may sound dull, the speaker is likely to say something that they can use. Do not allow your own biases or attitudes toward the subject or the speaker to influence your objectivity. Keep an open mind.
- Do not be distracted by a speaker's personality or speaking style; rather, respond thoughtfully to the speaker's words and avoid making judgments too quickly.
- Be prepared. On the job, think and talk about the subject of a meeting or a workshop ahead of time. Preparation should enable you to understand the material better and to remember it more easily.
- Analyze the speaker's words and ideas while you are listening, but don't become so engrossed in your own analysis that you miss important points. Try to spot inconsistencies between the facts and the ideas that you hear. Listen "between the lines." Is the speaker using emotionally charged words? If so, are they appropriate? Can you think of other points that support or reject what the speaker is advocating? Do your own attitudes match those of the speaker? Analyzing a speaker's words and ideas helps you not only to probe the meaning of the subject but to remember key points.
- Take notes. Being a good listener sometimes means being a good note-taker. You may wish to record your own thoughts and questions as you are listening, so that you will remember to verify or ask them after the speaker is finished. The best note-takers record only key words and phrases while they are listening, so that they won't miss anything that is being said.
- When you are not taking notes, look at the speaker. This is not only a courtesy but an aid to concentration and comprehension.

You may not have time or need to follow all these guidelines—if you don't, use the technique or techniques that best help *you* to absorb and remember. You may also find that some of these techniques work better when you are listening to formal oral presentations and others work better when you are listening to one or two people in conversations.

CHAPTER SUMMARY

Oral presentations are in many ways like written presentations.

First, you must analyze your audience. Who are they? Are they co-workers? Are they customers? Are they management? Whoever they are, you must gear your presentation specifically to them.

Then determine your objective: is it to inform? to persuade? to arouse your audience to action? Key your objective to the occasion and the audience, and fix it firmly in mind.

Then gather and organize your information as you would for any communication. Put your outline together using the most suitable method of development: for example, increasing order of importance, problem-solution, specific-to-general, or general-to-specific.

Prepare visual aids if they will help you to achieve your objective. Remember to keep them simple (one idea per visual) and legible. They must be readable by every member of the audience.

Once you have put your material together, rehearse your presentation until you have all the ideas and their order engraved on your mind. Practice with your visuals so that they become a part of your talk, not simply add-ons. Adequate rehearsal gives you the confidence you need to present your material effectively.

The easiest part comes last—the actual presentation. Look at your audience for a moment before you start, then begin talking to them. Watch the people in the audience as you speak—they'll give you the cues you need to adjust your delivery. Speak slowly and distinctly.

Refer to your notes when you need to; the audience expects it. Gesture when it is appropriate. If you have practiced sufficiently, these things will come naturally.

And, finally, conclude your presentation, don't just end it. Summarize your main points or make a firm recommendation.

Much of your time is spent listening to others. Listening is an acquired skill, just as writing and speaking are skills. Ways to increase your effectiveness as a listener are to be motivated to listen (by interest in the subject or by a desire to succeed), to develop a positive attitude toward the presentation, not to be distracted by the speaker's personality or speaking style, to be prepared to receive the information being given you, and to develop an active mind that anticipates and analyzes the information being received.

EXERCISES

1. Come to class prepared to discuss in detail the differences between writing a report and presenting one orally.

2. Deliver a 5- to 10-minute talk on an academic, business, or government policy of which you disapprove. State the reasons for your disapproval, and offer reasons why the policy should be changed or abolished.

3. Deliver a 5- to 10-minute talk explaining the purpose and function of a tool or piece of equipment typically used in your field. If possible, choose a device unfamiliar to someone outside your field. If the item is not too large, bring it to class; otherwise, rely on visual aids to clarify your explanation.

4. Deliver a 5- to 10-minute talk that describes a service that someone in your field provides to a customer, client, or patient. Ask a friend to play the role of the person being served, if such a role would aid the presentation.

5. Prepare a 10- to 15-minute talk that argues for or against a controversial issue in your career field. Typical topics would include training or accreditation practices, employment practices, professional or union affiliations, or any legislation, current or pending, that will affect your field.

6. Prepare a 10- to 15-minute talk in which you summarize the findings of a major report. Be prepared to respond to questions.

15

Finding a Job

Before you begin your search for a job, do some serious thinking about your future. Decide first what you would most like to be doing in the immediate future. Then think about the kind of work you'd like to be doing two years from now and five years from now. Once you have established your goals, you can begin your job hunt with greater confidence because you'll have a better idea of what kind of position you are looking for and in what companies or other organizations you are most likely to find that position.

The search for a job can be logically divided into five steps: (1) locating the job you want, (2) preparing an effective résumé, (3) writing an effective letter of application, (4) performing well in an interview, and (5) sending follow-up letters.

LOCATING THE JOB YOU WANT

A number of sources are available to help you locate the job you want: classified ads, letters of inquiry, trade and professional journals, school placement services, employment agencies, and the advice of friends and acquaintances.

Advertisements in Newspapers

Many employers advertise in the classified sections of newspapers. For the widest selection, look in the Sunday editions of local and big-city newspapers. Although reading dozens of want ads can be tedious, an item-by-item check is necessary if you are to do a thorough job search. The job you are looking for might be listed in the classified ads under any number of titles. A clinical medical technologist seeking a job, for example, might find the specialty listed under "Medical Technician," "Clinical Medical Technician," or "Laboratory Technician." Depending on a hospital's or a pathologist's needs, the listing could be more specific yet, such as "Blood Bank Technician," "Hematology Technician," or "Clinical Chemistry Technician." So play it safe— read *all* the ads. Occasionally, newspapers print special employment supplements that provide valuable information on many facets of the job market. Watch for these.

As you read the ads, take notes on such things as salary ranges, job locations, job duties and responsibilities, and even the terminology used in the ads to describe the work (a knowledge of the words and expressions that are generally used with regard to a particular type of work can be helpful when you prepare your résumé and letters of application).

Letters of Inquiry

If you would like to work for a particular firm, write and ask whether it has an opening for someone with your qualifications. Normally, you should send the letter either to the director of personnel or to the specific department head; for a small firm, however, you can write to the head of the firm. Your letter should present a general summary of your employment background or training. It should be brief and to the point, expressing interest in such a job but leaving everything else to your résumé, which you enclose with the letter.

Trade and Professional Journals

In many occupations there are associations that publish periodicals of general interest to members. Such periodicals often contain a listing of current job opportunities. If you were seeking a job in forestry, for example, you could check the job listings in the *Journal of Forestry*, published by the Society of American Foresters. To learn about the trade or professional associations for your occupation, consult the following reference books at a convenient library.

Encyclopedia of Associations
Encyclopedia of Business Information Sources
National Directory of Employment Services

School Placement Services

Check with the career counselors in your school's job-placement office. Government, business, and industry recruiters often visit job-placement offices to interview prospective employees; the recruiters also keep college placement offices aware of their company's current employment needs. While you are in the placement office, ask to see a current issue of the *College Placement Annual*. This publication lists the occupational requirements and addresses of over a thousand industry, business, and government employers.

State Employment Agencies

Most states operate free employment agencies that are in business specifically to match applicants and jobs. If your state has one, register with the local employment office. It may have just the job you want; if not, it will keep your résumé on file and call you if such a job comes along.

Private Employment Agencies

Private employment agencies are profit-making organizations that are in business to help people find jobs—for a fee. Choose a private employment agency carefully. Some are well established and quite reputable, but others have questionable reputations. Check with your local Better Business Bureau as well as with friends and acquaintances before signing an agreement with a private employment agency.

Reputable private employment agencies provide you with job leads and help to organize your campaign for the job you want. They may also provide useful information on the companies doing the hiring.

Who pays the fee if you are offered and accept a job through a private agency? Sometimes the employer will pay the agency's fee. Otherwise, you must pay either a set fee or a percentage of your first month's salary on the new job. Before signing a contract, be sure you understand who is paying the fee and, if *you* are, how much you are agreeing to pay. As with any written agreement, read the fine print carefully.

Friends and Acquaintances

Consult with people you know whose judgment you respect. It's especially useful to speak to people who are already working in your chosen field. Family members, friends, neighbors, teachers, members of the clergy—any one of these might provide exactly the job lead you need.

Other Sources

Local, state, and federal government agencies offer many employment opportunities. Local government agencies are listed in the white pages of your telephone directory under the name of your city, county, or state. For information about jobs with the federal government, contact the U.S. Office of Personnel Management and the Federal Personnel and Management Office, both of which have branches in most major cities. They are listed in the white pages of the telephone book under "U.S. Government."

If you are a veteran, local and campus Veterans' Administration offices can provide material on special placement programs for veterans. Such agencies can supply you with the necessary information about the particular requirements or entrance tests for your occupation.

PREPARING AN EFFECTIVE RÉSUMÉ[1]

A *résumé*, the key element in a job hunt, is a summary of your qualifications. It tells a prospective employer about your job objectives, your training and education, your work experience, and your personal data. A résumé itemizes, in one or two pages, the qualifications that you can mention only briefly in a letter of application. On the basis of the information that the résumé supplies, prospective employers can decide whether to ask you to come in for a personal interview. If you do have an interview, the interviewer can base specific questions on the data the résumé contains. For all these reasons, having a résumé is vital.

In preparing to write a résumé, determine what kind of job you are seeking. Then ask yourself what information about you and your background would be most important to a prospective employer in the field you have chosen. On the basis of your answers to this question, decide what sort of details you should include in your résumé and how you can most effectively present your qualifications. Analyze yourself and your background. What jobs have you held? What were your principal duties in each of them? What experience did you gain that

[1] When a regular typewriter is used, the word *résumé* is spelled without the accent marks (see Figure 15–1, for example).

would be of value in the kind of job you are seeking? When and how long were you on each job? Consider your education. List the college or colleges you attended, the dates you attended each one, the degree you received, your major field of study, and any academic honors you achieved. The significant details of your education or training and of any job experience you may have had—along with personal data (your name, address, and so on)—are what make up a résumé.

A number of different formats can be effectively used. The most important thing is to make sure that your résumé is attractive, well organized, easy to read, and free of errors. A common format contains the following:

Heading
Personal data
Employment objective
Education
Employment Experience
References

Underline or capitalize whatever headings you use to make them stand out on the page. Whether you list education or experience first depends on which is stronger in your background. If you are a recent graduate, list education first; if you have one or more years of related job experience, list experience first. In both cases, list the most recent education or job experience first, the next most recent experience second, and so on.

The Heading

Start with your name, address, and telephone number. These are usually centered on the page. Do not include a date in the heading; if you do, you'll have to keep changing it.

```
                David B. Edwards
              6819 Locustview Drive
              Topeka, Kansas 66614
                (913) 233-1552
```

Personal Data (Optional)

Recent federal legislation limits the inquiries an employer can make before hiring an applicant—especially requests for such personal information as age, sex, marital status, race, and religion. Consequently, some job seekers exclude this category because they feel their personal data could have a negative impact on the employer. You may also eliminate this category simply because you need the space for more significant information about your qualifications. However, if you believe the Personal Data category will help you to land a particular job, then include your date of birth and your marital status (it's better to give your date of birth than your age, so your résumé won't become out of date). In any case, you should see yourself through the eyes of your potential employers and provide whatever information would be most useful to them.

Employment Objective

State not only your immediate employment objective but the direction you hope your career will take.

EMPLOYMENT OBJECTIVE

A responsible position in an engineering department in which I may use my training in computer sciences to solve engineering-related problems.

The Employment Objective category enables the employer to identify your purpose quickly. However, avoid using an overly specific employment objective, since an employer might pass you over for similar or related positions in a large company. Ideally, you should write a well-focused, specific résumé for each job. Since this is not feasible, keep your Employment Objective well defined but flexible. If you do not have a clear objective and use one résumé to apply for several different positions, you may want to exclude the Employment Objective altogether.

Education

List the college or colleges you attended, the dates you attended each one, the degree or degrees you received, your major field of study, and any academic honors you earned. If your résumé is relatively short, also give the name of the high school you attended, its location, and the dates you attended.

EDUCATION

Georgia Institute of Technology, Atlanta; September 19-- to present.
Expect to receive a Bachelor of Science degree in Engineering in June 19--.

Major Courses: Calculus I, II, III, IV; Differ-
ential Equations; Methods of Digital Compu-
tations; Advanced Computer Techniques; Soft-
ware Utilization; Special Computer
Techniques; Graphic Display.
Activities and honors:
Phi Chi Epsilon--Honor Society for Women in
Business and Engineering
Society of Women Engineers--Secretary-Trea-
surer during Junior Year
American Institute of Industrial Engineers--
Secretary during Senior Year
Engineering Science Club
Doris Harlow Scholarship recipient--two con-
secutive years
Grade average: 3.46/4.00
Dean's List during 6 of 8 semesters

Butler County Community College, Butler, Pennsylvania; September 19-- to May 19--

Knoch High School, Saxonburg, Pennsylvania;
September 19-- to June 19--

Employment Experience

List all your full-time jobs, starting with the most recent and
working backward. If you have had little full-time work experience,
list part-time and temporary jobs too. Give the details of your employment, including the job title, dates of employment, and the name and
address of the employer. Provide a concise description of your duties
for those jobs with duties similar to those of the job you are seeking;
if a job is not directly relevant, give only a job title and a very brief
description. Specify any promotions you received. If you have been
with one company for a number of years, highlight your accomplishments during those years. List military service as a job: give the dates
you served, your duty specialty, and your rank at discharge. Discuss
the duties only if they relate to the job you are applying for.

EMPLOYMENT EXPERIENCE

September 19-- to Present

Participating in the Professional Training Program
at Computer Systems International, Atlanta, Georgia. Assigned to Design Department, as Production
Trainee; to Word Processing Department, as Cleri-

```
cal Assistant; to Engineering Department, as Pro-
gramer Trainee.

April 19-- to September 19--
Lifeguard at Vacationland Amusement Park,
    Hillstown, Pennsylvania.
Chief lifeguard at end of summer, supervising
    three other lifeguards.
```

Special Skills and Activities

This category usually comes near the end and provides an excellent replacement for the Personal Data category. You may include skills such as knowledge of foreign languages, writing and editing abilities, specialized technical knowledge (such as experience with word processing or a background in electronics), hobbies, student or community activities, professional or club memberships, and published works. Be selective: do not overdo this category, do not duplicate information given in other categories, and include only items that support your employment objective.

A variety of different headings can be used for this category, depending on which skills or activities you wish to emphasize. In Figure 15-2, for example, the heading "Professional Affiliations" is used.

References

You can include references as part of the résumé or provide a statement on the résumé that references will be furnished upon request. Either way, do not give anyone as a reference without first obtaining his or her permission to do so.

REFERENCES

```
Furnished upon request.
```

Some résumés, called functional résumés, are arranged not in reverse order of time but according to duties, starting with the job most closely related *in function* to the job you seek. Since this type of résumé relies heavily on experience, it is not one that a recent graduate would normally use.

Do not list your present salary in your résumé. If it is too high, you may automatically price yourself out of a job for which you are applying. If it is too low, any offer you receive might well be less than it might otherwise have been.

As you write your résumé, use action verbs and state ideas concisely. There is no reason to avoid *I* altogether, but it is best not to overuse it.

NOT   I was promoted to shop foreman in June 19--.

BUT   Promoted to shop foreman in June 19--.

Be truthful in your résumé. If you give false data and are found out, the consequences could be serious. At the very least, you will have seriously damaged your credibility with your employer.

Make your résumé flawless before mailing it. If you are not a skilled typist, you may want to have it professionally typed. Printing usually produces more professional-looking copies than does photocopying. This is no time to pinch pennies.

Following are two sample résumés: one by a recent community-college graduate and one by an applicant who has been employed for many years. The writer of the first résumé (Figure 15–1) has had only limited work experience and therefore puts the education section first and gives fairly detailed information about his college work. On the second sample résumé (Figure 15–2), work experience appears first because the applicant has had nine years of full-time employment—a fact that is much more important to a prospective employer than the applicant's educational data.

RESUME

David B. Edwards
6819 Locustview Drive
Topeka, Kansas 66614
(913) 233-1552

EMPLOYMENT OBJECTIVE

Position as entry-level programmer or data communications technician, leading to a career in systems analysis and management.

EDUCATION

Associate Degree in Computer Science. Fairview Community College, Topeka, Kansas.

FIGURE 15–1. Sample résumé.

Graduated June 1983. Dean's Honor List
Award received for six quarters.

Relevant course work:

Introduction to Cybernetics	Computer Graphics Operating Systems
Programming in COBOL	Design
Programming in FORTRAN	Data Structures
Data-Base Management	Technical Writing

Current course work: Programming in PASCAL
at Topeka Technical University Extension.

EMPLOYMENT EXPERIENCE

Computer Consultant--Fairview Community
College Computer Center: advised and
trained novice computer users at the College computer center; wrote and maintained
user documentation for the UNIX operating
system. November 1983 to present.

Tutor--Fairview Community College: tutored
and advised remedial students in mathematics and computer programming. January 1983
to June 1983.

SPECIAL SKILLS AND ACTIVITIES

Thorough knowledge of the UNIX operating
system, including its word-processing,
text-editing, and file-formatting programs.

Excellent writing and editing skills; practical experience in documenting computer
programs for beginning programmers and
users.

Ability to communicate well with both technical and nontechnical personnel.

Member of the Fairview Community Microcom-
puter User's Group, and helped to establish
and edit the Group's monthly newsletter.

References, college transcripts, portfolio
of computer programs, and writing samples
available upon request.

FIGURE 15–1, *continued*

RESUME

Robert Mandillo
7761 Shalamar Drive
Dayton, Ohio 45424
Home: (513) 255-4137
Business: (513) 255-3730

EMPLOYMENT OBJECTIVE

Position of greater responsibility and
growth potential in the field of technical
exhibit design.

EMPLOYMENT EXPERIENCE

Manager, Engineering Drafting Department.
Air Force Orientation Group, Wright-Patter-
son Air Force Base, Ohio: official exhibit
design, construction, and display agency
for the U.S. Air Force. Manage and control
the Engineering Drafting Department, supervising a staff of seventeen Drafting Mechanics. Support engineering design staff;
develop, judge, and improve the selection
of materials and equipment for design and
construction of exhibits. Write specifications, negotiate with vendors, initiate and
coordinate procurement procedures. June
19-- to present.

Supervisor, Graphic Illustrators. Henderson
Advertising Agency, Cincinnati, Ohio. Advanced from Illustrator to Graphic Technician, and was then promoted to supervisor
of five Illustrators and four Drafting Mechanics. Monitored and approved work orders
and analyzed work-order requirements. Selected appropriate media and techniques for
orders. Rendered illustrations in pencil or
ink.

FIGURE 15-2. Sample résumé.

```
EDUCATION

    Bachelor of Science in Mechanical Engineer-
    ing Technology. Edison State College,
    Wooster, Ohio. Graduated in June 19--.

    Associate Degree in Mechanical Drafting.
    Wooster Community College, Wooster, Ohio.
    Graduated in June 19--.

PROFESSIONAL AFFILIATIONS

    Member of the National Association of Me-
    chanical Engineers and Draftsman.

REFERENCES

    References, letters of recommendation, and
    portfolio of original designs and drawings
    available upon request
```

FIGURE 15–2, *continued*

WRITING AN EFFECTIVE LETTER OF APPLICATION

The letter of application is essentially a sales letter. In it, you are trying to sell your services and, in most cases, will be competing with other applicants. Your immediate objective is to have your letter read by someone in the organization who has authority to screen job applicants; your ultimate goal is to obtain an interview. Therefore, your letter must do three things: catch your reader's attention favorably, convince your reader that you are qualified for the position, and request an interview. Try to accomplish the three objectives in a one-page letter.

Your reader should be able to learn immediately what the purpose of your letter is—you should not waste his or her time with inappropriate formalities or unnecessary details. You should state clearly that you are looking for a job with the organization. It may be a specific job that was advertised or that you learned about from another source, or you may have heard that the company has the kind of position you seek and are writing to inquire whether it has any openings for a candidate with your background. Be sure to tell your reader why you feel you are qualified for the job and that you will be available for an interview. Provide the following information in your letter of application:

1. If you are applying for a specific job, identify the job by title and state how you heard about it. If you are not applying for a specific job, explain that you are seeking a particular kind of position and are writing to inquire whether the organization has any such openings.
2. List your qualifications for the job in summary form. If you are still a student or are a recent graduate and have had little work experience, stress your education; if you have been employed in a related field, emphasize your work background. Then refer the reader to the résumé for other important details.
3. State where you can be reached and when you will be available for an interview.

Send the letter of application to the organization to which you are applying. Include in the letter any information that is pertinent to the particular job you are applying for—details that you cannot include in the résumé because it is not written for a specific job.

The start of a letter of application is crucial in catching your reader's attention. One way to begin your letter is to state your employment objective and your interest in fulfilling your goal within the organization to which you are writing.

```
    I am looking for a responsible position in an
engineering department in which I may use my
training in computer sciences to solve engineer-
ing-related problems. I would be interested in
exploring the possibility of obtaining such a po-
sition within your firm.
```

Or you could begin the letter of application by naming someone you have met from the organization who has told you about a job (you may have met such a person at a conference or convention, through a friend, and so on). This kind of approach has the advantage of indicating that an employee evidently feels that you may be qualified for the job. Then in the next paragraph of your letter of application, you can give a summary of your qualifications.

```
    During the recent NOMAD convention in Washing-
ton, a member of your sales staff, Mr. Dale Jar-
rett, informed me of a possible opening for a
manager in your Dealer Sales Division. My exten-
sive background in the office machine industry,
```

```
I believe, makes me highly qualified for the
position.
```

Once you have opened the letter, your aim is to convince your reader that you are a highly qualified candidate for the position. Expand upon the qualifications you mentioned in the opening and present any additional qualifications that might be particularly appropriate for the specific job. Think carefully about the requirements of the job, and then stress those aspects of your background that would interest a prospective employer most. Highlight any related experience listed in your résumé that is especially pertinent to the job you are applying for. If you are applying for a sales job, for example, indicate that other jobs you have held have taught you how to present a product line effectively. If you are applying for a job as an office manager, indicate any supervisory experience you have had.

Close your letter with a direct request for an interview. If the prospective employer is located near you, you can request that the recipient of your letter either send you a note or call you to set up an appointment. If going on an interview would involve considerable travel expense, let the prospective employer bring up the subject of the interview.

Be sure to type the letter, and make it error-free and attractive.

Following are three sample letters of application. One is by a recent college graduate; the second is by a university student who is about to graduate; and the third is by someone who has had many years of work experience.

The opening paragraph of the first letter (Figure 15–3) states that the applicant read in a local newspaper about the company's plan to build a new data processing center. Since the writer is not applying for a specific job opening, he explains what sort of position he is looking for. The second paragraph contains a brief description of the writer's qualifications for the job. In the last paragraph, he indicates where he can be reached to arrange for an interview.

In the second sample letter of application (Figure 15–4), the writer does not specify where she learned of the opening because she does not know whether a position is actually available. Instead, because she is about to graduate, she uses the first paragraph to summarize her educational qualifications. She includes a description, in the second paragraph, of related work experience. In the last paragraph she indicates where she can be reached to set up an interview.

The third sample letter (Figure 15–5) opens with an indication of where the writer learned of the job vacancy. The second paragraph summarizes the candidate's qualifications for the job. The final paragraph asks for an interview and specifies where the writer can be reached.

6819 Locustview Drive
Topeka, Kansas 66614
June 14, 19--

Loudons, Inc.
4619 Drove Lane
Kansas City, Kansas 63511

Dear Personnel Manager:

The Kansas Dispatch recently reported that
Loudons is building a new data processing
center just north of Kansas City. I would
like to apply for a position as an entry-
level programmer at the center.

I am a recent graduate of Fairview Community
College in Topeka, with an Associate Degree
in Computer Science. In addition to taking a
broad range of courses, I have served as a
computer consultant at the college's computer
center, where I helped train novice computer
users. Since I understand Loudons produces
both in-house and customer documentation, my
technical writing skills (as described in the
enclosed resume) may be particularly useful.

I will be happy to meet with you at your convenience and provide any additional information you may need. You can reach me either at
my home address or at (913) 233-1552.

Sincerely,

David B. Edwards

David B. Edwards

Enclosure: Resume

FIGURE 15-3. Sample letter of application.

2701 Wyoming Street
Atlanta, Georgia 30307
May 29, 19--

Ms. Laura Goldman
Chief Engineer
Acton, Inc.
80 Roseville Road
St. Louis, Missouri 63130

Dear Ms. Goldman:

I am seeking a responsible position in an engineering department in which I may use my training in computer sciences to solve engineering problems. I would be interested in exploring the possibility of obtaining such a position within your firm.

I expect to receive a Bachelor of Science degree in Engineering from Georgia Institute of Technology in June, when I will have completed the Computer Systems Engineering Program of the Engineering Department. Since September 19-- I have been participating, through the university, in the Professional Training Program at Computer Systems International, in Atlanta. In the program I was assigned, on a rotating basis, to several staff sections in apprentice positions. Most recently I have been programmer trainee in the Engineering Department and have gained a great deal of experience in computer applications. Details of the academic courses I have taken are contained in the enclosed resume.

I look forward to hearing from you soon. I can be contacted at my office (415-866-7000, ext. 312) or at home (415-256-6320).

Sincerely yours,

Victoria T. Fromme

Victoria T. Fromme

Enclosure: Resume

FIGURE 15–4. Sample letter of application.

522 Beethoven Drive
Roanoke, Virginia 24017
November 15, 19—

Ms. Cecilia Smathers
Vice President, Dealer Sales
Hamilton Office Machines, Inc.
6194 Main Street
Hampton, Virginia 23661

Dear Ms. Smathers:

During the recent NOMAD convention in Washington, a member of your sales staff, Mr. Dale Jarrett, informed me of a possible opening for a Manager in your Dealer Sales Division. My extensive background in the office machine industry, I believe, makes me highly qualified for the position.

I was with the Technology, Inc., Dealer Division from its formation in 1969 to its phase-out last year. During this period, I was involved in all areas of dealer sales, both within Technology, Inc., and through personal contact with a number of independent dealers. Between 1967 and 1969 I served as Assistant to the Dealer Sales Manager as a Special Representative. My education and work experience are contained in the enclosed resume.

I would like to discuss my qualifications in an interview at your convenience. Please write to me or telephone me at 703-449-6743 any weekday.

Sincerely,

Gregory Mindukakis

Gregory Mindukakis

Enclosure: Resume

FIGURE 15–5. Sample letter of application.

CONDUCTING YOURSELF DURING THE INTERVIEW

A job interview may last for thirty minutes, or it may take several hours; you may be interviewed by one person or by several, either at one time or in a series of interviews. The job interview is too important to walk into unprepared.

Before the Interview

Learn everything you can about the potential employer before the interview. What kind of organization is it? Is the company locally owned? Is it a nonprofit organization? If it is public employment, at what level of government is it? Does it provide a service, and, if so, what kind? How large is the business? Is the owner self-employed? Is it a subsidiary of a larger operation? Is it expanding? Where will you fit in? This kind of information can be obtained from current employees, from such company literature as employee publications, or from the business section of back issues of local newspapers (available in the local library). You may be able to learn the company's size, sales volume, products, credit rating, plant locations, subsidiary companies, new products, building programs, and such information from its annual reports; from publications such as *Moody's Industrials, Dunn and Bradstreet, Standard and Poor's,* and *Thomas' Register;* and from other business reference sources a librarian might suggest. What you cannot find through your research, ask your interviewer.

Try to anticipate the questions your interviewer might ask, and prepare your answers in advance. Following are some of the questions that interviewers typically ask.

- What are your short-term and long-term occupational goals?
- What are your major strengths and weaknesses?
- Do you work better with others or alone?
- Why do you want to work for this employer?
- How do you spend your time?

Some of these questions are difficult. Give them careful thought.

During the Interview

Promptness is important. Be sure that you arrive for your interview at the appointed time. It's usually a good idea, in fact, to arrive ahead of time, since you may be asked to fill out an application before you meet your interviewer. Take a copy of your résumé and a pen with you. The résumé will be helpful because it contains much of the same information the application asks for: personal data, work experience, education. Read the form carefully before beginning to fill it out. The application form provides the company with a record for its files—it also gives the company an opportunity to see how closely you follow directions, how thoroughly you complete a task, and how neat you are. Therefore, fill the form out carefully, and proofread it when you are finished. Why risk a careless mistake now?

The interview will actually begin before you are seated: what you wear and how you act will be closely observed. The way you dress matters. The rule of thumb is to dress conservatively, avoiding extremes. Be well-groomed. For men, a recent haircut and a clean shave are essential; if you wear a beard, have a barber trim it. For women, basic clothes with simple jewelry look most businesslike. Avoid heavy perfume and gaudy lipstick and nail polish.

Remain standing until you are offered a seat. Then sit up straight (good posture suggests self-assurance), look at the interviewer, and try to appear relaxed and confident. Never chew gum. Don't smoke unless the interviewer invites you to do so. During the interview, you will be a little nervous. This is a natural reaction, and the interviewer expects it. Use this nervous energy to your advantage by channeling it into alertness. Listen carefully and record important information in your memory. Do not attempt to take extensive notes during the interview, although it is acceptable to jot down a few facts and figures.

When answering questions, don't ramble or stray away from the subject. Say only what you must in order to answer each question properly and then stop, but avoid giving just "yes" and "no" answers, which usually don't permit the interviewer to learn enough about you. Some interviewers allow a silence to fall just to see how you will react. The burden of conducting the interview is the interviewer's, not yours—and he or she may interpret it as a sign of insecurity if you rush in to fill a void in the conversation. If such a silence would make you uncomfortable, be ready to ask an intelligent question about the company.

Highlight your qualifications for the job you are seeking, but admit obvious limitations as well. Remember also that the job, the company, and the location must be right for *you*. Ask about such factors as opportunity for advancement and fringe benefits (but don't create the impression that your primary interest is security). If the employer seems clearly interested in you, you might also inquire about educational opportunities and, if accepting the job would require you to relocate, recreational and cultural activities in the community.

If the interviewer overlooks important points, bring them up. But, if possible, let the interviewer mention salary first. In the event that you are forced to bring up the subject, put it into a straightforward question. If you have taken the trouble to learn the prevailing salaries in your field, you will be better prepared to discuss salary. If you are a recent graduate, it is usually unwise to attempt to bargain. Many companies have inflexible starting salaries for beginners.

Interviewers look for a degree of self-confidence and for the candidate's apparent understanding of the field in which he or she is applying for a job. Less is expected of a beginner, but even a newcomer must show some command of the subject. One way to impress your interviewer is to ask questions about the company that are related to your line of work. Interviewers also respond favorably to applicants who can communicate, who can present themselves well. Jobs today require interaction of all kinds: person-to-person, department-to-department, division-to-division. Candidates who cannot look the interviewer in the eye or explain why they are applying for the job are not likely to do well in a work situation either.

At the conclusion of the interview, thank your interviewer for his or her time. Indicate that you are interested in the job (if true), and try to get an idea of when you can expect to hear from the company (but don't press too hard).

SENDING FOLLOW-UP LETTERS

After you leave the interview, jot down the pertinent information you obtained (this information will be especially helpful in comparing job offers). A day or two later, if the job is appealing, send the interviewer a brief note of thanks, saying that you find the job attractive and feel you can fill it well (see Figure 15–6).

If you are offered a job you want, write a brief letter of acceptance as soon as possible—certainly within a week. The format for such a letter is simple: begin by accepting the job you have been offered. Identify the job by title and state the exact salary, so that there will be no confusion on these two important points. The second paragraph might go into detail about moving dates and reporting for work. The details will vary, depending on the nature of the job offer. Conclude the letter with a statement that you are looking forward to working for your new employer. Figure 15–7 shows a typical letter of acceptance.

Since, in your job search, you will have applied to more than one organization (it is certainly legitimate to do so) and may receive more than one job offer, you may at some time need to write a letter

2647 Sitwell Road
Charlotte, North Carolina 28210
March 17, 19--

Mr. F. E. Vallone
Personnel Manager
Calcutex Industries, Inc.
3275 Commercial Park Drive
Raleigh, North Carolina 27609

Dear Mr. Vallone:

Thank you for the informative and pleasant interview we had last Wednesday. Please extend my thanks to Mr. Wilson of the Servocontrol Group as well.

I came away from our meeting most favorably impressed with Calcutex Industries. I find the position you are filling to be an attractive one and feel confident that my qualifications would enable me to perform the duties to everyone's advantage.

If I can answer any further questions, please let me know.

Sincerely yours,

Philip Ming

Philip Ming

FIGURE 15-6. Follow-up letter.

```
                        2647 Sitwell Road
                        Charlotte, North Carolina 28210
                        March 26, 19--


        Mr. F. E. Vallone
        Personnel Manager
        Calcutex Industries, Inc.
        3275 Commercial Park Drive
        Raleigh, North Carolina 27609

        Dear Mr. Vallone:

        I am pleased to accept your offer of $865 per
        month as a junior design draftsman in the
        Calcutex Group.

        After graduation on August 30, I plan to
        leave Charlotte on Tuesday, September 2. I
        should be able to find suitable living accom-
        modations within a few days and be ready to
        report for work on the following Monday, Sep-
        tember 8. Please let me know if this date is
        satisfactory to you.

        I look forward to what I am sure will be a
        rewarding future with Calcutex.

                            Very truly yours

                            Philip Ming
                            Philip Ming
```

FIGURE 15–7. Acceptance letter.

2647 Peters Road
Charlotte, North Carolina 28210
March 26, 19--

Mr. F. E. Vallone
Personnel Manager
Calcutex Industries, Inc.
3275 Commercial Park Drive
Raleigh, North Carolina 27609

Dear Mr. Vallone:

I enjoyed talking with you about your opening
for a junior design draftsman, and I was
gratified to receive your offer. Although I
have given the offer serious thought, I have
decided to accept a position with a commercial drafting agency. The job I have chosen
will provide me with a greater variety of duties, which I feel will develop my skills
more fully in the long run.

I appreciate your consideration and the time
you spent with me.

Sincerely,

Philip Ming

Philip Ming

FIGURE 15-8. Letter of refusal

of refusal. Be especially tactful and courteous because the employer you are refusing has spent time and effort interviewing you and may have counted on your accepting the job. Figure 15–8 shows an example of a job refusal letter. It acknowledges the consideration given the applicant, offers a logical reason for his refusal of the offer, and closes on a pleasant note.

CHAPTER SUMMARY

The search for a job consists of five steps: (1) locating the job you want, (2) preparing an effective résumé, (3) writing an effective letter of application, (4) conducting yourself well during the interview, and (5) sending a follow-up letter.

Sources you can use in locating a job include classified advertisements in newspapers, letters of inquiry, advertisements in trade and professional journals, school placement services, state and private employment agencies, the advice of friends and acquaintances, and local, state, and federal agencies.

Before writing your résumé, determine the exact type of job you are seeking and who the prospective employers are. Then ask yourself what information about you and your background would be most important to those employers. On the basis of your answer to this question, determine what details should be included in your résumé and how you can most effectively present your qualifications. Then prepare your résumé accordingly.

A letter of application must catch your reader's attention, create a desire for your services, and request an interview. Be sure that it includes the specific job for which you are applying (if known), a brief summary of your qualifications for the job, and when and where you can be reached to set up an interview.

Before going to the interview, learn everything you can about your prospective employer. Arrive for the interview promptly. During the interview, highlight strengths you have that could be used in the job you are applying for, demonstrate your knowledge of your field, and project self-confidence. After the interview, make notes of important information you learned during the interview. A day or two later, send the interviewer a brief note of thanks.

If you are offered a job that you plan to accept, send a letter of acceptance to the employer within a few days of receiving the offer. If you have decided to refuse the offer, send a letter as soon as possible, expressing your appreciation for the company's time and effort in considering you for the job.

EXERCISES

1. Prepare a résumé as it will read either at the end of the present semester or when you graduate. Type the résumé on high-quality white bond paper. Make sure it is error- and blemish-free.

2. Write a letter to a past or present teacher or an employer (or other appropriate person) asking permission to use him or her as a job reference. Be prepared to explain in class why you think this person is especially well qualified to comment on your job qualifications.

3. Write a letter to an actual firm for which you would like to work, asking whether there is a position available for someone with the qualifications you expect to have either at the end of the present semester or when you graduate.

4. Write a letter of application in response to an advertisement for a job for which you will be qualified upon graduation. Type it neatly on high-quality white bond paper.

5. Assume that you have been interviewed for the job in Exercise 4. Write a follow-up letter expressing thanks for the interview.

6. To prepare for an interview with a prospective employer, list three questions you think the interviewer may ask you, exclusive of the questions given in the text. Then list six questions you would like to ask the interviewer. Arrange both lists from most important to least important. Come to class prepared to discuss both lists.

part three

WRITER'S GUIDE

Section A

Spelling and Vocabulary

---

1 SPELLING

Personnel managers often reject candidates who make spelling errors on employment applications, résumés, and covering letters. Consider, for example, the true story of a college graduate who applied for the position of Assistant Director of Personnel and was rejected for misspelling the word *personnel*.

The reason potential employers react so strongly to spelling errors is simple. Poor spelling reflects negatively on an employee—and, by association, on the employer as well. Everyone makes an occasional error, of course, but a personnel manager may conclude that someone who has overlooked a spelling mistake on something as important as a job application may be careless in his or her work too. Keep in mind that when you apply for a job, an employer must make a judgment based primarily on your résumé, your letter of application, and your interview.

But an even more important reason to learn to be a careful speller is that accuracy in spelling can help you keep the bargain you, as a writer, make with your readers: to assist them in understanding what you are saying. Your job as a writer is to remove roadblocks from the path of communication between you and your readers—and spelling errors, because they can confuse and slow your readers down, create roadblocks.

As you write a first draft, you needn't be concerned about spelling words correctly. Your attention then should focus on what you are saying; to worry about spelling at that point would be a distraction. You can check for and correct spelling errors when you revise; in fact, you should proofread once *just for spelling.* Guard against the natural tendency to concentrate on complex words; pay as much attention to words in common use as you do to "hard" words. It is often the words you use most frequently that trip you up.

Learning to spell requires a systematic effort on your part. The following system will help you learn to spell correctly.

- Keep a dictionary handy, and use it regularly. If you are unsure about the spelling of a word, don't rely on memory or guess-work—consult the dictionary. When you look up a word, focus on both its spelling and its meaning.
- After you have looked in the dictionary for the spelling of the word, write the word from memory several times. Then check the accuracy of your spelling. If you have misspelled the word, repeat this step. If you do not follow through by writing the word from memory, you lose the chance of retaining it for future use. Practice is essential.
- Keep a list of the words you commonly misspell, and work regularly at whittling it down. Do not load the list with exotic words; many of us would stumble over *asphyxiation* or *pterodactyl.* Concentrate instead on words like *calendar, maintenance,* and *unnecessary.* These and other frequently used words should remain on your list until you have learned to spell them.
- Study the following common sets of words that sould alike but differ in spelling and meaning.[1]

affect (verb: to influence)
effect (noun: a result)

all ready (We are *all ready* to go.)
already (Have you finished the work *already?*)

brake (noun: device for stopping)
break (verb: to crack; noun: period of relaxation)

cite (verb: to refer to)
sight (noun: view; something to look at)
site (noun: location)

cent (noun: coin)
scent (noun: smell)
sent (verb: past tense of *send*)

---

[1] The meanings given here are for identification only—they are not intended to represent every meaning a word may have.

coarse (adjective: rough)
course (noun: direction; adverb in *of course*)

complement (noun: something that completes something else)
compliment (noun: praise; verb: to give praise)

fair (noun: exhibition; adjective: light-hued, beautiful)
fare (noun: cost of a trip; food served)

foreword (noun: introduction to a book)
forward (adjective and adverb: near or toward the front)

hear (verb: to listen to)
here (adverb: in this place)

its (possessive pronoun: Does the dog have *its* bone?)
it's (contraction[2] of *it is: It's* good to see you.)

lead (noun: a metal—rhymes with *bread*)
lead (verb: to be first—rhymes with *breed*)
led (verb: past tense of verb *to lead*)

may be (verb: It *may be* true, but it's hard to believe.)
maybe (adverb: perhaps—*Maybe* he will visit us.)

pair (noun: set of two)
pare (verb: to trim)
pear (noun: fruit)

peace (noun: absence of war)
piece (noun: small amount)

plain (adjective: ordinary-looking, simple; noun: large field)
plane (noun: aircraft)
plane (verb: to make smooth)

principal (adjective: primary, main; noun: school official)
principle (noun: a controlling idea or belief)

right (adjective: correct or a direction)
rite (noun: ritual)
write (verb: to create with words)

road (noun: passageway for vehicles)
rode (past tense of verb *to ride*)
rowed (past tense of verb *to row*—to propel a small boat)

stationary (adjective: not moving)
stationery (noun: writing paper and envelopes)

---

[2] In a *contraction*, two words are combined and one or more letters are omitted. An apostrophe (') indicates where the letter or letters have been dropped. Contractions are appropriate in some informal writing, but it is best to avoid them in formal contexts.

their (possessive pronoun—Do you know *their* telephone number?)

there (adverb: at that place)

they're (contraction of *they are*—*They're* going to meet us at the movies.)

to (preposition: toward)

too (conjunction: also; adverb: excessively)

two (number)

weak (adjective: not strong)

week (noun: seven days)

weather (noun: atmospheric conditions)

whether (conjunction: if)

who's (contraction of *who is*—Do you know *who's* coming?)

whose (possessive pronoun: *Whose* coat is this?)

your (possessive pronoun—Is this *your* book?)

you're (contraction of *you are*—*You're* a fine friend!)

The following pages contain a number of rules and some advice to help you improve your spelling (see also pages 104–107). It would be pointless to try to memorize all the rules and reminders. If you have specific problem areas in spelling, however, you would be wise to learn the rules that apply to your particular needs. Note that most of these rules also have exceptions.

1.1 THE SILENT *E* RULE OF THUMB

Words of one syllable that have a long vowel sound usually end in silent *e*. (A *long vowel* is one that is pronounced like the letter's name.) Adding silent *e* to a one-syllable word that has a *short vowel sound* ordinarily gives the vowel a long sound. (Dictionaries vary in the symbols they use to indicate how a word is pronounced. Examine the pronunciation key in the dictionary you use.)

Compare the words in the two lists below.

Short-Vowel Sounds	*Long-Vowel Sounds*
bit	bite
cut	cute
dot	dote
fat	fate
pet	Pete

The silent *e* rule also applies to the accented syllable in some longer words.[3]

com·plete′   con·trive′   re·fuse′

The silent *e* rule does not apply in longer words in which the final syllable is *not* accented.

com·pos′·ite   gran′·ite   hes′·i·tate   op′·pos·ite

If endings are added to the basic word, the silent *e* rule still holds, even if the silent *e* is dropped when the ending is added.

complete, completed   hope, hoping   late, later

1.2 HARD AND SOFT SOUNDS

The letter *c* can sound like a *k* ("hard" *c*) or like an *s* ("soft" *c*). The letter *g* can sound like "guh" ("hard" *g*) or like a *j* ("soft" *g*).

Hard Sound	*Soft Sound*
attic	ace
cog	cogent

1.2.1 Hard *C* and Soft *C*

Hard *c* and soft *c* cause problems mostly at the ends of words. The following guidelines will help you to distinguish between hard *c* and soft *c*.

- The sound of *c* is always hard when it is the last letter of a word.

  automatic   economic   electric   spastic   specific

- A long vowel followed by a *k* sound is always spelled with a *k* and a silent *e*.

  eke   fluke   like   take   woke

- A short vowel followed by a *k* sound is spelled *ck* when another syllable follows, except in certain words borrowed from French, such as *racquet.*

---

[3] An *accented syllable* receives the emphasis when the word is spoken. The symbol ′ is used here to indicate the accented syllable. Check your dictionary for the symbol it uses.

    beckon   bracket   picket   pocket   trucker

- An *e* after a *c* almost always indicates a soft *c*.

    ace   ice   piece   place   puce

1.2.2 Hard *G* and Soft *G*

Hard *g* and soft *g* cause problems mostly at the beginnings of words. The following guidelines should help you to distinguish between hard *g* and soft *g*.

- Any *g* followed by a consonant is a hard *g*.

    ghetto   gladly   grain   green

- The *g* in the combinations *gu* and *go* is always hard.

    cargo   goblet   guess   guide

- The *g* in the combination *ga* is always hard except in the word *margarine*.

    gale   gape   garage   gate

- The *g* in the combination *gi* can be either hard or soft.

    fragile   gibber   gift   give

- The *g* in the combination *ge* is usually soft.

    cage   garage   general   germinate   gesture

- The *g* in the combination *gy* is normally soft. Words such as *gynecology* are exceptions.

    gymnasium   gypsum   gyrate   gyroscope

1.3 ADDING TO BASIC WORDS

Words may change spelling according to the way they are used in a sentence. The following rules can serve as a guide in choosing the correct spelling of a plural noun, a verb form, an adverb formed from an adjective, and the comparative and superlative forms of some adjectives (*nicer, nicest*).

1.3.1 Plurals of Nouns

You may have no difficulty spelling a word like *tax, brush,* or *ox*. You may encounter some trouble, though, in spelling the plural forms of these and other words. The general rules for forming the plural of nouns are as follows.

- To form the plural of *most* nouns, add *s*.

  circumstance/circumstances   hat/hats   mule/mules
  pen/pens   tie/ties   tool/tools

- To form the plural of nouns that end in *ch, s, sh, ss, x, z,* or *zz,* add *es*.

  branch/branches   brush/brushes   bus/buses
  buzz/buzzes   glass/glasses   tax/taxes

- To form the plural of nouns that end in *y* preceded by a vowel, add *s*.

  boy/boys   monkey/monkeys

  But if the *y* is preceded by a consonant, change the *y* to *i* and then add *es*.

  filly/fillies   fly/flies

- To form the plural of most nouns that end in *f* and all nouns that end in *ff,* add *s*.

  reef/reefs   roof/roofs   cuff/cuffs

  For a few nouns that end in *f,* change the *f* to *v* and add *es*.

  leaf/leaves   loaf/loaves   wolf/wolves

  If a noun ends in *fe,* change the *f* to *v* and add *es*.

  knife/knives   life/lives   wife/wives

  Note: If there is a *v* in the plural form of a noun, you can usually hear it in the spoken word.

- Some commonly used nouns have a special plural form.

  child/children   foot/feet   ox/oxen
  tooth/teeth   woman/women

Consult your dictionary for other plural forms that may be troublesome: nouns ending in *o,* foreign words used in English, a number of scientific and medical terms, and so on.

1.3.2   Adding Verb, Adjective, and Adverb Endings

The general rules for adding endings to verbs, for forming adverbs from adjectives, and for adding the comparative (*er*) and superlative (*est*) endings to adjectives are as follows.

- If the word ends in a consonant, simply add the ending.

  burn + ing = burning   long + er = longer
  small + est = smallest   want + ed = wanted

- If the word ends in silent *e* and the ending begins with a vowel (including *e*), drop the silent *e* of the basic word.

  advise + ory = advisory   base + ic = basic
  desire + able = desirable   fine + est = finest
  landscape + er = landscaper   note + ed = noted

- If the basic word ends in silent *e* and the ending begins with a consonant, simply add the ending.

  care/carefully   like/likely   use/useless

  There are a few exceptions to this rule.

  argue/argument   nine/ninth   true/truly

- If the basic word ends in a consonant and the ending begins with the same consonant, keep both consonants.

  cool/coolly   jewel/jewellike   tail/tailless

- If the basic word ends in *y* preceded by a vowel, simply add the ending.

  betray/betrays/betrayed/betraying
  obey/obeys/obeyed/obeying

  Note: There are three important exceptions to this rule:

lay/lays/laying	*but*	laid
pay/pays/paying	*but*	paid
say/says/saying	*but*	said

- If the basic word ends in *y* preceded by a consonant, change the *y* to *i* before adding the ending, *unless the ending begins with i.*

  copy/copies/copied/copying
  try/tries/tried/trying

- If a verb ends in *ie,* add *s* or *d* directly to the word.

  die/dies/died   tie/ties/tied

  But change *ie* to *y* before adding *ing.*

  die/dying   tie/tying

- When you add *ly* to most adjectives to form an adverb, simply add the ending. The word *truly* is an exception to this rule.

careful/carefully   complete/completely   dim/dimly
nice/nicely   sure/surely   useless/uselessly

When you add the ending *ly* to most adjectives ending in *cal*, be sure to retain the *a* and both *l*'s.

magical/magically   practical/practically

- When you add *er, est,* or *ly* to an adjective that ends in *y*, change the *y* to *i* before adding the ending.

happy/happier/happiest/happily
noisy/noisier/noisiest/noisily

- When you add *ly* to adjectives ending in *ble*, drop the *e* and add only the *y*.

able/ably   favorable/favorably   incredible/incredibly

1.4 DOUBLING FINAL CONSONANTS

Knowing when and when not to double a final consonant before adding an ending is important. Three things affect the decision: (1) whether the vowel in the basic word is long or short, (2) whether the last syllable of the basic word is accented, and (3) whether the basic word ends in more than one consonant.

1.4.1 The Effect of the Vowel in the Basic Word

For most words of one syllable, double the final consonant only if the preceding vowel is *short*.

flop/flopped   ripe/ripen
let/letting   mate/mated
rip/ripped   tune/tuning

Never double the final consonant of a word if the consonant is immediately preceded by two vowels.

appear/appeared/appearing/appearance
treat/treated/treating/treatment

1.4.2 The Effect of the Word's Accent

In longer words, whether the final consonant is doubled depends on which syllable is accented. When the accent falls on the last syllable of a word, double the final consonant before adding the ending.

ad·mit'/admitted/admitting   com·pel'/compelled/compelling

When the accent does not fall on the last syllable, do not double the final consonant before adding the ending.

dif'fer/differed/differing   ex·hib'it/exhibited/exhibiting
fo'cus/focused/focusing   pro'fit/profited/profiting

1.4.3   The Effect of Final Consonants

When a word ends in more than one consonant, *do not double* the final consonant when adding an ending.

confirm/confirmed/confirming
depend/depended/depending/dependence

When a word ends in a double consonant, keep both consonants when adding the ending.

embarrass/embarrassed/embarrassing/embarrassment
enroll/enrolled/enrolling/enrollment

1.5   PREFIXES AND SUFFIXES

A *prefix* is a form like *dis, un,* or *anti* that is placed in front of a word to change its meaning. A *suffix* is a form like *able* or *ible* that is placed at the end of a word (or word part) to change its meaning. To avoid making spelling errors when you use words that contain prefixes and suffixes, study the following rules.

- When you attach a prefix like *dis, im, mis,* or *un* to a word that begins with the same letter as the *last* letter of the prefix, be sure to retain the double letters.

  dis + similar = dissimilar   im + movable = immovable
  mis + spell = misspell   un + natural = unnatural

- When you attach a suffix that begins with a vowel to a word that ends in silent *e,* you should usually drop the *e.*

  advise/advisory   continue/continual
  enclose/enclosure   sane/sanity

- When you attach the suffix *able* or *ible* to a word that ends in a soft *c* or a soft *g* sound, retain the *e* of the original word.

  change/changeable   manage/manageable
  notice/noticeable   service/serviceable

• When you attach suffixes like *ness* and *less,* do not change the spelling of the original word.

care + less = careless (retain the *e*—otherwise you are spelling *carless,* "without a car")
drunken + ness = drunkenness (retain both *n*'s)

Note: In a word like *lioness,* the suffix is *ess* (to indicate female), not *ness.*

1.6   WORDS WITH *IE* OR *EI*

Among the trickiest words in the English language to spell are *ie* and *ei* words. The following rules of thumb should help you to recognize the correct spelling of these words. The jingle "*i* before *e,* except after *c*" covers rules 1 and 2 below.

1. In most cases, the correct combination following the letter *c* is *ei.*

   ceiling   *conceive*   *perceive*   *receive*

2. Many words that are pronounced *ee* are spelled *ie.*

   achieve   brief   cashier   field
   piece   relieve   tier   yield

3. Many words that are pronounced as a long *a* are spelled *ei.*

   eight   freight   rein
   veil   vein   weight

4. Words that are pronounced as a long *i* are always spelled *ei.*

   height   seismograph   sleight

1.7   CONTRACTIONS

A *contraction* is a form that combines two words, omitting one or more letters, and uses an apostrophe (') to indicate where the letter or letters have been dropped.

cannot/can't   is not/isn't
it is/it's   they are/they're

Remember to place the apostrophe exactly where the letter or letters are deleted.

Be careful not to confuse contractions with words that have the same pronunciation as the contractions.

its/it's   their/they're   theirs/there's   whose/who's

And do not confuse the presence of the apostrophe to form a contraction with the use of the apostrophe to show possession.

Contraction	*Possession*
can't (can + not)	the woman's voice
don't (do + not)	a student's book

In a contraction, the apostrophe indicates that a letter has been left out. In a possessive form, the apostrophe indicates ownership.

1.8   ABBREVIATED SPELLINGS

In very informal writing, certain words are sometimes spelled in an abbreviated form: *thru* (*through*), *tho* (*although*), and *nite* (*night*). Such abbreviated spellings should be avoided in all job-related writing.

1.9   WORD GROUPS OF FREQUENTLY MISSPELLED WORDS

- Words Ending in *ery*

creamery	bravery	effrontery
hatchery	imagery	nursery

- Words Ending in *ary*

arbitrary	complementary	complimentary	documentary
elementary	fragmentary	imaginary	library
monetary	necessary	primary	tributary

- Words Ending in *able*

acceptable	agreeable	avoidable	changeable
dependable	manageable	profitable	valuable

  Note: Remember to keep the *e* in *changeable* and *manageable*.

- Words ending in *iable*

appreciable	enviable	justifiable
liable	reliable	variable

- Words Ending in *ible*

audible	combustible	compatible	credible
divisible	eligible	feasible	forcible

illegible   indelible   invincible   negligible
reducible   visible

- Words ending in *ise*

  advertise   advise   comprise   compromise
  excise   exercise   franchise   revise
  supervise

  Note: The noun form of *supervise* is *supervisor;* the noun
  form of advise is *adviser* or *advisor.*

- Words Ending in *ize*

  authorize   energize   familiarize   magnetize
  notarize   organize   specialize   stabilize
  standardize   subsidize   summarize   synchronize

- Words Ending in *yze*
  analyze   paralyze

  Note: The noun forms are *analysis* and *paralysis.*

- Words Ending in *eous*

  courteous   erroneous   gaseous
  heterogeneous   homogeneous   instantaneous
  outrageous   spontaneous

- Words Ending in *ious*

  cautious   contagious   curious   laborious
  mysterious   nutritious   previous   repetitious

- Words Ending in *ous*

  anonymous   callous   dangerous   disastrous
  grievous   hazardous   intravenous   mischievous
  monotonous

- Words Ending in *sion*

  compulsion   conclusion   conversion   diversion
  erosion   expansion   expulsion   extension
  occasion   persuasion   propulsion   provision
  reversion

- Words Ending in *ssion:*

  accession   admission   concession
  discussion   omission (note one *m*)   recession
  remission   succession   transmission

Note: Be sure to distinguish between *intersession* (the period between two *sessions* of the school year) and *intercession* (intervention on behalf of someone).

Words ending in *cede* and *ceed* are sometimes troublesome. Study the following lists.

- Words Ending in *cede*

accede	concede
intercede	precede (to go ahead of someone or something)
recede	secede

The *ing* forms of these words follow the silent *e* rule: *acceding, conceding, interceding, preceding, receding, seceding.*

- Words Ending in *ceed*

  exceed   proceed (to go forward)   succeed

The *ing* forms are *exceeding, proceeding, succeeding.*

Note: The word *supersede,* "to take the place of something that went before," is often misspelled. It is the only word in common use that has a *sede* ending.

- Words Ending in *ence*

magnificence	maleficence	permanence
persistence	pertinence	

- Words Ending in *ance*

  dissonance   malfeasance   perseverance

- Words Ending in *scence*

  effervescence   luminescence   phosphorescence

2 VOCABULARY

Trying to get along with a limited vocabulary is like trying to prepare a five-course meal with only one utensil and a pan. The limited equipment prevents you from dealing successfully with the range of situations you'll find yourself in. A limited vocabulary is a handicap, but it is one you can overcome. The emphasis here is on *you* because there is no magic formula for vocabulary building. It must be done because you want it done. It must also be done systematically and over a period of time. This chapter provides a system; you must provide the time and desire.

If you stop to think about it, you'll realize that you use at least three different vocabularies, perhaps four. Your largest vocabulary is your *recognition vocabulary,* which includes all the words you recognize and understand in your reading. Your next largest vocabulary is your *writing vocabulary,* which takes in all the words you use in your writing. The third largest is your *speaking vocabulary;* it is smaller than your writing vocabulary because you may consider some words from your writing vocabulary too formal for conversation. And, finally, you may have a limited vocabulary, of from 50 to 1,000 words, that are unique to the particular trade or profession in which you are (or will be) engaged.

You will probably have no trouble in learning your trade, or professional, vocabulary, but you may need to work on improving the other three—especially your writing and recognition vocabularies. One excellent way to do so is by increasing the amount of reading you do and keeping a good dictionary nearby for looking up unfamiliar words. The movement of a word from your recognition vocabulary to your writing vocabulary should be relatively easy. Another effective way to increase your vocabulary is to take a word-part approach, learning the meanings of prefixes and roots of words and, on the basis of those meanings, figuring out the meaning of a new word that contains them. The following pages explore these two methods of improving your vocabulary.

CHOOSING THE RIGHT WORD

Your guideline in choosing the right word should be appropriateness. Is the word or expression you are considering appropriate to both your reader and your purpose? When in doubt about the correct use, exact meaning, or pronunciation of a word, consult a recent edition of a good college or desk dictionary. A compact paperback dictionary may be convenient for checking the spelling of a word, but for a wide range of detailed information about a term, a hardback desk dictionary is essential. The following are considered good desk dictionaries.

- *The American Heritage Dictionary of the English Language.* New York: American Heritage Publishing Company, 1973.
- *Funk and Wagnall's Standard College Dictionary.* Rev. ed. New York: Funk and Wagnall's, 1977.
- *The Random House College Dictionary.* New York: Random House, 1975.

- *Webster's New Collegiate Dictionary.* Rev. ed. Springfield, Mass.: G. & C. Merriam Company, 1979.
- *Webster's New World Dictionary of the American Language.* Second college ed. Cleveland: William Collins, 1980.

Get into the habit of using a dictionary. As with any reference tool, the more you know about it, the more useful it will be to you. The following is a list of the kinds of information a dictionary entry may provide. Both the order in which the information is given and the form in which it is presented vary; most dictionaries supply a note near the beginning of the volume that explains how the information is arranged and presented in the work. Many dictionaries also include a key to the signs, symbols, and abbreviations that are used. In addition, most dictionaries include, before and after the entry section, a variety of information, such as a pronouncing gazetteer (names of places), a list of common English given names, the names of colleges and universities, and a history of the English language.

1. *Spelling.* Each entry is printed in **bold type.** Occasionally, when there is more than one acceptable spelling, both are given: *catalog, catalogue.*
2. *Syllables.* The word is divided into syllables (if it contains more than one): ox·y·gen. This division provides the correct *hyphenation* of the word—it indicates how the word is divided at the end of the line.
3. *Pronunciation.* The word's pronunciation (how it sounds when spoken) is given, usually in parentheses, by a combination of standard alphabet letters and symbols (the combination is called a *respelling*). Each letter and symbol represents one specific sound; a key to the symbols ordinarily appears at the bottom of every page or every second page of the dictionary. The pronunciation of the word *reserve,* for example, is indicated by the form rĭ·zûrv'.
4. *Accent.* An accent mark (' or ') indicates which syllable is emphasized when the word is spoken: pri·mar'i ly. The accent mark ordinarily appears as part of the *respelling* of the word.
5. *Part of speech.* An abbreviation identifies the part or parts of speech the word belongs to: *v.* for *verb; n.* for *noun; pron.* for *pronoun; adj.* for *adjective; adv.* for *adverb; prep.* for *preposition; conj.* for *conjunction; interj.* for *interjection.* If a word functions as more than one part of speech, the different parts of speech are included in the entry.
6. *Definition.* When a word has more than one meaning, each definition is listed, in numbered sequence. The order in which

a word's meanings are listed varies. Some dictionaries present the meanings in historical order, with the oldest meaning first and the most recent meaning last; other dictionaries list the most recent meaning first and the oldest meaning last. (The dictionary's explanatory notes will tell you in what order the meanings are arranged.) If a word has two or more fundamental, and unrelated, meanings, each word is listed as a separate entry; any additional *related* meanings of each word are numbered consecutively within the entry. The word *fan,* for instance, has two separate entries in *The Random House Dictionary:* the first entry includes both the noun that signifies "a device for moving air" and the verb meaning "to move the air"; the second entry applies to the noun *fan* that refers to an "enthusiastic follower."

When a word has one or more specific meanings in one or more special fields (biology, music, literature, architecture, religion, telecommunications, to name just a few), the definitions are introduced by a label that identifies the field. For example, the entry for the word *rest* in *The American Heritage Dictionary* first defines the word according to its most general use—the act of ceasing from work, sleep, death, and so on—and then goes on to define the word according to the way it is used in the specific fields of music, prosody, billiards, and the military.

7. *Example.* To help you understand exactly how a word may be used, some dictionaries provide examples of the word, usually in a phrase or a sentence. The word *serried,* for instance, is defined in *The American Heritage Dictionary* as "pressed together in rows; in close order." The sample sentence that follows is "Troops in *serried* ranks assembled." In examples, some dictionaries italicize the word in question, others abbreviate it, and still others represent the word with a tilde [~].

8. *Picture.* Occasionally, the definition of a word is accompanied by a drawing or a photograph of the object. *The American Heritage Dictionary* in particular has numerous pictures.

9. *Usage.* Usage labels provide information about the standing a word has in relation to current standards of speech. Such a label might indicate that a word is obsolete (no longer in use), primarily British, slang, and so on. Since usage standards change over time, the date of the dictionary is an important factor in determining the accuracy of a given label.

10. *Special uses.* Special uses of a word, or its use in certain expressions, may follow the main body of the definition. The entry for the word *court* in *The American Heritage Dictionary,* for

instance, indicates that the word appears in the expressions *out of court* and *pay court to;* each expression is defined.

11. *Synonyms.* For some words, *synonyms* (words that are similar in meaning) are listed and discussed; the discussion, by providing an explanation of the differences in meaning among the synonyms, can help you select the precise word you need.

12. *Antonyms.* For some words, *antonyms* (words that are opposite in meaning) are supplied. The listing may sometimes aid you in selecting the exact word for your context.

13. *Origin.* The origin and history of a word (its *etymology*) appears in some dictionaries following the last definition and in other dictionaries following the part-of-speech indicator.

The following is a typical dictionary entry. It is taken from *The Random House Dictionary* (revised edition, 1975).

> **op·er·a·tion** (op/ə rā/shən), *n.* **1.** the act or an instance, process, or manner of functioning or operating. **2.** the state of something that operates or is in effect (usually prec. by *in* or *into*): *a rule no longer in operation.* **3.** the exertion of force or influence: *the operation of alcohol on the mind.* **4.** a process of a practical or mechanical nature. **5.** *Surg.* a process or act of operating on the body of a patient. **6.** *Math.* a mathematical process, as addition, multiplication, etc., or an instance of its application. **7.** *Mil.* **a.** a campaign, mission, maneuver, or action. **b.** Usually, **operations.** the conduct of a campaign, mission, etc. **c. operations,** a place from which a military campaign or the like is planned and controlled. **8.** a business transaction in securities or commodities, esp. one of a speculative nature or on a large scale. [ME *operacioun* < L *operātiōn*- (s. of *operātiō*)]

Once you've become familiar with the dictionary, make using it a habit. A dictionary can provide great help to you as speaker, reader, and writer. Remember, too, that one of the most effective ways to build a good vocabulary is to read. You will, of course, sometimes run into terms that even a good desk dictionary does not define—especially those terms related to a particular occupation. Many occupations have created special vocabularies to serve their particular requirements, and a number of these vocabularies are large enough and widely enough used to necessitate the publication of specialized dictionaries. If such a dictionary exists in your field, locate one and use it regularly.

THE WORD-PART APPROACH

An effective way to increase your vocabulary is to call on the *word-part* approach when you come across a word you don't know. This technique enables you to work out the meanings of many words when you first see them. A large number of words contain a root, or part, that expresses its primary meaning. In the word *dictate,* for example, *dict-,* the root, means "say," "tell," "speak."

The meaning of a word frequently changes when a prefix or suffix is added to the root. A *prefix* is a word part that is placed in front of a root to modify the word's meaning. *Sure* is made *unsure* by the addition of the prefix *un-*. A *suffix* is a word part that is placed after a root. It often tells you what part of speech the word is. Nouns are formed by suffixes like *-ness (tightness)*, *-ment (impediment)*, and *-ion (coordination)*. Many verbs end in *-ate (dictate)*, *-ize (minimize)*, and *-ify (qualify)*. Adverbs are usually recognized by their *-ly* suffixes (*slowly, privately*), while for adjectives the endings *-ous, -ful*, and *-less* are common (*famous, colorful, colorless*).

Sometimes a root can have more than one prefix or suffix. The root *new* and the prefix *re-* form *renew*. The addition of the prefix *non-* and the suffix *-able* makes the word *nonrenewable*. Less common words follow the same pattern. The root *aqua* means "water." This root forms the basis for many words: An *aqualung* is a device used for breathing under water. An *aquacade* is a water sports spectacle in which an *aquaplane* (a board being towed swiftly across water) may be used. An *aquarium* is an enclosure for fish and other *subaqueous* creatures; chemicals dissolved in water form an *aqueous* solution. Once you learn to identify a group of roots and their prefixes and suffixes, you can often work out the meaning of a complex word you have never seen before.

The remainder of this section presents information on roots, prefixes, and suffixes. The word-part under study is listed, defined, and followed by examples of its use in typical sentences.

2.1 ROOTS

2.1.1 act

The root act means "do," "move," "put in motion." Typical words are *actuary* (one who calculates insurance premiums) and *activate* (to make active or more active; to put someone on active duty).

EXAMPLES
My insurance agent said that an *actuary* would have to determine the new rates.
To *activate* the mechanism, press the button.

2.1.2 cap, cip

The roots *cap* and *cip* mean "take." Typical words are *capacity* (the ability to take something; the amount that can be contained), *inca-*

pacitated (unable to take on usual work or responsibility), and *recipient* (one who takes or receives).

EXAMPLES

Most babies do not have a *capacity* for large amounts of food.

The injury kept Randall *incapacitated* for weeks.

The *recipients* of the questionnaire were asked to complete it and return it within ten days.

2.1.3   cede, ceed

The roots *cede* and *ceed* mean "go" or "move." Typical words are *precede* (to go before), *intercede* (to act on someone's behalf; to attempt to settle a dispute between two people or groups), *proceed* (to go forward), and *exceed* (to move or go beyond).

EXAMPLES

The union stated that negotiations must *precede* any decision.

The attorney attempted to *intercede* on behalf of the juvenile defendant.

After visiting the museum, we will *proceed* to a quaint little café for lunch.

The motorist had *exceeded* the speed limit.

2.1.4   chron

The root *chron* means "time." Typical words are *synchronize* (to arrange two or more things to make them come together in time), *chronic* (continuing over a period of time), and *chronology* (time sequence).

EXAMPLES

The two governments *synchronized* their announcements of the new treaty.

Johnson's *chronic* lateness to work prevented him from receiving a promotion.

The *chronology* of the events was clear from a reading of the pilot's log.

2.1.5   claim, clam

The roots *claim* and *clam* mean "shout." Typical words are *reclaim* (to make available for use; to rescue), *disclaim* (to deny responsibility for or association with something), and *proclamation* (an official public announcement).

EXAMPLES

The urban renewal project will *reclaim* many decaying areas of the city.

Norman *disclaimed* any knowledge of the mistake.

The governor's *proclamation* declared next Monday a state holiday.

2.1.6 clude

The root *clude* means "shut" or "close." Typical words are *include* (to close or contain within), *exclude* (to shut out or refuse admission), and *preclude* (to shut out, or make impossible, beforehand).

EXAMPLES

The warranty *included* both parts and labor.

The new warranty will *exclude* labor.

A busy schedule coming up in October will *preclude* our attending the national convention.

2.1.7 cred

The root *cred* means "believe." Typical words are *credible* (believable), *credence* (believability), *incredible* (not believable), and *credulous* (tending to believe too readily).

EXAMPLES

Vera's version of the event was the most *credible*.

The press gave little *credence* to the official's explanation.

The statistics, *incredible* as they seemed, were nonetheless accurate.

If you are too *credulous*—if you believe everything you hear—you may become the victim of many practical jokes.

2.1.8 cur

The root *cur* means "run." Typical words are *current* (that which runs or flows; at the present time), *cursory* (hasty, not thorough), *recurrent* (occurring or happening again), and *concurrent* (occurring together or at the same time).

EXAMPLES

The rate at which electric *current* flows through the conducting wire is measured in amperes.

The mechanic was not able to determine, from a *cursory* examination, just what had caused the machine to break down.

A *recurrent* dream haunted him all his life.

The *concurrent* scheduling of the meetings meant that we could attend only one of them.

2.1.9 dict

The root *dict* means "speak." Typical words are *dictate* (to speak for recording and transcription; to issue an order or command), *edict* (a proclamation or order), and *jurisdiction* (the area in which one is qualified or has the right to exercise power).

EXAMPLES

The executive *dictated* a letter; her secretary then typed it.

The presidential *edict* commanded citizens not to go out after 10 P.M.

The personnel manager's *jurisdiction* is not restricted to the hiring of employees; he or she administers the medical-insurance programs as well.

2.1.10   frag, fract

The roots *frag* and *fract* mean "break." Typical words are *fragile* (easily breakable) and *infraction* (the breaking of a rule).

EXAMPLES

The instrument is extremely *fragile* and must be handled with great care.

Although the *infraction* of the rule was not serious, the teacher felt that it should not be allowed to go unnoticed.

2.1.11   gress

The root *gress* means "step" or "go." Typical words are *progressive* (favoring change or improvement, especially in political or social affairs; increasing step by step), *digress* (to depart from the subject), and *egress* (the exit or the way out).

EXAMPLES

The *progressive* actions taken by the new administration were praised by the press.

The audience became restless when the speaker *digressed* from the announced topic.

The fire department considered the matter of an emergency *egress* from the building to be a primary concern.

2.1.12   ject

The root *ject* means "to throw." Typical words are *inject* (to force a fluid into a passage; to introduce something new or different into a conversation or other matter), *eject* (to throw out), and *reject* (to refuse to accept, or to throw back).

EXAMPLES

The infection can be controlled by *injecting* medication directly into the bloodstream.

The pilot survived because he was *ejected* from the cockpit and parachuted to earth.

Jerry worked hard on the proposal, but his boss *rejected* it.

2.1.13   mit

The root *mit* means "send." Typical words are *emit* (to send out or send forth), *remit* (to send back, especially money), and *transmit* (to send from one point to another).

EXAMPLES

The electronic cash register *emits* a signal to a central processor.

Please *remit* a total payment of $14.95.

The information is *transmitted* over commercial telephone lines.

2.1.14   sed

The root *sed* means "sit." Typical words are *sedentary* (involving much sitting) and *sediment* (substance that settles to the bottom of a liquid).

EXAMPLES

Desk work is by nature *sedentary*.

Sediment accumulated at the bottom of the pool.

2.1.15   solv

The root *solv* means "free from" or "loosen." Typical words are *absolve* (to free from, especially of guilt), *dissolve* (to loosen or break up), and *solvent* (an agent used to loosen or to dissolve).

EXAMPLES

After the car accident in which his passenger was killed, John never felt completely *absolved* of guilt.

A liquid *solvent* was used to *dissolve* the paint.

2.1.16   spec

The root *spec* means "look at." Typical words are *aspect* (the particular view from which something is considered), *inspect* (to look at closely and critically), *perspective* (a way of looking at things; a point of view that considers the relative proportion of the various elements of a scene), and *specification* (a detailed definition of the requirements of a project or a description of the parts of a whole).

EXAMPLES

The monetary *aspect* of the job was the least of his concerns.

The highway patrol arrived to *inspect* the scene of the accident.

From the *perspective* of the purchaser, the warranty was not a good one.

The *specifications* for the job were published for the benefit of all potential bidders.

2.1.17 tempor

The root *tempor* means "time." Typical words are *contemporary* (existing at the same time, of the same age; modern), *temporary* (for a short time), and *temporize* (to stall for time).

EXAMPLES

Although the two authors were *contemporaries,* their political attitudes were centuries apart.

Ms. Kenka has taken a *temporary* job, from June until September, when she plans to return to school.

The negotiator had instructions to *temporize* until more information could be obtained.

2.1.18 vis

The root *vis* means "to see." Typical words are *vision* (the ability to see) and *supervise* (to oversee the activities of others).

EXAMPLES

The patient was relieved that he still had full *vision* after the eye operation.

College students were hired to *supervise* the playgrounds.

2.2 PREFIXES

2.2.1 a-, an-

The prefixes *a-* and *an-* mean "without." Typical words are *anemia* (without sufficient red blood cells or volume of blood), *apathy* (complete lack of interest or feeling), and *anesthetic* (a drug that dulls the senses, especially the sense of pain).

EXAMPLES

A blood test revealed that the patient suffers from *anemia.*

When only 10 percent of the voting public go to the polls, civic *apathy* is evident.

Before pulling the tooth, the dentist administered an *anesthetic.*

2.2.2 ab-, abs-

The prefixes *ab-* and *abs-* mean "from." Typical words are *abnormal* (removed from the normal) and *abstain* (to keep oneself away from).

EXAMPLES
The man's *abnormal* behavior was caused by excessive drinking.
Drivers are advised to *abstain* from alcohol.

2.2.3 ad- (sometimes spelled ag-, al-, at- when combined with roots that begin with *g, l,* or *t*)

This prefix means "to" or "toward." Typical words are *adjoining* (joined to something else), *allocate* (to assign to; to distribute something according to a plan), and *attract* (to draw to or toward).

EXAMPLES
The two families knew each other well because they lived in *adjoining* apartments.
Every city must *allocate* a large sum of money for its transportation system.
Insects are *attracted* to food.

2.2.4 ante-

The prefix *ante-* means "before." Typical words are *anterior* (in or near the front), *anteroom* (a room that comes before another room, as a waiting room), and *antecedent* (an event that occurs before another; the word or phrase to which a pronoun refers).

EXAMPLES
The tumor was located in the *anterior* lobe of the brain.
Because many patients had come to see the doctor, the *anteroom* of the office was crowded.
My *antecedents* were farmers who lived in Wales.

2.2.5 anti-, ant- (before a vowel)

The prefix *anti-* (*ant-*) means "against" or "opposite." Typical words are *antibiotic* (a medicine that acts against bacteria), *antipathy* (a feeling of strong dislike), *antacid* (medicine that acts against acid in the body), and *antonym* (a word that means the opposite of another word).

EXAMPLES

Her fever was lower a few hours after she took the *antibiotic*.

Because I have an *antipathy* to crowds, I avoid the beach on July 4.

He felt better after taking the *antacid* to soothe his upset stomach.

Part of the assignment was to find *antonyms* for a given list of words.

2.2.6 bi-

The prefix *bi-* means "two." Typical words are *biped* (animals with two feet), *bigamy* (marriage to two people at the same time), *biannual* (two times each year), and *biennial* (every two years).

EXAMPLES

Humans and some apes are *bipeds*.

The man was charged with *bigamy* because he had one wife in Akron and another in Indianapolis.

The *biannual* event was held in December and June every year.

The *biennial* event was held in December of years ending in an odd number.

2.2.7 cata-

The prefix *cata-* means "down." Typical words are *catalogue* (a written list; to write down an orderly listing) and *catastrophe* (a sudden and severe downturn in fortune; a disaster).

EXAMPLES

The *catalogue* listed all the products manufactured by the company.

The sudden drop in the stock was a *catastrophe* for many small investors.

2.2.8 circum-

The prefix *circum-* means "around." Typical words are *circumference* (the distance around a circular object), *circumlocution* (a word or expression that says something in a roundabout rather than a straightforward way), *circumspect* (careful to look around at the possible consequences of a deed before acting), and *circumvent* (to go around a problem or an obstacle and thus avoid it).

EXAMPLES

After measuring the round library table, Jessica announced that its *circumference* was 12 feet.

A person who uses *circumlocution* is probably trying to avoid an issue.

Recognizing the importance of the question, the shop steward tried to be as *circumspect* as possible in answering it.

By apologizing to Ed, Martin hoped to *circumvent* further unpleasantness.

2.2.9 co-, col-, com-, con-

These prefixes all mean "with" or "together." Typical words are *cooperate* (to work together), *coordinate* (to act together), *collaborate* (to work jointly with someone else), *collate* (to put together in order), and *compound* (something formed by the joining of elements or parts).

EXAMPLES

The problem could be solved if the two sides would *cooperate.*

The nationwide United Fund is a *coordinated* attempt to raise funds for charitable organizations.

The two designers agreed to *collaborate* on the layout drawing.

The office bought a machine that can *collate* a sixteen-page document.

The glossy finish was achieved by the application of a rubbing *compound.*

2.2.10 contra-, contro-, counter-

These prefixes mean "against" or "opposite." Typical words are *contrary* (consistently against), *controversy* (a dispute between those of opposing views), and *countermand* (to cancel or reverse an order).

EXAMPLES

The views expressed in the book were *contrary* to everything Michael believed.

The school bond issue created a *controversy* in the town; there were strong feelings on both sides of the matter.

The superintendent *countermanded* the foreman's orders.

2.2.11 de-

The prefix *de-* means "down" or "reverse of." Typical words are *decelerate* (to slow down), *demote* (to move down to a lower rank), and *descend* (to go down).

EXAMPLES

He ran the car off the road because there was no time to *decelerate.*

Unfavorable sales figures forced the company to *demote* several of its junior officers.

The lineman *descended* from the pole after completing the repairs.

2.2.12 dia-

The prefix *dia-* means "across," "thoroughly," or "through." Typical words are *diagonal* (across from corner to corner, through the center), *diagnose* (to identify the nature of an illness; to investigate thoroughly the cause of something), and *diathermy* (a treatment that sends heat through the body).

EXAMPLES

The editor drew a *diagonal* line across the page that was to be omitted from the manuscript.

Lennie was examined by four specialists before one of them was able to *diagnose* his ailment.

A heating pad is one simple device for administering *diathermy*.

2.2.13 dis- (also spelled di-, dif-)

This prefix means "apart" or "not." Typical words are *dilate* (to make larger), *differentiate* (to tell apart), *disjointed* (disconnected, lacking unity), *dissent* (lack of agreement; to disagree), and *disrupt* (to interrupt, especially in a noisy way; to throw into confusion).

EXAMPLES

The medicine that the eye doctor administered caused the pupils of her eyes to *dilate*.

The students were taught to *differentiate* between the two chemicals.

His account of the incident was so *disjointed* that the police were hardly able to follow it.

Martha Sells was the only member of the committee to *dissent* from the majority report.

Sam seemed determined to *disrupt* the meeting because he did not want the resolution to be passed.

2.2.14 e-, ex-

The prefixes *e-* and *ex-* mean "out" or "outside." Typical words are *efficacy* (ability to produce a desired result or outcome), *exhale* (to breathe out), and *exorbitant* (exceeding the customary amount).

EXAMPLES

The chemist was testing a new cancer drug to determine its *efficacy*.

The doctor instructed the patient to take a deep breath and then *exhale*.

The price of the typewriter was *exorbitant;* we had never paid so much for such a machine.

2.2.15   in- (also spelled il-, im-, and ir-)

The prefix *in-*, as well as the alternate forms *il-, im-,* and *ir-,* means "not."[4] Typical words are *insolvent* (not able to pay one's debts; bankrupt), *illegible* (difficult or impossible to read, usually because of unclear or messy copy), *immune* (protected against a disease; not affected by an outcome), and *irrevocable* (irreversible; unable to be reversed or changed).

EXAMPLES

Jim had to move to a less expensive apartment because he had become *insolvent.*

Since the first draft of the paper was *illegible,* I decided to retype my work before I revised it.

Children who have taken flu shots should be *immune* to the disease.

Think carefully before you decide upon a course, since your decision will be *irrevocable.*

2.2.16   inter-

The prefix *inter-* means "between." Typical words are *intervene* (to come between; to interfere), *intermittent* (occurring from time to time; alternately starting and stopping), and *interlinear* (inserted between the lines).

EXAMPLES

Since the two lawyers could not settle the dispute, they asked the judge to *intervene* in the matter.

The patient complained of *intermittent* headaches that would come and go during periods of stress.

I've typed this draft triple-spaced so that you can easily make *interlinear* corrections or changes.

2.2.17   intra-, intro-

These prefixes mean "within." Typical words are *intrastate* (within a state), *intravenous* (within the veins), and *introspection* (examination of one's own thoughts and feelings).

EXAMPLES

The trucking firm was awarded a license to operate on an *intrastate* basis only.

The antibiotic can be taken only by *intravenous* injection.

---

[4] *In-* as a prefix meaning "in, into, within, or toward" is a separate form.

The *introspection* forced on him by a long period of illness made a striking change in his personality.

2.2.18   micro-

The prefix *micro-* means "small." Typical words are *microfilm* (a small film) and *micrometer* (an instrument for measuring small things).

EXAMPLES

Microfilm requires the use of special equipment to enable the viewer to see the material, the size of which has been reduced considerably.

The tiny specimen could be measured only with a *micrometer.*

2.2.19   para-

The prefix *para-* means "alongside." Typical words are *paraprofessional* (someone who works alongside a professional), *paraphrase* (to rephrase or restate something in one's own words), *parasite* (something that lives off another without giving anything useful in return), and *parallel* (alongside of but at an equal distance at every point, never meeting).

EXAMPLES

The use of *paraprofessionals* is becoming common in schools and hospitals.

When taking notes for a term paper, it is better to *paraphrase* the thinking of others than to quote them directly.

The tree was being slowly destroyed by two different *parasites.*

Railroad tracks are *parallel* to each other.

2.2.20   poly-

Poly- means "many." Typical words are *polygraph* (an instrument that measures changes in heartbeat, blood pressure, and so on and is used as a lie-detector device), *polytechnic* (pertaining to instruction in many arts and sciences), *polyphonic* (combining many different sounds), and *polychromatic* (having many colors).

EXAMPLES

The lie detector test is one of the most common uses of the *polygraph.*

The institute was dedicated to *polytechnic* studies.

The recording technique included a *polyphonic* procedure.

The art department ordered a *polychromatic* scale.

2.2.21   post-

The prefix *post-* means "after." Typical words are *posterity* (that which comes after; future generations), *postmortem* (after death), *postnatal* (after birth), and *postgraduate* (after graduation).

EXAMPLES

We owe it to *posterity* to preserve as much of our natural environment as possible.

The judge ordered a *postmortem* examination to determine the cause of the victim's death.

Postnatal complications can be serious for both the mother and the baby.

The university had acquired a fine reputation for the quality of its *postgraduate* program.

2.2.22   pre-

The prefix *pre-* means "before." Typical words are *preliminary* (going before and leading up to the main part), *preview* (to look at something before it is officially presented), and *preface* (a brief introduction before the text of a book).

EXAMPLES

The court must set a date for a *preliminary* hearing before the trial can be scheduled.

Employees were given a *preview* of the president's presentation to the stockholders.

The *preface* to the speech captured the audience's full attention.

2.2.23   pro-

The prefix *pro-* means "forward," or "forth." Typical words are *propose* (to put forward a suggestion), *proliferate* (to reproduce or increase rapidly), and *profusion* (that which is brought forth in large numbers; an abundance).

EXAMPLES

Frank wanted to *propose* a new method of handling the data, but he could not get the floor.

In the last decade, the use of calculators has *proliferated;* in many offices almost every executive has one.

Grasshoppers appeared that summer in *profusion.*

2.2.24 proto- (prot- before a root beginning with a vowel)

Proto- means "first" or "fundamental." Typical words are *prototype* (the first form of something, serving as a model for later forms) and *protozoa* (fundamental forms of animal life).

EXAMPLES

The committee voted funds to begin the project but withheld additional financing until the *prototype* proved whether the plan was practical.

Protozoa can be studied only through a microscope.

2.2.25 super-

The prefix *super-* means "over" or "beyond." Typical words are *superior* (far above average; higher in rank or authority), *supersede* (to take the place of something), and *superfluous* (more than what is needed).

EXAMPLES

The judges declared XYZ brand car wash to be *superior* to LMO brand.

The directive of June 12 *supersedes* the one dated May 5.

The shipwrecked sailors threw away everything that was *superfluous*.

2.2.26 sym-, syn-

The prefixes *sym-* and *syn-* mean "together" or "with." Typical words are *sympathy* (shared feeling; concern for another's distress), *symmetrical* (equal in size, shape, or position of parts on opposite sides of a dividing line), and *synthesis* (the combining of varied elements to form a meaningful whole).

EXAMPLES

The students appeared to be in *sympathy* with the protestors.

Organisms whose right and left sides are mirror images of each other are *symmetrical*.

Dr. Markon's theory of personality is a *synthesis* of psychological ideas taken from Freud, Jung, Horney, and Sullivan.

2.2.27 trans-

The prefix *trans-* means "across," "through," or "beyond." Typical words are *transport* (to carry from one place to another), *transfer* (to send from one person or place to another), *transcend* (to go beyond; to surpass), and *transient* (passing quickly, momentary; a visitor, especially to a hotel, who stays only briefly).

EXAMPLES

It is the company's responsibility to *transport* the goods to the customers.
The fee was payment for the *transfer* of the title from the seller to the buyer.
Each new generation of computers *transcends* the achievements of the last generation.
Although the thought was a *transient* one, it had made an impression.

2.3   SUFFIXES

Although individual suffixes do convey meaning, their chief function is to indicate a part of speech. For example, the suffixes *-ance, -ion, -ism, -ity,* and *-ment* indicate nouns; the suffixes *-ify* and *-ize* indicate verbs; and the suffixes *-able, -al, -ical, -ive,* and *-ous* indicate adjectives. (See Section 3 of this Guide for a discussion of parts of speech.)

Noun Markers
2.3.1   -ance, -ence

Typical words are *brilliance* (quality of light; great brightness) and *emergence* (act of coming out).

EXAMPLES

The *brilliance* of the stage lights made the keynote speaker appear unreal.
The river widened at the point of its *emergence* into the sea.

2.3.2   -ion, -ation, -tion

Typical words are *resolution* (the act of solving a problem), *litigation* (the process of taking court action), and *option* (the opportunity to choose; a choice).

EXAMPLES

The *resolution* of the problem was to be decided at a meeting of top management officials.
Ten persons who were seriously injured when the building collapsed began *litigation,* suing for medical expenses and lost wages.
The student has several career *options* after graduation: she can become a production trainee, enlist in the service, or take a degree in accounting.

2.3.3   -ism

Typical words are *anachronism* (something that is out of its place in time), *socialism* (a political theory that favors society's ownership of the means of production), and *individualism* (the assertion of one's specialness as an individual being).

EXAMPLES

The horse-drawn carriages of New York City are *anachronisms*.

Under *socialism*, all large industry is controlled by the government.

The company encouraged *individualism* in its employees.

2.3.4 -ity

Typical words are *facility* (the ability to do something easily), *authenticity* (the condition of being genuine), and *authority* (the power to command).

EXAMPLES

The *facility* with which Susan handled higher mathematics was remarkable.

Do you have proof of the *authenticity* of this painting—or might it be a fake?

The supervisor did not have the *authority* to dismiss an employee.

2.3.5 -ment

Typical words are *impediment* (an obstacle; something that stands in the way of something else) and *sentiment* (an opinion on a particular matter; a feeling based more on emotion than on thinking).

EXAMPLES

Not knowing how to operate some office machines can be an *impediment* to receiving a promotion.

The *sentiment* among the hospital administrative staff was in favor of working from 8:30 A.M. to 4:30 P.M. rather than from 9 A.M. to 5 P.M..

Verb Markers
2.3.6 -ify

Typical words are *testify* (to make a statement under oath), *justify* (to show that something is reasonable or correct), and *typify* (to be an example of).

EXAMPLES

Mavine was asked to *testify* during the trial, since she had been a witness to the accident.

You should not try to *justify* your action by claiming that the instructions were so poorly written that you misunderstood them.

I don't believe that the questionable acts of the manager *typify* the company's hiring policies.

2.3.7 -ize

Typical words are *legalize* (to make something lawful), *modernize* (to make something contemporary), and *anesthetize* (to make someone unable to feel pain).

EXAMPLES

The retail industry believed that stores would benefit from *legalized* shopping on Sundays.

The company decided to *modernize* its building, which was old and in poor condition.

The patient was *anesthetized* and felt no pain at all during surgery.

Adjective Markers
2.3.8 -able, -ible

Typical words are *comparable* (able to be compared; similar or equivalent), *indelible* (not able to be removed), *compatible* (able to live together in peace and harmony), and *inevitable* (incapable of being prevented; bound to happen).

EXAMPLES

Do you know in what ways soccer is *comparable* to football?

The tragic experience left an *indelible* mark on her memory.

The two technicians were *compatible* because they had had many similar experiences.

It seemed *inevitable* that the two companies would merge.

2.3.9 -al, -ial

Typical words are *spatial* (relating to space) and *radial* (relating to a radius).

EXAMPLES

An architect must have good *spatial* imagination.

The carpenter cut the bevels with a *radial* saw.

Section B

Handbook of Grammar, Punctuation, and Mechanics

Section 3 of this guide surveys the parts of speech—the functions performed by separate words or groups of words within sentences. Section 4 treats phrases, clauses, sentences, and paragraphs, the larger structures which words build. Section 5 reviews punctuation, the system of symbols that clarifies the structural relationships among words and parts of sentences. And Section 6 covers the mechanics of good writing, such as capitalization and the proper use of symbols.

3 PARTS OF SPEECH

Part of speech is a term used to describe the class of words to which a particular word belongs, according to its function in a sentence. If a word's function is to name something, it is a noun or pronoun. If a word's function is to indicate action or existence, it is a verb. If its function is to describe or modify something, the word is an adjective or an adverb. If its function is to join or link one element of a sentence to another, it is a conjunction or a preposition. And if its function is to express an exclamation, it is an interjection.

3.1 NOUNS

A noun names a person, place, thing, concept, action, or quality.

3.1.1 Types of Nouns

The two basic types of nouns are proper nouns and common nouns.

(a) **Proper nouns.** Proper nouns name specific persons, places, things, concepts, actions, or qualities. They are usually capitalized.

EXAMPLES New York, Abraham Lincoln, U.S. Army, Nobel Prize, Montana, Independence Day, Amazon River, Butler County, Magna Carta, June, Colby College

(b) **Common nouns.** Common nouns name general classes or categories of persons, places, things, concepts, actions, or qualities. The term *common noun* includes all types of nouns except proper nouns. Following are discussions of the basic types of common nouns. Note that many nouns can be placed in more than one of the overlapping categories.

Concrete nouns identify those things that can be detected by the five senses—by seeing, hearing, tasting, touching, or smelling. Concrete nouns can be either count nouns or mass nouns. *Count nouns,* as the term suggests, name things that can be counted or divided; their plurals often end in *s.*

EXAMPLES human, college, house, knife, bolt, carrot

Mass nouns name things that are not usually counted and do not usually appear in the plural.

EXAMPLES water, sand, air, copper, velvet

Many words, of course, can serve either as count nouns or as mass nouns, depending on the context in which they are used. If you were to say "I need one brick," *brick* would be a count noun. If you were to say "The building is built of brick," *brick* would be a mass noun.

Abstract nouns refer to things that cannot be detected by the five senses.

EXAMPLES love, loyalty, pride, valor, peace, devotion, harmony

Collective nouns indicate groups or collections of persons, places, things, concepts, actions, or qualities. They are plural in meaning but singular in form when they refer to groups as units.

EXAMPLES   audience, jury, brigade, staff, committee

3.1.2   Functions of Nouns

Nouns may function as subjects of verbs, as objects of verbs and prepositions, as complements, or as appositives.

EXAMPLES   The *metal* bent as *pressure* was applied to it. (subject of a verb, naming the thing about which the verb makes an assertion)

The bricklayer cemented the *blocks* efficiently. (direct object of a verb, naming the thing acted on by the verb)

The company awarded our *department* a plaque for safety. (indirect object of a verb, naming the recipient of the direct object)

The event occurred within the *year*. (object of a preposition, naming the thing linked by the preposition to the rest of the sentence)

An equestrian is a *horseman*. (subjective complement, renaming the subject of the sentence)

We elected the sales manager *chairman*. (objective complement, renaming the direct object)

George Thomas, the *treasurer*, gave his report last. (appositive, amplifying the noun that precedes it)

3.1.3   Forms of Nouns

With the general exception of mass nouns and abstract nouns, nouns can show number (singular or plural) and possession.

(a) **Singular and plural nouns.** The singular form of a noun refers to one thing, the plural to more than one. Most nouns form the plural by adding *s*.

EXAMPLE   *Dolphins* are capable of communication with humans.

Nouns ending in *s, z, x, ch,* and *sh* form the plural by adding *es*.

EXAMPLES   How many size *sixes* did we produce last month?

The letter was sent to all the *churches*.

Our company supplies cafeterias with *dishes* and *glasses*.

Those ending in a consonant plus *y* form the plural by changing the *y* to *ies*.

EXAMPLE   The store advertises prompt delivery but limits the number of *deliveries* scheduled on a single day.

Some nouns ending in *o* add *es* to form the plural; others add only *s*.

EXAMPLES   One tomato plant produced thirty *tomatoes*.

We installed two *dynamos* in the plant.

Some nouns ending in *f* or *fe* add *s* to form the plural; others change the *f* or *fe* to *ves*.

EXAMPLES   cliff/cliffs, fife/fifes, knife/knives, leaf/leaves

Some nouns require an internal change to form the plural.

EXAMPLES   goose/geese, man/men, mouse/mice, woman/women

Some nouns do not change in the plural form.

EXAMPLE   Several *fish* swam lazily in the clear brook while a few wild *deer* mingled with the *sheep* in a nearby meadow.

Most compound nouns joined by hyphens form the plural in the first noun.

EXAMPLE   He provided jobs for his two *sons-in-law*.

If you are in doubt about the plural form of a word, look up the word in a good dictionary. Most dictionaries give the plural form if it is made in any way other than by adding *s* or *es*.

(b) **Possessive nouns.** The possessive case, indicating ownership, is formed in two ways—either with an *of* clause, as in "the nature *of* the beast," or by adding *'s*. This discussion will address the *'s* construction, which is generally used with animate nouns.

EXAMPLES   The *chairman's* statement was forceful.

Henry's arm was broken.

The installation of the plumbing is finished except in the *men's* room.

Singular nouns ending in *s* may form the possessive by adding either an apostrophe alone or *'s*. The latter is now preferred.

EXAMPLES   a waitress's uniform *or* a waitress' uniform
             an actress's career *or* an actress' career

Plural nouns ending in *s* add only an apostrophe to form the possessive.

EXAMPLE   The architects' design manual contains many illustrations.

With word groups and compound nouns, add the *'s* to the last noun.

EXAMPLES   The *chairman of the board's* report was distributed.
             My *son-in-law's* address was on the envelope.

To show individual possession with a pair of nouns, use the possessive with both.

EXAMPLES   Both the *Senate's* and the *House's* galleries were packed for the hearings
             Mary's and *John's* presentations were the most effective.

To show joint possession with a pair of nouns, use the possessive with only the latter.

EXAMPLES   The *Senate and House's* joint committee worked out a compromise.
             Mary and John's presentation was the most effective.

Occasionally you will use both an *of* phrase and an *'s* construction.

EXAMPLE   Mary is a colleague *of John's*.

3.2   PRONOUNS

A pronoun is a word that is used as a substitute for a noun. The noun that a pronoun replaces is called its antecedent.

3.2.1   Types of Pronouns

Pronouns fall into several different categories: personal, demonstrative, relative, interrogative, indefinite, reflexive, intensive, and reciprocal.

(a) **Personal pronouns.**   The personal pronouns refer to the person or persons speaking (*I, me, my, mine; we, us, our, ours*); the person or persons spoken to (*you, your, yours*); or the person or thing (or persons or things) spoken of (*he, him, his; she, her, hers; it its; they, them, their, theirs*).

EXAMPLES   I wish *you* had told *me* that *she* was coming with *us*.

If *their* figures are correct, *ours* must be in error.

(b) Demonstrative pronouns.   The demonstrative pronouns (*this, these, that, those*) indicate or point out the thing being referred to. They also serve as adjectives. In good writing, demonstrative pronouns are avoided because they can lead to ambiguity. (As adjectives, however, demonstratives are not only acceptable but useful.)

EXAMPLES   *This* is my desk.

These are my co-workers.

That will be a difficult job.

Those are incorrect figures.

(c) Relative pronouns.   The relative pronouns (*who, whom, which, whose,* and *that*) perform two functions simultaneously. They substitute for nouns or preceding ideas, and they connect and establish the relationships between parts of sentences. (Refer to the discussion of dependent and independent clauses in Sections 4.2.1 and 4.2.2.)

EXAMPLES   The personnel manager told the applicants *who* would be hired.

The supervisor, *whose* office is next door, keeps those records.

(d) Interrogative pronouns.   Interrogative pronouns (*who, whom, which, whose, what*) ask questions.

EXAMPLES   *Who* went to the meeting in Detroit?

Which copier does two-sided copying?

(e) Indefinite pronouns.   Indefinite pronouns do not refer to a particular person or thing. They include *all, another, any, anyone, anything, both, each, either, everybody, few, many, most, much, neither, nobody, none, several, some,* and *such*.

EXAMPLE   Not *everyone* liked the new procedures; *some* even refused to follow them.

(f) Reflexive pronouns.   The reflexive pronouns (*myself, yourself, himself, herself, itself, oneself, ourselves, yourselves,* and *themselves*) always end with the suffix *-self* or *-selves*. Reflexive pronouns refer to the subject of the sentence, clause, or phrase in which they appear and turn the action of the verb back upon the subject.

EXAMPLE   I asked *myself* the same question.

(g) **Intensive pronouns.** The intensive pronouns are identical in form to the reflexive pronouns, but they perform a different function. They emphasize or intensify their antecedents.

EXAMPLE   I *myself* asked the same question.

(h) **Reciprocal pronouns.** The reciprocal pronouns (*one another* and *each other*) indicate relationships among people or things. Use *each other* when referring to two persons or things and *one another* when referring to more than two.

EXAMPLES   Sam and Ruth work well with *each other*.
The four crew members work well with *one another*.

3.2.2 Grammatical Properties of Pronouns

(a) **Person.** *Person* refers to the forms of a personal pronoun that indicate whether the pronoun represents the speaker, the person spoken to, or the person (or thing) spoken about. If the pronoun represents the speaker, the pronoun is in the first person.

EXAMPLE   *I* followed the directions in the manual.

If the pronoun represents the person or persons spoken to, the pronoun is in the second person.

EXAMPLE   *You* should report to Ms. Cooper before noon.

If the pronoun represents the person or persons spoken about, the pronoun is in the third person.

EXAMPLE   *They* followed the procedure that *he* had outlined.

Person	*Singular*	*Plural*
First	I, me, my	we, ours, us
Second	you, your	you, your
Third	he, him, his	they, them, their
	she, her, hers	
	it, its	

Identifying pronouns by person helps you avoid illogical shifts from one person to another. A very common error is to shift from the third person to the second person.

REVISE   *Employees* must sign the guard's logbook when *you* enter a restricted area.

TO   *Employees* must sign the guard's logbook when *they* enter a restricted area.

OR   *You* must sign the guard's logbook when *you* enter a restricted area.

(b) Gender.   *Gender* refers to forms of words that designate sex. English recognizes three genders: masculine, feminine, and neuter (to designate objects considered neither masculine nor feminine). The pronouns *he, she,* and *it* indicate gender; only a few nouns (such as *actor* and *actress*) do so.

Gender is important to writers because they must be sure that nouns and pronouns within a grammatical construction agree in gender. A pronoun, for example, must agree with its antecedent noun in gender.

EXAMPLE   Because Wanda Martin supervised *her* sales staff as effectively as Frank Martinez supervised *his,* the company doubled *its* profits.

(See also Section 3.2.3a for a discussion of how sexist language is best avoided.)

(c) Number.   *Number* signifies how many things a word refers to. A singular pronoun substitutes for a noun that names one thing; a plural pronoun replaces a noun that names two or more things.

EXAMPLE   The manager took *her* break after the employees took *their* breaks.

All singular pronouns (*I, he, she, it*) change form in the plural (*we, they*) except *you.*

EXAMPLE   Since *he* organizes efficiently and *she* supervises effectively, *they* are both valuable employees.

Number is a frequent problem with a few indefinite pronouns (*each, either, neither,* and those ending with *-body,* or *-one,* such as *anybody, anyone, everybody, everyone, nobody, no one, somebody, someone*). Since these pronouns are normally singular, they require singular verbs and are referred to by singular pronouns.

EXAMPLE   As *everyone* arrives for the meeting and takes *his* seat, please hand *him* a copy of the confidential report. *No one* should leave without returning *his* copy before *he* goes.

(d) **Case.** Pronouns have forms to show the subjective, objective, and possessive cases. A pronoun is in the *subjective case* when it is used as the subject of a clause or sentence, representing the person or thing acting or existing. The subjective case is also used when the pronoun follows a linking verb, such as *to be.* (A linking verb connects the pronoun with the subject it renames.)

EXAMPLES   *He* is my boss.
            My boss is *he.*

A pronoun is in the *objective case* when it indicates the person or thing receiving the action of a verb or when it follows a preposition.

EXAMPLES   Mr. Davis hired Tom and *me.* (not I)
            Between *you* and *me,* his facts are questionable.

To test whether a pronoun is in the subjective case or the objective case, try it with a transitive verb (one that requires a direct object— a person or thing to receive the action expressed by the verb). *Hit* is a useful verb for this test. If the form of the pronoun can precede the verb, it is in the subjective case. If it must follow the verb, it is in the objective case.

EXAMPLES   *She* hit the baseball. (subjective case)
            The baseball hit *her.* (objective case)

A pronoun in the *possessive case* expresses ownership.

EXAMPLE   He took *his* notes with him on the business trip.

Subjective	Objective	Possessive
I	me	my, mine
we	us	our, ours
you	you	your, yours
he	him	his
she	her	her, hers
it	it	its
they	them	their, theirs
who	whom	whose

If compound pronouns cause problems in determining case, try testing each separately.

EXAMPLES   In his letter, John mentioned *you* and *me*.

In his letter, John mentioned *you*.

In his letter, John mentioned *me*.

To determine the case of a pronoun that follows *as* or *than*, try mentally adding the words that are normally omitted.

EXAMPLES   The director does not have as much formal education as *he* [does]. (You would not write, "Him does.")

His friend was taller than *he* [was tall]. (You would not write, "Him was tall.")

An appositive is a noun or noun phrase that follows and amplifies another noun or noun phrase. A pronoun appositive takes the case of its antecedent.

EXAMPLES   Two systems analysts, *Joe* and *I*, were selected to represent the company. (*Joe and I* is in apposition to the subject, *systems analysts*, and therefore must be in the subjective case.)

The systems analysts selected two members of our department—Joe and *me*. (*Joe and me* is in apposition to *two members*, which is the object of the verb *selected*, and therefore must be in the objective case.)

The reverse situation can also present problems. To test for the proper case when the pronouns *we* and *us* are followed by an appositive noun that defines them, try the sentence without the noun.

EXAMPLES   (*We/Us*) pilots fly our own planes.

We fly our own planes. (You would not write, *"Us* fly our own planes.").

He addressed his remarks directly to (*we/us*) technicians.

He addressed his remarks directly to *us*. (You would not write, "He addressed his remarks directly to *we.*")

3.2.3   Usage of Pronouns

Pronouns must agree with and clearly refer to their antecedents.

(a)   **Pronoun–antecedent agreement.**   The noun for which a pronoun substitutes is called its antecedent. A personal pronoun in the first or second person does not normally require a stated antecedent.

EXAMPLES   *I* like my job.

You were there at the time.

We all worked hard on the project.

A personal pronoun in the third person usually has a clearly stated antecedent.

EXAMPLE   John presented the report to the directors. *He* (John) first read *it* (the report) to *them* (the directors) and then asked for *their* (the directors') questions.

Agreement, grammatically, means the correspondence in form between different elements of a sentence. A pronoun must agree with its antecedent in person, gender, and number. (See Section 3.2.2 for additional information about these properties of pronouns.)

A pronoun must agree with its antecedent in *person.* If you are describing the necessity of accurate data for laboratory technicians, for example, use either the third person or the second person. Don't mix them. The first sentence following suggests that the technicians are preparing data for someone else (you).

REVISE   If *laboratory technicians* do not update *their* records every day, *you* will not have accurate data.

TO   If *laboratory technicians* do not update *their* records every day, *they* will not have accurate data.

OR   If *you* do not update *your* records every day, *you* will not have accurate data.

A pronoun must agree with its antecedent in *gender.*

EXAMPLE   *Isabel* was already wearing *her* identification badge, but *Tom* had to clip on *his* badge before they could pass the security guard.

Traditionally, a masculine, singular pronoun has been used to agree with antecedents that include both sexes, such as *anyone, everybody, nobody, one, person, someone,* or *student.*

EXAMPLE   *Anyone* who meets this production goal will double *his* bonus.

Many people are now sensitive to an implied sexual bias in such usage. When graceful alternatives are available, use them. One solution is to use *he or she* instead of *he* alone, or *his or her* instead of *his* alone. Another possibility is to omit the pronoun completely if it isn't essential to the meaning of the sentence.

REVISE	*Everybody* completed *his* report on time.
TO	*Everybody* completed *his or her* report on time.
OR	*Everybody* completed a report on time.

Often, the best solution is to rewrite the sentence in the plural. Do not, however, attempt to avoid expressing gender by resorting to a plural pronoun when the antecedent is singular.

| REVISE | *Everybody* completed *their* report on time. |
| TO | The *employees* completed *their* reports on time. |

A pronoun must agree with its antecedent in *number*.

| REVISE | Because the *copier* has been used so much, *they* have been overheating. |
| TO | Because the *copier* has been used so much, *it* has been overheating. |

Use a singular pronoun with an antecedent like *anyone, each, everybody,* or *everyone* unless to do so would be illogical because the meaning is obviously plural.

| EXAMPLES | *Everyone* returned to *his or her* department. |
| | *Everyone* applauded when I demonstrated our new product for *them*. |

Collective nouns may be singular or plural, depending on meaning.

| EXAMPLES | The *staff* prepared *its* annual report. |
| | The *staff* returned to *their* offices after the meeting. |

A compound antecedent joined by *or* or *nor* is singular if both elements are singular and plural if both are plural.

| EXAMPLES | Either the *supervisor* or the *foreman* should present *his* report on the accident. |
| | Neither the *stockholders* nor the *executive officers* wanted *their* company to be taken over by Coast International. |

When one of the antecedents connected by *or* or *nor* is singular and the other plural, the pronoun agrees with the nearest antecedent.

| EXAMPLES | Either the *receptionist* or the *typists* should go on *their* lunch breaks. |
| | Either the *typists* or the *receptionist* should go on *her* lunch break. |

A compound antecedent with its elements joined by *and* requires a plural pronoun.

EXAMPLE   The *architect* and the *designer* prepared *their* plans.

If the two elements refer to the same person, however, use the singular pronoun.

EXAMPLE   The *architect and designer* prepared *his* plan.

(b) **Pronoun reference.** The noun to which a pronoun refers must be unmistakably clear. Pronoun references may be unclear if they are general, hidden, or ambiguous.

A *general (or broad) reference,* or one that has no real antecedent, may confuse your reader.

REVISE   He sold plumbing supplies in Iowa for eight years; *this* has helped him in his present job as sales manager.

TO   His eight years selling plumbing supplies in Iowa have helped him in his present job as sales manager.

A *hidden reference,* or one that has only an implied antecedent, is another problem.

REVISE   Electronics technicians must continue to study because *it* is a dynamic science.

TO   Electronics technicians must continue to study *electronics* because *it* is a dynamic science.

REVISE   A high-lipid, low-carbohydrate diet is called "ketogenic" because it favors *their* formation.

TO   A high-lipid, low-carbohydrate diet is called "ketogenic" because it favors the formation of ketone bodies.

The third basic problem is an *ambiguous reference,* or one that can be interpreted in more than one way.

REVISE   Susan worked with Jeanette on the presentation, but *she* prepared most of the slides. (Who prepared most of the slides, Susan or Jeanette?)

TO   Susan worked with Jeanette on the presentation, but Jeanette prepared most of the slides.

Ambiguous references frequently occur with the pronouns *it* and *they.*

REVISE   The fire marshal examined the stairway and inspected the basement storage room; *it* had suffered extensive smoke damage.

TO   The fire marshal examined the stairway, which had suffered extensive smoke damage, and inspected the basement storage room.

REVISE The inspector checked the scales and the time clocks; *they* needed to be leveled again.

TO The inspector checked the scales and the time clocks; the scales needed to be leveled again.

Do not repeat an antecedent in parentheses following the pronoun. If you feel that you must identify the pronoun's antecedent in this way, you need to rewrite the sentence.

REVISE The specialist met the patient's mother as soon as she (the specialist) arrived at the hospital emergency room.

TO As soon as the specialist arrived at the hospital emergency room, she met the patient's mother.

3.3 ADJECTIVES

An adjective modifies or describes a noun or pronoun.

3.3.1 Types of Adjectives

An adjective makes the meaning of a noun or pronoun more exact by pointing out one of its qualities (descriptive adjective) or by imposing boundaries upon it (limiting adjective).

EXAMPLES a *hot* iron (descriptive)

He is *cold*. (descriptive)

ten automobiles (limiting)

his desk (limiting)

Limiting adjectives include some common and important categories:

Articles (*a, an, the*)
Numeral adjectives (*one, two, first, second*)
Indefinite adjectives (*all, any, each, no, some*)
Demonstrative adjectives (*this, that, these, those*)
Possessive adjectives (*my, his, her, its, your, our, their*)
Interrogative and relative adjectives (*whose, which, what*)

Of these, the forms of the demonstrative, possessive, and interrogative and relative adjectives derive from pronouns and are sometimes called pronominal adjectives.

3.3.2 Comparison of Adjectives

Most adjectives add the suffix *-er* to show comparison with one other item and the suffix *-est* to show comparison with two or more other items. The three degrees of comparison are called the positive (the basic form of the adjective), the comparative (showing comparison with one other item), and the superlative (showing comparison with two or more other items).

EXAMPLES The first ingot is *bright*. (positive degree)

      The second ingot is *brighter*. (comparative degree)

      The third ingot is *brightest*. (superlative degree)

Many two-syllable adjectives and most three-syllable adjectives, however, are preceded by *more* or *most* to form the comparative or the superlative.

EXAMPLES The new facility is *more impressive* than the old one.

      The new facility is the *most impressive* in the city.

A few adjectives have irregular comparative and superlative degrees (*much, more, most; little, less, least*).

   Absolute words (such as *unique, perfect, exact,* and *infinite*) are not logically subject to comparison. After all, something either is or is not unique; it isn't more unique or most unique. Language, however, is not always logical, so these words are sometimes used comparatively.

EXAMPLE Phase-locked loop circuits make FM tuner performance *more exact* by decreasing tuner distortion.

3.3.3 Placement of Adjectives

When limiting and descriptive adjectives appear together, the limiting adjectives precede the descriptive adjectives, with the article usually in the first position.

EXAMPLE *the ten gray* cars (article, limiting adjective, descriptive adjective)

   Within a sentence, an adjective can precede its noun or follow its noun.

EXAMPLES The *small* jobs are given priority.

      Priority is given when a job is *small*.

In a larger, more complex construction, an adjective may shift from preceding its noun to following it.

EXAMPLES   We negotiated a *bigger* contract than our competitor did.

We negotiated a contract *bigger* than our competitor's.

An adjective is called a predicate adjective when it follows a linking verb, such as *to be*. By completing the meaning of a linking verb, a predicate adjective describes or limits the subject of the verb.

EXAMPLES   The job is *easy*.

The manager was very *demanding*.

An adjective also can follow a transitive verb and modify its direct object (the person or thing that receives the action of the verb).

EXAMPLES   The lack of lubricant rendered the bearing *useless*.

They painted the office *white*.

3.3.4 Usage of Adjectives

Nouns can sometimes function as adjectives, especially when precise qualification is necessary.

EXAMPLE   The *test* conclusions led to a redesign of the system.

Frequently, business and technical writing is weakened by too many nouns strung together to serve as modifiers. Therefore, exercise caution when you use nouns as adjectives.

REVISE   The test control group meeting was held last Wednesday.

TO   The meeting of the test control group was held last Wednesday.

OR   The test control group met last Wednesday.

Furthermore, you should avoid general adjectives (*nice, fine, good*) and trite or overused adjectives (a *fond* farewell). In fact, it is good practice to question the need for most adjectives in your writing. Often, your writing not only will read as well without an adjective but may even be better without it. If you need to use an adjective, select one that expresses your meaning as exactly as possible.

3.4 VERBS

A verb is a word, or a group of words, that specifies an action or affirms a condition or a state of existence.

EXAMPLES   The antelope *bolted* at the sight of the hunters.

She *was saddened* by the death of her friend.

He *is* a wealthy man now.

A verb is an essential part of a sentence since the verb makes an assertion about the action or existence of its subject, the someone or something that is its topic. Within a sentence, a verb alone is called a simple predicate; a verb with its modifiers and complements forms a complete predicate. When a subject and a predicate convey a complete thought, they form a sentence (or independent clause). When a subject and a predicate do not convey a complete thought, they form a dependent clause. In contrast to a clause, a phrase is a group of words without the subject-predicate combination.

3.4.1 Types of Verbs

Verbs may be described as either transitive or intransitive; the intransitive verbs include linking verbs.

(a) **Transitive verbs.** A transitive verb requires a *direct object* to complete its meaning. The direct object normally answers the question *whom* or *what* by naming the person or thing that receives the action of the verb.

> EXAMPLE   They *laid* the *foundation* on October 24. (*Foundation* is the direct object of the transitive verb *laid*.)

Some transitive verbs (such as *give, wish, cause,* and *tell*) may be followed by an *indirect object* as well as a direct object. The indirect object is usually a person and answers the question "to whom or what?" or "for whom or what?" The indirect object precedes the direct object.

> EXAMPLE   Georgiana Anderson *gave* the *treasurer* a *letter*. (*Treasurer* is the indirect object and *letter* is the direct object of the transitive verb *gave*.)

(b) **Intransitive verbs.** An intransitive verb is a verb that does not require an object to complete its meaning. It makes a full assertion about the subject without assistance (although it may have modifiers).

> EXAMPLES   The water *boiled*.
> The water *boiled* rapidly.
> The engine *ran*.
> The engine *ran* smoothly and quietly.

(c) **Linking verbs.** Although intransitive verbs do not have objects, certain intransitive verbs may take complements. These verbs are called linking verbs because they link the subject of a sentence to words following the verb. When this subjective complement is a noun (or pronoun), it refers to the same person or thing as the noun (or pronoun) that is the subject.

EXAMPLES   The conference table *is* an antique.

Maria *should be* the director.

When the complement is an adjective, it modifies the subject.

EXAMPLES   The study *was* thorough.

The report *seems* complete.

Such intransitive verbs as *be, become, seem* and *appear* are almost always linking verbs. Others, such as *look, sound, taste, smell,* and *feel,* may function either as linking verbs or as simple intransitive verbs.

EXAMPLES   Their antennae *feel* delicately. (simple intransitive verb meaning that they have a delicate sense of touch)

Their antennae *feel* delicate. (linking verb meaning that they seem fragile to the touch)

3.4.2   Forms of Verbs

By form, verbs may be described as either finite or nonfinite.

(a)   **Finite verbs.**   A finite verb is the main verb of a clause or sentence. It makes an assertion about its subject, and it can serve as the only verb in its clause or sentence. Finite verbs may be either transitive or intransitive (including linking) verbs. They change form to reflect person (I *see,* he *sees*), tense (I *go,* I *went*), and number (he *writes,* they *write*).

EXAMPLES   The telephone *rang,* and the secretary *answered* it.

When the telephones *ring,* you *answer* them.

A *helping verb* (sometimes called an *auxilliary verb*) is a verb that is added to a finite or main verb to help indicate mood, voice, and tense. (See the discussions of mood, voice, and tense in Sections 3.4.2b, 3.4.2c, and 3.4.2d, respectively.) Together, the helping verb and the main verb form a verb phrase.

EXAMPLES   The work *had* (helping verb) begun.

I *am* going.

I *was* going.

I *will* go.

I *should have* gone.

I *must* go.

The most commonly used helping verbs are the various forms of *have* (*has, had*), *be* (*am, is, are, was, were*), *do* (*did, does*), *can* (*could*), *may* (*might*), *shall* (*should*), and *will* (*would*). Phrases that function as helping verbs often include *to:* for example, *am going to* and *is about to* (compare *will*), *has to* (compare *must*), and *ought to* (compare *should*).

EXAMPLES   I *am going to* quit.

I *will* quit.

She *has to* get a raise.

She *must* get a raise.

The helping verb always precedes the main verb, although other words may come between them.

EXAMPLE   Machines *will* (helping verb) never completely *replace* (main verb) people.

(b) Nonfinite verbs or verbals. Nonfinite verbs are the verbals (gerunds, infinitives, and participles) which, although they are derived from verbs, actually function as nouns, adjectives, or adverbs.

When the *-ing* form of a verb functions as a noun, it is called a *gerund.*

EXAMPLE   *Seeing* is *believing.*

An *infinitive,* which is the root form of a verb, can function as a noun, an adverb, or an adjective. Because the word *to* usually precedes an infinitive, it is considered the sign of an infinitive.

EXAMPLES   He hates *to complain.* (noun, direct object of the verb *hates*)

The valve closes *to stop* the flow. (adverb, modifies the verb *closes*)

This is the proposal *to select.* (adjective, modifies the noun *proposal*)

A *participle* is a verb form that functions as an adjective. The present participle ends in *-ing.*

EXAMPLE   *Declining* sales forced us to close the branch office.

The past participle may end in *-ed, -t, -en, -n,* or *-d.*

EXAMPLES

What are the *estimated* costs?

Repair the *bent* lever.

Here is the *broken* calculator.

What are the *known* properties of this metal?

The story, *told* many times before, was still interesting.

The perfect participle is formed with the present participle of *have* and the past participle of the main verb.

EXAMPLE   *Having received* (perfect participle) a large raise, the *smiling* (present participle), *contented* (past participle) employee worked harder than ever.

3.4.3   Grammatical Properties of Verbs

Verbs can show person and number, mood, voice, and tense.

(a)   **Person and number.**   Verbs must agree with their subjects in *number* (singular or plural) and *person* (first, second, or third). In the present indicative of regular verbs (see Section 3.4.3b), only the third-person singular differs from the infinitive stem. The verb *to be,* however, is irregular: I *am,* you *are,* he *is,* we *are,* they *are.* (See section 3.4.4.)

EXAMPLES   I *see* (first-person singular) a yellow tint, but he *sees* (third-person singular) a yellow-green hue.

I *am* (first-person singular) convinced, and they *are* (third-person plural) convinced; unfortunately, he *is* (third-person singular) not convinced.

(b)   **Mood.**   *Mood* refers to the functions of verbs: making statements or asking questions (indicative mood), giving commands (imperative mood), or expressing hypothetical possibilities (subjunctive mood).

The *indicative* mood refers to an action or a state that is conceived as fact.

EXAMPLES   *Is* the setting correct?

The setting *is* correct.

The *imperative* mood expresses a command, suggestion, request, or entreaty.

EXAMPLES   *Install* the wiring today.

Please *let* me know if I can help.

The *subjunctive* mood expresses something that is contrary to fact, conditional, or hypothetical; it can also express a wish, a doubt, or a possibility. The verb *be* is the only one in English that preserves many changes in form to show the subjunctive mood.

EXAMPLES   The senior partner insisted that he (I, you, we, they) *be* in charge of the project.

I If the salesman (I, you, we, they) *were* to close the sale today, we would meet our monthly quota.

Most verbs other than *be* do not change form for the subjunctive. Instead, helping verbs show the subjunctive function.

EXAMPLE   *Had I known* that you were here, I would have come earlier.

The advantage of the subjunctive mood is that it enables you to express clearly whether or not you consider a condition contrary to fact. If you wish to express a contrary-to-fact condition or a highly doubtful hypothesis, use the subjunctive; if not, use the indicative.

EXAMPLES   If I *were* president of the firm, I would change several personnel policies. (subjuntive mood)

I *am* president of the firm, but I don't feel that I control every aspect of its policies. (indicative mood)

Be careful not to shift haphazardly from one mood to another within a sentence; to do so makes the sentence unbalanced as well as ungrammatical.

REVISE   Put the clutch in first (imperative); then you should put the truck in gear (indicative).

TO   Put the clutch in first (imperative); then put the truck in gear (imperative).

OR   You should put the clutch in first (indicative); then you should put the truck in gear (indicative).

(c) **Voice.** The grammatical term *voice* refers to whether the subject of a sentence or clause acts or receives the action. A sentence is in the active voice if the subject acts, in the passive voice if the subject is acted upon. The passive voice consists of a form of the verb *to be* and a past participle of the main verb.

EXAMPLES   The aerosol bomb *propels* the liquid as a mist. (active)

The liquid *is propelled* as a mist by the aerosol bomb. (passive)

In your writing, the active voice provides force and momentum, whereas the passive voice lacks these qualities. The reason is not difficult to find. In the active voice, the verb identifies what the subject is doing, thus emphasizing the subject and the action. On the other hand, the passive voice emphasizes what is being done to the subject, rather than the subject or the action. As a rule, use the active voice unless you have good reason not to.

EXAMPLES   The report *was written* by Joe Albright in only two hours. (passive voice) (The emphasis is on *report* rather than on Joe and the writing.)

Joe Albright *wrote* the report in only two hours. (active voice) (Here the writer and writing receive the emphasis.)

Things *are seen* by the normal human eye in three dimensions: length, width, and depth. (passive voice) (The emphasis is on *things* rather than on the eye's function.)

The normal human eye *sees* things in three dimensions: length, width, and depth. (active voice) (Here the eye's function—which is what the sentence is about—receives the emphasis.)

Sentences in the passive voice may state the actor, but they place the actor in a secondary position as the object of a preposition ("by the normal human eye").

The passive voice has its advantages, however; when the doer of the action is not known or is not important, use the passive voice.

EXAMPLE   The firm *was established* in 1929.

When the doer of the action is less important than the receiver of the action, use the passive voice.

EXAMPLE   Bill Bryant *was cited* for heroism by General Colby.

Be careful about shifting voice within a sentence.

REVISE   We *worked* late last night, and all the tests *were* finally *completed.*

TO   We *worked* late last night, and finally we *completed* all the tests.

(d) **Tense.**   *Tense* is the grammatical term for verb forms that indicate time distinctions. The six simple tenses in English are past, past perfect, present, present perfect, future, and future perfect. Each of these tenses has a corresponding progressive form that shows action in progress and is created by combining the helping verb *be*, in the appropriate tense, with the present participle (-*ing*) form of the main verb.

Simple	Progressive
I begin (present)	I am beginning (present)
I began (past)	I was beginning (past)
I will begin (future)	I will be beginning (future)
I have begun (present perfect)	I have been beginning (present perfect)
I had begun (past perfect)	I had been beginning (past perfect)
I will have begun (future perfect)	I will have been beginning (future perfect)

The *simple present tense* represents action occurring in the present, without any indication of time duration.

EXAMPLE   I *use* the calculator.

A general truth is always expressed in the present tense.

EXAMPLE   He learned that "time *heals* all wounds."

The present tense can be used to present actions or conditions that have no time restrictions.

EXAMPLE   Water *boils* at 212° F.

The present tense can be used to indicate habitual action.

EXAMPLE   I *pass* the paint shop on the way to the office every day.

The present tense can be used as the *historical present* to make things that occurred in the past more vivid.

EXAMPLE   It is 1865, and the founder of our company is pushing his cart through Philadelphia, delivering fish to his customers. He *works* hard, *expands* his business, and *builds* the firm that still bears his name.

The *simple past tense* indicates that an action took place in its entirety in the past. The past tense is usually formed by adding *-d* or *-ed* to the root form of the verb.

EXAMPLE   We *closed* the office early yesterday.

The *simple future tense* indicates a time that will occur after the present. The helping verb *will* (or *shall*) is used along with the main verb.

EXAMPLE   I *will finish* the job tomorrow.

The *present perfect tense* describes something from the recent past that has a bearing on the present—a period of time before the present but after the simple past. The present perfect tense is formed by combining a form of the present tense of the helping verb *have* with the past participle of the main verb.

EXAMPLES   He *has retired,* but he visits the office frequently.

We *have finished* the draft and are ready to begin revising it.

The *simple past perfect tense* indicates that one past event preceded another. It is formed by combining the helping verb *had* with the past participle of the main verb.

EXAMPLE   He *had finished* by the time I arrived.

The *future perfect tense* indicates an action that will have been completed at a future time. It is formed by linking the helping verbs *will have* to the past participle of the main verb.

EXAMPLE   He *will have driven* the test car 40 miles by the time he returns.

3.4.4   Conjugation of Verbs

When a verb is conjugated, all of its forms are arranged schematically so that the differences in tense, number, person, and voice are readily apparent. Following is the conjugation of the verb *drive.* Its principal parts, used to construct its various forms, are *drive* (infinitive and present tense), *drove* (past tense), *driven* (past participle), and *driving* (present participle).

Tense	*Number*	*Person*	*Active Voice*	*Passive Voice*
Present	Singular	1st	I drive	I am driven
		2nd	You drive	You are driven
		3rd	He drives	He is driven
	Plural	1st	We drive	We are driven
		2nd	You drive	You are driven
		3rd	They drive	They are driven
Progressive present	Singular	1st	I am driving	I am being driven
		2nd	You are driving	You are being driven
		3rd	He is driving	He is being driven
	Plural	1st	We are driving	We are being driven
		2nd	You are driving	You are being driven
		3rd	They are driving	They are being driven

Tense	Number	Person	Active Voice	Passive Voice
Past	Singular	1st	I drove	I was driven
		2nd	You drove	You were driven
		3rd	He drove	He was driven
	Plural	1st	We drove	We were driven
		2nd	You drove	You were driven
		3rd	They drove	They were driven
Progressive past	Singular	1st	I was driving	I was being driven
		2nd	You were driving	You were being driven
		3rd	He was driving	He was being driven
	Plural	1st	We were driving	We were being driven
		2nd	You were driving	You were being driven
		3rd	They were driving	They were being driven
Future	Singular	1st	I will drive	I will be driven
		2nd	You will drive	You will be driven
		3rd	He will drive	He will be driven
	Plural	1st	We will drive	We will be driven
		2nd	You will drive	You will be driven
		3rd	They will drive	They will be driven
Progressive future	Singular	1st	I will be driving	I will have been driven
		2nd	You will be driving	You will have been driven
		3rd	He will be driving	He will have been driven
	Plural	1st	We will be driving	We will have been driven
		2nd	You will be driving	You will have been driven
		3rd	They will be driving	They will have been driven
Present perfect	Singular	1st	I have driven	I have been driven
		2nd	You have driven	You have been driven
		3rd	He has driven	He has been driven
	Plural	1st	We have driven	We have been driven
		2nd	You have driven	You have been driven
		3rd	They have driven	They have been driven

Tense	Number	Person	Active Voice	Passive Voice
Past perfect	Singular	1st	I had driven	I had been driven
		2nd	You had driven	You had been driven
		3rd	He had driven	He had been driven
	Plural	1st	We had driven	We had been driven
		2nd	You had driven	You had been driven
		3rd	They had driven	They had been driven
Future perfect	Singular	1st	I will have driven	I will have been driven
		2nd	You will have driven	You will have been driven
		3rd	He will have driven	He will have been driven
	Plural	1st	We will have driven	We will have been driven
		2nd	You will have driven	You will have been driven
		3rd	They will have driven	They will have been driven

3.4.5   Subject-Verb Agreement

Agreement, grammatically, means the correspondence in form between different elements of a sentence. Just as a pronoun must agree with its antecedent in person, gender, and number (see Section 3.2.3a), so a verb must agree with its subject in person and number.

EXAMPLES   I *am* going to approve his promotion. (The first-person singular subject, *I,* requires the first-person singular form of the verb, *am*).

His colleagues *are* envious. (The third-person plural subject, *colleagues,* requires the third-person plural form of the verb, *are*).

Do not let phrases and clauses that fall between the subject and the verb mislead you.

EXAMPLES   Teaching proper oral hygiene to children, even when they are excited about learning, *requires* patience. (The verb *requires* must agree with the singular subject of the sentence, *teaching,* rather than with the plural subject of the preceding clause, *they.*)

Be careful to avoid making the verb agree with the noun immediately before it if that noun is not its subject. This problem is especially likely to occur when a modifying phrase containing a plural noun falls between a singular subject and its verb.

EXAMPLES   Each of the engineers *is* experienced. (The subject of the verb is *each,* not *engineers.*)

Only Bob, of all the district managers, *has doubled* his sales this year. (The subject of the verb is *Bob,* not *managers.*)

Proper cleaning of the machines and tools *takes* time. (The subject of the verb is *cleaning,* not *machines and tools.*)

Words like *type, part, series,* and *portion* take singular verbs even when such words precede a phrase containing a plural noun.

EXAMPLES   A *series* of directions *was given* to each branch manager.

A large *portion* of most employee handbooks *is devoted* to the responsibilities of the worker.

Subjects expressing measurement, weight, mass, or total often take singular verbs even though the subject word is plural in form. Such subjects are treated as a unit.

EXAMPLES   Ten pounds *is* the shipping weight.

Fifty dollars *is* her commission for each unit she sells.

However, when such subjects refer to the individual units that make up the whole, a plural verb is required.

EXAMPLE   If you need to make change, fifty dollars *are* in the office.

Similarly, collective subjects take singular verbs when the group is thought of as a unit, and take plural verbs when the individuals are thought of separately.

EXAMPLES   The staff *is* reaching its decision. (The staff is thought of as a unit.)

The staff *are* so divided in their opinions that a decision is unlikely to be reached soon. (The staff members are thought of as individuals.)

A book with a plural title requires a singular verb.

EXAMPLE   *Monetary Theories is* a useful source.

Some abstract nouns are singular in meaning though plural in form: examples are *mathematics, news, physics,* and *economics.*

EXAMPLES News of the merger *is* on page four of the *Chronicle.*

Textiles *is* an industry in need of import quotas.

Some words are always plural, such as *trousers* and *scissors.*

EXAMPLE His trousers *were* torn by the machine.

The scissors *were* on the table.

BUT A pair of trousers *is* on order.

A pair of scissors *was* on the table.

Modifiers such as *some, none, all, more,* and *most* may be singular if they are used with mass nouns or plural if they are used with count nouns. Mass nouns identify things that comprise a mass and cannot be separated into countable units; count nouns identify things that can be separated into countable units (See Section 3.1.1b).

EXAMPLES Most of the oil *has* been used.

Most of the drivers *know* why they are here.

Some of the water *has* leaked.

Some of the pencils *have* been used.

One and *each* are normally singular.

EXAMPLES One of the brake drums *is* still scored.

Each of the original founders *is* scheduled to speak at the dedication ceremony.

Following a relative pronoun such as *who, which,* or *that,* a verb agrees in number with the noun to which the pronoun refers (its antecedent).

EXAMPLES Steel is one of those industries that *are* hardest hit by high energy costs. (*That* refers to *industries.*)

She is an employee who *is* rarely absent. (*Who* refers to *employee.*)

She is one of those employees who *are* rarely absent. (*Who* refers to *employees.*)

A subjective complement is a noun or adjective in the predicate of a sentence, following a linking verb. The number of a subjective complement does not affect the number of the verb—the verb must always agree with the subject.

EXAMPLE The topic of his report *was* rivers. (The subject of the sentence is *topic,* not *rivers.*)

Sentences with inverted word order can cause problems with agreement between subject and verb.

EXAMPLE From this work *have come* several important improvements. (The subject of the verb is *improvements,* not *work.*)

A compound subject is one that is composed of two or more elements joined by a conjunction such as *and, or, nor, either . . . or,* or *neither . . . nor.* Usually, when the elements are connected by *and,* the subject is plural and requires a plural verb.

EXAMPLE Education and experience *are* valuable assets.

There is one exception to the *and* rule. Sometimes the elements connected by *and* form a unit or refer to the same person. In this case, the subject is regarded as singular and takes a singular verb.

EXAMPLES Ice cream and cake *is* his favorite dessert.

His lawyer and business partner *prepares* the tax forms. (His lawyer is also his business partner.)

A compound subject joined by *or* or *nor* requires a singular verb with two singular elements and a plural verb with two plural elements.

EXAMPLES Neither the *doctor* nor the *nurse is* on duty.

Neither the *doctors* nor the *nurses are* on duty.

A compound subject with a singular element and a plural element joined by *or* or *nor* requires that the verb agree with the element nearest to it.

EXAMPLES Neither the doctor nor the *nurses are* on duty.

Neither the doctors nor the *nurse is* on duty.

3.5 ADVERBS

An adverb modifies the action or condition expressed by a verb.

EXAMPLE The recording head hit the surface of the disk *hard.* (The adverb tells *how* the recording head hit the disk.)

An adverb may also modify an adjective, another adverb, or a clause.

EXAMPLES The graphics department used *extremely* bright colors. (modifying an adjective)

The redesigned brake pad lasted *much* longer than the original model. (modifying another adverb)

Surprisingly, the machine failed. (modifying a clause)

3.5.1 Functions of Adverbs

An adverb answers one of the following questions.

Where?

EXAMPLE Move the throttle *forward.*

When?

EXAMPLE Replace the thermostat *immediately.*

How?

EXAMPLE Add the solvent *cautiously.*

How much?

EXAMPLES The *nearly* completed report was lost in the move.
I *rarely* work on the weekend.
I have worked overtime *twice* this week.

Some adverbs (such as *however, therefore, nonetheless, nevertheless, consequently, accordingly,* and *then*) can join two independent clauses, each of which could otherwise stand alone as a sentence.

EXAMPLE I rarely work on the weekend; *nevertheless,* this weekend will be an exception.

Other adverbs, such as *where, when, why,* and *how,* ask questions.

EXAMPLE *How* many hours did you work last week?

3.5.2 Comparison of Adverbs

Adverbs, like adjectives, show three degrees of comparison: the positive (the basic form of the adverb), the comparative (showing comparison with one other item), and the superlative (showing comparison with two or more other items). Many adverbs indicate comparison with the suffixes *-er,* or *-est;* alternatively, *more* or *most* may be placed in front of an adverb to indicate comparison. One-syllable adverbs use the comparative ending *-er* and the superlative ending *-est.*

EXAMPLES This copier works *faster* than the old one.
This copier works *fastest* of the three tested.

Most adverbs with two or more syllables end in *-ly,* and most adverbs ending in *-ly* are compared by inserting the comparative *more* or the superlative *most* in front of them.

EXAMPLES   He moved *more quickly* than the other company's sales-
             man.

             Of all the salesmen, he moved *most quickly*.

Less and *least* are antonyms, or opposites, of *more* and *most*.

EXAMPLES   He moved *less quickly* than the other company's sales-
             man.

             Of all the salesmen, he moved *least quickly*.

A few irregular adverbs require a change in form to indicate comparison.

EXAMPLES   Our training program functions *well*.

             Our training program functions *better* than most others
             in the industry.

             Our training program functions the *best* in the industry.

3.5.3   Adverbs Made from Adjectives

Many adverbs are simply adjectives with *-ly* added, such as *dashingly*
and *richly*. Sometimes, the adverb form is identical to the adjective
form: examples are *early, hard, right,* and *fast*. Resist the temptation
to drop the *-ly* ending from such adverbs as *surely, differently, seriously,
considerably, badly,* and *really*.

REVISE   The breakdown of the air conditioning equipment dam-
             aged the computer system *considerable*.

TO   The breakdown of the air conditioning equipment dam-
             aged the computer system *considerably*.

On the other hand, resist the temptation to coin awkward adverbs
by adding *-ly* to adjectives (*firstly, muchly*).

REVISE   Firstly, I'd like to thank our sponsor; secondly, I'd like
             to thank all of you.

TO   First, I'd like to thank our sponsor; second, I'd like to
             thank all of you.

3.5.4   Placement of Adverbs

An adverb may appear almost anywhere in a sentence, but its position
can affect the meaning of the sentence. Avoid placing an adverb be-

tween two verb forms where it will be ambiguous because it can be read as modifying either.

REVISE   The man who was making calculations hastily rose from his desk and left the room. (Did the man calculate hastily or did he rise hastily?)

TO   The man who was making calculations rose hastily from his desk and left the room.

An adverb is commonly placed in front of the verb it modifies.

EXAMPLE   The accountant *meticulously* checked the figures.

An adverb may, however, follow the verb (or the verb and its object) that it modifies.

EXAMPLES   The accountant checked the figures *meticulously.*
             The gauge dipped *suddenly.*

An adverb may be placed between a helping verb and a main verb.

EXAMPLE   He will *surely* call.

If an adverb modifies only the main verb, and not any accompanying helping verbs, place the adverb immediately before or after the main verb.

EXAMPLES   The alternative proposal has been *effectively* presented.
             The alternative proposal has been presented *effectively.*

An adverb phrase, however, should not separate the parts of a verb.

REVISE   This suggestion has *time and time again* been rejected.
TO   This suggestion has been rejected *time and time again.*

To emphasize an adverb that introduces an entire sentence, you can put the adverb before the subject of the sentence.

EXAMPLES   *Clearly,* he was ready for the promotion when it came.
             Unfortunately, fuel rationing has been necessary.

In writing, such adverbs as *nearly, only, almost, just,* and *hardly* are placed immediately before the words they limit. A speaker can place these words earlier and avoid ambiguity by stressing the word to be limited; a writer, however, can ensure clarity only through correct placement of the adverb.

REVISE   The punch press *almost* costs $47,000.
TO   The punch press costs *almost* $47,000.

3.6   CONJUNCTIONS

A conjunction connects words, phrases, or clauses. A conjunction can also indicate the relationship between the two elements it connects. (For example, *and* joins together; *or* selects and separates.)

3.6.1   Types of Conjunctions

Conjunctions may be coordinating, correlative, or subordinating. In addition, certain adverbs act as conjunctions.

(a)   Coordinating conjunctions.   A coordinating conjunction is a word that joins two sentence elements that have identical functions. The coordinating conjunctions are *and, but, for, nor, or, so,* and *yet.*

EXAMPLES   Bill *and* John work at the Los Angeles office. (joining two proper nouns)

To hear *and* to obey are two different things. (joining two phrases)

He would like to include the test results, *but* that would make the report too long. (joining two clauses)

(b)   Correlative conjunctions.   Correlative conjunctions are used in pairs. The correlative conjunctions are *either . . . or, neither . . . nor, not only . . . but also, both . . . and,* and *whether . . . or.* To ensure not only symmetry but also logic in your writing, follow correlative conjunctions with parallel sentence elements that are alike in function and in construction.

EXAMPLE   Bill will arrive *either* on Wednesday *or* on Thursday.

(c)   Subordinating conjunctions.   A subordinating conjunction connects sentence elements of different weights, normally independent clauses that can stand alone as sentences and dependent clauses that cannot. The most frequently used subordinating conjunctions are *so, although, after, because, if, where, than, since, as, unless, before, that, though, when,* and *whereas.*

EXAMPLE   He left the office *after* he had finished writing the report.

(d)   Conjunctive adverbs.   A conjunctive adverb is an adverb that has the force of a conjunction because it is used to join two independent clauses. The most common conjunctive adverbs are *however, moreover,* *therefore, further, then, consequently, besides, accordingly, also,* and *too.*

EXAMPLE   The engine performed well in the laboratory; *moreover,* it surpassed all expectations during its road test.

3.6.2 Usage of Conjunctions

Coordinating conjunctions generally appear within rather than at the beginning of a sentence. There is, however, no rule against beginning a sentence with a coordinating conjunction. In fact, such conjunctions can be strong transitional words and at times can provide emphasis.

EXAMPLE   I realize that the project was more difficult than expected and that you have also encountered personnel problems. *But* we must meet our deadline.

Starting sentences with conjunctions is acceptable in even the most formal English. But, like any other writing device, this one should be used sparingly lest it become ineffective and even annoying.

3.7 PREPOSITIONS

A preposition is a word that links a noun or pronoun (its object) to another sentence element.

3.7.1 Functions of Prepositions

Prepositions express such relationships as direction (*to, into, across, toward*), location (*at, in, on, under, over, beside, among, by, between, through*), time (*before, after, during, until, since*), or figurative location (*for, against, with*). Although only about seventy prepositions exist in the English language, they are used frequently. Together, the preposition, its object, and the object's modifiers form a prepositional phrase, which acts as a modifier.

Many words that function as prepositions also function as adverbs. If a word takes an object and functions as a connective, it is a preposition; if it has no object and functions as a modifier, it is an adverb.

EXAMPLES   The manager sat *behind* the desk in his office. (preposition)

The customer lagged *behind;* then she came in and sat down. (adverb)

3.7.2 Usage of Prepositions

Do not use unnecessary prepositions, such as "off *of*" or "inside *of.*"

REVISE   *Inside of* the cave, the spelunkers turned on their headlamps.

TO   Inside the cave, the spelunkers turned on their headlamps.

Avoid adding the preposition *up* to verbs unnecessarily.

REVISE   Call *up* and see whether he is in his office.

TO   Call and see whether he is in his office.

However, do not omit needed prepositions.

REVISE   He was oblivious and not distracted by the view from his office window.

TO   He was oblivious *to* and not distracted *by* the view from his office window.

If a preposition falls naturally at the end of a sentence, leave it there.

EXAMPLE   I don't remember which file I put it *in.*

Be aware, however, that a preposition at the end of a sentence can indicate that the sentence is awkwardly constructed.

REVISE   Corn was the crop in the field that the wheat was planted *by.*

TO   The wheat was planted next to the corn in the field.

The object of a preposition—the word or phrase following the preposition—is always in the objective case. Despite this rule, a construction such as "between you and *me*" frequently and incorrectly appears as "between you and I."

REVISE   The whole department has suffered because of the quarrel between *he* and Bob.

TO   The whole department has suffered because of the quarrel between *him* and Bob.

Certain verbs (and verb forms), adverbs, and adjectives are used with certain prepositions. For example, we say "interested *in,*" "aware *of,*" "devoted *to,*" "equated *with,*" "abstain *from,*" "adhere *to,*" "conform *to,*" "capable *of,*" "comply *with,*" "object *to,*" "find fault *with,*" "inconsistent *with,*" "independent *of,*" "infer *from,*" and "interfere *with.*"

3.8 INTERJECTIONS

An interjection is a word or phrase of exclamation that is used independently to express emotion or surprise or to summon attention. *Hey! Ouch! Wow!* are strong interjections. *Oh, well,* and *indeed* are mild ones. An interjection functions much as *yes* or *no,* in that it has no grammatical connection with the rest of the sentence in which it appears. When an interjection expresses a sudden or strong emotion, punctuate it with an exclamation mark.

EXAMPLE   His only reaction was a resounding *"Wow!"*

Punctuate a mild interjection with a comma.

EXAMPLES   Well, that's done.

Oh, well, that's done.

Because they get their expressive force from sound, interjections are more common in speech than in writing. They are rarely appropriate to business or technical writing.

4 PHRASES, CLAUSES, SENTENCES, AND PARAGRAPHS

Good writing relies upon the writer's ability to put words together that convey a message to a reader in the most effective way. The writer can use a number of tools to help communicate ideas to a reader; among them are phrases, clauses, sentences, and paragraphs.

4.1 PHRASES

Although a phrase is the most basic meaningful group of words, it does not make a full statement. Unlike a clause, it does not contain both a subject (words that name someone or something) and a predicate (words that make an assertion about the subject). Instead, a phrase is based on a noun, a verbal (that is, a gerund, infinitive, or participle), or a verb without a subject.

EXAMPLES   *by August fifth*

operating the machine

has been working

A phrase may function as an adjective, an adverb, a noun, or a verb.

EXAMPLES   The subjects *on the agenda* were all discussed. (adjective)
We discussed the project *with great enthusiasm.* (adverb)
Hard work is her way of life. (noun)
The chief engineer *should have been notified.* (verb)

Even though phrases function as adjectives, adverbs, nouns, or verbs, normally they are named for the kind of word around which they are constructed—preposition, verb, noun, or the three verbals. For definitions of the parts of speech, refer to Section 3 of this Guide.

4.1.1 Prepositional Phrases

A preposition is a word that shows the relationship between the noun or pronoun that is its object and another sentence element. Prepositions express relationships such as direction, location, and time. A preposition, its object, and the object's modifiers form a prepositional phrase, which acts as a modifier.

EXAMPLE   After the meeting, the regional managers adjourned *to the executive dining room.*

4.1.2 Verb Phrases

A verb phrase consists of a main verb preceded by one or more helping verbs.

EXAMPLES   Company officials discovered that a computer *was emitting* more data than it *had been asked* for.
He *will file* his tax forms on time this year.

4.1.3 Noun Phrases

A noun phrase consists of a noun and its modifiers.

EXAMPLES   *Many large companies* use computers.
Have *the two new employees* fill out *these forms.*

4.1.4 Participial Phrases

A participial phrase consists of a participle plus its object and any modifiers. A participial phrase functions as an adjective, so it must modify a noun or pronoun and must be placed so that this relationship is clear.

EXAMPLE   *Looking very pleased with himself,* the sales manager reported on the success of the policies he had introduced.

4.1.5   Infinitive Phrases

An infinitive is the root form of a verb (*go, run, talk*), one of the principal parts that is used to construct the various forms of a verb. An infinitive generally follows the word *to,* called the sign of the infinitive. An infinitive phrase consists of the word *to* plus an infinitive and any objects or modifiers.

EXAMPLE   *To succeed in this field,* you must be willing *to assume responsibility.*

4.1.6   Gerund Phrases

When the *-ing* form of a verb functions as a noun, it is called a gerund. A gerund phrase, which also must function as a noun, consists of a gerund plus any objects or modifiers.

EXAMPLES   *Preparing an annual report* is a difficult task.
             She liked *running the department.*

4.2   CLAUSES

A clause is a part of a sentence that contains both a subject (the word or group of words that name someone or something as a topic) and a predicate (the main verb and its modifiers and complements that make an assertion about the subject).

Every subject-predicate word group in a sentence is a clause. Unlike a phrase, a clause can make a complete statement because it contains a finite verb (as opposed to a nonfinite verb or verbal) as well as a subject. Every sentence must consist of at least one clause. A clause that conveys a complete thought and thus could stand alone as a sentence is an independent clause.

EXAMPLE   *The scaffolding fell* when the rope broke.

A clause that could not stand alone without the rest of its sentence is a dependent or subordinate clause.

EXAMPLE   I was at the St. Louis branch *when the decision was made.*

A dependent clause may function as a noun, an adjective, or an adverb in a larger sentence; an independent clause may be modified by one or more dependent clauses.

EXAMPLE   While I was in college, I studied differential equations. (*While I was in college* is a dependent clause functioning as an adverb; it modifies the independent clause *I studied differential equations.*)

A clause may be connected with the rest of its sentence by a coordinating conjunction, a subordinating conjunction, a relative pronoun, or a conjunctive adverb. (Refer to Sections 3.2 and 3.6 for discussions of pronouns and conjunctions.)

EXAMPLES   Peregrine falcons are about the size of a large crow, *and* they have a wingspan of three to four feet. (coordinating conjunction)

Mission control will have to be alert *because* the space laboratory will contain a highly flammable fuel at launch. (subordinating conjunction)

It was Robert M. Fano *who* designed and developed the earliest "Multiple Access Computer" system at M.I.T. (relative pronoun)

It was dark when we arrived; *nevertheless,* we began to tour the factory. (conjunctive adverb)

4.2.1 Independent Clauses

Unlike a dependent clause, an independent clause is complete in itself. Although it might be part of a larger sentence, it always can stand alone as a separate sentence.

EXAMPLE   *We abandoned the project* because the cost was excessive.

4.2.2 Dependent Clauses

A dependent (or subordinate) clause is a group of words that has a subject and a predicate but requires a main clause to complete its meaning. A dependent clause can function in a sentence as a noun, as an adjective, or as an adverb.

As nouns, dependent clauses may function in sentences as subjects, objects, or complements.

EXAMPLES   *That human beings can learn to control their glands and internal organs by direct or indirect means* is now an established fact. (subject)

The trouble is *that we cannot finish the project by May.* (subjective complement)

I learned *that drugs ordered by brand name can cost several times as much as drugs ordered by generic name.* (direct object)

As adjectives, dependent clauses can modify nouns or pronouns. Dependent clauses are often introduced by relative pronouns and relative adjectives (*who, whom, whose, which, what, that*).

EXAMPLE   The man *who called earlier* is here. (modifying *man*)

As adverbs, dependent clauses may express relationships of time, cause, result, or degree.

EXAMPLES   You are making an investment *when you buy a house.* (time)

A title search was necessary *because the bank would not otherwise grant a loan.* (cause)

Consult an attorney *so that you will be aware of your rights and obligations.* (result)

Monthly mortgage payments should not be much more *than the buyer earns in one week.* (degree)

Dependent clauses clarify the relationships between thoughts. As a result, dependent clauses can present ideas more precisely than simple sentences (which contain one independent clause) or compound sentences (which combine two independent clauses).

REVISE   The sewage plant is located between Millville and Darrtown. Both villages use it. (two thoughts of approximately equal importance)

TO   The sewage plant, *which is located between Millville and Darrtown,* is used by both villages. (one thought, the plant's location, subordinated to the other, its service area)

REVISE   He arrived at his office early and was able to finish the report without any interruptions. (two thoughts of approximately equal importance)

TO   *Since he arrived at his office early,* he was able to finish the report without interruptions. (one thought, his early arrival, subordinated to the other, his completion of the report)

Subordinate clauses effectively express thoughts that describe or explain another statement. They can state where, when, how, or why an event occurred, thus supplying logical connections that may not be obvious from the context. Too much subordination, however, may be worse than none at all. A string of dependent clauses, like a string of simple sentences, may obscure the important ideas.

REVISE   He had selected classes *that* had a slant *that* was specifically directed toward students *who* intended to go into business. (three dependent clauses of approximately equal importance)

TO   He had selected classes *that* were specifically directed to business students. (one dependent clause emphasizing the most important of the three points)

4.3 SENTENCES

A sentence is a sequence of words that contains a subject and a predicate and conveys a complete thought. A sentence normally has at least two words: a subject (something or someone) and a predicate (an assertion about the action or state of existence of the subject).

EXAMPLE   Sales (subject) declined (assertion about the subject).

To the basic sentence can be added modifiers—words, phrases, and clauses that expand, limit, or make more exact the meanings of other sentence elements.

EXAMPLE   *Computer* sales declined *in August.*

In most sentences, the subject is a noun phrase rather than a single word, and the predicate is a verb or verb phrase with appropriate modifiers, objects, or complements.

EXAMPLE   A good personnel department (subject) screens job applicants carefully (predicate).

Sentences may be classified according to structure (simple, compound, complex) and intention (declarative, interrogative, imperative, exclamatory).

4.3.1 Structure

A simple sentence is often used to make its content stand out in the reader's mind. A compound sentence is used to show that the clauses in the sentence are of equal importance. And a complex sentence is used to show that the clauses in the sentence are of unequal importance.

(a) **Simple sentences.** A simple sentence has one clause. In its most basic form, the simple sentence contains only a subject and a predicate.

EXAMPLES   Profits rose.

The strike ended.

Both the subject and the predicate may be compounded to include several items without changing the basic structure of the simple sentence.

EXAMPLES   *Bulldozers and road graders* have blades. (compound subject)

Bulldozers *strip, ditch, and backfill.* (compound predicate)

Likewise, although modifiers may lengthen a simple sentence, they do not change its basic structure.

EXAMPLE   *The recently introduced* procedure works *very well.*

(b) **Compound sentences.** A compound sentence combines two or more related independent clauses that are of equal importance.

EXAMPLE   Drilling is the only way to collect samples of the layers of sediment below the ocean floor, but it is by no means the only way to gather information about these strata.[1]

The independent clauses of a compound sentence may be joined by a comma and a coordinating conjunction, by a semicolon, or by a conjunctive adverb preceded by a semicolon and followed by a comma.

EXAMPLES   The plan was sound, *and* the staff was eager to begin. (comma and coordinating conjunction)

The plan was sound; the staff was eager to begin. (semicolon)

The plan was sound; *therefore,* the staff was eager to begin. (conjunctive adverb)

(c) **Complex sentences.** A complex sentence contains one independent clause and at least one dependent clause.

EXAMPLE   We lost some of our efficiency (independent clause) when we moved (dependent clause).

---

[1] Bruce C. Heezen and Ian D. MacGregor, "The Evolution of the Pacific," *Scientific American* (November 1973), p. 103.

A dependent clause may occur before, after, or within the independent clause. The dependent clause can function within a sentence as a subject, an object, or a modifier.

EXAMPLES   *What he proposed* is irrelevant. (subject)

We know *where it is supposed to be.* (object)

Fingerprints, *which were used for personal identification in 200 B.C.,* were not used for criminal identification until about 1800. (modifier)

Because complex sentences offer more variety than simple ones, changing a compound sentence into a complex one can produce a more precise statement. When one independent clause becomes subordinate to another, the relationship between the two is more clearly established.

EXAMPLES   We moved, *and* we lost some of our efficiency. (compound sentence with coordinating conjunction)

When we moved, we lost some of our efficiency. (complex sentence with subordinating conjunction)

A complex sentence indicates the relative importance of two clauses and expresses the relationship between the ideas contained in them. Normally, the independent clause states the main point, and the dependent clause states a related but subordinate point.

EXAMPLE   Although the warehouse was damaged by the fire, all the employees escaped safely from the building.

4.3.2   Intention

By intention, a sentence may be declarative, interrogative, imperative, or exclamatory.

A declarative sentence conveys information or makes a factual statement.

EXAMPLE   This motor powers the conveyor belt.

An interrogative sentence asks a direct question.

EXAMPLE   Does the conveyor belt run constantly?

An imperative sentence issues a command.

EXAMPLE   Start the generator.

An exclamatory sentence is an emphatic expression of feeling, fact, or opinion. It is a declarative sentence that is stated with great force.

EXAMPLE   The heater exploded!

4.3.3   Construction

(a)   Parts of sentences.   Within a sentence, every word or word group functions as a sentence element. A *subject* names (and perhaps includes words that describe) the person or thing that is the topic of the sentence.

EXAMPLE   *The new machine* ran.

A verb describes an action or affirms the condition or state of existence of its subject.

EXAMPLE   The new machine *ran.*

A complement is used in the predicate (with the verb) to complete the meaning of a sentence. There are four kinds of complements. The first, the direct object, names the person or thing on which a transitive verb acts. The direct object normally answers the question *what* or *whom.*

EXAMPLES   He wrote *a letter.*
             I admire *the boss.*

The second type of complement, the indirect object, names the recipient of the direct object; that is, it names the person or thing that something is done to or for.

EXAMPLE   He wrote *the company* a letter.

The third type of complement, the objective complement, describes or renames a direct object.

EXAMPLE   I like my coffee *hot.*

The last type of complement, the subjective complement, describes or renames the subject of a sentence.

EXAMPLE   The director seems *confident.*

A modifier expands, limits, or makes more exact the meaning of other sentence elements.

EXAMPLE   *Automobile* production decreased *rapidly.*

A connective (a conjunction, a conjunctive adverb, or a preposition) ties together parts of sentences by indicating subordination or coordination.

EXAMPLE   I work hard each week, *but* I relax *when* I play racquetball.

An appositive is a noun or noun phrase that follows and amplifies another noun or noun phrase.

EXAMPLE   Bob, *the personnel director,* just interviewed another engineer.

An absolute is a participial or infinitive phrase that modifies a statement as a whole and is not linked to it by a subordinating conjunction or preposition.

EXAMPLE   *To speak bluntly,* the proposal is unacceptable.

An expletive is a word such as *it* or *there* that serves as a structural filler and reverses standard subject-verb order.

EXAMPLE   *It* is certain that he will go.

Because expletives are meaningless, they are best avoided in business or technical writing.

(b) **Sentence patterns.**   Subjects, verbs, and complements are the main elements of a sentence. Everything else is subordinate to them in one way or another. The following are the basic sentence patterns with which a writer works.

EXAMPLES   The cable snapped. (subject–verb)

Generators produce electricity. (subject–verb–direct object)

The test results gave us confidence. (subject–verb–indirect object–direct object)

Repairs made the equipment operational. (subject–verb–direct object–objective complement)

The metal was aluminum. (subject–linking verb–subjective complement)

Most sentences follow the subject–verb–complement pattern. In "The company dismissed Joe," for example, you recognize the subject and the object by their positions before and after the verb. In fact, readers interpret what they read more easily because they expect this sentence order. As a result, departures from it can be effective, if used sparingly for emphasis and variety, but annoying if overdone.

An inverted sentence places the elements in other than normal order.

EXAMPLES   A better job I never had. (direct object–subject–verb)

More optimistic I have never been. (subjective complement–subject–linking verb)

Inverted sentence order can be used in questions and exclamations; it can also be used for emphasis.

EXAMPLES   Have you a pencil? (verb–subject–complement)

How heavy your book feels! (complement–subject–verb)

In sentences introduced by expletives (*there, it*), the subject comes after its verb because the expletive occupies the subject's normal location before the verb. Because expletives are fillers, they are avoided in concise writing.

EXAMPLES   There (expletive) are (verb) certain principles (subject) of drafting that must not be ignored. (Compare: "Certain principles of drafting must not be ignored." The meaningful verb of the sentence, *be ignored*, which was buried in a relative clause in the expletive construction, becomes the only verb: the meaningless *are* is unnecessary.) It (expletive) is (verb) difficult (complement) to work (subject) in a noisy office. (Compare: "To work in a noisy office is difficult.")

Unusual sentence order, however, cannot be used often without tiring or puzzling the reader. Instead, a sentence that moves quickly from subject to verb to complement is clear and easy to understand. The writer's problem is to preserve the clarity and directness of this pattern but to write sentences that use more complicated forms to present more information. A skillful writer depends on subordination—the relative weighing of ideas—to make sentences more dense. As the following example shows, a sentence can be rewritten in several ways by subordinating the less important ideas to the more important ones.

REVISE   The city manager's report was carefully illustrated, and it covered five typed pages.

TO   The city manager's report, *which covered five typed pages,* was carefully illustrated. (adjectival clause)

OR   The city manager's report, *covering five typed pages,* was carefully illustrated. (participial phrase)

OR   The *carefully illustrated* report of the city manager covered five typed pages. (participial phrase)

OR   The *five-page* report of the city manager was carefully illustrated. (modifier)

OR   The city manager's report, *five typed pages,* was carefully illustrated. (appositive phrase)

The effective subordination of words, phrases, and clauses produces varied, concise, and emphatic sentences.

4.3.4 Common Sentence Problems

The most common sentence problems are faulty subordination, run-on sentences, sentence fragments, and dangling and misplaced modifiers.

(a) **Faulty subordination.** Faulty subordination occurs (1) when a grammatically subordinate element, such as a dependent clause, actually contains the main idea of the sentence; or (2) when a subordinate element is so long or detailed that it overpowers the main idea. You can avoid the first problem, expressing the main idea in a subordinate element, by deciding which idea is the main idea. Both of the following sentences, for example, appear logical, but each emphasizes a different point.

> EXAMPLES Although the new filing system saves money, many of the staff are unhappy with it.
>
> The new filing system saves money, although many of the staff are unhappy with it.

In this example, if the writer's main point is that *the new filing system saves money,* the second sentence is better. If the main point is that *many of the staff are unhappy,* then the first sentence is better.

The other major problem with subordination occurs when a writer puts so much detail into a subordinate element that it overpowers the main point by its sheer size and weight. In the following example, details are omitted in order to streamline the sentence.

> REVISE If company personnel do not fully understand what the new contract that was drawn up at the annual meeting of the district managers this past month in New Orleans requires of them, they should call or write the Vice President for Finance.
>
> TO If company personnel do not fully understand what the new contract requires of them, they should call or write the Vice President for Finance.

(b) **Run-on sentences.** A run-on sentence, sometimes called a fused sentence, is made up of two or more sentences without punctuation to separate them. The term sometimes includes pairs of independent clauses separated by only a comma, although these are usually called comma faults or comma splices. Run-on sentences can be corrected by (1) making two sentences, (2) joining the two clauses with a semicolon (if they are closely related and of equal weight), (3) joining the two clauses with a comma and a coordinating conjunction, or (4) subordinating one clause to the other.

REVISE   The training division will offer three new courses interested employees should sign up by Wednesday. (run-on sentence)

OR   The training division will offer three new courses, interested employees should sign up by Wednesday. (comma fault or comma splice)

TO   The training division will offer three new courses. Interested employees should sign up by Wednesday. (period)

OR   The training division will offer three new courses; interested employees should sign up by Wednesday. (semicolon)

OR   The training division will offer three new courses, so interested employees should sign up by Wednesday. (comma plus coordinating conjunction)

OR   Since the training division will offer three new courses, interested employees should sign up by Wednesday. (one clause subordinated to the other)

(c) **Sentence fragments and minor sentences.** A sentence that is missing an essential part (subject or predicate) is called a sentence fragment.

EXAMPLES   She changed jobs. (sentence)

And earned more money. (fragment; it lacks a subject)

But having a subject and a predicate does not automatically turn a clause into a sentence. The clause must also make an independent statement. "I work" is a sentence; "If I work" is a fragment because the subordinating conjunction *if* makes the statement a dependent clause.

Sentence fragments are often introduced by relative pronouns (*who, whom, whose, which, that*) or subordinating conjunctions (such as *after, although, because, if, when,* and *while*). When you use these introductory words, you can anticipate combining the dependent clause that follows with a main clause to form a complete sentence.

REVISE   The accounting department received several new calculators. After its order was processed.

TO   The accounting department received several new calculators after its order was processed.

A sentence must contain a main or finite verb; verbals (gerunds, participles, and infinitives) will not do the job. The following examples are sentence fragments because they lack main verbs. Their verbals (*working, to skip, expecting*) cannot function as finite verbs.

EXAMPLES   *Working* overtime every night during tax season.

To skip the meeting.

The manager *expecting* to place an order.

Fragments may reflect incomplete or confused thinking. The most common type of fragment is the careless addition of an afterthought.

REVISE   These are the branch tellers. *A dedicated group of employees.*

TO   These are the branch tellers, a dedicated group of employees.

The following examples illustrate common types of sentence fragments.

REVISE   Health insurance rates have gone up. *Because medical expenses have increased.* (adverbial clause)

TO   Health insurance rates have gone up because medical expenses have increased.

REVISE   The engineers tested the model. *Outside the laboratory.* (prepositional phrase)

TO   The engineers tested the model outside the laboratory.

REVISE   *Having finished the job.* We submitted our bill. (participial phrase)

TO   Having finished the job, we submitted our bill.

REVISE   We met with Jim Rodgers. *Former head of the sales division.* (appositive)

TO   We met with Jim Rodgers, former head of the sales division.

REVISE   We have one major goal this month. *To increase the strength of the alloy without reducing its flexibility.* (infinitive phrase in apposition with *goal*)

TO   We have one major goal this month: to increase the stength of the alloy without reducing its flexibility.

Occasionally, a writer intentionally uses an incomplete sentence. This kind of deliberate fragment, called a *minor sentence,* makes sense in its context because the missing element is clearly implied by the preceding sentence or is clearly understood without being stated.

EXAMPLES   In view of these facts, is new equipment really necessary? *Or economical?*

You can use the one-minute long-distance rates any time between eleven at night and eight in the morning. *Any night of the week.*

Minor sentences are elliptical expressions that are equivalent to complete sentences because the missing words are obvious to a reader from the context.

EXAMPLES   Why not?

How much?

Ten dollars.

At last!

This way, please.

So much for that idea.

Although they are common in advertising copy and fictional dialogue, minor sentences are not normally appropriate to business or technical writing.

(d) Dangling and misplaced modifiers. A *dangling modifier* is a word or phrase that has no clear word or subject to modify. Most dangling modifiers are phrases with verbals (gerunds, participles, or infinitives). Correct this problem by adding the appropriate noun or pronoun for the phrase to modify or by making the phrase into a clause.

REVISE   After finishing the negotiations, dinner was relaxing.

TO   After finishing the negotiations, we relaxed at dinner.

REVISE   Entering the gate, the administration building is visible.

TO   As you enter the gate, the administration building is visible.

A *misplaced modifier* refers, or appears to refer, to the wrong word or phrase. The misplaced element can be a word, a phrase, or a clause.

REVISE   Our copier was used to duplicate materials for other departments that needed to be reduced.

TO   Our copier was used to duplicate materials that needed to be reduced for other departments.

You can avoid this problem by placing modifiers as close as possible to the words they modify. Position each modifier carefully so that it says what you mean.

REVISE   We *just* bought the property for expansion.

TO   We bought *just* the property for expansion.

A *squinting modifier* is ambiguous because it is located between two sentence elements and might refer to either one. To correct the problem, move the modifier or revise the sentence.

REVISE	The union agreed during the next week to return to work.
TO	During the next week, the union agreed to return to work.
OR	The union agreed to return to work during the next week.

Occasionally, a subject and verb are omitted from a dependent clause; the result is known as an *elliptical clause*. If the omitted subject of the elliptical clause is not the same as the subject of the main clause, the construction dangles. Simply adding the subject and verb to the elliptical clause solves the problem. (Or you can rework the whole sentence.)

REVISE	When ten years old, his father started the company. (Could his father have started the company at age ten?)
TO	When *Bill Krebs was* ten years old, his father started the company.
OR	Bill Krebs was ten years old when his father started the company.

(e) **Other sentence faults.** The assertion made by the predicate of a sentence about its subject must be logical.

REVISE	Mr. Wilson's *job* is a salesman.
TO	*Mr. Wilson* is a salesman.
REVISE	Jim's *height* is six feet tall.
TO	*Jim* is six feet tall.

Do not omit a required verb.

REVISE	The floor is swept and the lights out.
TO	The floor is swept, and the lights *are* out.
REVISE	I never have and probably never will write the annual report.
TO	I never have *written* and probably never will write the annual report.

Do not omit a subject.

REVISE	Although he regarded price-fixing as wrong, he engaged in it until abolished by law.
TO	Although he regarded price-fixing as wrong, he engaged in it until *it was* abolished by law.

Avoid compound sentences containing clauses that have little or no logical relationship to each other.

REVISE	My department is responsible for all company publications, and the staff includes twenty writers, three artists, and four typists.

TO   My department is responsible for all company publications. The staff includes twenty writers, three artists, and four typists.

4.3.5 Effective Sentences

Effective sentences guide the reader and engage his or her attention. They can alert a reader to ideas weighted equally (through parallel structure) or differently (through subordination). In addition, carefully constructed and revised sentences clarify ideas for the reader. Besides highlighting especially significant information, sentences can be varied in length, pattern, and style to avoid boring the reader. Most writers wait until they are revising to concentrate on effective sentences. Then, they can try to eliminate confusion and monotony by building clear, precise, and varied sentences.

(a) **Sentence parallelism.** Express coordinate ideas in similar form. The very construction of a sentence with parallel elements helps the reader to grasp the similarity of its parts.

EXAMPLE   Similarly, atoms come and go in a molecule, but the molecule remains; molecules come and to in a cell, but the cell remains; cells come and go in a body, but the body remains; persons come and go in an organization, but the organization remains.[2]

(b) **Emphatic sentences.** Subordinate your minor ideas to emphasize your more important ideas.

REVISE   We had all arrived, and we began the meeting early.

TO   Since we had all arrived, we began the meeting early.

The most emphatic positions in a sentence are the beginning and the end. Do not waste these spots by burying the main idea in the middle of the sentence between less important points or by tacking on phrases and clauses almost as afterthoughts. For example, consider the following original and revised versions of a statement written for a company's annual report to its stockholders.

REVISE   Sales declined by 3 percent in 1983, but nevertheless the company had the most profitable year in its history, thanks to cost savings that resulted from design improvements in several of our major products; and we expect

[2] Kenneth Boulding, *Beyond Economics* (Ann Arbor: University of Michigan Press, 1968), p. 131.

1984 to be even better, since further design improvements are being made. (The sentence begins with the bad news, buries the good news, and trails off at the end.)

TO   Cost savings from design improvements in several major products not only offset a 3 percent sales decline but made 1983 the most profitable year in the company's history. Further design improvements now in progress promise to make 1984 even more profitable. (The sentence beginnings emphasize *cost savings* and *design improvements;* the ends stress profits.)

Reversing the normal word order is also used to achieve emphasis, though this tactic should not be overdone.

REVISE   I will never agree to that.

TO   *That* I will never agree to.

OR   *Never* will I agree to that.

(c) **Clear sentences.** Uncomplicated sentences are most effective for stating complex ideas. If readers must unravel a complicated sentence in addition to a complex idea, they are likely to become confused.

REVISE   Burning fuel and air in the production chamber causes an expansion of the gases formed by combustion, which in turn pushes the piston down in its cylinder so that the crankshaft rotates and turns the flywheel, which then transmits to the clutch the power developed by the engine.

TO   Burning fuel and air in the production chamber causes an expansion of the gases formed by combustion. These gases push the piston down in its cylinder so that the crankshaft rotates. Then the flywheel on the end of the crankshaft transmits to the clutch the power developed by the engine.

Just as simpler sentences can make complex ideas easier to understand, so more complex sentences can make groups of simple ideas easier to read.

REVISE   The industrial park was designed carefully. A team of architects and landscape designers planned it. It has become a local landmark.

TO   The carefully designed industrial park, planned by a team of architects and landscape designers, has become a local landmark.

(d) Sentence length. Variations in sentence length make writing more interesting to the reader because many sentences of the same length become monotonous.

Short sentences often can be combined effectively by converting verbs to adjectives.

REVISE The steeplejack was *exhausted*. He collapsed on the scaffolding.

TO The *exhausted* steeplejack collapsed on the scaffolding.

Sentences that string together short, independent clauses may be just as tedious as a series of short sentences. Either connect such clauses with subordinating connectives, thereby making some of them dependent, or turn some clauses into separate sentences.

REVISE This river is 60 miles long, *and* it averages 50 yards in width, *and* its depth averages 8 feet.

TO This river, *which* is 60 miles long and averages 50 yards in width, has an average depth of 8 feet.

OR This river is 60 miles long. It averages 50 yards in width and 8 feet in depth.

Although too many short sentences make your writing sound choppy and immature, a short sentence can be effective at the end of a passage of long ones.

EXAMPLE I believe that man is about to learn that the most practical life is the moral life and that the moral life is the only road to survival. He is beginning to learn that he will either share part of his material wealth or lose all of it; that he will respect and learn to live with other political ideologies if he wants civilization to go on. This is the kind of argument that man's actual experience equips him to understand and accept. This is the low road to morality. *There is no other.*[3]

In general, short sentences are good for emphatic statements. Long sentences are good for detailed explanations and support. Nothing is wrong with a long sentence, or even with a complicated one, as long as its meaning is clear and direct. A sentence that is either noticeably short or noticeably long can be used to good effect because its length will draw the reader's attention. When varied for emphasis or contrast, sentence length becomes an element of style.

[3] Saul Alinsky, *Rules for Radicals* (New York: Random House, 1971), p. 25.

(e) **Word order.** When successive sentences all begin in exactly the same way, the result is likely to be monotonous. You can make your sentences more interesting by occasionally starting with a modifying word, phrase, or clause.

EXAMPLES *Fatigued,* the project director slumped into a chair. (adjective)

Lately, our division has been very productive. (adverb)

Smiling, he extended his hand to the irate customer. (participle)

To learn, you must observe and ask questions. (infinitive)

Work having already begun, there was little we could do. (absolute construction)

In the morning, we will finish the report. (prepositional phrase)

Following the instructions in the manual, she located and repaired the faulty parts. (participial phrase)

To reach the top job, she introduced constructive alternatives to unsuccessful policies. (infinitive phrase)

Because we now know the results of the survey, we may proceed with certainty. (adverb clause)

Overdoing this technique can also be monotonous; use it with moderation.

Be careful in your sentences to avoid confusing separations of subjects and verbs, prepositions and objects, and the parts of verb phrases. Your reader expects the usual patterns and reads more quickly and easily when they are clear.

REVISE The manager worked closely with, despite personality differences, the head engineer. (preposition and object separated)

TO Despite personality differences, the manager worked closely with the head engineer.

This is not to say, however, that subject and verb never should be separated by a modifying phrase or clause.

EXAMPLE John Stoddard, who founded the firm in 1943, is still an active partner.

Vary the positions of modifiers in your sentences to achieve variety as well as different emphases or meanings. The following examples illustrate four different ways in which the same sentence could be written by varying the position of its modifiers.

REVISE   Gently, with the square end up, slip the blasting cap down over the time fuse.

TO   With the square end up, gently slip the blasting cap down over the time fuse.

OR   With the square end up, slip the blasting cap gently down over the time fuse.

OR   With the square end up, slip the blasting cap down over the time fuse gently.

(f) Loose and periodic sentences. A loose sentence makes its major point at the beginning and then adds subordinate phrases and clauses that develop the major point. You express yourself most naturally and easily in this pattern. A loose sentence could seem to end at one or more points before it actually ends, as the periods in parentheses illustrate in the following example.

EXAMPLE   It went up (.), a great ball of fire about a mile in diameter(.), an elemental force freed from its bonds(.) after being chained for billions of years.

A compound sentence is generally classed as loose since it could end after its first independent clause.

EXAMPLE   Copernicus is frequently called the first modern astronomer, since he was the first to develop a complete astronomical system based on the motion of the earth.

Complex sentences are loose if their subordinate clauses follow their main clauses.

EXAMPLE   The installation will not be completed on schedule(.) because heavy spring rains delayed construction.

A periodic sentence delays its main idea until the end by presenting subordinate ideas or modifiers first. Skillfully handled, a periodic sentence lends force, or emphasis, to the main point by arousing the reader's anticipation and then presenting the main point as a climax.

EXAMPLE   During the last decade or so, the attitude of the American citizen toward automation has undergone a profound change.

Do not use periodic sentences too frequently, however, for overuse may irritate a reader who tires of waiting for your point. Likewise, avoid the sing-song monotony of a long series of loose sentences, particularly a series containing coordinate clauses joined by conjunctions. Instead, experiment in your writing, especially during revision, with shifts from loose sentences to periodic sentences.

4.4 PARAGRAPHS

A paragraph is a group of sentences that supports and develops a single idea. Like an essay in miniature, it expands upon the central idea stated in its topic sentence (*italicized* below).

> *The arithmetic of searching for oil is stark.* For all his scientific methods of detection, the only way the oilman can actually know for sure that there is oil in the ground is to drill a well. The average cost of drilling an oil well is over $100,000, and drilling a single well may cost over $1,000,000! And once the well is drilled, the odds against its containing any oil at all are 8 to 1![4]

Paragraphs perform three essential functions: (1) they develop the central ideas stated in their topic sentences; (2) they break material into logical units; and (3) they create physical breaks on the page, which visually assist the reader.

4.4.1 Topic Sentences

A topic sentence states the central idea of a paragraph; the rest of the paragraph then supports and develops that statement with pertinent details.

The topic sentence is most often the first sentence of the paragraph. It is effective in this position because it lets the reader know immediately what subject the paragraph will develop.

> *The fundamental conception of statistics is that of an infinitely large series of measurements, or population.* Since all observable data is subject to influence by uncontrollable and variable change factors, the values recorded in a series of measurements exhibit corresponding variations. If the mean value is calculated the individual values will be seen to be more or less closely distributed around it. Since the chance factors operate equally in a positive or negative fashion, the distribution is symmetrical. The larger the number of measurements the closer will mean value approach the "true" value of the measured object. Only with an infinite number of measurements, however, will it be identical with the "true" value.[5]

On rare occasions, the topic sentence logically falls in the middle of a paragraph.

---

[4] *The Baker World,* Baker Oil Tools, Inc.

[5] *Documenta Geigy,* 5th ed. (Ardsley, N.Y.: Geigy Pharmaceuticals, 1956), p. 31.

It is perhaps natural that psychologists should awaken only slowly to the possibility that behavioral processes may be directly observed, or that they should only gradually put the older statistical and theoretical techniques in their proper perspective. But it is time to insist that science does not progress by carefully designed steps called "experiments," each of which has a well-defined beginning and end. *Science is a continuous and often a disorderly and accidental process.* We shall not do the young psychologist any favor if we agree to reconstruct our practices to fit the pattern demanded by current scientific methodology. What the statistician means by the design of experiments is design which yields the kind of data to which *his* techniques are applicable. He does not mean the behavior of the scientist in his laboratory devising research for his own immediate and possibly inscrutable purposes.[6]

Although the topic sentence is usually most effective early in the paragraph, a paragraph can lead up to the topic sentence to achieve emphasis. When a topic sentence ends a paragraph, it also can serve as a summary or conclusion, based on the details that were designed to lead up to it.

Energy does far more than simply make our daily lives more comfortable and convenient. Suppose you wanted to stop—and re-verse—the economic progress of this nation. What would be the surest and quickest way to do it? Find a way to cut off the nation's oil resources! Industrial plants would shut down; public utilities would stand idle; all forms of transportation would halt. The country would be paralyzed, and our economy would plummet into the abyss of national economic ruin. *Our economy, in short, is energy-based.*[7]

Because several paragraphs are sometimes necessary to develop different aspects of an idea, not all paragraphs have topic sentences. In this situation, transitions between paragraphs are especially important so the reader knows that the same idea is being developed through several paragraphs.

To conserve valuable memory space, a large portion of the software package remains on disk; only the most frequently used portion resides in internal memory all of the time. The disk-resident software is orga-nized into small modules that are called into memory as needed to perform specific functions.

Transition *The disk-resident portion* of the operating system contains rou-tines that are used less frequently in system operation, such as periph-

[6] B. F. Skinner, "A Case History in Scientific Method," *American Psychologist* 2 (May 1956), p. 232.

[7] *The Baker World,* Baker Oil Tools, Inc.

eral-related software routines that are used for correcting errors encountered on the various units, and the log and display routines that record unusual operating conditions in the system log. The disk-resident portion of the operating system also contains Monitor, the software program that supervised the loading of utility routines and the user's programs.

Transition   *The memory-resident portion* of the operating system maintains strict control of processing. It consists of routines, subroutines, lists, and tables that are used to perform common program functions, such as processing input/output operations, calling other software routines from disk as needed, and processing errors.[8]

In this example, the idea expressed in the topic sentence is developed in three paragraphs, rather than one, so that the reader can more easily assimilate the two separate parts of the main idea.

4.4.2   Paragraph Coherence and Unity

A good paragraph has unity and coherence. Unity means singleness of purpose, based on a topic sentence that states the central idea of the paragraph. When every sentence in the paragraph contributes to the central idea, the paragraph has unity. Coherence means being logically consistent throughout the paragraph so that all parts naturally connect with one another. Coherence is advanced by carefully chosen transitional words that tie together ideas as they are developed. In the following paragraph, the topic sentence and the transitions are italicized.

> *Any company which operates internationally today faces a host of difficulties.* Inflation is worldwide. Most countries are struggling with *other* economic problems *as well. In addition,* there are many monetary uncertainties and growing economic nationalism directed against multinational companies. *Yet* there is ample business available in most developed countries if you have the right products, services, and marketing organization. To maintain the growth NCR has achieved overseas, we recently restructured our international operations into four major trading areas. *This* will improve the services and support which the Corporation can provide to its subsidiaries around the world. *At the same time* it established firm management control, insuring consistent policies around the world. *So* you might say the problems of doing business abroad will be more difficult this year but we are better organized to meet those problems.[9]

[8] *NCR Century Operating Systems Manual,* NCR Corporation.
[9] *1974 Annual Report,* NCR Corporation.

A good paragraph often uses details from the preceding paragraph, thereby preserving and advancing the thought being developed. Appropriate conjunctions and the repetition of key words and phrases can help to provide unity and coherence among, as well as within, paragraphs.

Six high power thyristors connected in a three-phase bridge configuration form the basic armature module. When necessary, the modules are paralleled to meet higher power requirements. The basic armature module is constructed as a convenient *pull-out tray*. All *armature trays* are interchangeable.

For optimum shovel performance it is also desirable to use thyristors in the control of motor fields. These smaller thyristors are also arranged in a *pull-out tray* arrangement called a *field tray*.

Should a fault ever occur in a tray, an *indicator tray* is provided, which by means of pilot lights indicates which tray is the source of the trouble. Through the *pull-out* tray concept, the mine electrician can quickly replace the faulty tray and need not troubleshoot.[10]

5 PUNCTUATION

Punctuation is a system of symbols that help the reader to understand the structural relationships within (and the intention of) a sentence. Marks of punctuation may link, separate, enclose, terminate, classify, and indicate omissions from sentences. Most of the thirteen punctuation marks can perform more than one function. The use of punctuation is determined by grammatical conventions and by the writer's intention. Misuse of punctuation can cause your reader to misunderstand your meaning. The following are the thirteen marks of punctuation.

apostrophe	'
brackets	[ ]
colon	:
comma	,
dash	—
exclamation mark	!
hyphen	-
parentheses	( )

[10] Harnischfeger Corporation.

period	. (including ellipses and leaders)
question mark	?
quotation marks	" "(including ditto marks)
semicolon	;
slash	/

5.1 COMMAS

The comma is used more often than any other mark of punctuation because it has such a wide variety of uses: it can link, enclose, separate, and show omissions. Effective use of the comma depends on your understanding of how ideas fit together. Used with care, the comma can add clarity and emphasis to your writing; used carelessly, it can cause confusion.

5.1.1 To Link

Coordinating conjunctions (*and, but, for, or, so, nor, yet*) require a comma immediately preceding them when they are used to connect independent clauses.

EXAMPLE   Human beings have always prided themselves on their unique capacity to create and manipulate symbols, but today computers are manipulating symbols.

Exceptions to this rule sometimes occur when the two independent clauses are short and each has a single subject and single predicate. However, even in such cases, a comma is preferred.

EXAMPLE   The cable snapped and the power failed.

BETTER   The cable snapped, and the power failed.

5.1.2 To Enclose

(a) **Nonrestrictive and parenthetical elements.**   Commas are used to enclose nonrestrictive and parenthetical sentence elements. Nonrestrictive elements provide additional, nonessential information about the things they modify; parenthetical elements also insert extra information into the sentence. Each is set off by commas to show its loose relationship with the rest of the sentence.

EXAMPLES   Our new Detroit factory, *which began operations last month,* should add 25 percent to total output. (nonrestrictive clause)

We can, *of course,* expect their lawyer to call us. (parenthetical element)

Similarly, commas enclose nonrestrictive participial phrases.

EXAMPLE   The lathe operator, *working quickly and efficiently,* finished early.

In contrast, restrictive elements—as their name implies—restrict the meaning of the words to which they apply and cannot be set off with commas.

RESTRICTIVE   The boy *in the front row* is six years old.

NON-   The boy, *who is sitting in the front row,* is six years old.
RESTRICTIVE

In the first sentence, *in the front row* is essential to the sentence: the phrase identifies the boy. In the second sentence, the nonrestrictive relative clause *who is sitting in the front row* is incidental: the main idea of the sentence can be communicated without it.

Phrases in apposition (which are nonrestrictive and follow and amplify an essential element) are enclosed in commas.

EXAMPLE   Our company, *the Blaylok Precision Company,* is doing well this year.

(b)   Dates.   When complete dates appear with sentences, the year is enclosed in commas.

EXAMPLE   On November 11, 1918, the Armistice went into effect.

However, when only part of a date appears, do not use commas.

EXAMPLE   In November 1918 the Armistice went into effect.

When the day of the week is included in a date, the month and the number of the day are enclosed in commas.

EXAMPLE   On Friday, November 11, 1918, the Armistice went into effect.

(c)   Direct address.   A direct address should be enclosed in commas if it appears anywhere other than at the beginning or end of a sentence.

EXAMPLE   You will note, *Mark,* that the surface of the brake shoe complies with the specifications.

5.1.3   To Separate

Commas are used to separate introductory elements from the rest of the sentence, to separate items from each other, to separate subordinate clauses from main clauses, and to separate certain elements for clarity or emphasis.

(a) **To separate introductory elements.** In general, use a comma after an introductory clause or phrase unless it is very short. This comma helps indicate to a reader where the main part of the sentence begins.

EXAMPLE   *Since many rare fossils never occur free from their matrix,* it is wise to scan every slab with a hand lens.

When long modifying phrases precede the main clause, they should always be followed by a comma.

EXAMPLE   *During the first field-performance tests last year at our Colorado proving ground,* the new motor failed to meet our expectations.

When an introductory phrase is short and closely related to the main clause, the comma may be omitted.

EXAMPLE   *In two seconds* a 20° temperature rise occurs in the test tube.

Certain types of introductory words must be followed by a comma. One such is a name used in direct address at the beginning of a sentence.

EXAMPLE   *Bill,* here is the statement you asked me to audit.

A mild introductory interjection (such as *oh, well, why, indeed, yes,* and *no*) must be followed by a comma.

EXAMPLES   *Yes,* I will make sure your request is approved.
Indeed, I will be glad to send you further information.

An introductory adverb, like *moreover* or *furthermore,* must be followed by a comma.

EXAMPLE   *Moreover,* this policy will improve our balance of payments.

Occasionally, when adverbs are closely connected to the meaning of an entire sentence, they should not be followed by a comma. (Test such sentences by reading them aloud. If you pause after the adverb, use the comma.)

EXAMPLE   *Perhaps* we can still solve the environmental problem.
Certainly we should try.

(b) **To separate items from each other.** Commas should be used to separate words in a series.

EXAMPLE   Basically, plants control the wind by *obstruction, guidance, deflection,* and *filtration.*

Phrases and clauses in coordinate series, like words, are punctuated with commas.

EXAMPLE   It is well known that plants absorb noxious gases, act as receptors of dust and dirt particles, and cleanse the air of other impurities.

Although the comma before the last item in a series is sometimes omitted, it is generally clearer to include it. The following sentence illustrates the confusion that may result from omitting the comma.

EXAMPLE   Random House, Allyn and Bacon, Doubleday and Dell are publishing companies. (Is "Doubleday and Dell" one company or two? "Random House, Allyn and Bacon, Doubleday, and Dell" removes the doubt.)

When adjectives modifying the same noun can be reversed and make sense, or when they can be separated by *and* or *or,* they should be separated by commas.

EXAMPLE   The *dull, cracked* tools needed to be repaired.

When an adjective modifies a noun phrase, no comma is required.

EXAMPLE   He was investigating the *damaged radar beacon system.* (*damaged* modifies the noun phrase *radar beacon system.*)

Never separate a final adjective from its noun.

REVISE   He is a conscientious, honest, reliable, worker.
TO   He is a conscientious, honest, reliable worker.

Commas are conventionally used to separate distinct items. Use commas between the elements of an address written on the same line.

EXAMPLE   Walter James, 4119 Mill Road, Dayton, Ohio 45401

Use a comma to separate the numerical elements of a complete date. When the day is omitted, however, the comma is unnecessary. (When a date appears in a sentence, a comma also follows the year. See Section 5.1.2b.)

EXAMPLES   July 2, 1949
July 1949

Use commas to separate the elements of Arabic numbers.

EXAMPLE   1,528,200

Use a comma after the salutation of a personal letter.

EXAMPLE   Dear John,

Use commas to separate the elements of geographical names.

EXAMPLE   Toronto, Ontario, Canada

Use a comma to separate names that are reversed.

EXAMPLE   Smith, Alvin

(c) **To separate subordinate clauses.**   Use a comma between the main clause and a subordinate clause when the subordinate clause comes first.

EXAMPLE   While the test ramp was being checked a final time, the driver reviewed his checklist.

Use a comma following an independent clause that is only loosely related to the dependent clause that follows it.

EXAMPLE   The plan should be finished by July, even though I lost time because of illness.

(d) **To separate elements for clarity or emphasis.**   Two contrasting thoughts or ideas can be separated by commas for emphasis.

EXAMPLES   The project was finished on time, but not within the cost limits.

The specifications call for 100-ohm resistors, not 1,000-ohm resistors.

It was Bill, not Matt, who suggested that the names be changed.

Use a comma to separate a direct quotation from its introduction.

EXAMPLE   Morton and Lucia White said, "Men live in cities but dream of the countryside."

Do not use a comma, however, when giving an indirect quotation.

EXAMPLE   Morton and Lucia White said that men dream of the countryside even though they live in cities.

Sometimes commas are used simply to make something clear that might otherwise be confusing.

REVISE   The year after Xerox and 3M outproduced all the competition.

TO   The year after, Xerox and 3M outproduced all the competition.

If you need a comma to separate two consecutive uses of the same word, rewrite the sentence.

REVISE   The assets we had, had surprised us.

TO   We were surprised at the assets we had.

5.1.4 To Show Omissions

In certain coordinate constructions, a comma can replace a missing, but implied, sentence element.

EXAMPLE   Some were punctual; others, late. (comma replaces *were*)

5.1.5 Conventional Use with Other Punctuation

In American usage, a comma always goes inside quotation marks.

EXAMPLE   Although he called his presentation "adequate," the audience thought it was superb.

Except with abbreviations, a comma should not be used with a period, question mark, exclamation mark, or dash.

REVISE   "I have finished the project.," he said.

TO   "I have finished the project," he said. (omit the period)

REVISE   "Have you finished the project?," I asked.

TO   "Have you finished the project?" I asked. (omit the comma)

5.1.6 Comma Problems

The most frequent comma problems are the comma fault and the use of superfluous commas.

(a) **Comma faults.**   Do not attempt to join two independent clauses with only a comma; this is called a "comma fault" or "comma splice." (See also Section 4.3.4b.)

REVISE   The new medical plan was comprehensive, the union negotiator was pleased.

Such a comma fault could be corrected in several ways:

Substitute a semicolon.

TO   The new medical plan was comprehensive; the union negotiator was pleased.

Add a conjunctive adverb preceded by a semicolon and followed by a comma.

TO   The new medical plan was comprehensive; *therefore,* the union negotiator was pleased.

Add a conjunction following the comma.

TO   The new medical plan was comprehensive, *so* the union negotiator was pleased.

Create two sentences. (Be aware, however, that putting a period between two closely related and brief statements may result in two weak sentences.)

TO   The new medical plan was comprehensive. The union negotiator was pleased.

Subordinate one clause to the other.

TO   *Because* the new medical plan was comprehensive, the union negotiator was pleased.

(b) Superfluous commas. A number of common writing errors involve placing commas where they do not belong. These errors often occur because writers assume that a pause in a sentence should be indicated by a comma. It is true that commas usually signal pauses, but it is not true that pauses *necessarily* call for commas.

 Be careful not to place a comma between a subject and its verb or between a verb and its object.

REVISE The extremely wet weather throughout the country, makes spring planting difficult.

TO   The extremely wet weather throughout the country makes spring planting difficult.

REVISE The advertising department employs, four writers, two artists, and one photographer.

TO   The advertising department employs four writers, two artists, and one photographer.

 Do not use a comma between the elements of a compound subject or a compound predicate consisting of only two elements.

REVISE The chairman of the board, and the president prepared the press release.

TO	The chairman of the board and the president prepared the press release.
REVISE	The production manager revised the work schedules, and improved morale.
TO	The production manager revised the work schedules and improved morale.

Placing a comma after a coordinating conjunction (such as *and* or *but*) is an especially common error.

REVISE	We doubled our sales, and, we reduced our costs.
TO	We doubled our sales, and we reduced our costs.
REVISED	We doubled our sales, but, we still did not dominate the market.
TO	We doubled our sales, but we still did not dominate the market.

Do not place a comma before the first item or after the last item of a series.

REVISE	We are purchasing new office furniture, including, desks, chairs, and tables.
TO	We are purchasing new office furniture, including desks, chairs, and tables.

5.2 SEMICOLONS

The semicolon (;) links independent clauses or other sentence elements that are of equal weight and grammatical rank. The semicolon indicates a greater pause between clauses than a comma would, but not so great a pause as a period would.

When the independent clauses of a compound sentence are not joined by a comma and a conjunction, they are linked by a semicolon.

EXAMPLE	No one applied for the position; the job was too difficult.

Make sure, however, that the relationship between the two statements is so clear that a reader will understand why they are linked without further explanation. Often, such clauses balance or contrast with each other.

EXAMPLE	Our last supervisor allowed only one long break each afternoon; our new supervisor allows two short ones.

Use a semicolon between two main clauses connected by a coordinating conjunction (*and, but, for, or, nor, yet*) if the clauses are long and contain other punctuation.

EXAMPLE   In most cases these individuals are corporate executives, bankers, Wall Street lawyers; but they do not, as the economic determinists seem to believe, simply push the button of their economic power to affect fields remote from economics.[11]

A semicolon should be used before conjunctive adverbs (such as *therefore, moreover, consequently, furthermore, indeed, in fact, however*) that connect independent clauses.

EXAMPLE   I won't finish today; moreover, I doubt that I will finish this week.

The semicolon in this example shows that *moreover* belongs to the second clause.

Do not use a semicolon between a dependent clause and its main clause. Remember that elements joined by semicolons must be of equal grammatical rank or weight.

REVISE   No one applied for the position; even though it was heavily advertised.

TO   No one applied for the position, even though it was heavily advertised.

A semicolon may also be used to separate items in a series when they contain commas within them.

EXAMPLE   Among those present were John Howard, president of the Omega Paper Company; Carol Martin, president of Alpha Corporation; and Larry Stanley, president of Stanley Papers.

5.3 COLONS

The colon (:) is a mark of anticipation and introduction that alerts the reader to the close connection between the first statement and the one following. A colon may be used to connect a clause, word, or phrase to the list or series that follows it.

EXAMPLE   We carry three brands of watches: Timex, Bulova, and Omega.

A colon may be used to introduce a list.

---

[11] Robert Lubar, "The Prime Movers," *Fortune* (February 1960), p. 98.

EXAMPLE   The following corporations manufacture computers:
Control Data Corporation
NCR Corporation
Burroughs

Do not, however, place a colon between a verb and its objects.

REVISE   The three fluids for cleaning pipettes are: water, alcohol, and acetone.

TO   The three fluids for cleaning pipettes are water, alcohol, and acetone.

Do not use a colon between a preposition and its object.

REVISE   I would like to be transferred to: Tucson, Boston, or Miami.

TO   I would like to be transferred to Tucson, Boston, or Miami.

A colon may be used to link one statement to another that develops, explains, amplifies, or illustrates the first. A colon can be used in this way to link two independent clauses.

EXAMPLE   Any large organization must confront two separate, though related, information problems: it must maintain an effective internal communication system, and it must maintain an effective external communication system.

Occasionally, a colon may be used to link an appositive phrase to its related statement if special emphasis is needed.

EXAMPLE   Only one thing will satisfy Mr. Sturgess: our finished report.

Colons are used to link numbers in Biblical references and time designations.

EXAMPLES   Genesis 10:16 (refers to chapter 10, verse 16)
9:30 A.M.

In a ratio, the colon indicates the proportion of one amount to another. (The colon replaces *to*.)

EXAMPLE   The cement is mixed with the water and sand at a ratio of 7:5:14.
7:3 = 14:6

A colon follows the salutation in business letters.

EXAMPLES   Dear Ms. Jeffers:
Dear Sir:
Dear George:

The first word after a colon may be capitalized if the statement following is a complete sentence, a formal resolution or question, or a direct quotation.

EXAMPLE   This year's conference attendance was low: We did not advertise widely enough.

If a subordinate element follows the colon, however, use a lowercase letter following the colon.

EXAMPLE   There is only one way to stay within our present budget: to reduce expenditures for research and development.

5.4 PERIODS

A period (.) usually indicates the end of a declarative sentence. Periods also link (when used as leaders) and indicate omissions (when used as ellipses).

5.4.1 Uses of Periods

Although their primary function is to end declarative sentences, periods also end imperative sentences that are not emphatic enough for an exclamation mark.

EXAMPLE   Send me any information you may have on the subject.

Periods may occasionally end questions that are really polite requests and questions that assume an affirmative response.

EXAMPLE   Will you please send me the specifications.

Periods end minor sentences (deliberate sentence fragments). These sentences are common in advertising but are rarely appropriate to business or technical writing.

EXAMPLE   Bell and Howell's new Double-Feature Cassette Projector will change your mind about home movies. *Because if you can press a button, now you can show movies. Instantly. Easily.*

Do not use a period after a declarative sentence that is quoted within another sentence.

REVISE   "The project has every chance of success." she stated.

TO   "The project has every chance of success," she stated.

A period, in American usage, is placed inside quotation marks.

EXAMPLES   He liked to think of himself as a "tycoon."

He stated clearly, "My vote is yes."

Use periods after initials in names.

EXAMPLES   W. T. Grant, J. P. Morgan

Use periods as decimal points with numbers.

EXAMPLES   109.2, $540.26, 6.9%

Use periods to indicate abbreviations.

EXAMPLES   Ms., Dr., Inc.

Use periods following the numbers in numbered lists.

EXAMPLE   1.
2.
3.

5.4.2   Periods as Ellipses

When you omit words from quoted material, use a series of three spaced periods—called ellipsis marks—to indicate the omission. Such an omission must not change the essential meaning of the passage.

EXAMPLE   "Technical material distributed for promotional use is sometimes charged for, particularly in high-volume distribution to educational institutions, although prices for these publications are not uniformly based on the costs of developing them." (without omission)

"Technical material distributed for promotional use is sometimes charged for . . . although prices for these publications are not uniformly based on the costs of developing them." (with omission)

When introducing a quotation that begins in the middle of a sentence rather than at the beginning, you do not need ellipsis marks; the lowercase letter with which you begin the quotation already indicates an omission.

EXAMPLE   "When the programmer has determined a system of runs, he must create a systems flowchart to trace the data flow through the system." (without omission)

The booklet states that the programmer "must create a systems flowchart to trace the data flow through the system." (with omission)

If there is an omission following the end of a sentence, retain the period at the end of the sentence and add the three ellipsis marks to show the omission.

EXAMPLES "During the year, every department participated in the development of a centralized computer system. The basic plan was to use the computer to reduce costs. At the beginning of the year, each department received a booklet explaining the purpose of the system." (without omission)

"During the year, every department participated in the development of a centralized computer system. . . . At the beginning of the year, each department received a booklet explaining the purpose of the system." (with omission)

5.4.3 Periods as Leaders

When spaced periods are used in a table to connect one item to another, they are called leaders. The purpose of leaders is to help the reader align the data.

EXAMPLE

Weight		Pressure
150 lbs.	. . . .	1.7 psi
175 lbs.	. . . .	2.8 psi
200 lbs.	. . . .	3.9 psi

5.4.4 Period Fault

The incorrect use of a period is sometimes called a period fault. When a period is inserted prematurely, the result is a sentence fragment. (See Section 4.3.4c.)

REVISE After a long day at the office during which we finished the report. We left hurriedly for home.

TO After a long day at the office during which we finished the report, we left hurriedly for home.

When a period is left out, the result is an incorrect fused (or run-on) sentence.

REVISE The work plan showed the utility lines they might interfere with construction.

TO The work plan showed the utility lines. They might interfere with construction.

5.5 QUESTION MARKS

The question mark (?) indicates questions. Use a question mark to end a sentence that is a direct question.

EXAMPLE   Where did you put the specifications?

Use a question mark to end any statement with an interrogative meaning (a statement that is declarative in form but asks a question).

EXAMPLE   The report is finished?

Use a question mark to end an interrogative clause within a declarative sentence.

EXAMPLE   It was not until July (or was it August?) that we submitted the report.

When used with quotations, the question mark may indicate whether the writer who is doing the quoting or the person being quoted is asking the question. When the writer doing the quoting asks the question, the question mark is outside the quotation marks.

EXAMPLE   Did she say, "I don't think the project should continue"?

On the other hand, if the quotation itself is a question, the question mark goes inside the quotation marks.

EXAMPLE   She asked, "When will we go?"

If the writer doing the quoting and the person being quoted both ask questions, use a single question mark inside the quotation marks.

EXAMPLE   Did she ask, "Will you go in my place?"

Question marks may follow each item in a series within an interrogative sentence.

EXAMPLE   Do you remember the date of the contract? its terms? whether you signed it?

A question mark should never be used at the end of an indirect question.

REVISE   He asked me whether sales had increased this year?
TO   He asked me whether sales had increased this year.

When a directive or command is phrased as a question, a question mark usually is not used, but a request (to a customer or a superior, for instance) would almost always require a question mark.

EXAMPLES Will you please make sure that the machinery is operational by August 15. (directive)

Will you please telephone me collect if your entire shipment does not arrive by June 10? (request)

5.6 EXCLAMATION MARKS

The exclamation mark (!) indicates an expression of strong feeling. It can signal surprise, fear, indignation, or excitement but should not be used for trivial emotions or mild surprise. Exclamation marks cannot make an argument more convincing, lend force to a weak statement, or call attention to an intended irony—no matter how many are stacked like fence posts at the end of a sentence.

The most common use of an exclamation mark is after an interjection, phrase, clause, or sentence to indicate strong emotion.

EXAMPLES Ouch! Oh! Stop! Hurry!

The subject of this meeting—note it well!—is our budget deficit.

The gas line is leaking! Clear the building!

When used with quotation marks, the exclamation mark goes outside unless what is quoted is an exclamation.

EXAMPLE The boss yelled, "Get in here!" Then Ben said, "No, sir"! (Ben's statement was not emphatic; the writer is highlighting the unusual nature of his negative reply)

5.7 PARENTHESES

Parentheses ( ) are used to enclose words, phrases, or sentences. Parentheses can suggest intimacy, implying that something is shared between the writer and the reader. Parentheses deemphasize (or play down) an inserted element. The material within parentheses can clarify a statement without changing its meaning. Such information may not be essential to a sentence, but it may be interesting or helpful to some readers.

EXAMPLE Aluminum is extracted from its ore (called bauxite) in three stages.

Parenthetical material pertains to the word or phrase immediately preceding it.

EXAMPLE   The development of IBM (International Business Machines) is an American success story.

Parentheses may be used to enclose the figures or letters that mark items in a sequence or list. When they appear within a sentence, enclose the figures or letters with two parentheses rather than only one parenthesis.

EXAMPLE   The following sections deal with (1) preparation, (2) research, (3) organization, (4) writing, and (5) revision.

Parenthetical material does not change the punctuation of a sentence. A comma following a parenthetical word, phrase, or clause appears outside the closing parenthesis.

EXAMPLE   These oxygen-rich chemicals, including potassium permanganate ($KMnO_4$) and potassium chromate ($KCrO_4$), were oxidizing agents.

If a parenthesis closes a sentence, the ending punctuation appears after the parenthesis. When a complete sentence within parentheses stands independently, however, the ending punctuation goes inside the final parenthesis.

EXAMPLES   The institute was founded by Harry Denman (1902–1972).

The project director outlined the challenges facing her staff. (This was her third report to the board.)

Use parentheses with care because they are easily overused. Avoid using parentheses where other marks of punctuation are more appropriate.

5.8   HYPHENS

The hyphen (-) functions primarily as a spelling device. The most common use of the hyphen is to join compound words. Check your dictionary if you are uncertain about whether to hyphenate a word.

EXAMPLES   able-bodied, self-contained, carry-all, brother-in-law

A hyphen is used to form compound numbers and fractions when they are written out.

EXAMPLES   twenty-one, one-fifth

Two-word and three-word unit modifiers that express a single thought are frequently hyphenated when they precede a noun (a *clear-cut* decision). If each of the words could modify the noun without the aid of the other modifying word or words, however, do not use a hyphen (a *new digital* computer—no hyphen). If the first word is an adverb ending in *-ly,* do not use a hyphen (*hardly* used, *badly* needed). Finally, do not hyphenate such modifying phrases when they follow the nouns they modify.

EXAMPLES   Our office equipment is *out of date.*

Our *out-of-date* office equipment will be replaced next month.

A hyphen is always used as part of a letter or number modifier.

EXAMPLES   15-cent stamp, 9-inch ruler, H-bomb, T-square

When each item in a series of unit modifiers has the same term following the hyphen, this term need not be repeated throughout the series. For smoothness and brevity, add the term only to the last item in the sequence.

REVISE   The third-floor, fourth-floor, and fifth-floor offices have been painted.

TO   The third-, fourth-, and fifth-floor offices have been painted.

When a prefix precedes a proper noun, use a hyphen to connect the two.

EXAMPLES   pre-Sputnik, anti-Stalinist, post-Newtonian

A hyphen may (but does not have to) be used when the prefix ends and the root word begins with the same vowel. When the repeated vowel is *i,* a hyphen is almost always used.

EXAMPLES   re-elect, re-enter, anti-inflationary

A hyphen is used when ex- means "former."

EXAMPLES   ex-partners, ex-wife

The suffix *-elect* is connected to the word it follows with a hyphen.

EXAMPLES   president-elect, commissioner-elect

Hyphens identify prefixes, suffixes, or syllables written as such.

EXAMPLE   *Re-, -ism,* and *ex-* are word parts that cause spelling problems.

Hyphens should be used between letters showing how a word is spelled (or misspelled).

EXAMPLE   In his letter, he spelled "believed" b-e-l-e-i-v-e-d.

To avoid confusion, some words and modifiers should always be hyphenated. *Re-cover* does not mean the same thing as *recover,* for example; the same is true of *re-sent* and *resent, re-form* and *reform, re-sign* and *resign.*

A hyphen can stand for *to* or *through* between letters, numbers, and locations.

EXAMPLES   pp. 44-46

The Detroit-Toledo Expressway

A-L and M-Z

Finally, hyphens are used to divide words at the ends of typed or printed lines. Words are divided on the basis of their syllable breaks, which can be determined by consulting a dictionary. If you cannot check a word in a dictionary, pronounce the word to test whether each section is pronounceable. Never divide a word so near the end that only one or two letters remain to begin your next typed line. If a word is spelled with a hyphen, divide it only at the hyphen break unless this division would confuse the reader. In general, unless the length of your typed line will appear awkward, avoid dividing words.

5.9 QUOTATION MARKS

Quotation marks (" ") are used to enclose direct repetition of spoken or written words. Under normal circumstances, they should not be used to show emphasis. Enclose in quotation marks anything that is quoted word for word (direct quotation) from speech.

EXAMPLE   She said clearly, "I want the progress report by three o'clock."

Do not enclose indirect quotations—usually introduced by *that*—in quotation marks. Indirect quotations paraphrase a speaker's words or ideas.

EXAMPLE   She said that she wanted the progress report by three o'clock.

Handle quotations from written material the same way: place direct quotations within quotation marks, but not indirect quotations.

EXAMPLES   The report stated, "During the last five years in Florida, our franchise has grown from 28 to 157 locations."

The report indicated that our franchise now has 157 locations in Florida.

When a quotation is longer than four typed lines, indent each line ten spaces from the left margin. Do not enclose the quotation in quotation marks.

Use single quotation marks (the apostrophe key on a typewriter) to enclose a quotation that appears within another quotation.

EXAMPLE   John said, "Jane told me that she was going to 'hang in there' until the deadline is past."

Slang, colloquial expressions, and attempts at humor, although infrequent in business and technical writing in any case, seldom rate being set off by quotation marks.

REVISE   Our first six months in the new office amounted to little more than a "shakedown cruise" for what lay ahead.

TO   Our first six months in the new office amounted to little more than a shakedown cruise for what lay ahead.

Use quotation marks to point out that particular words or technical terms are used in context for a special purpose.

EXAMPLE   What chain of events caused an "unsinkable" ship like the *Titanic* to sink on its maiden voyage?

Use quotation marks to enclose titles of short stories, articles, essays, radio and television programs, short musical works, paintings, and other art works.

EXAMPLE   Did you see the article "No-Fault Insurance and Your Motorcycle" in last Sunday's *Journal?*

Titles of books and periodicals are underlined (to be typeset in italics).

EXAMPLE   Articles in the <u>Business Education Forum</u> and <u>Scientific American</u> quoted the same passage.

Some titles, by convention, are neither set off by quotation marks nor underlined, although they are capitalized.

EXAMPLES   the Bible, the Constitution, the Gettysburg Address

Commas and periods always go inside closing quotation marks.

EXAMPLE   "We hope," said Ms. Abrams, "that the merger will be announced this week."

Semicolons and colons always go outside closing quotation marks.

EXAMPLES   He said, "I will pay the full amount"; this was a real surprise to us.

The following are his favorite "sports": eating and sleeping.

All other punctuation follows the logic of the context: if the punctuation is part of the material quoted, it goes inside the quotation marks; if the punctuation is not part of the material quoted, it goes outside the quotation marks.

Quotation marks may be used as ditto marks, instead of repeating a line of words or numbers directly beneath an identical set. In formal writing, this use is confined to tables and lists.

EXAMPLE
A is at a point equally distant from L and M.
B " " " " " " " S and T.
C " " " " " " " R and Q.

5.10 DASHES

The dash (—) is a versatile, yet limited, mark of punctuation. It is versatile because it can perform all the functions of punctuation (to link, to separate, to enclose, and to show omission). It is limited because it is an especially emphatic mark that is easily overused. Use the dash cautiously, therefore, to indicate more informality, emphasis, or abruptness than the conventional punctuation marks would show. In some situations, a dash is required; in others, a dash is a forceful substitute for other marks.

A dash can indicate a sharp turn in thought.

EXAMPLE
That is the end of the project—unless the company provides additional funds.

A dash can indicate an emphatic pause.

EXAMPLE
Consider the potential danger of a household item that contains mercury—a very toxic substance.

Sometimes, to emphasize contrast, a dash is also used with *but*.

EXAMPLE
We may have produced work more quickly—but our results have never been as impressive as these.

A dash can be used before a final summarizing statement or before repetition that has the effect of an afterthought.

EXAMPLE
It was hot near the ovens—steaming hot.

Such a thought may also complete the meaning of the sentence.

EXAMPLE   We try to speak as we write—or so we believe.

A dash can be used to set off an explanatory or appositive series.

EXAMPLE   Three of the applicants—John Evans, Mary Stevens, and Thomas Brown—seem well qualified for the job.

Dashes set off parenthetical elements more sharply and emphatically than do commas. Unlike dashes, parentheses tend to reduce the importance of what they enclose. Contrast the following sentences.

EXAMPLES   Only one person—the president—can authorize such activity.

Only one person, the president, can authorize such activity.

Only one person (the president) can authorize such activity.

Use dashes for clarity when commas appear within a parenthetical element; this avoids the confusion of too many commas.

EXAMPLE   Retinal images are patterns in the eye—made up of light and dark shapes, in addition to areas of color—but we do not see patterns; we see objects.

A dash can be used to show the omission of words or letters.

EXAMPLE   Mr. A— told me to be careful.

The first word after a dash is never capitalized unless it is a proper name. When typing, use two consecutive hyphens (--) to indicate a dash.

5.11 APOSTROPHES

The apostrophe (') is used to show possession, to mark the omission of letters, and to indicate the plural of letters.

5.11.1 Possession

An apostrophe is used with an *s* to form the possessive case of many nouns. (See Section 3.1.3b.)

EXAMPLE   A recent scientific analysis of *New York City's* atmosphere concluded that a New Yorker on the street inhaled toxic materials equivalent to 38 cigarettes a day.

Singular nouns ending in *s* may form the possessive either by an apostrophe alone or by *'s*. The latter is now preferred.

EXAMPLES   a waitress's uniform, an actress's career

a waitress' uniform, an actress' career

Use only an apostrophe with plural nouns ending in *s*.

EXAMPLES   a managers' meeting, the technicians' handbook, a motorists' rest stop

When a noun ends in multiple consecutive *s* sounds, or when the word following the possessive begins with an *s,* the possessive is often formed by adding only an apostrophe. Your ear should tell you when you are stacking up too many sibilants.

EXAMPLES   Jesus' disciples, Moses' sojourn, for goodness' sake, Euripides' plays

With word groups and compound nouns, add the *'s* to the last noun.

EXAMPLES   The chairman of the board's statement was brief.

My daughter-in-law's business has been thriving.

With a series of nouns, the last noun takes the possessive form to show joint possession.

EXAMPLE   Michelson and *Morley's* famous experiment on the velocity of light was made in 1887.

To show individual possession with a series of nouns, each noun should take the possessive form.

EXAMPLE   *Bob's* and *Susan's* promotions will be announced Friday.

The apostrophe is not used with possessive pronouns. (*It's* is a contraction of *it is,* not the possessive form of *it.*)

EXAMPLES   yours, its, his, ours, whose, theirs

In names of places and institutions, the apostrophe is usually omitted.

EXAMPLES   Harpers Ferry, Writers Book Club

5.11.2 Omission

(a) **Contractions.** An apostrophe is used to mark the omission of letters in a word. Omission of letters in a word and their replacement with an apostrophe produce a *contraction.* Contractions are most often shortened forms of the most common helping verbs. In addition, contractions can reflect negation, combining elements of the word *not* with elements of the helping verb (*don't* for *do not*, for example). Although contractions are in no sense wrong, they are less formal than the longer forms and should therefore be used with caution in writing.

(b) Abbreviated dates. An apostrophe can also stand for the first two digits of a year when these digits can be inferred from the context. This device is most common in alumni newsletters and in informal writing; it should be avoided in formal situations.

EXAMPLES   the class of '61
the crash of '29

5.11.3 Plurals

An apostrophe and an *s* may be added to show the plural of a word as a word. (The word itself is underlined or italicized.)

EXAMPLE   There were five *and's* in his first sentence.

However, if a term consists entirely of capital letters or ends with a capital letter, the apostrophe is not required to form the plural.

EXAMPLES   The university awarded seven *Ph.D.s* in engineering last year.
He had included 43 *ADDs* in his computer program.

Do not use apostrophes to indicate the plural forms of letters and numbers unless confusion would result without one.

EXAMPLES   5s, 30s, two 100s, seven I's

5.12 SLASHES

Although not always considered a mark of punctuation, the slash (/) performs punctuating functions by separating and showing omission. The slash has various names: slant line, virgule, bar, shilling sign.
    The slash is often used to separate parts of addresses in continuous writing.

EXAMPLE   The return address on the envelope was Ms. Rose Howard/62 W. Pacific Court/Claremont/California/91711.

The slash often indicates omitted words and letters.

EXAMPLES   miles/hour (for "miles per hour")

c/o (for "in care of")

w/o (for "without")

The slash separates the numerator from the denominator of a fraction.

EXAMPLES   2/3 (2 of 3 parts); 3/4 (3 of 4 parts); 27/32 (27 of 32 parts)

In informal writing, the slash is also used in dates to separate day from month and month from year.

EXAMPLE   2/28/84

The slash is sometimes used to indicate brackets when a typewriter has no bracket key.

EXAMPLE   The reports stated that "the success of the affirmative action plan at the Westchester/New York/plant should be an inspiration for the industry."

The horizontal lines for the brackets are then penned in neatly.

5.13 BRACKETS

The primary use of brackets ([ ]) is to enclose a word or words inserted by an editor or writer into a quotation from another source.

EXAMPLE   He stated, "Wheat prices will continue to rise [no doubt because of the Russian wheat purchase] until next year."

Brackets are also used to set off a parenthetical item within parentheses.

EXAMPLE   We have all been inspired by the energy and creativity of our president, Roberta Jacobs (a tradition she carries forward from her father, Frederick Jacobs [1910–1966]).

6 MECHANICS

Certain mechanical questions tend to confound the writer on the job. Such questions as whether a number should be written as a word or as a figure, how and where acronyms should be used, whether a date should be stated day-month-year or month-day-year, and many others frequently arise when you are writing a letter or a report. This section of the Writer's Guide is provided to give you the answers to those and other perplexing questions concerning the mechanics of writing on the job.

6.1 NUMBERS

6.1.1 When to Write Out Numbers

The general rule is to write numbers from zero to ten as words and numbers above ten as figures. There are, however, a number of exceptions.

Page numbers of books, as well as figure and table numbers, are expressed as figures.

EXAMPLE   Figure 4 on page 9 and Table 3 on page 7 provide pertinent information.

Units of measurement are expressed in figures.

EXAMPLES   3 miles, 45 cubic feet, 9 meters, 27 cubic centimeters, 4 picas

Numbers that begin a sentence should always be spelled out, even if they would otherwise be written as figures.

EXAMPLE   One hundred and fifty people attended the meeting.

If spelling out such a number seems awkward, rewrite the sentence so that the number does not appear at the beginning.

REVISE   Two hundred seventy-three defective products were returned last month.

TO   Last month, 273 defective products were returned.

When several numbers appear in the same sentence or paragraph, they should be expressed alike regardless of other rules and guidelines.

EXAMPLE   The company owned 150 trucks, employed 271 people, and rented 7 warehouses.

When numbers measuring different qualities appear together in the same phrase, write one as a figure and the other as a word.

REVISE   The order was for *12* 6-inch pipes.

TO   The order was for *twelve* 6-inch pipes.

Approximate numbers are normally spelled out.

EXAMPLE   More than two hundred people attended the conference.

In business or technical writing, percentages are normally given as figures.

EXAMPLE   Exactly 87% of the stockholders approved the merger.

In typed manuscripts, page numbers are written as figures, but chapter or volume numbers may appear either way.

EXAMPLES   page 37
Chapter 2 *or* Chapter Two
Volume 1 *or* Volume One

6.1.2   Dates

The year and day of the month should be written as figures. Dates are usually written in month-day-year sequence, but businesses and industrial corporations sometimes use the European and military day-month-year sequence. Note that in the latter sequence, elements are not separated by a comma.

EXAMPLES   August 24, 1983
24 August 1983

The slash form of expressing dates (8/24/83) is used in informal writing only.

6.1.3   Time

Hours and minutes are expressed as figures when A.M. or P.M. follows.

EXAMPLES   11:30 A.M., 7:30 P.M.

When not followed by A.M. or P.M., however, times should be spelled out.

EXAMPLES   four o'clock, eleven o'clock

6.1.4   Fractions

Fractions are expressed as figures when written with whole numbers.

EXAMPLES   27 1/2 inches, 4 1/4 miles

Fractions are spelled out when they are expressed independently.

EXAMPLES   one-fourth, seven-eighths

Numbers with decimals are always written as figures.

EXAMPLE   5.21 meters

6.1.5 Addresses

Numbered streets from one to ten should be spelled out except where space is at a premium.

EXAMPLE   East Tenth Street

Building numbers are written as figures. The only exception is the building number *one*.

EXAMPLES   4862 East Monument Street
One East Tenth Street

Highway numbers are written as figures.

EXAMPLES   U.S. 70, Ohio 271, I94

6.1.6 Writing the Plurals of Numbers

The plural of a written number is formed by adding *s* or *es* or by dropping *y* and adding *ies*, depending on the last letter, just as the plural of any other noun is formed. (See Section 1.3.1.)

EXAMPLES   sixes, elevens, twenties

The plural of a figure should be written with *s* alone.

EXAMPLES   5s, 12s

6.1.7 Redundant Numbering

Do not follow a word representing a number with a figure in parentheses that represents the same number.

REVISE   Send five (5) copies of the report.
TO   Send five copies of the report.

6.2   ACRONYMS AND INITIALISMS

An acronym is an abbreviation that is formed by combining the first letter or letters of two or more words. Acronyms are pronounced as words and are written without periods.

EXAMPLES   radar (*r*adio *d*etecting *a*nd *r*anging)

COBOL (*C*ommon *B*usiness-*O*riented *L*anguage)

scuba (*s*elf-*c*ontained *u*nderwater *b*reathing *a*pparatus)

An initialism is an abbreviation that is formed by combining the initial letter of each word in a multiword term. Initialisms are pronounced as separate letters. When written lowercase, they generally require periods; when written uppercase, they generally do not.

EXAMPLES   e.o.m. (*e*nd *o*f *m*onth)

COD (*c*ash *o*n *d*elivery)

In business and industry, acronyms and initialisms are often used by people working together on particular projects or having the same specialties—as, for example, engineers or accountants. So long as such people are communicating with one another, the abbreviations are easily recognized and understood. However, if the same acronyms or initialisms were used in correspondence to someone outside the group, they might be incomprehensible to those readers.

Acronyms and initialisms can be convenient—for the reader and the writer alike—if they are used appropriately. Business writers, however, often overuse them, either as an affectation or in a misguided attempt to make their writing concise.

6.2.1   When to Use Acronyms and Initialisms

Two guidelines apply in deciding whether or not to use acronyms and initialisms.

1. If you must use a multiword term an average of once each paragraph, introduce the term and then use its acronym or initialism. (See Section 6.2.2.) For example, a phrase such as "primary software overlay area" can become tiresome if repeated again and again in one piece of writing; it would be better, therefore, to use PSOA.
2. If something is better known by its acronym or initialism than by its formal term, you should use the abbreviated form. The initialism A.M., for example, is much more common than the formal *ante meridiem*.

If these conditions do not exist, however, always spell out the full term.

6.2.2 How to Use Acronyms and Initialisms

The first time an acronym or initialism appears in a written work, write out the complete term and then give the abbreviated form in parentheses.

EXAMPLE   The Capital Appropriations Request (CAR) controls the spending of the money.

Thereafter, you may use the acronym or initialism alone. In a long document, however, you will help your reader greatly by repeating the full term in parentheses after the acronym or initialism when the term has not been mentioned for some time. This saves the reader the trouble of searching back to the first time the acronym or initialism was used to find its meaning.

EXAMPLE   As noted earlier, the CAR (Capital Appropriations Request) controls the spending of money.

Write acronyms in capital letters without periods. The only exceptions are those acronyms that have become accepted as common nouns; these terms are written in lowercase letters.

EXAMPLES   laser, scuba, sonar

Initialisms that do not stand for proper nouns may be written either uppercase or lowercase. In general, do not use periods when the letters are uppercase; always use periods when they are lowercase. Two exceptions are geographic names and academic degrees.

EXAMPLES   COD/c.o.d., FOB/f.o.b., CIF/c.i.f., EOM/e.o.m.

CIA, FBI, NASA

U.S.A., U.S.S.R.

B.A., M.B.A.

Form the plural of an acronym or initialism by adding an *s*. Do not use an apostrophe unless confusion could result.

EXAMPLES   MIRVs, CRTs, seven GI's

6.3   ABBREVIATIONS

An abbreviation is a shortened form of a word, formed by omitting some of its letters. Most abbreviations are written with a period; however, in technical and business writing, abbreviations of measurements are generally an exception. In cases where an abbreviation of measurement might be confused with an actual word, the period is used.

EXAMPLES   Mister/Mr.

Avenue/Ave.

September/Sept.

centimeter/cm

inch/in. (the abbreviation *in* could be misread as the word *in*)

Abbreviations, like symbols, can be important space savers in business writing, where it is often necessary to provide the maximum amount of information in limited space. Use abbreviations, however, only if you are certain that your reader will understand them as readily as he would the terms for which they stand. Remember also that a memorandum or report addressed to a specific person may be read by others, and you must consider those readers as well. Use common sense to decide when abbreviations are appropriate. Do not use them if they might become an inconvenience to the reader. A good rule of thumb is: When in doubt, spell it out.

In general, use abbreviations only when space is limited. For example, abbreviations are often useful space savers in charts, tables, graphs, and other illustrations. Normally you should not make up your own abbreviations, for they will probably confuse your reader. Except for commonly used abbreviations (U.S.A., P.M.), a term to be abbreviated should be spelled out the first time it is used, with the abbreviation enclosed in parentheses following the term. Thereafter, the abbreviation may be used alone.

EXAMPLE   The annual report of the National Retail Dry Good Association (NRDGA) will be issued next month. In it, the NRDGA will detail shortages of several widely used textiles.

6.3.1 Measurements

When you abbreviate terms that refer to measurement, be sure your reader is familiar with the abbreviated form. The following list contains some common abbreviations used with units of measurement. Notice that, except for *in.* (inch), *bar.* (barometer), and other abbreviations that might be mistaken for other words, abbreviations of measurements do not require periods.

amp   ampere

atm   atmosphere

bbl   barrel

bhp   brake horsepower

Btu   British thermal unit

bu   bushel

cal   calorie

cm   centimeter

cos   cosine

ctn   cotangent

doz or dz   dozen

emf or EMF   electromotive force

F   Fahrenheit

fig.   figure (illustration)

ft   foot (or feet)

gal   gallon

gm   gram

hp   horsepower

hr   hour

in.   inch

kc   kilocycle

kg   kilogram

km   kilometer

lb   pound

mg   milligram

min   minute

oz   ounce

pt   pint

qt   quart

rad   radian

rev   revolution

sec   second or secant

tan.   tangent

yd   yard

yr   year

Abbreviations of units of measurement are identical in the singular and plural: one *cm* and three *cm* (not three *cms*).

6.3.2   Personal Names and Titles

Personal names should generally not be abbreviated.

REVISE   Chas., Thos, Wm, Geo.

TO   Charles, Thomas, William, George

An academic, civil, religious, or military title should be spelled out when it does not precede a name.

EXAMPLE   The *doctor* asked for the patient's chart.

When it precedes a name, the title may be abbreviated.

EXAMPLES   Dr. Smith, Mr. Mills, Capt. Hughes

Reverend and *Honorable* are abbreviated only if the surname is preceded by a first name.

EXAMPLES   The Reverend Smith, Rev. John Smith (but not Rev. Smith)

The Honorable Commissioner Holt, Hon. Mary J. Holt

An abbreviation of a title may follow the name; however, be certain that it does not duplicate a title before the name.

REVISE   Dr. William Smith, Pn.D.

TO   Dr. William Smith

OR   William Smith, Ph.D.

The following is a list of common abbreviations for personal and professional titles.

Atty.	Attorney
B.A. or A.B.	Bachelor of Arts
B.S.	Bachelor of Science
B.S.E.E.	Bachelor of Science in Electrical Engineering
D.D.	Doctor of Divinity
D.D.S.	Doctor of Dental Science
Dr.	Doctor (used with any doctor's degree)
Ed.D.	Doctor of Education
Hon.	Honorable
Jr.	Junior
LL.B.	Bachelor of Law
LL.D.	Doctor of Law
M.A. or A.M.	Master of Arts
M.B.A.	Master of Business Administration
M.D.	Doctor of Medicine
Messrs.	Plural of Mr.
Mr.	Mister (spelled out only in the most formal contexts)
Mrs.	Married woman
Ms.	Woman of unspecified marital status
M.S.	Master of Science
Ph.D.	Doctor of Philosophy
Rev.	Reverend
Sr.	Senior (used when a son with the same name is living)

6.4 AMPERSANDS

The ampersand (&) is a symbol sometimes used to represent the word *and,* especially in the names of organizations.

EXAMPLES   Chicago & Northwestern Railway

Watkins & Watkins, Inc.

You may use the ampersand in footnotes, bibliographies, lists, and references. However, when writing the name of an organization in sentences or in an address, spell out the word *and* unless the ampersand appears in the official name of the company.

An ampersand must always be set off by normal word spacing but should never be preceded by a comma.

REVISE   Carlton, Dillon, & Manchester, Inc.

TO   Carlton, Dillon & Manchester, Inc.

Do not use an ampersand in the titles of articles, journals, books, or other publications.

REVISE   Does the bibliography include Knoll's *Radiation Detection & Measurement?*

TO   Does the bibliography include Knoll's *Radiation Detection and Measurement?*

6.5 CAPITAL LETTERS

The use of capital letters (or uppercase letters) is determined by custom and tradition. Capital letters are used to call attention to certain words, such as proper nouns and the first word of a sentence. Care must be exercised in using capital letters because they can affect the meaning of words (march/March, china/China, turkey/Turkey). For the same reason, however, capital letters can help eliminate ambiguity.

6.5.1 First Words

The first letter of the first word in a sentence is always capitalized.

EXAMPLE   Of all the plans you mentioned, the first one seems the best.

The first word after a colon may be capitalized if the statement following is a complete sentence or if it introduces a formal resolution or question.

EXAMPLE   Today's meeting will deal with only one issue: What is the firm's role in environmental protection?

If a subordinate element follows the colon, however, use a lowercase letter following the colon.

EXAMPLE   We had to keep working for one reason: pressure from above.

The first word of a complete sentence in quotation marks is capitalized.

EXAMPLE   He said, "When I arrive, we will begin."

Complete sentences contained as numbered items within a sentence may also be capitalized.

EXAMPLE   He recommended two ways to increase sales: (1) Next year we should spend more on television advertising, and (2) Our quality control should be improved immediately.

The first word in the salutation or complimentary close of a letter is capitalized.

EXAMPLES   Dear Mr. Smith:
             Sincerely yours.
             Best regards,

6.5.2 Specific People and Groups

Capitalize all personal names.

EXAMPLES   Walter Bunch, Mary Fortunato, Bill Krebs

Capitalize names of ethnic groups and nationalities.

EXAMPLES   American Indian, Italian, Jew, Chicano
             Thus Italian immigrants contributed much to the industrialization of the United States.

Do not capitalize names of social and economic groups.

EXAMPLES   middle class, working class, ghetto dwellers

6.5.3 Specific Places

Capitalize the names of all political divisions.

EXAMPLES   Chicago, Cook County, Illinois, Ontario, Iran, Ward Six

Capitalize the names of geographical divisions.

EXAMPLES   Europe, Asia, North America, the Middle East, the Orient

Do not capitalize geographic features unless they are part of a proper name.

EXAMPLE   The mountains in this area make television transmission difficult, which is also true in the Great Smoky Mountains.

The words *north, south, east,* and *west* are capitalized when they refer to sections of the country. They are not capitalized when they refer to directions.

EXAMPLES   I may travel south when I relocate to Delaware.

We may build a new plant in the South next year.

State Street runs east and west.

Capitalize the names of stars, constellations, and planets.

EXAMPLES   Saturn, Andromeda, Jupiter, Milky Way

Do not capitalize *earth, sun,* and *moon,* however, except when they are used with the names of other planets.

EXAMPLES   Although the sun rises in the east and sets in the west, the moon may appear in any part of the evening sky when darkness settles over the earth.

Mars, Pluto, and Earth were discussed at the symposium.

6.5.4   Specific Institutions, Events, and Concepts

Capitalize the names of institutions, organizations, and associations.

EXAMPLE   The American Management Association and the Department of Housing and Urban Development are cooperating in the project.

An organization usually capitalizes the names of its internal divisions and departments.

EXAMPLES   Faculty, Board of Directors, Accounting Department

Types of organizations are not capitalized unless they are part of an official name.

EXAMPLES   Our group decided to form a writers' association; we called it the American Association of Writers.

I attended Post High School. What high school did you attend?

Capitalize historical events.

EXAMPLE   Dr. Jellison discussed the Boston Tea Party at the last class.

Capitalize words that designate specific periods of time.

EXAMPLES   Labor Day, the Renaissance, the Enlightenment, January, Monday, the Great Depression, Lent

Do not, however, capitalize seasons of the year.

EXAMPLES   spring, autumn, winter, summer

Capitalize scientific names of classes, families, and orders, but do not capitalize species or English derivatives of scientific names.

EXAMPLES   Mammalia, Carnivora/mammal, carnivorous

6.5.5   Titles of Books, Articles, Plays, and Films

Capitalize the initial letters of the first and last words of a title of a book, article, play, or film, as well as all major words in the title. Do not capitalize articles (*a, an, the*), conjunctions (*and, but, if*), or short prepositions (*at, in, on, of*) unless they begin the title. Capitalize prepositions that contain more than four letters (*between, because, until, after*).

EXAMPLES   The author worked three years writing the book, *The Many Lives of an Organization.*

The article "Year After Year" describes the life of a turn-of-the-century industrialist.

6.5.6   Personal Titles

Titles preceding proper names are capitalized.

EXAMPLES   Ms. March, Professor Galbraith, Senator Church

Appositives following proper names are not normally capitalized. (The word *President,* however, is usually capitalized when it refers to the chief executive of a national government.)

EXAMPLE   Frank Jones, senator from New Mexico (but Senator Jones)

The only exception is an epithet, which actually renames the person.

EXAMPLES   Alexander the Great, Solomon the Wise

Use capital letters to designate family relationships only when they occur before a name or substitute for a name.

EXAMPLES   One of my favorite people is Uncle Fred.

My uncle is one of my favorite people.

Jim and Mother went along.

Jim and my mother went along.

6.5.7 Abbreviations

Capitalize abbreviations if the words they stand for would be capitalized. (See also Section 6.3.)

EXAMPLES   OSU (Ohio State University)

p. (page)

Ph.D. (Doctor of Philosophy)

6.5.8 Letters

Certain single letters are always capitalized. Capitalize the pronoun *I* and the interjection *O* (but do not capitalize *oh* unless it is the first word in a sentence).

EXAMPLES   When I say writing, O believe me, I mean rewriting.

When I say writing, oh believe me, I mean rewriting.

Capitalize letters that serve as names or indicate shapes.

EXAMPLES   X-ray, vitamin B, T-square, U-turn, I-beam

6.5.9 Miscellaneous Capitalizations

The word *Bible* is capitalized when it refers to the Christian Scriptures; otherwise, it is not capitalized.

EXAMPLE   He quoted a verse from the Bible, then read from Blackstone, the lawyer's bible.

All references to deities (Allah, God, Jehovah, Yahweh) are capitalized.

EXAMPLE   God is the One who sustains us.

A complete sentence enclosed in dashes, brackets, or parentheses is not capitalized when it appears as part of another sentence.

EXAMPLES   We must make an extra effort in sales this year (last year's sales were down 10%).

Extra effort in sales should be made next year. (Last year's sales were down 10%.)

When certain units, such as chapters of books or rooms in buildings, are specifically identified by number, they are normally capitalized.

EXAMPLES   Chapter 5, Ch. 5, Room 72, Rm. 72

Minor divisions within such units are not capitalized unless they begin a sentence.

EXAMPLES   page 11, verse 14, seat 12

When in doubt about whether or not to capitalize, check a dictionary.

6.6   DATES

In business and industry, dates have traditionally been indicated by the month, day, and year, with a comma separating the figures. (See also Section 5.1.2.)

EXAMPLE   October 26, 1981

The day-month-year system used by the military does not require commas.

EXAMPLE   26 October 1981

A date can be written with or without a comma following the year, depending on how the date is expressed. If the date is in the month-day-year format, set off the year with commas.

EXAMPLE   October 26, 1981, was the date the project began.

If the date is in the day-month-year format, do not set off the date with commas.

EXAMPLE   26 October 1981 was the date the project began.

The strictly numerical form for dates (10/26/81) should be used sparingly, and never on business letters or formal documents, since it is less immediately clear. When this form is used, the order in American usage is always month/day/year. For example, 5/7/81 is May 7, 1981.

Confusion often occurs because the spelled-out names of centuries do not correspond to the numbers of the years.

EXAMPLES   The twentieth century is the 1900s (1900–1999).
The nineteenth century is the 1800s (1800–1899).
The fifth century is the 400s (400–499).

6.7   ITALICS (UNDERLINING)

Italics (indicated on the typewriter by underlining) are a style of type used to denote emphasis and to distinguish foreign expressions, book titles, and certain other elements. *This sentence is printed in italics.*

You may need to italicize words that require special emphasis in a sentence.

EXAMPLE   Contrary to projections, sales have *not* improved since we started the new procedure.

Do not overuse italics for emphasis, however.

REVISE   This will hurt *you* more than *me.*

TO   This will hurt you more than me!

6.7.1   Titles

Italicize the titles of books, periodicals, newspapers, movies, and paintings.

EXAMPLES   The book *Statistical Methods* was published in 1981.
The *Cincinnati Enquirer* is one of our oldest newspapers.
The *Journal of Marketing* is published monthly for those engaged in marketing.

Italicize abbreviations of such titles if their spelled-out forms would be italicized.

EXAMPLE   The *WSJ* is the business community's journal of record. (reference is to the *Wall Street Journal*)

Put titles of chapters or articles that appear within publications in quotation marks, not italics.

EXAMPLE   The article "Does Advertising Lower Consumer Prices?" was published in the *Journal of Marketing.*

Do not italicize titles of holy books and legislative documents.

EXAMPLE   The Bible and the Magna Carta changed the history of Western civilization.

Italicize titles of long poems and musical works, but enclose titles of short poems and musical works and songs in quotation marks.

EXAMPLES   Milton's *Paradise Lost* (long poem)
Handel's *Messiah* (long musical work)
T. S. Eliot's "The Love Song of J. Alfred Prufrock" (short poem)
Leonard Cohen's "Suzanne" (song)

6.7.2 Proper Names

Italicize the names of ships, trains, and aircraft, but not the names of companies that own them.

EXAMPLE   They sailed to Africa on the Onassis *Clipper* but flew back on the TWA *New Yorker*.

Exceptions are craft that are known by model or serial designations, which are not italicized.

EXAMPLES   DC-7, Boeing 747

6.7.3 Words, Letters, and Figures

Italicize words, letters, and figures that are discussed as such.

EXAMPLES   The word *inflammable* is often misinterpreted.
I should replace the *s* on my old typewriter.

6.7.4 Foreign Words

Italicize foreign words that have not been assimilated into the English language.

EXAMPLES   *sine qua non, coup de grâce, in res, in camera*

Do not italicize foreign words that have been fully assimilated into the language.

EXAMPLES   cliché, etiquette, vis-à-vis, de facto, siesta

When in doubt about whether or not to italicize a foreign word, consult a current dictionary.

6.7.5 Subheads

Subheads in a report are sometimes italicized; on a typewriter, they are generally underlined.

EXAMPLES   There was no publications department as such, and the writing groups were duplicated at each plant or location. Wellington, for example, had such a large number of publications groups that their publications effort can only be described as disorganized. Their duplication of effort must have been enormous.

Training Writers

We are certainly leading the way in developing first-line managers (or writing supervisors) who not only are technically competent but can train the writers under their direction and be responsible for writing quality as well.

6.8 SYMBOLS

From highway signs to mathematical equations, people communicate in written symbols. When a symbol seems appropriate in your writing, either be certain that your reader understands its meaning or place an explanation in parentheses following the symbol the first time it appears. However, never use a symbol when your reader would more readily understand the full term. Following is a list of symbols and their appropriate uses.

Symbol	Meaning and Use
£	pound (basic unit of currency in the United Kingdom)
$	dollar (basic unit of currency in the United States)
O	oxygen (for a listing of all symbols for chemical elements, see a periodic table of elements in a dictionary or handbook)
+	plus
−	minus
±	plus or minus
∓	minus or plus
×	multiplied by
÷	divided by
=	equal to
≠ or $\doteq$	not equal to
≈ or ≑	approximately (or nearly equal to)
≡	identical with
≢	not identical with
>	greater than
≯	not greater than
<	less than
≮	not less than
:	is to (or ratio)
≐	approaches (but does not reach equality with)
∥	parallel
⊥	perpendicular
√	square root
∛	cube root

Symbol	Meaning and Use
∞	infinity
π	*pi*
∴	therefore (in mathematical equations)
∵	because (in mathematical equations)
( )	parentheses
[ ]	brackets
{ }	braces (used to group two or more lines of writing, to group figures in tables, and to enclose figures in mathematical equations)
°F or °C	degree (Fahrenheit or Celsius)
′	minute *or* foot
″	second *or* inch
#	number
*	asterisk (used to indicate a footnote when there are very few)
&	ampersand
♂	male
♀	female
©	copyright
%	percent
c/o	in care of
a/o	account of
@	at (sometimes used in tables, but never in writing)
´	acute (accent mark in French and other languages)
`	grave (accent mark in French and other languages)
^	circumflex (accent mark in French and other languages)
~	tilde (diacritical mark identifying the palatal nasal in Spanish and Portuguese)
¯	macron (marks a long phonetic sound, as in *cāke*)
˘	breve (marks a short phonetic sound, as in *brăcket*)
¨	dieresis or umlaut (mark placed over the second of two consecutive vowels indicating that the sound is to be pronounced—*coöperate*)
¸	cedilla (mark placed beneath the letter *c* in French, Portuguese, and Spanish to indicate the letter is pronounced as *s*—*garçon*)
∧	caret (proofreader's mark used to indicate inserted material)
FR	franc (basic unit of currency in France)
Mex $	peso (basic unit of currency in Mexico)
$	peso (Phillippine peso)
R	ruble (basic monetary unit of the U.S.S.R.)
¥	yen (basic unit of currency in Japan)

6.9 PROOFREADERS' MARKS

Publishers have established symbols, called proofreaders' marks, which writers and editors use to communicate with printers in the production of publications. A familiarity with these symbols makes it easy for you to communicate your changes to others.

Mark in Margin	Instruction	Mark on Manuscript	Corrected Type
	Delete	the ~~lawyer's~~ bible	the bible
lawyers	Insert	The bible	The lawyer's bible
stet	Let stand	the ~~lawyer's~~ bible	the lawyer's bible
cap	Capitalize	the bible	the Bible
lc	Make lower case	the Law	the law
ital	Italicize	the lawyer's bible	the *lawyer's* bible
tr	Transpose	the bible lawyer's	the lawyer's bible
⌒	Close space	the Bi ble	the Bible
sp	Spell out	② bibles	two bibles
#	Insert space	TheBible	The Bible
¶	Start paragraph	¶ The lawyer's...	The lawyer's...
run in	No paragraph	...marks Below is a....	....marks. Below is a....
sc	Set in small capitals	The bible	The BIBLE
rom	Set in roman type	The bible	The bible
bf	Set in boldface	The bible	The **bible**
lf	Set in lightface	The bible	The bible
⊙	Insert period	The lawyers have their own bible	The lawyers have their own bible.
⌄	Insert comma	However we cannot....	However, we cannot....
⌐=/=⌐	Insert hyphens	half and half	half-and-half
O	Insert colon	We need the following	We need the following:
⌐;	Insert semicolon	Use the law don't....	Use the law; don't....
⌄	Insert apostrophe	Johns law book	John's law book
⌄/⌄	Insert quotation marks	The law is law.	The "law" is law.
(/)	Insert parentheses	John's law book	John's (law) book
[/]	Insert brackets	John 1920-1962 went....	John [1920-1962] went....

Mark in Margin	Instruction	Mark on Manuscript	Corrected Type
$\frac{/}{N}$	Insert en dash	1920ᴧ1962	1920-1962
$\frac{/}{M}$	Insert em dash	Our goalᴧvictory	Our goal—victory
$\overset{2}{\diagup}$	Insert superior type	$3^{\vee}= 9$	$3^2 = 9$
$\diagup\!2\!\diagdown$	Insert inferior type	HᴧSO4	H_2SO_4
$\overset{*}{\diagup}$	Insert asterisk	The law$^{\vee}$	The law*
$\dagger$	Insert dagger	The lawᴧ	The law†
$\ddagger$	Insert double dagger	The bibleᴧ	The bible‡
$\S$	Insert section symbol	ᴧResearch	§Research

Index

Abbreviated dates, 542
Abbreviated spellings, 436
Abbreviations, 548–551
  capital letters for, 556
  in heading of letters, 131
  list of, in formal reports, 283, 286
Absolute, 504
Abstract, in formal reports, 280–282
Abstract nouns, 461
Accent mark, 440
Accident reports (trouble reports), 211–213
  chronological sequence in, 26–27
Accountability, in job descriptions, 343
Accuracy
  in business letters, 130
  checking for, 93
  of instructions, 177
  in spelling, 425
Acknowledgment letters, 155, 156
Acquaintances, job leads from, 399–400
Acronyms, 547–548
  in title of formal reports, 278
Active voice, 480–481
  for emphasis, 58–61
  in letter writing, 120
Address(es)
  in heading of letters, 131
  inside, in letters, 131
  numbers in, 546
Adjective endings, spelling, 431–433
Adjective markers, 459
Adjectives, 473–475
  adverbs made from, 490
  comparison of, 474
  placement of, 474
  usage of, 475
Adjustment letters, 158, 160–162
Adverb endings, spelling, 431–433
Adverbs, 488–491
  from adjectives, 490
  comparison of, 489
  conjunctive, 492–493
  functions of, 489
  placement of, 490–491
Advertisements, job, 397–398
Affectation, 86–87, 89–90, 92–93
Agreement
  definition of, 94
  pronoun-antecedent, 96, 97, 469–472
  subject-verb, 94–96, 485–488

Alphabetizing bibliographic entries, 268
Ambiguity, 78–80
Ambiguous pronoun reference, 81, 472–473
American Statistics Index, 234–235
Ampersands, 551–552
Analogy, definition by, 197
Antecedent
  agreement of pronoun with, 96, 97, 469–472
  of a pronoun, 80
Antonyms, 442
Apostrophes, 540–542
Appearance
  of business letters, 130–131
  See also Physical appearance
Appendixes, in formal reports, 308
Appositive, 503–504
  pronoun, 469
Argumentative writing
  increasing order of importance in, 31–33
  See also Persuasive writing
Atlases, 235–236
Attention-getting devices, in instructions, 180
Attention line, in place of a salutation, 133
Audience
  of oral presentations, 383–384
  See also Readers
Author card, 236
Author/date notation system, 267

Background information, in oral presentations, 391
Back matter of formal reports, 307–308
"Bad news" letters, 122–125
  See also Refusal letters
Bar graphs, 362–365
Bibliographies, 240–243
  alphabetizing, 268
  at the end of a report or research paper, 267–272
  in formal reports, 307
  forms for, 268–270
  full, selected, and annotated, 268
  sample, 270–272
  typing, 268
Body of informal reports, 211

Body of formal reports, 277, 286–307
  conclusions, 302–303
  explanatory footnotes, 306–307
  introduction, 290–293
  recommendations, 303–306
  references, 307
  summary, 287–290
  text, 293, 301
Body of letters, 133
Body of proposals, 312, 315–316
Body of tables, 356
Books, *see* Library research
Brackets, 543
Brainstorming, 9
Buffer
  in "bad news" letters, 124
  in refusal letters, 160
Business forms, *see* Forms
Business letters, *see* Letters

Call number, 238
Capital letters, 552–557
  for emphasis, 71
  for heads, 300
Captions in forms, 347
Card catalog, 236–240
Case of pronouns, 468–469
Cause-and-effect analysis, 200–203
Cause-and-effect development, in oral
  presentations, 385
Chalkboard, for oral presentations, 388
Charts
  flip, 389
  organizational, 376–377
Checklist, revision, 108–109
Chronological sequence, 26–27
Circular definitions, 199
Claim letters, *see* Complaint letters
Clarifying definitions, 197–199
Classification, as method of development,
  191–195
Classification systems of libraries, 238
Classified ads, 397–398
Clauses, 497–500
  elliptical, 510–511
  independent, 62, 498
  misplaced, 80
  subordinate (dependent), 62, 498–500,
    524
Climatic order, 70
Closing, 51–54
  See also Conclusion
Coherence of paragraph, 44–48
Collection letters, 163, 165–166
Collective nouns, 462
College placement offices, 399
Colons, 528–530
Comma faults, 525–526
Commands, instructions as, 178

Commas, 520–527
  to enclose, 520–521
  errors in use of, 102–104
  to link, 520
  with other punctuation, 525
  problems with, 525–527
  to separate, 521–525
  to show omissions, 535
  superfluous, 526–527
Comma splice, 102–103
Common knowledge, 251
Common nouns, 461–462
Comparison(s), 189–191
  of adjectives, 474, 489
  of adverbs, 489
  faulty, 79
  part-by-part method for, 190, 191
  whole-by-whole method for, 190–191
Complaint letters, 155, 157–158
Complements, 503
Completeness, checking for, 93
Complex sentences, 501–502
Complimentary close, in letters, 134
Compound antecedent, 96
Compound sentences, 501, 510–511
Compound subject, 95–96
Computerized information retrieval,
  243–244
Conciseness
  checking for, 86–93
  of instructions, 178
  in letter writing, 127
Conclusion(s)
  in formal reports, 302–303
  of informal reports, 211
  of oral presentations, 393
  of proposals, 312, 316–317
Concrete nouns, 461
Confidence, generating, 389–390
Conjugation of verbs, 483–485
Conjunctions
  coordinating, 492, 520, 527
  correlative, 492
  function of, 492
  subordinating, 492
  usage of, 493
Conjunctive adverbs, 492–493
Connectives, 503
Consistency
  of tense and person, 97–99
  See also Agreement
Consonants, doubling final, 433–434
Continuation page of letters, 134
Contractions, 541–542
  spelling, 435–436
Cooling period
  in letter writing, 119
  before revising, 77

Coordinating conjunctions, 492, 520
  commas after, 527
Copy notation, 135–136
Correlative conjunctions, 492
Correspondence, *see* Letters
Cost analysis, in sales proposals, 331–333
County and City Data Book, 235
Courtesy, in "bad news" letters, 122, 124
Cover letter, for sales proposals, 324–325
Customer Relations Departments, 158

Danger, warnings of, 71
Dangling modifiers, 99–100, 509
Dash(es), 539–540
  within sentence, for emphasis, 71
Date(s), 557
  abbreviated, 542
  commas in, 521
  of formal reports, 278
  on letters, 131
  numbers in, 545
Decimal numbering system, for heads,
    294
Declarative sentences, 502
Decreasing order of importance, organi-
    zation of information in, 29–31
Definitions, 195–200
  by analogy, 197
  circular, 199
  clarifying, 197–199
  dictionary, 440–441
  extended, 196–197
  formal, 195, 198
  glossary, 308
  informal, 195–196
  "is when" and "is where," 199–200
  in oral presentations, 390
  problems in, 199–200
  with unfamiliar terms, 200
Delivering an oral presentation, 389–393
Delivery schedule, in sales proposals,
    331, 334
Demonstrative pronouns, 465
Dependent clauses (subordinate clauses),
    62, 498–500, 524
Descriptions, 186–189
  general, in sales proposals, 328–329
  job, 343–345
  purchase-order, 186
  spatial sequence in, 27–29
  vendor, in sales proposals, 334, 338
  whole-to-parts technique in, 187
  See also Process descriptions
Descriptive abstract, 280, 281
Detailed solution, in sales proposals,
    330–331
Dewey Decimal System, 238
Dictionaries, 233–234, 439–442
Direct address, commas in, 521

Direct quotation, 245–247
Directions, *see* Instructions
Directness of letters, 121–127
Division, 191–195
Documentation, 261–272
  in bibliographies, 267–272
  in footnotes, 261–267
Double spacing, in letters, 133
Doubling final consonants, 433–434
Draft, 41–57
  closing of, 51–54
  of letters, 119
  opening of, 48–51
  paragraph length in, 48
  paragraph unity in, 42–44
  revising, *see* Revising
Drawings, 369–371
  instructions with, 180
  See also Illustrations

Educational background, in resumes,
    402–403
Elite typewriters, 350
Ellipses
  in direct quotations, 247
  periods as, 531–532
Elliptical clauses, 510–511
Emphasis, 58–75
  active voice for, 58–61
  climatic order for, 70
  commas for, 524–525
  introductory words and phrases for,
    66–67
  labeling ideas as important for, 70–71
  lists for, 69–70
  mechanical devices for, 71–72
  parallel structure for, 67–69
  subordination for, 61–66
  unusual word order for, 66
Emphatic sentences, 511–512
Employment search, *see* Job search
Employment agencies, 399
Employment experience, in resumes,
    403–404
Employment objective, in resumes, 402
Enclosure notations, 135
Encyclopedias, 232–233
Endnotes, 262
  See also Footnotes
English-language dictionaries, 233
  See also Dictionaries
Enthusiasm, generating, 389–390
Entry lines, in forms, 348–349
Enunciation, 392
Envelopes, 136, 139
Evidence
  in cause-and-effect analysis, 200–203
  in persuasive writing, 204
Exclamation marks, 534

Exclamatory sentences, 502
Executive summaries, 287
  in sales proposals, 327–328
Experience, 260
Explanation of a process, 180, 183–185
Explanatory footnotes, 262
  in formal reports, 306–307
  for graphs, 363, 365
Expletives, 504, 505
Exploded-view drawing, 370
Extemporaneous speech, 383
  See also Oral presentations
Extended definitions, 196–197
External proposals, *see* Sales proposals
Eye contact, in oral presentations, 392

Facts
  generating ideas and recording, 8–11
  interesting, in oral presentations, 390–391
  See also Information; Research
Faulty comparisons, 79
Faulty subordination, 506
Figures
  in formal reports, 309
  See also Illustrations
Final consonants, doubling, 433–434
Finite verbs, 477–478
First draft, *see* Draft
First-hand observation, 260
Flip charts, 389
Flowcharts, 373–376
Follow-up letters
  after job interviews, 416–420
  for order letters, 145, 147
Follow-up questions, in interviews, 253
Footnotes, 261–267
  author/date system for, 267
  explanatory, *see* Explanatory footnotes
  numbered references, 266
  numbers of, 262
  second-and-later, 265–266
  for tables, 356
  traditional, 261–262
Forecast, in oral presentations, 392
Foreign words, italics for, 559
Formal definitions, 195, 198
Formal reports, 209, 276–310
  graphic and tabular matter in, 308–309
  order of elements in, 276–277
  See also Back matter of formal reports; Body of formal reports; Front matter of formal reports
Formality, excessive, 90–92, 127
Formality of memos, 141
Formal style, in letter writing, 127
Format of letters, 119

Forms, 344, 346–350
  captions in, 347
  designing, 348–350
  instructions in, 346–347
  main portion of, 347–348
  planning for responses in, 347
  preliminary information in, 347
  sequencing of data in, 347–348
  spacing in, 349–350
  typeset, 350
Fractions, 545–546
Fragments, sentence, 100–101, 507–508
Friends, job leads from, 399–400
"From" line of memo, 139
Front matter of formal reports, 277–286
  abstract, 280–282
  list of abbreviations and symbols, 283, 286
  preface, 283, 285
  table of contents, 280, 283, 284
  title page, 278–280
Full block style, 136, 137
Fused sentences, *see* Run-on sentences

Gender
  pronoun-antecedent agreement in, 97
  of pronouns, 467
General description, in sales proposals, 328–329
General encyclopedias, 232
General (or broad) pronoun reference, 81, 472
General-to-specific sequence, 33–34
  of oral presentations, 385
Generating ideas, 8–11
Gerund phrases, 497
Glossary, in formal reports, 308
"Good news" letters, 124, 126–127
Goodwill
  "good news" letters and, 124
  letter writing and, 119–121
Governmental agencies and organizations
  employment opportunities in, 400
  free or inexpensive materials from, 260–261
Grammar, checking, 93–104
Graphs, 356–369
  bar, 362–365
  line, 357–362
  picture, 366–369
  pie, 363, 366
Greeting, in letters, 131–133
Grid lines, of line graphs, 361

Handbooks, 234
Hard and soft sounds, spelling, 429–430
Hazardous materials, warnings concerning, 179–180

Heads (headings)
  in formal reports, 293, 300–301
  of letters, 131
  of resumes, 401
  of second page, 134
  of tables, 356
Hidden pronoun reference, 81–82, 472
Hyphenation, 440
Hyphens, 535–537

Ideas
  generating, 8–11
  organization of, 12–13
Ie or *ei* words, spelling, 435
Illustrations, 353–354
  in descriptive writing, 188–189
  in formal reports, 308, 309
  instructions with, 180
  See also Drawings
Imitation, affectation and, 92
Imperative mood, 479
Imprecision, affectation and, 92
Impression, wishing to create an, 92
Impromptu speech, 382–383
  See also Oral presentations
Inaccuracies
  checking for, 93
  See also Accuracy
Increasing order of importance, organi-
    zation of information in, 31–33
  in oral presentations, 385
Indefinite pronouns, 465
Independent clauses, 62, 498
Indexes, periodical, 240–243
Indicative mood, 479
Indirectness of letters, 121–127
Indirect object, 503
Infinitive phrases, 497
Informal definitions, 195–196
Informal reports, 209–230
  conclusion of, 211
  introduction of, 210–211
  investigative, 212, 214–217
  parts of, 210–211
  periodic, 218, 220–221
  progress, 217–220
  recommendations in, 211
  special-purpose, 214–217
  taking notes for, 210
  test (laboratory), 223–227
  trip, 222–223
  trouble (accident), 211–213
  types of, 211–227
Informal style in business letters, 127
Information
  checking for accuracy of, 93
  organization of, 19–20
  See also Facts; Research
Informative abstract, 280, 282

Initialisms, 547–548
Initials of writer and typist, on letters,
    135
Initiation, affectation and, 92
Inquiry letters, 145, 148, 149
  response to, 148, 150–152
Insecurity, affectation and, 92
Inside address of letters, 131
Institutional sales pitch, in sales propos-
    als, 334, 338–339
Instructions, 176–182
  accuracy of, 177
  in active versus passive voice, 60
  conciseness of, 178
  in forms, 346–347
  "Materials Required" or "Tools Re-
    quired" section in, 179
  spatial method of organization in, 28
  step-by-step organization of, 24–26, 178
  warnings in, 179–180
Intensive pronouns, 466
Interesting facts, in oral presentations,
    390–391
Interjections, 495
Internal proposals, 313–320
Interrogative pronouns, 465
Interviews, 251–254
  conducting, 253–254
  job, 414–416
  preparation for, 252–253
  See also Questionnaires
Intimidation, affectation and, 92
Intransitive verbs, 476
Introduction
  of formal reports, 290–293
  of informal reports, 210–211
  of internal proposals, 314–315
  of proposals, 312
Introductory words and phrases, 66–67
Inverted sentence order, 504–505
Investigative report, 212, 214–217
Italics (underlining), 557–560
  for emphasis, 71

Jargon, 85–86
Job descriptions, 343–345
Job interviews, 414–416
Job search, 397–421
  follow-up letters, 416–420
  interview, 414–416
  letter of application, 408–413
  locating the job, 397–400

Kipling, Rudyard, 9

Leaders, periods as, 532
Legalese, 90
Length of paragraph, 48

Letters, 117–175
  accuracy in, 130
  acknowledgment, 155, 156
  additional information in, 135–136
  adjustment, 158, 160–162
  appearance in, 130–131
  "bad news," 122–125
  body of, 133
  collection, 163, 165–166
  complaint, 155, 157–158
  complimentary close of, 134
  cooling period in writing, 119
  cover, for sales proposals, 324–325
  direct and indirect patterns for, 121–127
  double-spacing in, 133
  draft of, 119
  envelope for, 136, 139
  follow-up, after job interviews, 416–420
  follow-up, for order letters, 145, 147
  format of, 119, 136
  full block style, 136, 137
  "good news," 124, 126–127
  heading of, 131
  inquiry, 145, 148, 149
  inquiry, responses to, 148, 150–152
  inside address of, 131
  job application, 408–413
  job inquiry, 398
  margins of, 133
  modified block style, 136, 138
  order, 144–146
  outlines for, 119
  parts of, 131–136
  refusal, 160, 163
  rejection, 122–125
  revising, 119
  sales, 166, 169–170
  salutation in, 131–133
  second page of, 134
  signature on, 134
  steps in writing, 118–119
  style of, 127–130
Letter writer's initials, 135
Library of Congress System, 238
Library research, 232–244
  card catalog, 236–240
  computerized information retrieval, 243–244
  periodical indexes and bibliographies, 240–243
  reference works, 232–236
Line graphs, 357–362
Linking verbs, 476–477
Listeners of oral presentations, 383–384
Listening to oral presentations, 393–395
Lists, for emphasis, 69–70
Loose sentences, 515

Manuals, 234
Maps, 377–378
Margins of letters, 133
Mass nouns, 461
"Materials Required" section, in instructions, 179
Measurements, abbreviations for, 549–550
Mechanics, 543–562
Meetings, minutes of, *see* Minutes of meetings
Memorandum (memo), 136, 139–142
  openings of, 49
  persuasive, 204–205
  preparation for writing, 4–16
  special-purpose report, 214–217
Minor sentences, 508–509
Minutes of meetings, 339–343
  chronological sequence in, 26
Misplaced clauses, 80
Misplaced modifiers, 79–80, 509
Misplaced phrases, 80
Misspelled words, commonly, 104–107, 426–428, 436–438
MLA Handbook for Writers of Research Papers, Theses, and Dissertations, 261
Modified block style, 136, 138
Modifiers, 503
  dangling, 99–100, 509
  misplaced, 79–80, 509
  redundant, 87
  single, 63
  squinting, 80, 509–510
  See also Adjectives; Adverbs; Prepositional phrases; Subordinate clauses
Mood of verbs, 479–480
Ms. in salutation of letters, 132

Nervous mannerisms, in oral presentations, 392
Newspapers, job advertisements in, 397–398
Nonfinite verbs, 478–479
Nonrestrictive and parenthetical elements, commas used to enclose, 520–521
Note-taking, 244–251
  direct quotation in, 245
  for informal reports, 210
  in interviews, 253–254
  paraphrasing in, 247–249
  summary in, 249–251
Notes, 262
  for oral presentations, 393
  See also Footnotes
Noun markers, 457–458
Noun phrases, 496
Nouns, 461–464

Number
    pronoun-antecedent agreement in, 96
    of pronouns, 467–468
    of verbs, 479
Numbers (numerals)
    plurals of, 546
    redundant, 546
    when to write out, 544–546

Objective case of pronouns, 468
Objective complement, 503
Objective of a project, in oral presenta-
    tions, 391
Observation, first-hand, 260
Omissions
    apostrophes used to mark, 541–542
    commas used to show, 525
Opening, 48–51
Oral presentations, 382–396
    concluding, 393
    delivering, 389–393
    listeners of, 383–384
    listening to, 393–395
    outlines for, 384–387
    preparing, 383–389
    purpose of, 384
    question-and-answer period after, 393
    types of, 382–383
    visual aids in, 387–389
Order letters, 144–146
    follow-up letters for, 145, 147
Organization
    of ideas, 12–13
    of information, 19–20
    See also Outlines
Organizational charts, 376–377
Organization methods (sequence), 23–36
    chronological, 26–27
    decreasing order of importance, 29–31
    general-to-specific, 33–34
    increasing order of importance, 31–33
    spatial, 27–29
    specific-to-general, 34–36
    step-by-step, 24–26
Origin of a word (etymology), 442
Outlines, 19–23
    for letters, 119
    for memos, 141
    for oral presentations, 384–387
Overhead projectors, 389

Padded phrases, 86, 88–89
Page numbers, in bibliographic entries,
    269
Paragraph(s), 516–519
    coherence of, 44–48, 518–519
    definition and functions of, 516
    length of, 48
    topic sentences in, 516–518

transitions between, 47–48
    unity of, 42–44, 518–519
Parallel structure, 67–69
Paraphrase, 247–249
Parentheses, 534–535
Parenthetical elements, commas used to
    enclose, 520–521
Part-by-part method for comparisons,
    190, 191
Participial phrases, 496–497
Parts of speech, 460–495
    adjectives, 473–475
    adverbs, 488–491
    conjunctions, 492–493
    in dictionary, 440
    interjections, 495
    nouns, 461–464
    prepositions, 493–494
    pronouns, 464–473
    verbs, 475–488
Passes, revising in, 78
Passive voice, 58–61, 480–481
    in letter writing, 120
Period fault, 532
Periodical indexes, 240–243
Periodicals, job opportunities in, 398
Periodic reports, 218, 220–221
Periodic sentences, 515
Periods, 530–532
Person
    consistency of, 97–99
    of pronouns, 466–467
    of verbs, 479
Personal data, in résumés, 401–402
Personal names, abbreviations of, 550
Personal pronouns, 464–465
    See also Pronouns
Personal titles
    abbreviations of, 550–551
    capitalized, 555
Persuasive writing, 203–205, 312–313
    See also Proposals
Photographs, 371–373
Phrases, 495–497
    definition of, 62–63
    for emphasis, 62–63, 66–67
    introductory, 66–67
    misplaced, 80
    padded, 86, 88–89
    subordination, 62–63
Physical appearance
    of business letters, 130–131
    checking, 107–108
    at job interviews, 415
Pica typewriters, 350
Picture graphs, 366–369
Pie graphs, 363, 366
Placement offices, 399
Plagiarism, 251

Plurals
apostrophe used to show, 542
of numbers, 546
Plurals of nouns, 462–463
spelling, 430–431
Points of view
opposing, persuasive writing and, 205
reader's, in letter writing, 120–121
Possessive case
apostrophe used to form, 540–541
of pronouns, 468
Possessive nouns, 463–464
Postal Service abbreviation of state
names, 131, 132
Posters, for oral presentations, 388–389
Precision
checking for, 78–86
See also Accuracy
Preface of formal reports, 283, 285
Prefixes, 434–435, 448–457
Preparation for writing, 4–16
Prepositional phrases, 496
Prepositions, 493–494
Private agencies and organizations, free
or inexpensive materials from, 260–
261
Private employment agencies, 399
Problem-solution pattern, for oral pre-
sentations, 385
Problems, statement of, in oral presenta-
tions, 390
Process descriptions, step-by-step sequence in, 24–26
Process explanation, 180, 183–185
Professional journals, job opportunities
in, 398
Progress reports, 217–220
spatial method of organization in, 28
Projectors, for oral presentations, 389
Pronoun-antecedent agreement, 96, 97,
469–472
Pronoun reference, 472–473
unclear, 80–82
Pronouns, 464–473
antecedents of, 80
case of, 468–469
demonstrative, 465
gender of, 467
indefinite, 465
intensive, 466
interrogative, 465
number of, 467–468
person of, 466–467
personal, 464–465
reciprocal, 466
reflexive, 465–466
relative, 465
as transitional device, 46
usage of, 469–473

Pronunciation, 440
Proofreaders' marks, 562
Proofreading for spelling, 426
Proper names, italics for, 559
Proper nouns, 461
Proposals, 311–339
for capital appropriations, 317, 320
internal, 313–320
purpose of, 311
sales, *see* Sales proposals
transmittal letters accompanying, 150
Punctuation, 519–543
apostrophes, 540–542
brackets, 543
colons, 528–530
commas, 520–527
dashes, 539–540
exclamation marks, 534
hyphens, 535–537
parentheses, 534–535
periods, 530–532
question marks, 533–534
quotation marks, 537–539
semicolons, 527–528
slashes, 542–543
Purchase order, descriptive writing in,
186
Purpose
determining your, 4, 5, 176
generating ideas and, 9
of oral presentations, 384
statement of, *see* Statement of purpose

Question and answer, as transitional de-
vice, 47–48
Question-and-answer period, 393
Question marks, 533
Questionnaires, 254–260
Quotation, direct, 245–247
Quotation marks, 537–539
commas inside, 525
Quotations, in oral presentations, 391

Reader's needs
determining your, 5–6
generating ideas and, 9
letter writing and, 119–121
Reader's point of view
letter writing and, 120–121
Readers, identifying your, 4, 6
Read speeches, 382
See also Oral presentations
Reciprocal pronouns, 466
Recognition vocabulary, 439
Recommendations
in formal reports, 303–306
in informal reports, 211
Recording secretary, 339
Redundancy, 86, 87

Reference section, 267
Reference works, 232–236
    atlases, 235–236
    dictionaries, 233–234
    encyclopedias, 232–236
    handbooks and manuals, 234
    statistical sources, 234–235
References
    in formal reports, 307
    numbered, 266
    in resumes, 404–405
Reflexive pronouns, 465–466
Refusal letters, 160, 163
Rejection letters, 122–125
Relative pronouns, 465
Repetition of key words and phrases, as
    transitional device, 46–47
Reports, 209
    See also Formal reports; Informal re-
    ports
Request for proposals, 322
Research, 231–275
    documentation of, *see* Documentation
    first-hand observation and experience
    in, 260
    free or inexpensive materials from pri-
    vate and governmental agencies and
    organization, 260–261
    interviewing for, 251–254
    library, *see* Library research, note-tak-
    ing for, 244–251
    plagiarism and, 251
Responses
    in forms, 347
    to inquiry letters, 148, 150–152
Responsibilities
    scope of, in job descriptions, 344
    statement of, in sales proposals, 334,
    337
Restrained style, in business letters, 127
Résumés, 400–408
    educational background in, 402–403
    employment experience in, 403–404
    employment objective in, 402
    personal data in, 401–402
    references in, 404–405
    sample, 405–408
    special skills and activities in, 404
Revising, 76–114
    "cooling" period before, 77
    affected writing, 89–90, 92–93
    ambiguous writing, 78–80
    checking for accuracy, 93
    checking for completeness, 93
    checking for conciseness, 86–93
    checking for precision, 78–86
    checking grammar, 93–104
    checking physical appearance, 107–
    108

checking spelling, 104–107
    distancing yourself from your writing
    and, 77–78
    effective, 77–78
    excessive formality, 90–92
    final checklist for, 108–109
    jargon, 85–86
    letters, 119
    padded phrases, 88–89
    in passes, 78
    redundant modifiers, 87
    technical terms, 84–85
    unclear pronoun reference, 80–82
    word choice, 82–84
    your most frequent errors, 78
Roots of words, 443–448
Rough draft, *see* Draft
Run-on sentences, 101–102, 506–507

Sales letters, 166, 169–170
Sales proposals, 320–339
    cost analysis and delivery schedule in,
    331–334
    detailed solution in, 330–331
    executive summary in, 327–328
    general description in, 328–329
    long, 324–339
    Request for, 322
    simple (short), 322–324
    site preparation description in, 331,
    335
    solicited and unsolicited, 321–322
    statement of responsibilities in, 334,
    337
    training section in, 331, 336
    vendor descriptions in, 334, 338
Salutation in letters, 131–133
School placement services, 399
Scope
    establishing your, 11–12
    stating the, in introduction of formal
    reports, 293
Second page of letters, 134
"See also" subject card, 237–238
Semicolons, 527–528
Sentence fragments, 100–101, 507–508
Sentence patterns, 504–505
Sentences, 500–515
    clear, 512
    common problems with, 506–511
    complex, 501–502
    compound, 501, 510–511
    construction of, 503
    declarative, 502
    effective, 511–515
    emphatic, 511–512
    exclamatory, 502
    faulty subordination in, 506
    intention of, 502

length of, 513
loose and periodic, 515
minor, 508–509
overloaded with subordination, 64–66
paragraph unity and, 42–44
with parallel elements, 511
parts of, 503–504
run-on, 101–102, 506–507
simple, 501
structure of, 500–502
topic, 43–44, 516–518
transitions between, 45–47
ungrammatical, 100–104
word order in, 514–515
Sequence, *see* Organization methods
Sequencing of data in forms, 347–348
Sexist language, 97
Signature on letters, 134
Silent *e* rule, 428–429
Simple sentences, 501
Single modifiers, 63
Singular nouns, 462–463
Site preparation description, in sales proposals, 331, 335
Skills, in resumes, 404
Slashes, 542–543
Slide projectors, 389
Source line, in tables, 356
Source notes, 262
Spatial sequence, 27–29
Speaking vocabulary, 439
Special-purpose report, 214–217
Specific-to-general sequence, 34–36
in oral presentations, 385
Speeches, *see* Oral presentations
Spelling, 425–438
abbreviated forms of words, 436
checking, 104–107
contractions, 435–436
doubling final consonants, 433–434
hard and soft sounds, 429–430
ie or *ei* words, 435
plurals of nouns, 430–431
prefixes and suffixes, 434–435
proofreading for, 426
silent *e* rule of thumb, 428–429
verb, adjective, and adverb endings, 431–433
Squinting modifiers, 80, 509–510
State employment agencies, 399
State names, Postal Service abbreviations of, 131, 132
Statement of purpose, 5
in introduction of formal report, 293
Statement of responsibilities, in sales proposals, 334, 337
Statistical Abstract of the United States, 235

Statistical sources, 234–235
Step-by-step sequence, 24–26, 178
of process explanations, 183
Stub of tables, 356
Style, in letter writing, 127–130
Subheads, italics for, 559–560
Subject, in introduction of formal reports, 290
Subject card, 236–237
Subject dictionaries, 233–234
Subject encyclopedias, 232–233
Subject line
of memo, 139
in place of a salutation, 133
Subjective case of pronouns, 468
Subjective complement, 503
Subjects of sentences, 503
Subject-verb agreement, 94–96, 485–488
Subjunctive mood, 480
Subordinate clauses (dependent clauses), 62, 498–500
commas used to separate, 524
Subordinating conjunctions, 492
Subordination
for emphasis, 61–66
faulty, 506
methods of, 62–63
sentences overloaded with, 64–66
Suffixes, 434–435, 457–459
Summarizing sentence, as transitional device, 47
Summary
in formal reports, 287–290
in note-taking, 249–251
Syllables, 440
Symbols, 560–561
list of, in formal reports, 283, 286
Synonyms, 442

Table of contents of formal reports, 280, 283, 284
Tables, 353–356
in formal reports, 308, 309
Taking notes, *see* Note-taking
Technical terms, 84–85
See also Jargon
Tense, 481–483
consistency of, 97–98
Test report (laboratory report), 223–227
Text of formal reports, 293–301
Time, numbers to express, 545
Title
of formal reports, 278
in salutation of letters, 131–132
table, 356
Title card, 236, 237
Title pages, for formal reports, 278–280

Titles
    capital initial letters for, 555
    italics for, 558
    personal, *see* Personal titles
"Tools Required" section, in instruc-
    tions, 179
Topic, development of, in introduction of
    formal reports, 293
Topic sentences, 43–44, 516–518
Trade journals, job opportunities in, 398
Training section, in sales proposals, 331,
    336
Transitional devices, 45–48
    in process explanations, 184–185
Transitions
    between paragraphs, 47–48
    between sentences, 45–47
Transitive verbs, 476
Transmittal letters, 150, 153–155
Trip report, 222–223
    chronological sequence in, 26
Trouble report (accident report), 211–213
Twain, Mark, 82
Typefaces
    for emphasis, 71
    for warnings or cautions in instruc-
        tions, 180
Typing
    appearance of letters and, 130
    a bibliography, 268
    envelopes, 136, 139
    forms, 350
    quotations, 245–247
Typist's initials, 135

Unabridged dictionaries, 233
Underlining, *see* Italics
Unity of paragraphs, 42–44, 518–519
Unnumbered heading system, 294, 300–
    301
Unusual word order, 66
Uppercase letters, *see* Capital letters
Usage labels in dictionaries, 441

Vendor descriptions, in sales proposals,
    334, 338
Verbals, 478–479
Verb endings, spelling, 431–433
Verb markers, 458–459
Verb phrases, 496
Verbs, 475–488, 503
    conjugation of, 483–485
    finite, 477–478

    forms of, 477–478
    grammatical properties of, 479–480
    intransitive, 476
    linking, 476–477
    mood of, 479–480
    nonfinite, 478–479
    person and number of, 479
    tense of, 481–483
    transitive, 476
    types of, 476–477
    voice of, 480–481
    See also Tense
Veterans, placement programs for, 400
Visual aids, 353–381
    drawings, 369–371
    flowcharts, 373–376
    graphs, *see* Graphs
    maps, 377–378
    in oral presentations, 387–389
    organizational charts, 376–377
    photographs, 371–373
    tables, 353–356
    See also Illustrations
Vocabulary, 438–459
    dictionaries as aid in increasing, 439–
        442
    word-part approach to increasing, 442–
        459
Voice of verbs, 480–481

Warnings of danger, 71
    in instructions, 179–180
Weeks, Francis W., 121–122
Whole-by-whole method for compari-
    sons, 190–191
Whole-to-parts technique, 187
Word choice, 82–84, 439–442
    See also Vocabulary
Word order
    in passive versus active voice, 59
    unusual, 66
Word-part approach to increasing your
    vocabulary, 442–459
Wordiness
    checking for, 86–93
    See also Conciseness
Work schedules, chronological sequence
    in, 26
Writing block, in forms, 349
Writing line, in forms, 348
Writing vocabulary, 439

Zero point of graph, 359

Correction Chart

The following symbols are commonly used in correcting written work. Most of the symbols are keyed to the pages in the text where the problem is discussed.

Symbol	Problem	Page
ab	abbreviation	436, 547–51, 556
adj	adjective	473
adv	adverb	488–91
agr	agreement	94–97, 479, 485–88
amb	ambiguity	78–80, 472–73, 491
ap	apostrophe	540–42
awk	awkward	
[ ]	brackets	543
cap	capital letter	552–57
lc	no capital letter (lower case)	552–57
case	grammatical case	468–69
coh	coherence	42–48, 518–19
:/	colon	528–30
⌃	comma	102, 520–27
cf	comma fault	525–26
dm	dangling modifier	99–100, 509–10
dash	dash	71, 539–40
def	define term	195–200
⌐	delete	86–93
div	word division (syllabication)	537
el	ellipsis (ellipses)	531–32
emph	emphasis	58–72, 511–12
excl	exclamation mark	534
fn	footnote	261–67
frag	sentence fragment	100–1, 495, 507–9
h	hyphen	535–37
ital	italics (underlining)	71, 557–60